Regionalism and the Humanities

Regionalism *and* *the* Humanities

Edited and with an introduction by
Timothy R. Mahoney
and Wendy J. Katz

University of Nebraska Press
Lincoln & London

Library of Congress Cataloging-
in-Publication Data
Regionalism and the humanities / edited and with an
introduction by Timothy R. Mahoney and Wendy J. Katz.
p. cm.
Includes bibliographical references and index.
ISBN 978-0-8032-7634-5 (pbk. : alk. paper)
1. Regionalism—United States. 2. Humanities—Study
and teaching—United States. 3. Regionalism in literature.
4. National characteristics, American, in literature.
I. Mahoney, Timothy R., 1953– II. Katz, Wendy Jean.
E179.5.R44 2008
320.973—dc22
2008029369
Set in Sabon by Kim Essman.

Contents

Illustrations

Introduction

Regionalism and the Humanities: Decline or Revival?

WENDY J. KATZ & TIMOTHY R. MAHONEY

In November 2003 nearly 150 poets, writers, geographers, musicologists, literary critics, and historians of all fields—from agriculture and architecture to women and immigration—gathered in Lincoln, Nebraska, at a national conference of the Consortium of Regional Humanities Centers to explore the general theme of "Regionalism and the Humanities." The papers in this volume reflect the general perception shared by most of the humanists at the conference: in a modern world increasingly homogenized and standardized by the forces of globalization, the regionalist impulse is still very much alive. Once viewed as a reaction against the forces of modernism, it has emerged in a globalized world as a repackaged, more-aggressive endeavor to make a claim for the role of place and space—as opposed to gender, race, ethnicity, class, demography, or other cultural or physical distinctions—in the effort to understand ourselves and what it means to be human. What distinguishes regionalism from these other efforts at self-understanding is its focus on locating oneself in the space lived in, inhabited, made home, or traveled through. This emphasis is itself rooted in man's fundamental interaction with nature: the land, climate, flora and fauna, and the physical environment.

Most of the essays in this collection, though they position themselves in quite diverse ways, agree that the ongoing erosion of space and place as factors in identity formation in modern life has given regionalism its continuing impetus, indeed, its renewed urgency and vitality. In some ways, in a shrinking global life connected by instant communications and integrated into an international economy, one's sense of place or the role of one's geographic location on one's sense of identity may seem to matter less than ever before, in terms of ideas, news, and production and exchange of goods and services. Yet, as these essays attest, amid such perceived sameness, region and place—nature and custom—have come to matter even more for many people, as they struggle to hold on to that which makes them distinct. Together, they represent some of the most innovative and intriguing explorations of the history and contemporary value of regionalism in humanistic investigation.

To understand the ironies and even contradictions within this simultaneous decline and revival of regionalism, it's useful to consider the different political, social, economic, and aesthetic purposes to which theorizing about region has been put. This introduction therefore attempts to provide an interpretive framework for comparing and contrasting the regionalist analyses employed by the authors in this volume. One place to begin is by defining several related terms used in this volume: space, place, region, regionalism, regionality, local, landscape, and regional identity. Each discipline tends to wield such terms differently, but for humanists, even humanist geographers, while space evokes a more neutral quality of spaciousness, positioning oneself amid openness or an unbounded expanse of terrain, place is something constructed by people. Place is space that has been given meaning and borders, and so a location with a human-created ensemble of features.

A similar relationship exists between land and landscape, in that the term landscape always implies that the land has already been ordered and shaped by human perceptions and action. In giving a portion of the earth limits, whether creating a place or a landscape, John Findlay and Richard White rightly observe that people are also asserting control or power over the environment, as well as over other people who might have different mental concepts of the same physical space. So the concept of a region itself—the concept of an observable uniformity of certain cultural attitudes, behaviors, and artifacts in a socially and naturally defined place and time—is itself an assertion of power. Regionalism and regionalist, then, refers to practices and agendas in cultural, political, economic, or other realms, which are identified with regional interests and affirm regional particularities or a particular regional identity. Local and localism are terms used less frequently in this volume, but suggest an even greater particularity of interest and identity, an even smaller or narrower geographic base for group or individual identity; local color and local history are often considered a subset of region and regionalism, though they share a focus on the ordinary or common person whose activities and features emerge more clearly on a smaller spatial or microhistorical level of analysis. Often it is part of the regionalist's project to describe the local as part of or imbedded within a larger set of natural or cultural relationships.[1]

A regional identity then, is a sense of belonging, an awareness of similar traits among people living under similar conditions, or not coincidentally, of how their cultural patterns are distinctive in comparison to other regions or places. Such an identity is subjective by nature and so might appear either as a perception of residents (a region's consciousness of itself), or might appear among those outside a region. In either case, the assertion of a belief in a common identity and common interest across a region represents a struggle over the properties, natural or human, that determine the right to be in and possess that place, to determine its unifying elements. Any regionalist discourse, including this one, is a performance that imposes its own definitions and boundaries and aims to get people to recognize them as legitimate; any utterance about region is always an argument that either favors or hampers the chances of the region (and its ascribed traits or nature and supposed interests) acquiring recognition and so any "real" existence.[2] As Douglas Powell asserts in *Critical Regionalism*, to acquire a sense of place, one has to help create that place; and for him, a critical regionalism is a way to assert what the relationships among places should or ought to be, not merely to identify objective and static characteristics.[3]

As this suggests, regionalism as an approach in the humanities is not necessarily an effort to produce a consensual history of a place, a period, or a people. It can equally or instead emphasize pluralism and conflict among and between competing identities. In fact, the great contribution of the humanities to the study of regions is derived from its insistence that nature matters, but matters particularly or insofar as that nature is transformed by various human categories. Accordingly, different disciplines target a range of apparently subjective and unscientific criteria for region: the political, legal, economic, and symbolic marks with which various groups of humans establish their territorial boundaries, under the assumption that these shape the region as much or more than patterns of rainfall. Annie Proulx, in "Dangerous Ground, Landscape in American Fiction," is thus able to identify one author as a regionalist who based his literary landscapes on an artist's paintings, but never actually saw the countryside he described.[4]

The history of regionalism has been addressed by several notable authors and collections. For example, in their introduction to their important anthology, *All Over the Map: Rethinking American Regions* (1996), Edward Ayers and Peter Onuf find the origins of regions and regionalism both in modes of thinking brought from Europe and in the structure of the federal system itself.[5] Robert Dorman's equally influential *Revolt of the Provinces*, though focusing on the period between the world wars, similarly traces regionalism to the desire already expressed in the colonial period for a communitarian ethos, a desire frequently revived since then.[6] If one attends to a history of how regions have been theorized in the U.S. rather than a history of regionalism, however, a somewhat different trajectory emerges, from what could be called a nineteenth-century geographical determinism to a twentieth-century modernist "sense of place" regionalism to the even more fluid postmodern notion that region is a dynamic and relative construction. With each of these viewpoints, one moves from concentration on a sensibility available only to residents, particularly those who seem deeply rooted in the land itself, to the sensibility of ever more mobile people, who live somewhere for a while or pass through, and finally, to anyone who cares to relate his or her work to a certain place, whether they were residents or not, the last being an issue addressed in the essay by Steve Behrendt in this collection.

At the risk of oversimplifying this shift, geographic determinism in the humanities has typically defined a region by apparently neutral or objective criteria (through the selection of factors such as water distribution or geological formation) and then given this environment credit for molding human activity and perception in certain ways. As an antebellum booster of western regional culture noted, Cincinnati's location (then the West) on east–west and north–south river transportation routes meant that it would inevitably mix the economies and characters of all the regions into a western composite, nevertheless capable of truly representing, and unifying, the nation.[7] On one level this type of argument seems just common sense. Many assume that people living in a place with a particular topography, climate, and resources will become conditioned by it and that, in some way—economic, psychological, or otherwise—it will become part of them and shape their behavior. Such determinism, too, may be rooted, as William Slaymaker suggests, in our tendency to project ourselves into nature and become both sympathetic and empathetic with the environment we experience, though this point of view tends to be adopted more by conservationists than advocates of regional development.

For later and more influential western boosters and geographical determinists such as Frederick Jackson Turner and Walter Prescott Webb, the interaction between environment and inhabitant was more forceful. In his most deterministic moments, Turner seems to have suggested that westward moving Euro-American settlers simply "poured their plastic pioneer life into geographic moulds."[8] As Kurt Kinbacher characterizes Turner's hypothesis in this volume, the wilderness environment of the frontier shaped Americans anew, endowing them with the characteristics of individualism and democracy. Because Turner's theory provided fodder for American exceptionalism in a period of cultural nationalism and democratic interest in the "folk," the result was the triumph in the 1920s of a geographical determinism whose "grand narrative" of the West both defined it as a region and credited it with shaping national character. As Robert Dorman observes,

Henry Nash Smith, the founder of American Studies and author of 1950's *Virgin Land: The American West in Symbol and Myth*, was educated in this form of regionalism.[9]

Most regionalists and western historians today, including those in this collection, eschew Turner's brand of geographical determinism as insufficiently pluralist. To Guy Reynolds, this type of regionalism leads to the view that a region consists of a certain clutch of features that mark everyone from the region in much the same way. Yet as the frequent references in this volume attest, Turner's influence is still felt, even as scholars argue that he overemphasizes place at the expense of culture, perhaps particularly disregarding the variety of cultures, among men and women, whites and nonwhites, active on the frontier. Barbara Handy-Marchello's essay on a female booster in the West is an example of how gender creates fissures in regionalism's potentially monolithic definitions of place and coherent social groups.[10]

Even those often ecologically conscious historians and writers who take seriously Turner's premises about the importance of the frontier environment's uniqueness come to different conclusions: for example, that its aridity led to a hierarchical concentration of capital rather than democracy, high urbanization and depopulization rather than levelling.[11] So too, Proulx notes that Turner may still be ironically relevant because he was wrong. The frontier, which he defined by a population density of less than two people per square mile and which he declared closed in 1893, in fact still existed in the 1990 census—and, with continuing declining population, certainly must still exist today—in 132 counties, mostly arid, across the western states. Travel books like Dayton Duncan's *Miles from Nowhere* agree with Proulx, observing that the contemporary frontier's vast distances are attracting a new wave of pioneers and that the retirees moving to its sunny, low-tax realm are still attracted to the ideas and values of the mythic west.[12] Michael Steiner and David Wrobel, while supportive of the New Western History's inclusion of much greater human diversity in its picture of the frontier, confirm that Turner's mythic West retains its grip on American and European imaginations and so still exercises influence on the West's future development.[13]

Edward Watts in turn asserts that Turner's idea that the Midwest, as a region, emerged in a colonial framework rooted in interregional asymmetries remains useful. Because Turner sought to establish an interaction between regional or sectional stories and national ones (a process-oriented approach some construe as antiregional), his impulse was to put place—the land, climate, topography, region—and its diversity back into a history governed by a spaceless national politics. This asymmetric model understands regionalism as a form of dependence on already-existing national norms, in which a place is recognized as a region precisely because of its deviance from standards that are themselves created elsewhere—usually in eastern urban milieus that control the national market for publishing, capital, art—and so can and do equate their own region with the nation.

Like colonies, regions, then, may be produced for the eastern market, for outsiders and by outsiders, who define others' cultural peculiarities in order to enforce and reinforce "national" norms as well as a ruling elite's control over establishing those norms.[14] Both the role of the federal government as a patron of "nonpartisan" regionalism and the role of the outsider—the regionalist writer or artist is almost always someone who leaves the region for a time or for good, or an outsider who immerses him or herself in a locality—are undeniable factors in the various historical flowerings of regionalism, just as the National Endowment for the Humanities has been important for its twenty-first-century revival. Willa Cather, a quintessential regionalist, emerges in the studies of both Guy Reynolds and Mark Robison as someone who understood the dependence of the Plains and the West on eastern markets. The newly arrived European settlers in the Plains or the Northwest Territory described by Kurt Kinbacher and Patrick Lucas, like Cather and the other authors and artists in this volume, similarly create regional identities while not being themselves "homegrown."

At the same time, individuals of any origin in a place may adopt regionalism as a way of achieving control over economic and political life and of resisting outside coercion or intervention. Nicolas Witschi's discussion of how a Nevada town hoaxed travelers with fake gunfights is an innovative analysis of the tension operating within postcolonial models of regionalism: capital and imagery produced outside the region aimed to define it in ways useful to them, while inhabitants, in order to be understood, must rely on the same set of regional concepts but put them to purposes of resisting outside incursions or of resolving their own internal tensions. Ginette Aley turns not to a performative—signifying—model but to a biographic one, but she shares Witschi's aim of figuring out how a region can achieve a kind of internal representation. Like other regional historians, notably Andrew Cayton and Susan Gray, she endeavors to treat region as an autonomous entity, with its own turning points and defining moments that are not necessarily derived from national narratives.[15] Warren Hofstra, in advocating this approach, notes that the National Endowment for the Humanities might have similarly benefited from dropping the externally imposed structure of its initiative to establish regional centers in the humanities, where states were assigned to various regions, in favor of allowing regions to self-identify (midwesterners, Appalachians, Angelenos, southerners, etc.). Such a tactic might indeed have helped more regional centers achieve greater regional recognition.[16] Cheryll Glotfelty's essay directly, and many others in the volume indirectly, highlights this problem of regional definition, whether it is defined on a geographical basis or imposed by external agencies without taking into account the inhabitants' self-perceptions.

The legacy of Turner, along with some of his essentialist assumptions, also survives in the ideas of many regionalists who subscribe to a "sense of place," or a spirit that defines a particular regional perspective. The roots of contemporary notions of sense of place in regionalist studies lie in the humanist geography of Yi-Fu Tuan and other theorists of the everyday landscape, particularly John Brinckerhoff Jackson and Donald W. Meinig.[17] Yi-Fu Tuan describes the transmission of the "essential" characteristics of the land via one's subjective perceptions of or interaction with the external world.[18] Yi-Fu Tuan called it "topophilia," a perception of a *genii loci* of a place, and his work provided an important corrective to geographers who posed such entities as the "Great Plains," a region that can be justified ecologically, but which exists neither as an economic nor a political unit, nor is understood as a regional identity for the vast majority of its supposed inhabitants. Yi-Fu Tuan's emphasis on how surroundings (place) provide individuals with a sense of the coherence of inner lives with the outer world, a reassuring sense that selfhood and culture are interrelated (rather than the world as alienating), has been key for writers and scholars interested in keeping nature primary without succumbing to determinism. That is, for thinkers who value rootedness, who wish to resist change, or "progress," who feel nostalgic for a home that has been destroyed, topophilia reorients American culture around environment and the importance of preserving a human relationship with that environment. Art and culture, in this formulation, help people integrate their lives with the environment and, in doing so, validate those very ordinary aspects of life that are part of daily living in a place.[19]

But as with Turner, this idea of a place's pervading spirit can carry the baggage of the nineteenth- and early twentieth-century conviction that human culture and human nature are determined by evolution, biology, and even national boundaries. For discussions of region are almost always implicitly also discussions of ethnicity, race, and the possibility of pluralism: of who "naturally" belongs. Or as D. H. Lawrence said in his influential mystification of American regions, "Every people is polarized in some particular locality, which is home, the homeland. Different places on the face of the earth have different vital effluence, different vibration, different chemical exhalation, different polarity with different stars: call it what you like."[20] In such formulations of a nation or a people as organically rooted in the land, their very blood and breath united with the natural world, it can be a short jump from regionalism to varieties of essentialism that have historical connections to ethnic cleansing and scientific as well as romantic racism, in their common assumption that cultural components can be biologically or environmentally transmitted.

Accordingly, most advocates for spirit of place also incorporate the model J. B. Jackson offers, which acknowledges that place is only created over the course of time; this acknowledgement reconfigures

Lawrence's homeland as the product of human habit and custom more than any mysterious effluence. Similarly, writers in this volume like Larry Moore, who suggest that region is the outward and visible sign of the underlying spirit of place, see this process of signification as a result of lived experience, akin to Michel de Certeau's view that "place is practiced space."[21] Region thus becomes cultural construction, like any other feature of human identity and no more important, rather than a geographically and environmentally defined place.

If "sense of place" regionalists explore the transaction between people and a space and how people gradually create a place through their interactions and habits, then others in this volume regard a region as something less natural and more mediated from the start—a space of representation manufactured in the course of commodity exchanges or in the politics of a regional competition that is both created by locals and imposed on them by outsiders. By discarding an essentialist notion of regionalism that argues that the direction of culture is determined by a particular natural environment or that core values or characteristics define an "authentic" place or identity, contemporary scholarship has been able to demonstrate precisely how social interests determine competing identities, including those of place. Yet, if region is wholly a construction, it risks turning regionalism into a wholly imaginary framework, discounting the very real effects of life in a particular place. But considered from such a fluid, relational, even subjective perspective, regionalism and regionality are naturally dynamic, contested, unfinished, and ever changing. This conclusion is less surprising when it is understood that contemporary regionalism is far more tied to questions of identity politics than in its earlier revivals.

In particular, the regionalists of the 1920s and 30s—those decades of mass migration from the farm to the city and of anti-immigration laws—with assistance from federal government programs, developed regional literature and art as an antidote or response to the forces of consumerism and standardization as well as to the universalizing and cosmopolitan aesthetics of modernist art and literature. As Charles Reagan Wilson observes, however, interest in regionalism declined during the consensus era of the 1950s, when scholars and planners stressed the continuity and unity of experience in America and the homogenizing forces that promised to continue to bridge social divisions in the future.[22] However, an anthology of interdisciplinary papers from a 1949 symposium, itself designed to show the utility of regions as a concept for research and public administration, was reissued in 1965, and the foreword by Supreme Court Justice Felix Frankfurter explains why it seemed relevant once again in an age of expanding civil rights: the goal of regionalism is recognition of the "intractable diversities among men derived from the different reactions of men to nature."[23] In the 1960s and 1970s, and even in the 1990s when Wilson's anthology *The New Regionalism* was published, revivals in regional studies reinvigorated both these legacies (linking regionalism to cultural and environmental diversity) in ecocritical and postmodernist forms. This resulted in the creation of some regional centers, giving regionalism a new institutional home in the academy, and a resurgence in regional and nature writing and folklore studies.

While people acted from concern about both vanishing diversity and eroding community in each of those earlier regionalist moments, from a twenty-first-century vantage point, regional life seems vibrant and alive in the 1890s, 1920s, or 1960s as compared to today. Yet to be fully breached by national or international media, markets, and mobility, different American regions seemed more grounded and surrounded by borders and markers, and were more different, parochial, or provincial—for good or bad—than they are today. As recently as the 1960s, a relatively significant percentage of goods and services consumed in local and regional markets were still made there by local and regional people in locally or regionally owned or based companies; local and regional news had some vitality; states and municipalities took care of themselves while resisting federal intervention; travel across the country from region to region retained a sense of adventure and was often fraught with difficulties; and regional differences remained more distinctive and "authentic." The West and Southwest loomed as exotic, arid lands of opportunity. The South was a place in social turmoil with its special problem—recall that it took years for many Americans to be convinced that the civil rights movement was a "national" as opposed to just a "southern" movement. The Midwest was the comfortable, confident, solid core of the nation. And the East remained the home of the "Establishment" that ran the country. Today regional barriers, borders, and markers of difference have all been irrevocably breached, awash in the nationalizing and globalizing flood of the economy, polity, population, and culture. And, in spite of the hardening of national borders in an age of heightened security, the forecast is for the flood to continue unabated. Indeed, it is hard to imagine when this might not be the case in the foreseeable future.

While those earlier strains of regionalist thought that concentrated on preserving the American "folk" persist today, what is emphasized by most of the essays in this volume is that regionalism, in contextualizing human endeavor spatially, draws distinctions between one's here and another's there as a route to attaching individuals to group identities. Larry Moore suggests that most such efforts to construct identity emerge from our natural tendency to distinguish ourselves from others by mediating the difference between us and them, self and other. Maggie Valentine affirms, "focusing on regionalism allows us to discover how we are different and how we are the same. It helps us identify who we are."[24] At the most extreme, this involves negotiating between the self and the other, but for most it involves eliciting grounds for sameness as well as distinctions. Such an effort, Michael Saffle observes in his essay, is rooted in the human as well as scholarly necessity of selecting one part of reality from all of reality, as a way of making distinctions. And Behrendt (quoting William Shakespeare) notes that truisms about human imagination and behavior must find "local habitation and a name" in order to become real and that the project of the humanities—mapping the human condition—cannot be resolved without a productive tension between general and specific, cosmopolitan and provincial, global and local, national and regional, the homogenous and the distinctive, and even modernism (or postmodernism) and the "backward."[25]

Behrendt and other scholars see a productive dualism, a dialectic between space and place, individual freedom and social constraint, between Kathleen Norris's literary embrace of monastic asceticism in *Dakota* and the fears of isolation expressed in the sociological study *Bowling Alone*.[26] But these theses and antitheses are not innocent; rather, they reveal the terms of the debate over what is sometimes still called multiculturalism, of whether the nation itself ought to be inclusive or exclusive, and to what extent. In discussing the "spatial turn" of American studies, Karen Halttunen advocates regionalism's potential to create activist scholarship, humanists who contribute to making their own communities more egalitarian and inclusive.[27] But she also notes the parallel presence of a long-standing tradition of promoting place in America that operates through a jeremiad about its disappearance. In these critical studies of American life, the strategy of identifying national uniqueness in terms of the land, rather than republican principles, expresses a conservative desire to set "natural" limits on individual economic and geographic mobility (particularly that of immigrants) and on individual choices, particularly moral ones, like gambling or other elements of a "decent" social order, but also on decisions about such things as natural resources. Place thus acts as a check on the individual, offering (instead of the lure of self-fulfillment) a sense of belonging to something larger, which in turn operates to stabilize communities by controlling individual interest.

William Leach's *A Country of Exiles* is one of the most persuasive articulations of the dangerous and "unhealthy" results for labor, for American Indians, for the public sphere generally of capitalism's atomizing influences; it proposes place as a new haven in this heartless world of cosmopolitan escapists who do not acknowledge their own social location.[28] A "constructed" community—of minds or of shared principles or tastes, such as one online—if it lacks a relationship to a geographic place with a history, cannot impose sufficient accountability to act as a brake on individuals. Regionalists who might define themselves as conservationist rather than conservative also often aim to instill a sense of connectedness to place as a means of creating support for environmental controls on development.

For contemporary scholars who compare what they see as the diversity of the past with modern day homogeneity, the Midwest becomes an increasingly important source of origins. This may explain why this volume as a whole is marked by a striking absence of the two regions conventionally seen as most important to national history: New England and the South. Instead, it is dominated by the Plains/Midwest (nine essays) and the Southwest (four essays). This is due partly to the economies of travel and academic conference structure; the conference that originated these essays took place in Lincoln, Nebraska. But there is more to this emphasis than that: the Midwest and the Southwest represent two important poles of current thinking about regionalism. The Midwest is a classic example of a nonexistent region, as Aley notes; or as Kinbacher says, the Plains exposed the fault lines in previous American institutions without clearly replacing them with new ones. Instead, its endless prairie, grids, transportation corridors, and cash crops seem to have bred the genteel standardization or rationalization of social and business life that epitomize the middle-class American society that most twentieth-century humanists traditionally critiqued. But humanists who see the middle class and man-made systems as playing a role in regionalism have recently begun to embrace the Midwest's featurelessness, at least as an object of study; as Louise Erdrich ruefully confesses, if the modern writer cannot call on a sacred mountain to create a cultural identity, then mass culture and bland suburbs provide a replacement as a common reference.[29]

The Southwest serves a very different purpose for humanist scholars of region. Its desert, as a supremely harsh environment, provides reassurance of the overriding importance of nature in a culture that otherwise flaunts its ability to escape nature, through means such as air conditioning or irrigation. The Southwest and Midwest do have in common, however, the fact that they were both home early on to an internal regionalism of boosters who specifically and self-consciously felt marginalized or alienated from centers of power; and so they promoted their regions as distinctive or superior in order to advance interests that they believed were being ignored. In trying to make sense of this long history of boosterism, which often aimed at commercializing the region for tourists and markets outside the region in just the way southwestern-style ATMs and fast food restaurants do today, Maggie

Valentine, writing on southwestern architecture, returns to the land as a more authentic source of defining characteristics, while Barbara Handy-Marchello, writing on the Northern Plains, does not. Cheryll Glotfelty's essay on Nevada literature is particularly valuable in this context of the Southwest as a more determining environment, by highlighting the ambivalent rather than adaptive responses the southwestern desert also aroused.

The regionalism reflected in these essays has relatively little interest in putting a finger in the dike holding back the flood of globalism. Rather than hunkering defensively and resisting for all the wrong reasons, they acknowledge the forces of nationalism and globalism and the efficiency, convenience, diversity, prosperity, and cosmopolitan understanding they promote or at least hope to promote. But while accepting these, they recognize, as many others have, that in the face of all these forces people still understand themselves from the perspective of the place in which they live and may want to do so more, rather than less, as material and physical life becomes more and more similar around the world. As what might be called humanist environmentalists, they seek to cultivate and enhance our appreciation of how bringing space and place into our efforts to define ourselves enriches our lives. Just as paving or building over all the land and cutting down all the forests is not necessarily considered positive progress, so too eliding all regional distinctiveness, or rampant "delocalization" leading to banal homogeneity amid touristically manufactured difference, is dreaded and disparaged by most regionalists, if not by most people.[30]

In the end much of today's scholarly and perhaps even popular interest in regionalism is closely related to the motives that drove it in the 1850s, 1890s, 1920s, and 1960s. That is, people still feel their identity is threatened by homogenization, now inevitably represented by Wal-Mart or McDonald's, international chains that threaten to put local firms out of business, and they often look to the past and to local nature in hopes of finding a model for survival in which those economies of scale are not so inevitable, even if it means turning to marketable symbols of regional distinctiveness, like ceramic saguaros made in China. These people find in regional systems, human and natural, a model in which markets seem to play a smaller role in determining human life so that distinctiveness and authentic selfhood can flourish.

Regionalism as a scholarly and cultural category works to be inclusive when it is not used to draw distinctions between the middle class who can afford the expensive local microbrew and the working class who cannot and when the regional preference for the homogenous chain is understood as valid regionalism because it is the result not only of the area's integration into larger markets but of its relatively low wages. As Lucy Lippard pointedly observes, to romanticize rootedness or the locally made is to be blinded by the way that the wealthy or socially elevated can escape—from a place or economic necessity or their culture—and the way that the poor are tied to environments and circumstances, no matter how untenable.[31] Equally, to deny certain populations a connection with the land can disenfranchise them economically and politically, as Sylvia Rodriguez notes of a southwestern regionalism that privileges picturesque American Indians over Mexican Americans.[32]

For that matter, Glotfelty's extensive citations of twentieth-century Nevada literature represent what might have been considered middle-brow or genteel fiction in an earlier time; one wonders what Nevada's politically determined exceptionalism might have looked like had her survey, in addition to covering literary fiction set in Nevada or by Nevada writers, included category fiction (mysteries, romances, westerns, etc.) or fiction written in languages other than English. The result might have conformed more to the usual Southwest tropes— or perhaps it might have evoked a different understanding of the purposes those tropes can serve. This is because, as Andrew Cayton and Susan Gray have noted, region is a vital part of popular, not just academic, narratives of identity; and studies of regionalism, whether in art, literature, music, or history, tap into these widespread cultural ideas and stereotypes, along with all the interests and exclusions they represent.[33] At the same time, the impulse that motivates current regionalism is a broadly shared one: the desire to belong somewhere is as common as the impetus to find ways of doing so, to wield regional art and literature and music and architecture to establish a connection to a place and community, regardless of that connection's "authenticity." Perhaps by enriching our understanding, appreciation, and indeed our tolerance and respect for this somewhat benign kind of difference, we may be better able to navigate other more intractable kinds of difference with a similar degree of understanding, appreciation, and respect. Viewed as such, cultivating regionalism lies at the center of even the most universal humanist endeavor.

Notes

1. There are numerous definitions of space and place, but for ones that emphasize power relationships, see John M. Findlay and Richard White, introduction to *Power and Place in the North American West*, ed. Richard White and John M. Findlay (Seattle: University of Washington Press, 1999), ix–xx; and Virginia Scharff, "Lighting Out for the Territory: Women, Mobility, and Western Place," in *Power and Place in the North American West*, ed. Richard White and John M. Findlay (Seattle: University of Washington Press, 1999), 287–303. There are good definitions of regionalism and related terms in Robert L. Dorman, *Revolt of the Provinces: The Regionalist Movement in America, 1920–1945* (Chapel Hill: University of North Carolina Press, 1993), 1–25; Heike Schaefer, introduction to *Mary Austin's Regionalism: Reflections on Gender, Genre and Geography* (Charlottesville: University of Virginia, 2004), 1–18; Barbara Allen, "Regional Studies in American Folklore Scholarship," in *Sense of Place: American Regional Cultures*, ed. Barbara Allen and Thomas Schlereth (Lexington: University of Kentucky Press, 1990), 1–13; and Thomas Schlereth, "Regional Culture Studies and American Culture Studies," in *Sense of Place: American Regional Cultures*, ed. Barbara Allen and Thomas Schlereth (Lexington: University of Kentucky Press, 1990), 164–83. For discussion on the local, see June Howard, "Unraveling Regions, Unsettling Periods: Sarah Orne Jewett and American Literary History," *American Literature* 68, no. 2 (June 1996), 365–84.

2. Pierre Bourdieu, "Identity and Representation: Elements for a Critical Reflection on the Idea of Region," in *Language and Symbolic Power*, ed. John Thompson, trans. Gino Raymond and Matthew Adamson (Cambridge MA: Harvard University Press, 1991), 220–28.

3. Douglas Reichert Powell, *Critical Regionalism: Connecting Politics and Culture in the American Landscape* (Chapel Hill: University of North Carolina Press, 2007), 34–35.

4. Annie Proulx, "Dangerous Ground, Landscape in American Fiction," (this volume), 23n1.

5. Edward Ayers and Peter Onuf, introduction to *All Over the Map, Rethinking American Regions*, ed. Edward Ayers and others (Baltimore: Johns Hopkins University Press, 1996) 1–10.

6. Dorman, *Revolt of the Provinces*, 1–25; see also Michael Steiner and David

Wrobel, "Many Wests: Discovering a Dynamic Western Regionalism," in *Many Wests: Place, Culture, and Regional Identity*, ed. David M. Wrobel and Michael C. Steiner (Lawrence: University Press of Kansas, 1997), 1–30.

7. See Wendy Katz, *Regionalism and Reform: Art and Class Formation in Antebellum Cincinnati* (Columbus: Ohio State University Press, 2002), 13–21, 95–96.

8. Frederick Jackson Turner, *The Significance of Sections in American History* (New York: Henry Holt, 1932; repr. New York: Peter Smith, 1950), 38.

9. Kurt Kinbacher, "Imagining Place: Nebraska Territory, 1854–1867," (this volume), 252. On Turner's importance to 1920s cultural nationalism, see Dorman, *Revolt of the Provinces*, 13–15, and on Smith's importance, see Dorman, *Revolt of the Provinces*, 311.

10. On "women's place" in the world disrupting regionalism's presumption of shared values, see Kathleen Wallace, "Roots, Aren't They Supposed to Be Buried? The Experience of Place in Midwestern Women's Autobiographies," in *Mapping American Culture*, ed. Wayne Franklin and Michael Steiner (Iowa City: University of Iowa Press, 1992), 168–87.

11. Donald Worster, *Rivers of Empire: Water, Aridity, and the Growth of the American West* (New York: Oxford University Press, 1985).

12. Dayton Duncan, *Miles From Nowhere: Tales from America's Contemporary Frontier* (Lincoln: University of Nebraska Press, 1993), 7.

13. Steiner and Wrobel, "Many Wests," 1–30. See also William Kittredge, *Who Owns the West?* (San Francisco: Mercury House, 1996).

14. There is considerable literature on the concept of regionalism as dependence. See particularly Henry Shapiro, *Appalachia on Our Mind: The Southern Mountains and Mountaineers in the American Consciousness, 1870–1920* (Chapel Hill: University of North Carolina Press, 1978); Henry Shapiro, "The Place of Culture and the Problem of Identity," in *Appalachia and America: Autonomy and Regional Dependence*, ed. Allen Batteau (Lexington: University of Kentucky Press, 1983), 111–41; and Allen Batteau, "Rituals of Dependence in Appalachian Kentucky," in Batteau, *Appalachia and America*, 142–67. Angela Miller offers a case study of a regionalist artist's dependence on eastern markets in "The Mechanisms of the Market and the Invention of Western Regionalism: The Example of George Caleb Bingham," in *American Iconology: New Approaches to Nineteenth-Century Art and Literature*, ed. David Miller (New Haven CT: Yale University Press, 1993), 112–34.

15. Andrew R. L. Cayton and Susan E. Gray, eds., *The American Midwest: Essays on Regional History* (Bloomington: Indiana University Press, 2001).

16. Warren Hofstra, "Reconsidering Regional History," *OAH Newsletter* 34, no. 1 (February 2006), 15–22. In 1999 the National Endowment for the Humanities, led by William Ferris, the former director of the Center for Southern Studies, initiated a multi-million-dollar competition to establish nine regional centers for the humanities. By 2005, however, most of the federal funding was cut and the nine centers, typically located at state universities, primarily serve in-state populations, albeit often with productive and exciting interdisciplinary programs.

17. Jackson is discussed below, but for humanists, Meinig's most influential book

is probably still his edited volume, *The Interpretation of Ordinary Landscapes* (New York: Oxford University Press, 1979).

18. Yi-Fu Tuan, *Space and Place: The Perspective of Experience* (Minneapolis: University of Minnesota Press, 1977).

19. See also Yi-Fu Tuan, *Topophilia: A Study Of Environmental Perception, Attitudes, and Value* (Englewood Cliffs NJ: Prentice-Hall, 1974); and Yi-Fu Tuan, "Place and Culture: Analeptic for Individuality and the World's Indifference," in Franklin and Steiner, *Mapping American Culture*, 27–49, and Schaefer, *Mary Austin's Regionalism*, 40–47.

20. Lawrence quoted in Mark Busby, "'I Don't Know, but I Ain't Lost': Defining the Southwest," (this volume), 45.

21. For this aspect of J. B. Jackson's broad-ranging ideas, see John Brinckerhoff Jackson, *A Sense of Place, a Sense of Time* (New Haven CT: Yale University Press, 1994); and Michel de Certeau, *The Practice of Everyday Life* (Berkeley: University of California Press, 1984), 117.

22. Charles Reagan Wilson, ed., introduction to *The New Regionalism: Essays and Commentaries* (Jackson: University Press of Mississippi, 1998), xi–xiii.

23. Felix Frankfurter, "Foreword," in *Regionalism in America*, ed. Merrill Jensen (Madison: University of Wisconsin Press, 1951/1965), xvi. Jensen's structural pairing of the humanities and the social sciences as equally relevant for regionalism is preserved in Michael Steiner and Clarence Mondale, *Region and Regionalism in the United States: A Source Book for the Humanities and Social Sciences* (New York: Garland Publishing Inc., 1988), though not in Wilson's anthology, which stresses the power relationships involved in the construction of regional identities.

24. Valentine, "A Border Runs through It: Regional Architecture of the Southwest," (this volume), 57.

25. Stephen C. Behrendt, "Regionalism and the Realities of Naming," (this volume), 160.

26. Kathleen Norris, *Dakota: A Spiritual Geography* (New York: Ticknor and Fields, 1993); and Robert Putnam, *Bowling Alone: The Collapse and Revival of American Community* (New York: Simon and Schuster, 2000).

27. Karen Halttunen, "Groundwork: American Studies in Place; Presidential Address," *American Quarterly* 58, no. 1 (March 2006), 1–15. The revival of regionalism in American studies is, as earlier, paired with concern about internationalism; see for example Shelley Fishkin, "Crossroads of Cultures: The Transnational Turn in American Studies; Presidential Address to the American Studies Association," *American Quarterly* 57, no. 1 (March 2005) 17–57, and Alfred Hornung, "Transnational American Studies: Response to the Presidential Address," *American Quarterly* 57, no. 1 (March 2005), 67–73.

28. William Leach, *A Country of Exiles* (New York: Pantheon Books, 1999).

29. Louise Erdrich, "A Writer's Sense of Place," in *A Place of Sense: Essays in Search of the Midwest*, ed. Michael Martone (Iowa City: University of Iowa Press, 1988), 34–44. See also Nicole Etcheson, *The Emerging Midwest: Upland Southerners and the Political Culture of the Old Northwest, 1787–1861* (Bloomington: Indiana University Press, 1996) 140–43.

30. Watts, "The Midwest as a Colony," (this volume), 181.

31. Lucy R. Lippard, *The Lure of the Local: Senses of Place in a Multicentered Society* (New York: The New Press, 1997).

32. Sylvia Rodriguez, "Art, Tourism, and Race Relations in Taos," in *Discovered Country*, ed. Scott Norris (Albuquerque: Stone Ladder Press, 1994), 143–60.

33. Andrew R. L. Cayton and Susan E. Gray, "The Story of the Midwest: An Introduction," in *The American Midwest: Essays on Regional History*, ed. Andrew R. L. Cayton and Susan E. Gray (Bloomington: Indiana University Press, 2001), 1–26.

I

Sensing Place: The Authority of Nature

Insisting on the power and authority a specific regional nature exerts over human life has particular value for writers committed to environmental conservation. Thus Annie Proulx regrets the way authors of books about middle-class life dismiss that authority of nature; the mark of middle-class existence for these modern antiregionalists is apparently its economic conquest of and consequently its distance from nature. This distance is just what makes these suburban lives feel unreal and interiorized, at least in comparison with novels of rural or poor folk upon whom nature—described in detail, which grounds the work in physical truths—still exerts force, demanding visceral responses. The country that is "jackstrawed with highways," in Proulx's vivid description, is one in which standardized consumer products and their signs are more crucial to middle-class consciousness than trees and birds; and accordingly, any sense of what's real or specific or what belongs to a place is dulled, since all such physical reality is filtered through a homogenizing web of human (not natural) interdependence.[1] For Proulx, the idea of a regionalism based on J. B. Jackson's definition of landscape as a synthetic or man-made space, a space modified to suit humans that then orders their perceptions, means that there has been a loss of an authentic and powerful natural environment that connects with and impacts human life and thus the loss of a true regional landscape.

More particularly, this erasure of "true" regionalism and the authority of its landscapes is a bad thing for anyone who is interested in preserving wild nature, separated from relationships with humans (e.g., envisioning rivers without dams or bridges). Proulx cites as a model Leslie Silko's iteration of the idea that nonwestern (true natives, in this construction) peoples do not objectify nature from outside it, but instead they form an inextricable part of the landscape. The writers like Silko whom Proulx praises as making specific landscapes an essential part of their fictions—writing rooted in "a sense of place based on regional landscape," whether it is environmental literature or novels—project human consciousness into those landscapes; the cancerous brain, for example, becomes a metaphor of nuclear tests in the Southwest—or vice versa.[2] Thus insistence on the importance of details of soil, insects, plants, weather, while at times anthropomorphizing those features, is a tradition designed to preserve (or conserve) nature from becoming another commodity. The promotion of a regionalism founded on man-made systems is less hospitable to a conservationist mission, though it offers benefits for regions like the Midwest (by privileging them in the regionalist discourse), which seem to lack just such a powerfully determining natural environment and whose distinctive features instead seem much more the product of human manipulation.

William Slaymaker's "The Ec(h)ological Conscience" is a case study of how late twentieth-century nature writers project themselves into a regional landscape, with the goal of encouraging readers to "put down roots" in particular ecosystems. In his discussion of the Plains naturalist writings of John Janovy, Loren Eiseley, and Wes Jackson, Slaymaker argues that they connect themselves emotionally to nature by personifying it and endowing it with their feelings. As Slaymaker astutely notes, the intent is to make us "like"—to feel an affinity with and a desire for—local animals and plants and to perceive our resemblance to them. Doing so is specifically an antidote to a view of nature that treats it as an economic object to be efficiently used and manipulated, because it offers instead a view of nature as a model for how *humans* should exist in a place. However, these authors also seek to recover the "wildness" of nature, its difference from human mentalities, in order to hold on to what is being ruined by human activity.

Slaymaker's examples are all scientists, often with academic affiliations, who are writing about the Plains not for scholarly peers but for a general audience, for whom their scholarly credentials presumably underwrite the accuracy and objectivity of their observations of nature, as precise botanical illustrations do for their texts. Titles like *Back in Keith County* seem designed for a regional audience who might feel particular loyalties to a specific place and so be more readily motivated to find themselves in its nature. These readers might also be willing to preserve baby owls rather than build roads that run them over. Though humans are the adversary in such "pathetic" discourses, those who interact with the nature, the land, the flora and fauna, and the climate in analogously intensive and emotional ways, even as they farm it, build on it, and construct modern life on it, are also acknowledged by these writers as constructing a deeply rooted regionalism based on the land and climate.[3]

Slaymaker sees this genre of regional naturalist writing as a continuing national literary strategy—he cites a lineage of white male writers back to Henry David Thoreau—designed to demonstrate the individual's existence as an unhomogenized and free spirit apart from or beyond any limiting human and social constraints. The usefulness of this version of regionalism, not just to conservationists but to naturalizing definitions of American manhood, is made evident by the contrast with several essays on the Midwest and Plains in the next section of this volume, where women play a much more active role in the regionalist argument and, not surprisingly, networks of social and economic dependence very much akin to crisscrossed highways are considered to be integral producers of regionalist identity, rather than barriers to it.

Because the Southwest's harsh landscape appears so inescapable, it encourages humanists to outline its seemingly most permanent and stable natural features in order to show how cultures or individuals have necessarily adapted to them. Mark Busby's study of a diverse set of Texas and Oklahoma writers—Ralph Ellison, Katherine Anne

Porter, and Cormac McCarthy—argues that the landscape's vastness, for example, induces certain recurring literary forms in these writers. Because architecture *must* respond to specific conditions of place, Maggie Valentine's survey of the Southwest convincingly establishes certain continuities in the designs of those who live there. It was clever of the National Endowment for the Humanities to include Las Vegas in the Southwest, however, as a triumphant example of how even architectural responses to place may involve as much absolute denial of place as any more "organic" relationship like those Valentine perceives in earlier settlements. For a counterexample of how humanists can tackle both regionalist literature and architecture as the product of politics rather than nature, see Cheryll Glotfelty on Nevada and Patrick Lucas on the Greek Revival in Part IV: Place is Political.

Notes

1. Proulx, "Dangerous Ground," (this volume), 18.
2. Proulx, "Dangerous Ground," (this volume), 6.
3. Slaymaker, "The Ec(h)ological Conscience," (this volume), 33.

1. Dangerous Ground

Landscape in American Fiction

ANNIE PROULX

L andscape description was once an important element in novels not only to give meaning and shape to the story but for its strange ability to carry the reader deeply and intimately inside the fiction, to establish the fiction's truth. There is a description of this literary transport in critic James Stern's account of his first reading in 1948 of a review copy of *The Aunt's Story* by the Australian writer Patrick White, then unknown. Stern wrote later, "The author's name was new to me. Within an hour my whole world had changed. I had never been to Australia, yet here was prose which, by its baroque richness, its plasticity and wealth of strange symbols, made an unknown landscape so real that I felt I could walk out into it as into country. I could see the black volcanic hills, the dead skeleton trees. . . . I could all but touch the rock, scrub, bones, the sheep's carcass, the ox's skull, as they lay bleached in Australia's eternal greyness . . . under the immense blue of its skies."[1]

A sense of place based on regional landscape—something rather different than the contemporary political boundaries of state and nation—dominated American perceptions and writing until recent decades. Referring to the literature of pretelevision days, Alfred Kazin wrote in *A Writer's America: Landscape in Fiction*:

The enduring sense of place . . . fills American writing with the sight and fury of different American settlements. And how different from each other, how often speechless with each other, these 'Americas' remain. A nation composed of many nations, a people who often have nothing in common but their being American . . . have produced a literature united only by the sense of difference within the country itself.

Yet behind all these writers still lies some everlasting background that we call "Nature"—land, the land that was here before there was anything else.[2]

American landscape novels—set in, and moved by, specific and identifiable places—bloomed in the golden period that fell in roughly the first half of the twentieth century.[3] In most of these novels landscape seemed fixed and immutable, ordering the lives of the characters who moved within it, forcing the events of the story. This use of landscape as a massive presence in a novel to shape and control the content, direction, plot, and the characters' psychological profiles distinguishes it from mere regionalism or local color and is more profound than the determinism of geography that illustrates a Turnerian combat between virgin land and strong-willed pioneers.[4] In such novels the story cannot be removed from the place any more than the unfolding of our own lives can be pulled from the places where we live and work.

Today that kind of deep landscape novel, in which the story that unfolds can only happen because of *where* it happens, is rarely written. In 1948—the same year that Ross Lockridge's *Raintree County*, rural midwestern lives seen behind a scrim of mythic dream sequences, was published—Norman Mailer's *The Naked and the Dead* appeared, its characters not within the landscape, not locked in a struggle with the climate, but in contemptuous dismissal of the authority of the natural world.[5] Mailer's novel revealed the gap that was opening between Americans who lived in cities and suburbs and those who lived in the rural countryside, a gap that is now a vast chasm. Today most Americans live in fairly dense population centers and regard the sparsely populated regions of the country as empty. They define the hinterlands only in terms of utility: scenic vistas of tourism and outdoor adventure trips; sites for seasonal vacation homes; the locus of the raw stuff of extractive industries such as timber and coal; good places for nuclear testing and missile silos, and now, for the storage of nuclear waste. They see rural and frontier regions as economically backward, without culture or the amenities of life, as unreasonably hostile to government. And the larger body of our contemporary literature, with its emphasis on middle-class suburban life, has come to reflect those attitudes.

The cognitive scientists tell us what we already know—that all human knowledge and understanding rises from stories. Information comes from us and to us as narrative. Fiction reflects our perception of ourselves in our time, our general human and individual position in the universe. For millennia the human imagination has pulled literature and mythologies from the glassy cliffs and burning ground of the wilderness, the unknown territories. The idea that geography, climate, and time dictate human culture is very old.

Landscape, Regional Writing, Local Color

We loosely use the word 'landscape' to describe the geography of a particular region. Although the phrase 'landscape writer' does not mean much, to call someone a 'regional writer' carries a certain weight. In one sense we mean a writer who uses and describes a physical landscape to make a fictional world meaningful. A regional writer is also someone whose work is identified with a specific place—William Faulkner with Mississippi; Patrick White with Australia; Frederick Phillip Grove with the Canadian prairie; John Graves, Cormac McCarthy, and Larry McMurtry with Texas; James Joyce with Dublin; Thomas Hardy with the West Country of England. Additionally, regional fiction may have a kind of representative value to local newspapers, television stations, arts councils, schools and universities, even tourism boards, a representative iconic marker of regional character that may override the writer's personal vision or the literary value of the work.

There is another category of regional literature—the collective work of a number of writers who represent a particular cultural or ethnic ethos as opposed to the main culture. Sometimes this literature springs from a specific cultural enclave (as in the works of John Fante, William Saroyan, and Sandra Cisneros) or it may exist in scattered fragments. In the late 1960s Edward Simmen, a literature teacher at the University of Texas—85 percent of his students were of Mexican descent—began looking for short stories that revealed something about the Mexican American experience. He found nothing in the national magazines nor in the small literary reviews. It took him three years to scratch up enough stories for an anthology and fourteen rejection slips before the collection was published in 1971.[6] Now, almost thirty years later, there are literally hundreds of anthologies of Mexican American writing, a subgenre of an extensive Latino literature.

The ethnic, or outsider, novels by the so-called emerging colonial voices are some of the most interesting contemporary fiction, not only in the United States but in all the old, dominant Western culture countries. In this country over the last two decades Dagoberto Gilb, Lois Ann Yamanaka, Amy Tan, Junot Diaz, Francisco Goldman, Diana Abu-Jaber, Ha Jin, Michelle Cliffe, Sherman Alexie, and many others have made reputations in American outsider literature, what cultural historian Lucy Lippard refers to in *The Lure of the Local* as the "hybrid space" between two cultures and what Chicana artist Amalia Mesa Bains sees rather differently as "a landscape of longing."[7]

The poor cousin of landscape writing and regional writing is local color—"the use of detail peculiar to a particular region and environment to add interest and authenticity to a narrative . . . description of the locale, dress, customs, music . . . for the most part decorative."[8] Decorative is the key word here. The descriptions illustrate the story but do not move it along. Local color, an almost exclusively American writing technique, was very much in vogue in the United States in the nineteenth century, usually in the form of humorous fiction that captured quaint rural customs and amusing country dialects. Contemporary mystery and horror writers continue to make good use of local color, found in Janwillem Van De Wetering's chief constable's garden with its eternal turtle or Stephen King's lonely New England roads. The novels of Graham Greene, Somerset Maugham, and sometimes

Ernest Hemingway also presented landscape as a kind of literary travel poster (or cultural signpost)—exotic backdrops against which native types moved and where, in the foreground, the main story unfolded around the European or American protagonists. Tony Hillerman's *romans policier*—which draw all of their considerable power from an inextricable knit of character, plot, climate, weather, landscape, and culture, in the specific southwest landscape of the Hopi and Navajo— go far beyond local color, and are true landscape novels.

Defining Landscape

Landscape is what is out there, what was out there, and, for the futurologists, what may be out there some day. Traversing ocean and plain was the original plot material. The *Iliad* and the *Odyssey* were accounts of adventures in strange territory. Landscape is geography, geology, archaeology, astrophysics, agronomy, agriculture, the violent character of the atmosphere, climate, black squirrels and wild oats, folded rock, bulldozers; it is jet trails and barbwire, government land, dry stream beds; it is politics, desert wildfire, introduced species, abandoned vehicles, roads, ghost towns, nuclear test grounds, swamps, a bakery shop, mine tailings, bridges, dead dogs. Landscape is rural, urban, suburban, semirural, small town, village; it is outports and bedroom communities; it is a remote ranch. Landscape is neither pure nor static. We may speak of the rural landscape as an independent (though shrinking) entity, but it is only possible to isolate rural countryside in the mind. For everything is linked.

Estelle Jussim and Elizabeth Lundquist-Cock, in their provocative *Landscape as Photograph*, name the ways we define landscape; and although they are concerned with photography—where the illusion of pure landscape *sans* humans is possible in a way it is not in fiction— there are parallel types of literary landscapes.[9] Those parallels are genre, spiritual values, landscape as fact, as symbol, as pure form, as popular culture, as concept, as politics, as propaganda. To this list we might add environmental artist Robert Smithson's concept of "absent presence"—landscape erased by storm, clear-cut, erosion, rockslide, or housing development. Smithson's act of photographing rocks *in situ* then removing them and photographing the holes in which they rested illustrates the concept.

For nearly two decades contemporary landscape photographers (the so-called new topographers) have refused to make sensuously pure landscapes, have insisted on showing the pipelines, refineries, housing developments on mountain slopes, nuclear blast grounds. There is an equivalent eye in literature, but it is in nonfiction. The few novelists who try to write about "pure" landscape today must indulge in reactionary fantasy.

Jack Kerouac's 1959 *On the Road* prefaced the work of the new topographers, although where the photographers are determinedly neutral, or objective or even documentarily censorious, Kerouac shouted in celebratory amazement at highways, car lots, billboards, the seedy outskirts of cities. He described the great rivers solely by the bridges that crossed them, the strip of landscape streaming past in a jittery, twitching roll against the spread of amorphous country, the early entry in what we now call "road books."

By the sixties a harder reflection of place glanced from American literature's mirror. Norman Mailer in his 1965 *An American Dream* wrote:

> The heat wave held. I went into two atmospheres. Five times a day, or eight, or sixteen, there was a move from hotel to car, a trip through the furnace with the sun at one hundred and ten, a sprint along the Strip (billboards the size of a canyon) a fast sprint to the car, the best passenger car in America . . . and then an aces fast turn off the Strip to land in the parking lot of the next hotel where the second atmosphere was on, the cold atmosphere, the seventy degrees of air-conditioned oxygen, that air which seemed to have come a voyage through space . . . lived in this second atmosphere for twenty-three hours of the twenty-four. . . . Nobody knew that the deserts of the West, the arid and empty wild blind deserts, were producing again a new breed of man.[10]

Landscape historian Christopher Tunnard was interested in literary landscapes, and he noted that Kerouac, Lawrence Ferlinghetti, and later, Tom Wolfe pulled the sense of urban America with them on their cross-country journeys. He added in his 1978 *World With a View: An Inquiry into the Nature of Scenic Values*, "Since the departure of the Beat Generation, modern fiction has added little to our knowledge of the physical world. The best writing has been concerned with the devastation of war, ethnic determinism, and dynamic social change. . . . One looks outside literature nowadays for signs of a deeper appreciation of landscape. 'Protect against the wrong' (the rape of the environment) has become the prerogative of a new generation of young people. They may not be able to write well, but they will not remain silent."[11]

There were certainly new nonfiction writers concerned with landscape out there, set on fire by Rachel Carson and Edward Abbey—*Silent Spring* appeared only five years before *Desert Solitaire*—and some of them wrote very well indeed. The 1970s mark the point where landscape and place descriptions began to shift out of the novel and into essays and nonfiction—Edward Hoagland's *Walking the Dead Diamond River*, John McPhee's *Coming into the Country*, Peter Mathiesson's *The Cloud Forest*, Simon Schama's *Landscape and Memory*, David Quammen's *The Song of the Dodo*, and the books of Wendell Berry, Barry Lopez, and many others. In these nonfiction works, landscape is mutable, fragile, damaged, and endangered. Fiction, meanwhile, has taken a narrower path, exploring the personal interior landscape and the family. What is *out there* seems increasingly irrelevant.

John Brinckerhoff Jackson, Tunnard's colleague at Yale and a pioneer in the history of landscape studies, describes himself as one who like "millions of other Americans . . . [has] . . . no great liking for wilderness and forest"; he is a critic of save-the-wilderness movements and inclines toward "that old fashioned but surprisingly persistent definition of landscape: 'a portion of the earth's surface that can be comprehended at a glance.'" For Jackson, landscape "is not a natural feature of the environment but a synthetic space, a man-made system of spaces superimposed on the face of the land, functioning and evolving not according to natural laws but to serve a community—for the collective character of the landscape is one thing that all generations and all points of view have agreed on."[12]

If landscape as space modified to suit humans orders our perceptions, it may partially explain why place description in fiction can draw the reader into the story. Jackson writes, "every landscape, no matter how exotic, also contains elements which we at once recognize and understand."[13] Those elements include boundaries, roads and paths, plazas and open public gathering places, sacred places, the forest, open grasslands, various habitats. Every reader instantly recognizes these ancient, globally common elements in the fictional landscape.

Jackson's handy dictionary definition of landscape, "a portion of the earth's surface that can be comprehended at a glance," is thin and only a little useful to the writer. The glance, superficial and shallow, occurs in the present tense, though there are writers who use glance landscape effectively.[14] The trend in current intellectual observation and thinking is to recognize the complexities, the stunningly intricate linkages, of the natural world with humans in it. That interest has not much stirred American fiction writers.

In objection to the simple definition of landscape, Leslie Silko, in her essay "Landscape, History and the Pueblo Imagination," wrote, "So long as the human consciousness remains within the hills, canyons, cliffs, and the plants, clouds, and the sky, the term landscape, as it has entered the English language, is misleading. . . . '[A] portion of territory the eye can comprehend in a single view' does not correctly describe the relationship between the human being and his or her surroundings. This assumes the viewer is somehow outside or separate from the territory he or she surveys. Viewers are as much a part of the landscape as the boulders they stand on."[15]

The viewers may be characters within a literary work, but they are also, by virtue of memory and prior experience and the creative demands of the work, the writer and the reader, the latter because of the reader's peculiar participatory role as receiver and interpreter of the story. The viewer and writer and reader stand metaphorically in both the unwritten and the written landscapes and enter the territory on the page at the same time it is created in the mind—a profound involvement with place through real three-dimensional landscapes and the described and imagined landscape.

Beyond Definition

Traditionally, landscape in fiction is more than what the eye quickly sees. It includes what Kazin was getting at when he wrote of that "everlasting background that we call 'Nature'—land, the land that was here before there was anything else."[16] Everything of the natural place may swell into the story: the underlying geology, insects, temperature extremes, shoreline, seasonal shift of daylight. Landscape is the sum of accumulated changes wrought by the inhabitants and their marks on the land, as the farmer protagonist Leszek in Charles T. Powers's *In the Memory of the Forest* understood when he remarked, "memories recurred; like stones in a path—they pushed up. Memory had a future as well as a past."[17] Rural people, such as the characters in John Berger's novels, are *of* the landscape, their lives ruled by place. And when landscape is presented in detail in fiction, it literally grounds the work, gives it a strength and sense of truth not possible to achieve through words on the page in any other way.

Marjorie Kinnan Rawlings's novels of the 1930s (e.g., *South Moon Under* and *The Yearling*), where the lives of backwoods Florida crackers are inextricably meshed with scrub country, show deep use of landscape. Rawlings struggled to write fiction for years, and it was only when she moved to Florida that she found her voice. In a 1931 letter to Scribner editor Maxwell Perkins, she wrote about the landscape and the people who were the focus of her work.

> There is no human habitation—there never has been and probably never will be—in the scrub itself. As far as I can determine, there is no similar section anywhere in the world. The scrub is a silent stretch enclosed by two rivers, deeply forested with southern spruce (almost valueless), scrub oak, scrub myrtle and ti-ti, occasional gall-berry and black-jack. . . . There is an occasional small lake. . . . The only settlement is here and there on these bodies of water, and along the river edges, where the natural hammock growth

has been bitten into by the settlers' clearings. It is a fringe of life, following the waterways.

Many [of the inhabitants'] expressions are very beautiful. The fish and deer, in fact most of the game, feed 'on the moon'—at moonrise, moon-down, south-moon-over and south-moon-under. The people are conscious at all times of the positions of the sun and moon and stars and wind. They *feel* the moon under the earth—south-moon-under.[18]

The West in Fiction

In literature the American west has been variously seen as "feminine" in the sense of conquerable; as a hard testing ground for men; as empty and unmarked and, by virtue of this quality, able to erase the signs of human endeavor and passage; as the grief-haunted place of destruction of Native American lives and culture; as an ecological disaster zone for bison, native grasses, soil, native plants, and free-running rivers; and, in the last few years, as neutered and defenseless territory threatened by humans, their domestic livestock, and technologies. Today we are beginning to recognize that the inimical force which subdues all is not the landscape but humankind. Victim and oppressor have exchanged places.

Many of the earlier American fiction writers working in western landscapes depended on a simple call- and-response approach. In their works the landscape was almost always frontier and hostile—*malpais*, chasmed, unknown, inhabited by dangerous tribes with deep understanding of the terrain and place. The survival of the white protagonists (and the continuation of the story) depended on nick-of-time luck, ability to withstand physical hardship, or the help of wise man or woman characters. Almost never did the protagonist display any sense of belonging to or understanding of the country through which he journeyed, nor did he try to learn much about it. The situation of place was always antithetical; the protagonist, always surprised and at the worst advantage but ultimately victorious.

In American literature the western landscape has sometimes functioned as a substitute for the European forest. That old forest (and the eastern American forest) was tenebrous; difficult to find one's way through for lack of sightlines; inhabited by brigands and thieves, wolves and evil mythological creatures with magic powers; moist and claustrophobic; full of squeaking trees and hoo-hooing owls. The outside world was distant and shuttered. By contrast, the American West was brilliantly lit and treeless, vast and featureless, especially the *llano estacado* of Texas and New Mexico. The immensity was broken by badlands and towering mountains, watered by poisonous springs and boiling fumaroles. There were grizzlies and mountain lions. The weather—wind, tornado, thunderstorm, earthquake, paralyzing cold, blizzard—outclassed any forest in vindictive malevolence. The matter of concern was not losing one's way (a central theme in traditional and religious literature) but staying alive. In the end, the aim of the new-comers was to subdue both landscape and its wild inhabitants.

Some of these old signs can be recognized in Cormac McCarthy's books. *Blood Meridian, or the Evening Redness in the West* is set in a monstrous place of dust, rock, "little patches of twisted grass," and landscape whose impersonal vastness forces the stunted characters to commit acts of atrocity.[19] Landscape functions here as it does in much western landscape writing—as godlike force. The band of nihilist conquerors pushes blindly westward, driven only by the necessity to move against the evening redness. When at last they reach the sea, when at last there is no more landscape, nothing more to take, to crush, to cat-alog, to know, to possess, the book ends. The western American land-scape literally shapes this novel structurally, historically, and mythi-cally; *Blood Meridian* is a complex map drawn in words.

Travelers moving through the high plains states today are impressed with the seemingly empty land and the huge sky that shows multiple thunderstorms a hundred miles away. The landscape seems overpower-ingly massive. The eye glides over the thready fence lines and the dusty side roads. The place seems unchanged when photographs from a hun-dred years ago are held up against it—the same buttes, the same long draws, the same sharp mountain profiles. Yet every inch of this land, used primarily as sheep and cattle range, is partitioned, leased, owned, and jealously watched. Writers working with this terrain understand that exotics have replaced native grasses; that domestic cattle graze instead of bison; that nomadic tepee camps are no more, reservations in their place; that many species of animals are sliding toward extinction; that streams and surface water are less, dams more; that roads and railroad tracks and irrigation ditches cut everywhere; and that barbwire fence in hundreds of thousands of rectilinear miles divides it to the last inch. This, too, is a cultural landscape.

The Frontier

The center of historian Frederick Jackson Turner's western expansion thesis held that the empty frontier—locus of the free-for-all chance to own land and make good—closed around 1890. The chances were gone, the westward push ended. Revisionist historians have challenged his concept of the closed frontier in recent decades. The open range may have closed with the introduction of barbwire, ending the long trail drives north; but if the accepted definition of frontier is a population index, the frontier persisted and still exists.

The crucial identification of frontier is a population of less than two inhabitants per square mile. Dayton Duncan, in his 1993 *Miles From Nowhere*, found that the 1990 U.S. census "counted 132 counties within fifteen western states . . . that still had fewer than two people per square mile."[20] Those extremely rural frontier areas comprise 13 percent of the landmass of the contiguous United States, strikingly similar to the population map of 1890. (This is the region blocked out on television weather broadcasts by the body of the announcer who stands before the map—such sparsely populated country hardly matters.)

The invention and manufacture of the automobile and paved highways provided the national psyche with a surrogate frontier. By 1927, 26 million cars stank and jarred around the country, each driver a pioneer. For the following generation, the mythic drive from coast- to-coast became a rite of passage; and the road book, an important American literary form. Dwight Eisenhower, who had led a rough expedition of troops across the country after the First World War to demonstrate (for military purposes) the ghastly condition of American roads, didn't get his chance until a decade after the Second World War. In 1956, as President, he signed into law the Interstate Highway Act, which was described at the time as the most expensive public works project in the history of the world. Our perception of landscape and the parts that make up a landscape changed violently and forever.

From inside the automobile, the landscape was transformed into a swiftly streaming mass of soft color, whether thick tunnels of eastern maple and oak, the pale soil and spiky herbage of the southwest, the khaki-colored plains, or the massy conifers of the northwest rainforest. In a landscape always receding or approaching, individual trees, small animals, and lesser streams disappeared in the blur. The pictorial, the framed but vague windshield view, replaced the particular and the specific. Today the country, jackstrawed with highways, is easily traversed—no place in the continental United States lies more than twenty-one miles from a road.[21] It is a rare American who, on a ten minute walk, can identify and describe common birds, trees, or wildflowers. On a long journey the landmarks we look for and at are motels, signs, eateries, gas stations. The larger landscape is simply amorphous background. This fading view produces novels where streets, feelings, body language, contemporary manners, interiors, clothes, and consumer products are the salient features of a place.

Time

It is a writer's thought that nothing we see has meaning unless we understand how it was in the past—the element of time, the slow accretion of change, the seeming immutability of rural land forms. The southern novelist Mary Lee Settle uses landscape in layers of time to unfold a story that spans some generations in her *Beulah* quintet. Critic Brian Rosenberg comments:

> the sense of permanence created by the continued presence throughout the novels of such recognizable landmarks as the river, which as it flows through the quintet virtually takes on the personality of a character, or the shape of a valley itself. Even human additions to the landscape reappear and are reunderstood. When the grave of the

SENSING PLACE

murdered con man Squire Raglan that was dug in *O Beulah Land* is romanticized in *Know Nothing* into an Indian burial mound, the sense of timelessness created by the invulnerability of the grave itself seems inseparable from the sense of evolution created by its misrepresentation. Like many imaginative historians of the nineteenth century, Settle uses the sheer physical presence of the land to place in perspective the changes wrought by time and man.[22]

Curiously, this dynamic feature of landscape is missing in most contemporary fiction; writers present us with a static description of the world through which the characters move, only occasionally relieved by flashbacks or flash-forwards, despite the examples of Italo Calvino, Franz Kafka, Alain Robbe-Grillet, and William Golding, and more recently Mary Lee Settle, Donald Antrim, Alan Lightman, Salman Rushdie, and Orhan Pamuk, all of whom have written novels shot through with metamorphosis and change, damage and repair, with elements of time as slippery as eels. Yet never has there been a time in human history when landscapes have changed and disappeared with such rapidity. Gone or going are the chestnut trees, elms, and old-growth forests; prairie potholes and swamps; vast flights of passenger pigeons; codfish; night skies black and without planes, satellites, or urban glow; unclimbed mountains; rivers without dams or bridges.

The old Pequot Path was an ancient and wooded Indian trail that ran along the southern New England coast before bending north to what is now Maine. As white settlements grew, it metamorphosed into a stagecoach road, then became The Old Post Road and eventually a turnpike. In 1925 it became U.S. Route 1, the first named road in the federal government's new numbering system. A 1938 WPA writer described it as "depressingly ugly, being characterized by hideous shacks, enormous signs, dumps and raw cuts."[23] Yet it follows the same route and serves the same purpose as it did 350 years earlier: to carry human traffic. The Pequot Path is an example of the living dynamism of place, a type of historical observation that does not interest many contemporary writers.

Often the past is carried in the names of landscape parts, indicators of old events but also of the workings of other humans' minds, others' eyes. Years ago Robert Smithson walked through Passaic, New Jersey, and said it was as though he were walking on an enormous aerial photograph; the river was a monstrous blank movie film playing a continuous loop. And seen from the air, the Midwest is mile-squared by roads, a circular urban conglomeration appearing every thirty or forty miles like pancake batter on a griddle. There are unseen landscapes in gazetteers and on maps—Knife Point Mountain, Teapot Dome, Death Valley, Book Cliffs, Joe Batt's Arm, Seldom-Come-By—landscapes as fantastic as that glimpsed by the blind man, sight restored, in the Gospel of St. Mark who saw "men like trees, walking."[24]

Flight from Fiction

Today it is almost impossible to write about landscape without reference to economics, politics, and human manipulation of the environment. Parallel with these critical and investigative perceptions, landscape description has shifted out of the novel and into the essay, especially into the new, nonfiction genre of environmental literature. Most Americans believe that landscapes are no longer the fixed and monolithic underpinnings of everything in life and instead accept them as vulnerable and damaged in innumerable places. The novels of Don DeLillo extend the damage to American culture, which exists in a landscape of disintegrating values. If one tries to think about McCarthy's *Blood Meridian* while seated on a night jet booming over the rivers of light that are highways or of *South Moon Under* while driving through the billboards of Florida, the power of the novels ebbs away, diminished by what we see. The worlds inside these novels are no longer true.

Roderick Nash's *Wilderness and the American Mind*, Bill McKibben's *End of Nature*, and scores of other books by observers of landscape, by preservationists and conservationists have repeated the lesson if we cannot see it with our own eyes. It is difficult now for geography to define a contemporary novel because we believe there is little true landscape left. David Quammen began his *The Song of the Dodo* with an arresting image of a fine Persian carpet and a hunting knife.

The carpet is cut into dozens of pieces, still recognizable carpet-stuff, still roughly the same total area. What, he asks, have we got? "Have we got thirty-six nice Persian throw rugs? No. All we're left with is three dozen ragged fragments, each one worthless and commencing to come apart. . . . An ecosystem is a tapestry of species and relationships. Chop away a section, isolate that section, and there arises the problem of unraveling."[25]

This unraveling is visible in Dayton Duncan's sentimentalized frontier—the sparsely settled regions are indeed still there, but they fall in a pattern of isolate pieces economically connected to, and controlled by, some urban center where one can enjoy a cappuccino, buy a computer, get the vehicle repaired, see a movie, visit a doctor, get one's hair dyed magenta. For many rural people the nearest Wal-Mart serves as a substitute for a town.

This common acceptance of spoiled rural landscape is reflected in Canadian writer Moira Farr's essay, "The Death of Nature Writing."

> Only a very naive or dishonest writer would head off today into what he or she took to be the unspoiled wilderness, and engage with it in the manner of a Dillard or a Thoreau. It would be self-indulgent, to say the least, to write of one's communion with a mighty river, while failing to mention that the last remaining fish in it bulge with cancerous tumours. A contemporary writer would probably hesitate to find in leaves, vegetable mould or maple keys uplifting metaphors for the transcendent self; at the edge of the imagination sways a chorus of furies crying Acid Rain! Global Warming! Deforestation! Desertification! Dead Dolphins in Drift Nets! Species Extinction! Nuclear Meltdown! Dioxins in (Your) Breast Milk![26]

And from that viewpoint, how disturbing becomes the phrase from one of Yasunari Kawabata's novels—"my life, a fragment of a landscape."[27]

Today's fiction writers who wish to use landscape description as the underpinning of a work must face down a common belief that pristine wildernesses and even rural regions are eroded and ravaged, as well as a swelling tide of urban and suburban readers and critics who have little or no experience of the natural world. They cannot connect. To millions of Americans, "Nature" is a reference to a chain of stores that sells rocks and fossils and T-shirts stamped with images of eagles in flight. To millions, "landscape" is something done by a merchant who deals in cookie-cutter shrubs and bedding plants. The vast number of readers, editors, booksellers, critics—and writers themselves—have little knowledge or recognition of landforms, regional differences, wilderness areas, or even the existence of extensive rural and frontier locales.

A decade ago in an introduction to Susan Lowell's short story collection, *Ganado Red*, Phillip Lopate reiterated the urban assumption that landscape in literature is little more than window trimming. "I should say something solemn here about the author's feeling for the land, but since I am a thorough urbanite who feels more comfortable with subways than wildflowers, and who usually falls asleep when reading what I am tempted to call the 'narcissism of landscape,' I will only add that Susan Lowell's place descriptions do not put me to sleep."[28]

Yet the first story in Lowell's collection, "White Canyon," deals with a young family in the 1950s in Utah, where "parents roused their children from bed to watch the atomic explosions bubble up in the sky."[29] The story concerns a uranium geologist's daughter, who spent her childhood in White Canyon but developed brain cancer as an adult. The story is built on and draws its meaning specifically from the southwestern desert swept by fallout storms in the days of nuclear tests. Without this landscape the story could not exist, and it is depressingly clear that Lopate does not recognize this.

In the last few decades, novels and stories rooted in and sustained by deep landscape have become dangerous ground.[30] Even the minor use of place to control and move the story seems in decline. For example, Jane Smiley's 1991 novel, *A Thousand Acres*, begins with a description of the farm in terms of its boundary roads. Yet except for presenting the land as a vague substance to be worked by agricultural machinery, there are almost no passages linking the events of the story to soils, insects, plant growth, weeds, weather, or climate (aside from a mediocre storm), which are all crucial elements in farming since time

SENSING PLACE

immemorial. The omission, deliberate, one supposes, has the effect of transforming the land(scape) into quantitative commodity.

Perhaps one can say that the absence of landscape description where it might serve is a contemporary writer's twist in the techniques and tricks of the novel. So too may be the use of repetitive and interchangeable details of the coast- to-coast nowhere and the substitution of the steering wheel for the curve of the earth. Or is it a reflection of the highway society that we have become, proof of our growing insensitivity to the complex parts of the natural world, of our proud ignorance, of our inability to understand any of the deep meanings of place and time?

Notes

An early, unpublished version of this article was circulated for colloquium discussion at Yale University's Program in Agrarian Studies, October 30, 1998. A later version was presented as the Van der Leeuw Lecture in Groningen, Holland, October 22, 1999. The proceedings were published as Annie Proulx, *Gevaarlijk terrein: het landschap in de Amerikaanse literatuur*, also including Jan Donkers, *En dan: wat is natuur nog in dit land?*, ed. Paul Brill (Amsterdam: De Volkskrant Boekenfonds, 1999).

1. James Stern, "Patrick White: The Country of the Mind," *London Magazine*, 5, no. 6, June 1958, 49, cited in David Marr, *Patrick White: A Life* (New York: Knopf, 1992), 304. White had returned to Australia to find his literary voice, his place, after years of living abroad; and for the rest of his life, hating Australia and Australians, a self-condemned prisoner, he wrote his savagely beautiful novels. Yet he never ventured into the Australian outback but, instead, studied Sidney Nolan's paintings, which he first saw in 1949, and used them as the basis of the vivid landscape descriptions for that red, seared land in *Voss*.

2. Alfred Kazin, *A Writer's America: Landscape in Literature* (New York: Knopf, 1988), 8.

3. Jack London's *Call of the Wild* (1903), Willa Cather's *My Antonia* (1918), William Faulkner's *The Sound and the Fury* (1929), Marjorie Kinnan Rawlings's *South Moon Under* (1933), H. L. Davis's *Honey in the Horn* (1935), Walter Edmond's *Drums Along the Mohawk* (1936), Kenneth Roberts's *Northwest Passage*, John Steinbeck's *Grapes of Wrath* (1939), Walter Van Tilburg Clark's *The Ox Bow Incident* (1940), Flannery O'Connor's *Wise Blood* (1952), Ross Lockridge's *Raintree County* (1948), and much of what Ernest Hemingway wrote resonated with the sense of place.

4. Diane Dufra Quantic's *The Nature of the Place: A Study of Great Plains Fiction* (Lincoln: University of Nebraska Press, 1995) is a valuable examination of the land and human confrontation in the novels of Wright Morris, Willa Cather, Marie Sandoz, Laura Ingalls Wilder, and O. E. Rolvaag.

5. Ross Lockridge, *Raintree County* (Boston: Houghton Mifflin Company, 1948); Norman Mailer, *The Naked and the Dead* (New York: Rinehart, 1948).

6. Edward Simmen, *The Chicano: From Caricature to Self-Portrait* (New York: New American Library, 1971).

7. Lippard, *The Lure of the Local*, 8.

8. J. A. Cuddon and Claire Preston, *A Dictionary of Literary Terms and Literary Theory*, 4th ed. (Cambridge MA: Blackwell, 1998), 476.

9. Estelle Jussim and Elizabeth Lindquist-Cock, *Landscape as Photograph* (New Haven CT: Yale University Press, 1985).

10. Norman Mailer, *An American Dream* (New York: Dial Press, 1965), 268–69; see also Aaron Betsky, "Emptiness on the Range: Western Spaces," in *Crossing the Frontier: Photographs of the Developing West, 1949 to the Present* (San Francisco: Chronicle Books, 1996).

11. Christopher Tunnard, *A World with a View: An Inquiry into the Nature of Scenic Values* (New Haven CT: Yale University Press, 1978), 65.

12. John Brinckerhoff Jackson, *Discovering the Vernacular Landscape* (New Haven CT: Yale University Press, 1984), 12.

13. Jackson, *Discovering the Vernacular Landscape*, 11.

14. The definition is persistent because it is a dictionary definition. Jackson has his critics. James Howard Kunstler, *The Geography of Nowhere* (New York: Touchstone, 1994), 122–123, excoriates him as an academic apologist for "the ubiquitous highway crud" and finds him lacking in "critical faculties." See Bret Easton Ellis, *Less Than Zero* (New York: Simon and Shuster, 1985); Stephen Wright, *Going Native* (New York: Farrar, Straus, and Giroux, 1993).

15. Cited in A. Carl Bredahl, "Landscape: The Perceiver and the Coursing of Human Events," in *The Big Empty: Essays on Western Landscapes as Narrative*, ed. Leonard Engel (Albuquerque: University of New Mexico Press, 1994), 304.

16. Kazin, *A Writer's America*, 8.

17. Charles T. Powers, *In the Memory of the Forest* (New York: Scribner, 1997), 282.

18. Marjorie Kinnan Rawlings, *The Marjorie Kinnan Rawlings Reader* (New York: Scribner, 1956), xii–xiii.

19. Cormac McCarthy, *Blood Meridian, or the Evening Redness in the West* (New York: Vintage, 1992).

20. Duncan, *Miles from Nowhere*, 7.

21. Alexander Wilson, *The Culture of Nature* (Cambridge MA: Blackwell, 1992), 40.

22. Brian Rosenberg, *Mary Lee Settle's Beulah Quintet: The Price of Freedom* (Baton Rouge: Louisiana State University Press, 1991), 20.

23. Federal Writers' Project, *U.S. One: Maine to Florida* (New York: Modern Age Books, Inc., 1938), xv.

24. Robert Smithson, "The Monuments of Passaic," *Artforum* 7 no. 4 (December 1967): 48–51. Mark 8:22–26.

25. David Quammen, *The Song of the Dodo: Island Biogeography in an Age of Extinction* (New York: Scribner, 1996), 11.

26. Moira Farr, "The Death of Nature Writing," *Brick*, no. 47 (Winter 1993): 19.

27. Yasunari Kawabata, *The Master of Go*, trans. Edward G. Seidensticker (New York: Knopf, 1972), 149.

28. Phillip Lopate, foreword to *Ganado Red*, by Susan Lowell (Minneapolis: Milkweed, 1988).

29. Lowell, *Ganado Red*, 13.

30. There are a number of contemporary American writers who use landscape as a powerful and central engine in their fiction. Notable are the novels of Peter Mathiesson, Tim O'Brien's *The Things They Carried*, the stories of Lydia Davis, and Joyce Carol Oates's *What I Lived For*, a rare example of urban landscape and architecture used to shape and move the protagonist's life.

2. The Ec(h)ological Conscience

Reflections on the Nature of Human Presence in Great Plains Environmental Writing

WILLIAM SLAYMAKER

Since Aristotle, philosophers have modeled human behavior on what could be discovered in nature. The "natural" became the standard for human thought and action. Aquinas made this paradigmatic strategy an important part of Roman Catholic dogma.

The British linguistic philosopher G. E. Moore argued that such naturalistic normative propositions could be either true or false, because they were imprecisely structured and expressed. Accordingly, the attempt to derive what ought to be and what we ought to do based on what naturally exists was especially flawed, and he labeled such thinking "the Naturalistic Fallacy."[1]

Similarly, some literary critics and aestheticians, such as the nineteenth-century British art critic John Ruskin, have objected to graphic, rhetorical, or any aesthetic ploys and strategies that would intrude the human into nature. Ruskin's term for mirroring human emotive and affective states in natural scenes and animal behavior was "the Pathetic Fallacy." Ruskin and his intellectual sympathizers thought it was false to make nature a parabolic reflector of human emotions and states of mind. Unlike the Naturalistic Fallacy, the Pathetic Fallacy is not based on an error in logic but on an improper aesthetic judgment. Ruskin and like-minded critics claim that the Pathetic Fallacy is an invasive form of personification and an exaggerated rhetorical use of the tropological figure traditionally labeled prosopopoeia.[2]

Creative writers utilizing nature and the environment, even those with advanced degrees in the natural sciences, usually pay little mind to these theoretical objections. Rather, scientifically trained writers often project themselves into nature, evincing sympathy and empathy with what they environmentally experience. They focus on, amplify, and echo landscapes and their human, animal, and vegetable inhabitants. Anthropomorphism abides in their work, illogically some have argued and immorally others would claim. The debate about the legitimacy of anthropomorphic portraits of animals itself has a long and complex history. Eileen Crist's *Images of Animals* offers an academic overview of the opposing sides. In her study of linguistic representations of the animal mind and behaviors by naturalists, ethologists, and sociobiologists from Charles Darwin to E. O. Wilson (mid-nineteenth century to the end of the twentieth century), she concludes that while many scientifically trained nature writers have eschewed anthropomorphism, this approach "discloses the nature of animal life with the power and internal cohesion that real worlds possess."[3] In her view, ascribing emotions and intentions to animals is acceptably affective and thus an effective way to write about nature. Using affective anthropomorphic language reduces human-animal distance and constructs a normative natural world in which humans are less likely to be alienated or remote from the nonhuman other.

It seems quite natural for writers, especially those with substantial scientific backgrounds, to thrust their points of view into the scheme of the palpable world and just as logical and ethical to derive what ought to be from what is. Such naturalistic strategies in the creative narrative essay lead nature writers to portray human consciousness and moral conscience as reflections or echoes of animal and even plant behaviors. And since most nature writers with extensive scientific qualifications accept a Darwinian evolutionary paradigm as an explanatory model of what exists in the biological world, mirroring the human mind in nonhuman beings and events appears quite natural, even if they are only a dim or even distorted reflection of what appears to the human eye and impinges on the human ear. Echoes are never perfect reproductions of original sounds, just as mirrors disfigure images. Still, we recognize our own and other voices and sounds in the mutations of the original. Further, we delight in perceiving what we think is a part of human history, even though it is really natural history that has been manifoldly but recognizably transcribed as a part of the process of translating, transforming, and inserting the alien other into human mental processes, which then record what we think exists.

How could it be otherwise for nature writers? How else could a nature writer think or write? How could it be false—a Pathetic or Naturalistic Fallacy—to make nature into a symbol or metaphor of how humans think and live? Projecting the conscious and conscientious self into an unconscious environment is quite naturally the way we represent ourselves and animals and plants that are integral parts of our experiential world. This projection is of course a dominating and colonizing one, even a patronizing project. Here is the objection for those who resist anthropomorphism and its more objectionable cousin, anthropocentrism. The former means that we "morph" or transform the natural world to meet our expectations and to support our limited understanding and representation of the "other" or alien world of nonlingual, unconscious nature. The latter seems more insidious for it makes humans—the *anthropoi*—the center of all value and the proper judges of natural values, inventing an inventory of what is natural and acceptable and what is not. But, as Lorraine Daston and Gregg Mitman point out in the introduction to their essay collection *Thinking with Animals*, "[t]he advent of evolutionary theory, which posits phylogenetic continuities between humans and other animals, has made the ban on anthropomorphism difficult to sustain in principle as well as in practice in the life sciences."[4]

In examining four nature writers who help us to imagine Great Plains landscapes and life—Loren Eiseley, John Janovy, Paul Johnsgard, and Wes Jackson, all of whom have PhD's in a scientific discipline—it becomes obvious that these trained observers are not just parabolic antennae amplifying signals from nature. Rather, they are focused on what is beautiful and admirable and amazing in the natural world and what humans ought to see and do in order to preserve this rich world of familiar beings that are not alien after all but instead are natural "family" members. They are deeply embedded and integrated into their scientific disciplines, but even more they are interested and involved in the nature they investigate and communicate to students and general audiences. This is the case even though they are aware of the alienation of human consciousness from its natural environment. They know that most undomesticated wild animals avoid us and are estranged from us. The vegetable world is unconsciously remote, unaware of our existence—seemingly uncaring, cold, and distant. They are well educated and sophisticated readers of both natural and human texts and dramas. As professional nature writers and as professors, they are well apprised of the traps and pitfalls of anthropomorphism and especially anthropocentrism. They have been trained to recognize—and perhaps warned to avoid—the Naturalistic and the Pathetic fallacies. Nonetheless, the creative intent of these four Great Plains writers is to make us like animals and plants, in both senses of the word "like": we both feel affinity with them and desire their presence as well as resemble them and perceive natural homologies. We like them and we are like them in the dual sense of resemblance and affection. But we also are very aware of the gulf that divides the conscious and the unconscious worlds. Our thinking and linguistic capabilities exclude us from nonhuman communities. We admire birds and want to imaginatively enter their worlds. However, they dislike or suspect us and want to fly from our presence, or they are unconcerned or uninterested in us except at feeding time.

These four environmental writers often hear a different message in bird songs and visualize a different lesson in bird migrations or movements. They do not write exclusively about birds, yet birds often are the indicator species for environmental health or disease. Birds are creatures that they often associate with or intersect with and that reflect their own states of mind, becoming the anthropomorphized avatars of the natural world. In any case, they are thinking and writing about and with the animals on the Great Plains landscapes. In Wes Jackson's case, he does not promote prairie animals so much as he does prairie grasses. He is an animated defender of prairie grasses, even in consciously re-created biogenetic forms that may serve human more than natural prairie interests; for prairie grasses have no interests except survival and certainly no voluntary or willful strategies for their own adaptive success.[5]

Consumers and audiences for Great Plains nature writing look for and long for this sort of intimate and authenticated imaging of the life forms on the prairie. The education, experience, and abilities of these four Great Plains nature writers validate their entries into and speculations about nonhumans, even if their nature tales are "fabulous," in the sense of fables that are fabricated for our entertainment and moral instruction but not objectively or scientifically true. To make nature into an "echo" of humans is not necessarily bad science or logically or rhetorically fallacious, rather it is what we expect of good nature writers who have a commitment to saving an environment and in this case, to the restoration of an ecoregion.

Loren Eiseley, the Lincoln, Nebraska, nature essayist and paleontologist, was one of the most popularly read and imitated writers during the third quarter of the twentieth century. Because of his training, he accused himself of being a "revolving eye," which, like a beacon in a "desiccated skull," sees the natural world with the unimpassioned neutrality of the scientist.[6] The chapter "The Star Thrower" from his *Unexpected Universe* is bent on disproving the hypothesis, which was made early in that chapter, that science and human consciousness look upon the "debris of life" with analytic skepticism amounting almost to nihilism.[7] Eiseley shows us in the course of narrating "The Star Thrower" that he is really connected with the natural universe through his implication in natural life and his human hope to maintain nonhuman life, specifically the lives of starfish washed up on the beach by the surf.

The reverse is true for birds. While the human mind and imagination are fascinated by avian life forms, the birds in Eiseley's essays remain remote or disturbed by human intrusion into their domains. For example, his essay "The Judgment of the Birds" in the collection *The Immense Journey* depicts white pigeons as surreal inhabitants of tall buildings and skyscrapers—dreamlike denizens of nighttime cityscapes. A crow has a painful encounter with him in the fog; and Eiseley speculates that the crow, disoriented by the thick curtain of fog, is surprised to find a human in a realm only birds are supposed to inhabit. Eiseley projects himself into the unconscious and nonlinguistic crow, in order to represent himself to the crow as an alien and disconcerting unnatural event and object. His clever narrative rhetorical strategy diverts the echo and deflects his own image in the crow's ears and eyes. By such means, he is able to make the human self strange and an interloper in an otherwise perfectly natural world of birds and fog.

Another essay in *The Immense Journey*, "The Bird and the Machine," repeats this natural process of personification. The human narrator recounts the capture of a sparrow hawk that rejoins its mate in a fierce and passionate sky dance when released the next day. For Eiseley this anthropomorphized loyalty and hope, which are rewarded with reunion, are evidence that birds and humans—and not machines—share a complex of emotions that unite them even though the distance that separates their conscious understanding of each other is immense. As the book title points out, humans have traveled through time, made an immense journey; but despite the temporal and evolutionary gulfs that divide us from our avian ancestors, we have the cognitive capacity to imagine and project our feelings into birds or anything else nonhuman. The ecstatic recoupling of the sparrow hawks, their shrieks of reengagement, resound through time and break the human-animal barrier to remind Eiseley of the shared joy and passion of the birds, his and theirs. To make matters worse for the defenders of the Naturalistic or Pathetic fallacies, Eiseley is obviously suggesting that what we humans ought to do in our own lives is to live with the same passionate loyalty to our mates. Deriving ought from what naturally is or interpreting our thoughts and feelings about bird behaviors as evidence of natural truth creates the fallacies and drives the controversy.

John Janovy, professor of parasitology at the University of Nebraska–Lincoln, has mirrored and echoed Eiseley's moralistic naturalism with his own experiences, which are richly embedded in the living landscapes of the Great Plains. Two of his early essay collections,

Keith County Journal and *Back in Keith County*, show how birds move snails to remote places like Sand Hills stocktanks and even to fountain pools in Lincoln, several hundred miles away. In his essay "Pioneers," in *Keith County Journal*, he compares the migrations of snails and their evolving natural adaptive abilities to his own desires to move and resettle and experience new environments. He envies the "Snail King" (*Stagnicola elodes*) because it has found its place in the "calm, serene, warm" waters of Keith County and secured its time in evolutionary history. But like the snail, Janovy wants to do some pioneering. He concludes his two chapters on the snail by shifting the landscape from western Nebraska to Lincoln in the late fall. He hears geese going over his house, migrating south. They represent migrating snail eggs to him. And he vows to do what they are doing: "I will pioneer somewhere, perhaps somewhere in the mind, but somewhere; I will take that time, simply, forcibly if necessary, take that time, to pioneer in some way."[8] Janovy's conclusion: Snails "R" Us! Humans share with snails, birds, and all migrating creatures the capacity to change environments and adapt to them. Even more, humans share with other complex living organisms the desire and the need to move, hence Janovy's recurring metaphor of pioneering as a natural human impulse shared by nonhuman beings.

Many of the chapters in *Keith County Journal*, as well as in his sequel *Back in Keith County*, dwell on birds. As a parasitologist, he communes with the avian hosts of parasites and serves them up to his students and readers as evidence of the braided insinuations of all life forms into human consciousness. His detailed pencil drawings of the birds he studies reinforce his intrusion into the lives of the birds whose beauty and utility fascinate him. Wrens, swallows, herons, owls, kingfishers, all the birds he encounters on his collecting trips grab his attention. He tries to get his observations of them right and make his drawings anatomically accurate. Like Eiseley, he pours his soul into the apparitions of the birds yet confesses that collecting swallows is the most alienating experience a biologist can have. Touching and collecting swallow nests, he experiences the radical wildness and otherness of birds. It is a disturbing feeling.

The chapter "Owls," in *Back in Keith County*, is a revelation of death and the apocalyptic end of a burrowing owl family. They live too near a curve in the highway, and all the fledglings are run over, squashed flat by cars negotiating the curve, unable or unwilling to avoid the jaywalking owls. Janovy ascribes to the owls a sort of freedom of choice in their choice of a roadside burrow. Thus, they become somehow responsible for the consequences of their site selection. The owls also become the focus of intense human attention and concern for their growth and survival. He and his students are disheartened and demoralized with each flattened, ant-riddled owlet they find on the highway. While the story of the owls illustrates the lesson of the fragility of natural lives and the loss of investment of time and energy by parent owls, the real underlying impact of the essay is the emotional investment of Janovy and his students in the survival of this owl family. For their part, the owls have no clue that one hundred humans are observing them and rooting for their survival. The emotional osmosis membrane is one way: from humans to owls. Ecologically speaking, the deaths of the young owls were no great loss. Logically examined, death always wins sooner or later. Emotionally considered, the loss of owls was a sad lesson. It was all natural, quite logical, and within the parameters of expected owlet mortality rates. But neither Janovy nor his students could stoically accept the massacre of avian life. Empathy is a natural form of the Pathetic Fallacy.

The recognition and acceptance of avian mortality rates is not the message that comes across in Janovy's essay. Rather the reader feels the intensity of his interest and direct emotional involvement in the lives of the owls. As an engaged nature writer, Janovy is sympathetic and, even more, empathetic to the lives of nonhuman beings. And this is what readers of nature essays expect from this type of writing and this point of view. We expect to be intimately involved in the narrator's pathetic perspectives. Indeed we as an audience (hearing the words) and as readers and viewers (seeing the words and line drawings on the pages) would agree that the death of the young owls is pathetic in the dual sense of what we feel and the unnecessary tragic deaths they experience. The communication of shared personal perspectives and the rhetorical staging of emotive states are some of the narrative strategies that make Janovy's essays intimate and intensely interesting to the author and to the reader. Cool scientific terminology and judgment give way to intrusive and invasive human feelings that interpret nature with sympathy and empathy.

Ultimately, the reason Janovy is out in Keith County is not to justify his salary and position as professor of biology by teaching students to empathize with owls. Rather, he is out there, not in the classroom or lab, to discover and maintain the "inner Keith County," the space within him that expands to meet the natural spaces allotted to it. And his lucky allotment is a large piece of Sand Hills prairie, as well as the lakes and reservoirs on this land. The last chapter of *Back in Keith County* carries the title "The Experiment," for it refers to the political and psychological testing of America and Americans. When Janovy encounters the restrictions and unpleasantness of bureaucracies and their destructive behavior—in this land and overseas—he retreats into his "inner Keith County" cocoon (as a parasitologist) or nest (as an amateur ornithologist). This escape is not a wormlike retreat, wound tight in itself never to emerge. Rather, it is encased in an environment that he has spun out of his own mind from the landscape and its inhabitants, where he discovers and unravels answers to his moral and political doubts. He concludes that the individualistic American conscience needs wildness and space to support its unique life forms. He echoes important American nature writers—Henry David Thoreau's *Walden* comes to mind—with his insistence that "the sight of wild fields is essential to the healthy mind." More powerfully, he argues: "I must have that freedom and wildness symbolized by the marsh."[9] His stubborn insistence on the preservation of a wildness—inner and outer—which is resistant to economic destruction by business and technological interests, strikes a conscientious chord that resonates from most American environmentalists and nature writers.

If he can't manage to defend and save the wren or the watershed and the wilderness in the physical world and if they become sacrifices to the dynamo of modernity, then Janovy will preserve them psychologically in the inner Keith County of his mind. Bird calls will echo in the cerebral cave of his private consciousness; but unlike the singing canaries in coal mines that succumbed to methane, he is determined not to let the notes die out in the subterranean folds of his brain. Hence the concluding justification for writing his two books on Keith County. It's a living place. So long live the thoughts and books of man, so long live the songs of birds, the sounds and sights of the land that are fading fast out of human existential experiences into that silent spring. If Janovy were innocent of Naturalistic and Pathetic fallacies, he simply would not care what happened to the nature he studied beyond the results and data he obtained. Such is obviously not the case. Janovy is a passionately committed nature writer. His nature is loaded with his feelings for it. Nature is echoed by his emotive states, which have been translated into words and transcribed onto paper.

Paul Johnsgard shares Janovy's self-insertion into the lives of birds and his passion for the natural continuities of Nebraska landscapes. Johnsgard, a professor of ornithology at the University of Nebraska–Lincoln, has authored or edited more than forty books on birds and the biology of the Great Plains. While much of his writing is professional and technical, there are a number of essays that express his emotive relationships to the environment. Johnsgard's books for the general reader, such as *The Nature of Nebraska* or *Prairie Dog Empire*, are informational and straightforward accounts of animal and plant lives on the landscapes of the Great Plains. While, in the essays of these two collections, he expresses regret, even anger and impatience, with the forces of civilization that have plowed under, ripped up, and shot down whatever grew, walked, or flew on and over the prairie grass empire, he maintains a balanced observer's eye in a rhetorically measured and cool style. The title of the last chapter, "Sad Stories and Short Visions," from *The Nature of Nebraska* sets the reader up for expressions of remorse and injunctions for natural remediation of Nebraska's disappearing flora and fauna. What we read is instead rather prosaic: there are few preachments and no salvific narrative posturings in this finale. But he does become eloquent in the antepenultimate summary sentence that preaches, "Nebraska is our spiritual home, our own self-chosen Nirvana, our prairie-born paradise, and the natural surviving legacy of long-forgotten winds, immense amounts of water, now vanished glacial ice, and unfathomable eons of time."[10] His hope is that humans will not reverse evolution and undo millennia with millennial interventionism and an end-of-the-world mentality that is set on preparing the way for the rule of human interests over the land. Mainly, Johnsgard keeps his passionate devotion to preservation of nature in reserve. Even his pencil drawings of birds and other animals that populate most of his publications are accurate, detailed, and usually (but not always) lack the anthropomorphic drama that are often evident in nineteenth-century naturalist John James Audubon's depictions of birds and animals.

The collection of essays *Earth, Water, and Sky*, however, contains short personal and emotive narratives about his encounters with birds in their natural habitats. Even the drawings seem to have more life and momentum. In these essays, he emphasizes the importance of linking the history of bird species and their behaviors to human genealogy and evolution. In the essay "Sacred Places and the Voices of the Ancestors," he relates the "hypnotic calling and somewhat human like dancing behavior" of male prairie chickens, which he recorded in the presence of his two young sons.[11] Now, twenty years later, he takes his granddaughter to the same site at Burchard Lake, near Pawnee, Nebraska, to witness the prairie chicken mating ritual. Johnsgard makes the point that ancestral voices are both avian and human, that participating in the annual mating ceremony is a sacred reenactment for generations of his relatives and for generations of prairie chickens. The echoes of both human and avian ancestors have been recorded by Johnsgard on tape and on the page. The prairie chickens replay their genetically encoded mating behaviors. Humans are witnesses and accomplices in this rite of spring, though humans participate at a higher level of consciousness and awareness and thus must assume greater responsibility for the preservation and maintenance of the dance.

Johnsgard repeats this anthropomorphic view in the essay "The Gifts of the Cranes." Taking his granddaughter to experience the migration of the sandhill cranes on the Platte River in Nebraska, he feels the connection to his own biological offspring. This essay compares

SENSING PLACE

crane calls and choruses to celestial singing and the majesty of symphonic harmonies of Ludwig van Beethoven or Maurice Ravel. In the transcendent and spiritualized language of this essay, Johnsgard humanizes, even etherealizes, the cranes, making their exuberant calls into echoes of previous generations of cranes and humans as well as reverberations of the aesthetic conventions of classical music and Renaissance painting. The cranes appear "miraculously from incredible heights like celestial seraphim" and resemble the "angels painted on the ceiling of the Sistine Chapel."[12] He concludes his crane essay with inspiration from the natural sublime. Again the link between human and animal generations is his key theme: "Holding the hand of a small grandchild, as a flock of cranes passes overhead, and telling her that if she is very lucky she might also one day show these same sights to her own grandchild are a powerful lesson in faith, hope, and love. And beauty, touched by love, is somehow transformed into magic."[13]

Birds, and other nonhuman life forms, remind Johnsgard of the evolutionary great chain of being, in which humans are linked to all life from top to bottom. Crane calls remind him of this connection, and he feels the call in order to remind us of this biological and spiritual connection. Call and response is the rhetorical frame for the ecological ethical echoes Johnsgard records and replays for the benefit of the living and the ancestors who brought them forth.

Wes Jackson's essay collection *Becoming Native to This Place* takes up many of the same nagging issues of human (and inhumane) treatment of land and its denizens. Like Eiseley and Janovy and Johnsgard, Jackson is a scientist (PhD in genetics) with a speculative inclination that leads him to ask all sorts of questions far beyond the pale of his discipline and expertise. He is famous for promoting the preservation of Kansas prairie and for his experiments with prairie grasses. He founded the Land Institute in Salina, Kansas, where he and other plant geneticists and students are trying to make native grasses into high yield perennialized grain producers that would replace corn and bean monocultures. Reestablishing grasses would restore the prairie yet make it economically sustainable for human habitation and agriculture.

Becoming Native to This Place deals more with Matfield Green, Kansas, a vestigial prairie village near Interstate 35, halfway between Wichita and Topeka. Jackson and the Land Institute bought up a good portion of this dying prairie town and attempted to restore it, not like it was but with the practical goal of sheltering and sustaining people who want to live and work there in order to understand human lives in the process of conforming to prairie soil and climate. Like Jackson, those who move to Matfield Green want to see and study what monocultures such as corn and beans and alfalfa have done to prairie, and how to restore native grasses because they belong there. Wes Jackson would like to see rural landscapes repopulated and good farming practices returned. He is a scientist who is concerned with the emptying out of the prairie. Not only have people left, but many species of grasses as well as animals have gone with them, or more accurately, because of them.

Jackson rarely draws inspiration from birds, as Eiseley and Janovy and Johnsgard did. Rather, it is the prairie and its soils and grasses that inspire him. Like Eiseley, Janovy, and Johnsgard, Jackson doesn't favor governmental or institutional macrosolutions as remediators of the destruction, degradation, and depopulation of the Great Plains. Like the rest of this stubborn lot of environmental individualists, he favors dedication to the best rural American ideas and ideals and loyalty to the land that has been ruined. Hence the name of the title essay, "Becoming Native to our Places." Just as Janvoy ended *Back in Keith County* with a thought experiment about wildness, so Jackson describes his nonhostile takeover of Matfield Green as an experiment in the regeneration of ideals regarding sustainability and self-sufficiency. In his view the new inhabitants and inheritors of the prairie need to be scientists, artists, and accountants with devotion to the recouping and recoupling of agriculture and culture.

In Jackson's moral model of land use, modernity is the mismeasure; instead, nature is the measure we should use and follow. As a geneticist, Jackson is quite obviously in favor of modern science, but he is obstinately against modern economics and agricultural production systems and theories. The extractive conscience that wants to mine the prairie for its golden treasures—sun and corn—is inimical to the natures of prairie life forms that have evolved and succeeded. Jackson favors a light-handed human domestication of what exists in a place. Going native does not exclude human arranged change; going native means to let grass, people, and animals put down roots that will hold onto the soil and flourish under the sun.

Becoming Native to This Place is an ecological echo of Ecclesiastes, and Jackson is its prophet. He preaches profit as the point source for moral ruination of land and people. The restoration of a pastoralist piety is the salvation he believes in. To sum it up, Jackson's cry in, to, and for the wilderness is not just a cry for returning to a holy land blessed by God, but to a more scientific perspective that can be practiced by farmers and communicants with the land. It is a sort of moral mimicry. He explains this conscientious approach to land love and restoration in the chapter "Science and Nature." Sustainable agriculture would domesticate and mimic those plants and animals that traditionally have done well without human intervention in this bioregion. Jackson supports a rigorous and scientific accounting of what has been in order to produce what should be. Thus, he cultivates the Naturalistic Fallacy with the same assiduity and industry as the row-crop Great Plains farmer, whom he hopes to replace or reform. In Jackson's reconception and revision of modern agriculture, prairie plants that have flourished should be imitated and promoted. He wants to maintain an organic and moral model of flourishing, not an industrial, unnatural one. As he concludes in this chapter, "We need a way to arrest consumerism. We need a different form of accounting so that both sufficiency and efficiency have standing in our minds."[14] God's ledger of rights and wrongs is replaced by a human tally of what works for us and nature without too much damage and with limitations on excessive extraction. Jackson's eleventh commandment then would be a scientific sectarian prohibition of usurious usufruct: thou shall not steal or force nature's bounty!

Jackson commits the same Pathetic and Naturalistic fallacies as Eiseley, Janovy, and Johnsgard. Prairie lands, soil, and native grasses are nonhuman things for which Jackson has extraordinary sympathy.

It hurts to see them plowed under or blown away or extinguished or banished. He makes this bioregion and ecosystem a living entity that deserves not only respect but love. He has put down roots and is doing his best to hold on to what is left. Much more than his scientific reports and plant physiological studies, his essays have gained an audience because of the depth of his commitment and the natural feelings he has for prairie grass. His successes, like any nature writer with a popular audience, are founded on the capacity to elicit similar emotions from his readers. Stylistically, this rapprochement with readers occurs when they hear from an informed expert on plant genetics an impassioned ex cathedra condemnation of contemporary agricultural practices. Persuasion occurs when the audience is led to believe in the words of the rhetorician. Jackson has the academic credentials as well as the narrative skills to make his plea for preservation and restoration believable. He believes in the prairie soils he extols and criticizes the dirty hands of human rapacity on the Great Plains. This sort of soapbox rhetoric may seem deceptive or untrustworthy to those careful readers who want precise objective information and not emotive judgments or preachy pastorals. But without the passion and a language that occasionally is more loaded with sentiment than science, Jackson's moral commitment to the environment of the Great Plains would be suspect.

Eiseley, Janovy, Johnsgard, and Jackson do what we expect of nature and environmental writers: they write themselves into the living landscapes that they create with words. Their naturalistic, logical ploys are indeed pathetic: sympathetic and empathetic. The spaces they imaginatively create are photogenic; the animals they study and describe are anthropomorphic; the landscapes they invent and investigate are anthropogenic. Nature may be alien, but it is not alienation we sense or value in the essays of these four writers. Scientists and academic purists might cavil, but average readers—the majority of us—feel intimately connected to environments and regions by means of the conscientious authorial echoing both of nature's sights and sounds and of the artistic representation of unconscious life.

Eiseley, Janovy, Johnsgard, and Jackson rarely disappoint. They echo our own sentiments with greater precision, deeper knowledge, and stronger emotion.

In their prose nature pieces, the fallacies fall because they fail to elicit readerly skepticism or distance. Anthropomorphism is a way into nature and an enduring human perspective and record of seeing, hearing, and remembering—and cherishing.

Notes

1. The Naturalistic Fallacy is most often associated with the writings of the philosopher G. E. Moore. The entry "Naturalism in Ethics" in the *Routledge Encyclopedia of Philosophy* outlines the central assumptions of naturalism: ethical facts are natural facts and ethical thought can uncover them. Moore argued that such naturalistic ethical thinking led to false conclusions. Nature does not supply humans with firm moral lessons that are logically valid. *Routledge Encyclopedia of Philosophy*, vol. 6, ed. Edward Craig (London: Routledge, 1998), s.v. "Naturalism in Ethics."

2. The Pathetic Fallacy has a long and illustrious history of controversy and debate. For an accurate and comprehensive definition, see *Princeton Encyclopedia of Poetry and Poetics*, ed. Alex Preminger (Princeton: Princeton University Press, 1965), s.v. "Pathetic Fallacy" (by James K. Robinson).

3. Eileen Crist, *Images of Animals: Anthropomorphism and the Animal Mind* (Philadelphia: Temple University Press, 1999), 7, 202–22. A more recent collection of essays, *Thinking with Animals*, edited by Lorraine Daston and Gregg Mitman, explores the issues and controversies behind anthropomorphism in popular as well as academic nature writing, documentaries, and major films. See Lorraine Daston and Gregg Mitman, eds., *Thinking with Animals: New Perspectives on Anthropomorphism* (New York: Columbia University Press, 2005). Unlike Crist's monograph, there is no single conclusion about the ethical permissibility or linguistic effectiveness of featuring animal mental states or animal behavior as similar to humans.

4. Daston and Mitman, *Thinking with Animals*, 8.

5. The rest of this essay draws from the following works: Loren Eiseley, *The Immense Journey* (New York: Random House, 1956) and *The Unexpected Universe* (New York: Harcourt Brace Jovanovich, 1964); Wes Jackson, *Becoming Native to This Place* (Washington DC: Counterpoint, 1996); John Janovy, *Back in Keith County* (New York: St. Martins, 1981) and *Keith County Journal* (New York: St. Martins, 1978); and Paul Johnsgard, *Earth, Water, and Sky: A Naturalist's Stories and Sketches* (Austin: University of Texas Press, 1999), *The Nature of Nebraska* (Lincoln: University of Nebraska Press, 2001), and *Prairie Dog Empire: A Saga of the Shortgrass Prairie* (Lincoln: University of Nebraska Press, 2005).

6. Eiseley, *Unexpected Universe*, 68.

7. Eiseley, *Unexpected Universe*, 69.

8. Janovy, *Keith County Journal*, 30, 36.

9. Janovy, *Back in Keith County*, 177–78.

10. Johnsgard, *Nature of Nebraska*, 191.
11. Johnsgard, *Earth, Water, and Sky*, 3.
12. Johnsgard, *Earth, Water, and Sky*, 4.
13. Johnsgard, *Earth, Water, and Sky*, 112.
14. Jackson, *Becoming Native*, 60.

3. "I Don't Know, but I Ain't Lost"

Defining the Southwest

MARK BUSBY

An old joke finds an easterner driving over the back roads of western Texas until he's hopelessly lost. Finally, he sees a house set back off the road, and he drives up to find an old man sitting on the porch. He leans out the window of his Cadillac and asks the old man which way is north, to which the old man says he doesn't know. The easterner then asks, "Well, which way is east?" The old man again answers he doesn't know. The easterner then asks about south and west and gets the same response. The frustrated easterner then blurts out, "Hell, old man, you don't know nothing." And the old man says, "Nope, I don't know, but I ain't lost."

This joke points to the value of being grounded in place, the principle at the center of regional studies, the focus of this collection. Before discussing the American Southwest, I first want to cover some of the ground on which regional studies stands and to examine some of the underlying principles of interdisciplinary and regional studies. As director of an interdisciplinary program that focuses on region, I particularly want to consider interdisciplinarity and then regional studies as one type of interdisciplinary study.

In *Consilience: The Unity of Knowledge*, biologist Edward O. Wilson argues passionately for what he calls "consilience," by which he means a concurrence of results from different fields of knowledge.[1]

Wilson uses the term to call for an intellectual program of full disciplinary integration. Enlightenment thinkers believed in a grand union of knowledge built upon a set of universal laws. While Wilson thinks that consilience has been attained across a broad range of the natural sciences, he argues that the social sciences and the humanities have remained outside the integration. He contends that the humanities and social sciences need to join with the natural sciences, that the time has come to revive the Enlightenment vision.

Clearly, as the twentieth century drew to a close, education based on discrete disciplines was being challenged. At a 1993 meeting sponsored by the Pew Higher Education Roundtable, university presidents agreed that a fundamental restructuring of higher education was underway, made necessary by rising costs, new technology, and, more important, the need to rethink fundamental assumptions about knowledge. As universities throughout the country looked for new ways to examine and impart knowledge, interdisciplinary programs such as regional studies became increasingly important. In *Interdisciplinarity: History, Theory, and Practice*, Julie Thompson Klein writes, "New divisions of intellectual labor, collaborative research, team teaching, hybrid fields, comparative studies, increased borrowing across disciplines, and a variety of 'unified,' 'holistic' perspectives have created pressures upon traditional divisions of knowledge. There is talk of a growing 'permeability of boundaries,' a blurring and mixing of genres, a postmodern return to grand theory and cosmology, even a 'profound epistemological crisis.'"[2] As Glen Lich pointed out in *Regional Studies: The Interplay of Land and People*, a particularly fertile interdisciplinary approach is regional studies: "Amid arguments about cultural literacy and the holistic development of students, regional studies afford concrete yet interdisciplinary approaches to the ideal education."[3]

Regional studies is just one type of interdisciplinary study. Across the country and internationally, interdisciplinary studies—including cultural studies, feminist studies, gender studies, ethnic studies, and regional studies—have all grown in the last decade, almost to the point that "interdisciplinarity" became a buzz word and naturally gave rise to countercurrents and opposition. The primary argument against interdisciplinarity recently has been that it is fine in theory but that few people have actually been intellectually capable of putting it into practice and that disciplinary knowledge still maintains priority.

In the United States, one of the more established interdisciplinary programs is American studies, of which regional studies is logically a branch. American studies has been under attack for different reasons, most of which revolve around the question of American Exceptionalism, an argument that America is special or different from the rest of the world and therefore exceptional. The job of an American studies scholar has been accordingly to find an overarching theme that explains American culture, such as the American Adam or the machine in the garden. With a loss of faith in national innocence and in the possibility of a transcendent national character, Ed Ayers and Peter Onuf suggest that Americans have decided that places closer to home than the nation-state are worthy of study.[4] Additionally, American studies scholars have tried to redefine the discipline to acknowledge *difference* more than an all-inclusive synthesis, and that too is where regional studies comes in.

Regional studies centers grew out of an understanding of the "concrete" importance of place and have explored the elements that characterize different places. Two quotations highlight the necessary role of environment and history in forming a region. The first is from noted British writer D. H. Lawrence's *Studies in Classic American Literature*: "Every people is polarized in some particular locality, which is home, the homeland. Different places on the face of the earth have different vital effluence, different vibration, different chemical exhalation, different polarity with different stars: call it what you like. But the spirit of place is a great reality."[5] The second one comes from the dean of Texas literature, John Graves, in *Goodbye to a River*: "If a man couldn't escape what he came from, we would most of us still be peasants in Old World hovels. But if, having escaped or not, he wants in some way to know himself, define himself, and tries to do it without taking into account the thing he came from, he is writing without any ink in his pen. The provincial who cultivates only his roots is in peril, potato-like, of becoming more root than plant. The man who cuts his roots away and denies that they were ever connected with him withers into half a man."[6] These writers refer to the spirit of their place, which they and other writers have attempted to capture in their works—the symbiotic relationship between places and writing. The geographer Yi-Fu Tuan calls this feeling "topophilia," by which he means the perception of sacred place and *genii loci*, the spirits that inhabit particular places in the landscape.[7] J. Frank Dobie, in *The Mustangs*, prefers to use the Spanish word *querencia* (from *querer*, "to love") to refer to the feelings that some living things have for special places.[8]

To be sure, some of these are essentialist definitions of place, suggesting that qualities are irrevocably bound in the wind and soil to be imbibed by those who live there. Of course, places are mutable and reactions to them are far from universal. One person's El Dorado is another's hell. But even if definitions of the Southwest shift like the Hill Country breeze, places are nonetheless real; and they elicit reactions that make it possible to generalize what distinguishes one place from another. Those similarities in reactions stem largely from the changing physical environment and human interaction with it. Regional definitions are human constructions—language intertwined with a physical environment altered by time—as J. B. Jackson makes clear: "Sense of place, a sense of being at home in a town or city, grows as we become accustomed to it and learn to know its peculiarities. . . . [A] sense of place is something that we ourselves create in the course of time. It is the result of habit or custom."[9]

These quotations undergird the current reemergence of regional studies programs across the country. In the introduction to *All Over the Map: Rethinking American Regions*, Edward Ayers and Peter Onuf write, "The resurgence of interest in and loyalty to region is reflected in the impassioned localism of environmentalism and historic preservation; the new regionalism appears, too, in the form of regional magazines and festivals, in the packaging of local particularities by tourist boards and chambers of commerce."[10] They also point to the resurgence of interest in regionalism in academia with the growth of regional studies centers in universities around the country. Regional studies centers address both the importance of understanding place, at a time when increased mobility leads to the loss of a sense of rootedness, and the major problems facing education on America's college campuses: (1) the need for coordinated interdisciplinary courses of study that reduce the fragmentation produced by rigid academic disciplines; (2) the need for programs that promote collaboration among faculty from varied disciplines; (3) the need for programs that strengthen understanding among various racial and cultural divisions in distinct regions of the country; (4) the need to comprehend the fundamental connection to one's own sense of place, of being in the world.

Each regional program has developed certain criteria that define its region. John Graves, in an address at Texas State University in 1978, emphasized the detailed knowledge that a regional study permits with its consequent revelation of new kinds of connections: "A sense of place is . . . bound up even more with physical and natural detail, with trees and grass and soil, creatures, weather, water, sky, wild sounds, the way some weed smells when you walk on it."[11] Students in regional studies programs thus learn to approach knowledge in a new way, seeing the connections that bind history, literature, art, music, architecture, anthropology, sociology, and other disciplines through the clarifying lens of region. An interdisciplinary approach increases awareness of and sensitivity to the diversity of ethnic and cultural traditions in the area by emphasizing the historical, social, and environmental interaction among cultures. Students are prepared to return to the region with an awareness of the natural and cultural factors that have shaped it. These interdisciplinary programs lead students out of traditional departmental limitations and increase their understanding of how the branches of knowledge are intertwined rather than separated.

Defining Region: The Southwest

Like other regions of the United States, the American Southwest exists clearly in the imagination but is often difficult to define. Geographers have three methods for defining regions, which provide a starting point: (1) Formal—based upon specified elements, such as national origin of residents; (2) Vernacular—based upon how people define their own regions (e.g., Texans have designated such areas as "Big Country," "Metroplex," "Golden Triangle," "Heart of Texas," and "Hill Country"); (3) Functional—based upon political designation such as state, county, city, school district, or subdivision. Humanists tend to define regions by cultural traits—the values and beliefs that have developed over time. To understand any region requires knowing the specific elements of both kinds of territory, natural and social. Accordingly, the Southwest has been variously defined based on different political or state boundaries, physical characteristics (particularly aridity), and cultural qualities. When the National Endowment for the Humanities created ten regions to be served by regional humanities centers around the country in 1998, it designated the Southwest as four states: Texas, New Mexico, Arizona, and Nevada. Others had used Texas, Oklahoma, New Mexico, and Arizona (e.g., Eugene Hollon) or just New Mexico and Arizona (e.g., Kenneth Kurtz).[12]

Though no one can agree on which states constitute the Southwest, scholars have identified various qualities over the years that typify southwestern culture—warts and all. Larry Goodwyn recognized early on how the frontier myth determined important elements of the literary Southwest: the frontier legend values the pastoral, open landscape and emphasizes male experience, particularly the triumphant conquest of nature and racial "others."[13] Following Goodwyn's emphasis on the frontier myth, with its tendency to immerse men in the nature they battle, a key trait of southwestern literature is its visualization of a severe if diverse landscape of desert, canyon, and plain. Later writers, particularly those excluded from the frontier legend, criticize the sexism, racism, and primitivism of the cowboy mythos but still celebrate other elements, often the nature of the landscape itself.

Another important quality in southwestern literature, the journey, results from the expanse of that landscape, because traveling is a natural act in a region as large as the Southwest, which also has such a scattered population. For example, it is 801 miles from the northern Texas panhandle to Brownsville in the south and 773 miles from the easternmost bend in the Sabine River to the westernmost point of the

Rio Grande near El Paso. On one hand, the vastness of the area seems to negate borders; on the other is the reality of bordering—the long Rio Grande border with Mexico—as fact and metaphor. Both the borders and the frontier suggest a line where differing cultures, attitudes, and factions meet. In fact, one of the major features of southwestern writing is ambivalence—the act of being at once torn in several directions and crossing varying borders. This duality was already part of early settlers' experience as they conquered nature and felt simultaneously at one with it.

Three Literary Examples

Three southwestern writers, Katherine Anne Porter, Ralph Ellison, and Cormac McCarthy, have been recognized as being among the most significant American writers of the last one hundred years; and like the Southwest, they are diverse—a woman writer, an African American writer, and a contemporary Anglo writer. Each deals with and helps shape the themes central to southwestern writers. All three also show how a regional understanding often results from seeing a region set in relief against others, for they all left their native lands before they settled on writing about the Southwest.

Porter was born in 1890 in Indian Creek, Texas, and moved to Kyle, Texas, just five miles north of Texas State University in San Marcos to live with her grandmother after her mother died when she was two. She left Kyle when she was eleven, lived in San Antonio for a while, had an early ill-fated marriage at sixteen, and left Texas for good when she was twenty-eight. Later in a letter, she told fellow expatriate-Texan William Humphrey, "I got out of Texas like a bat out of hell at the earliest possible moment and stayed away cheerfully half a life-time."[14] But she returned to Texas again and again in her fiction, creating a young Texan alter ego in Miranda Rhea. Like other southwesterners, then, she demonstrated a strong ambivalence about her Texas home territory, excoriating yet embracing it.[15] She created strong female characters that challenged southwestern sexism. Porter lived a similarly independent life, traveling widely and boasting once of having had "thirty-seven lovers"; yet she held in high regard the more traditional female values of beauty and cooking.[16]

Although Porter kept coming back to Texas in her fiction, she was thwarted in her desire to return with her literary archive later in life. She thought Harry Ransom, when he was building the archive that became the Humanities Research Center at the University of Texas, was going to name a library for her. Porter went to Austin to lecture and left believing she had been promised a library in her name. She made plans to be buried underneath the library in a brightly painted Mexican wooden coffin, but when the plans never materialized, she gave her materials to the McKeldrin Library in Maryland. Still, on a last, late trip, Porter decided that her own remains would be interred next to her mother's in Indian Creek. So it is fitting that her literary remains—including that coffin—are in Maryland and that her own remains, her ashes, are in Texas.

The ambivalence that Porter displayed in her life toward the Southwest—an especially clear trait of that region—appears in her work as well, perhaps most explicitly in her presentation of the grandmother, Sophia Jane Rhea. In most of the stories in which Miss Sophia appears, Porter draws her in both positive and negative terms. In "The Source," the first story of *The Old Order*, for example, Porter's ambivalence toward the character is evident. The story concerns how every spring Miss Sophia needs to return to the farm to relax. On one level, then, the title refers to the farm as a primitivistic source of Miss Sophia's power and indicates the positive side of the character—a woman who is the source of order in a natural world where entropy overcomes without a counter force. But when Miss Sophia revisits the farm, she is a martinet, a returning general who becomes a "tireless, just and efficient slave driver of every creature on the place."[17] Similarly, in "Old Mortality," one of the most disagreeable characters is the new-woman feminist, Cousin Eva; yet Porter's alter ego, Miranda, sets out to re-create herself at the end of the story, clearly a type of new woman as well.

Since almost all of the stories in *The Old Order* are built on dualities, this uncertainty about the rightness of the "natural" southwestern order enter throughout. "The Grave," one of the most anthologized stories in twentieth-century American literature, is set in frontier Texas and turns on the dualities of birth and death, youth and age, innocence and experience, past and present, fertility and infertility, male and female, guilt and innocence—all intertwined through the power of memory. Porter's characters thus negotiate metaphorical borders; and like other southwesterners, Porter was strongly influenced by growing up close to the United States–Mexico border. Stories such as "Old Mortality" acknowledge the border's significance in the United States' Southwest, whereas other stories, such as "Maria Conception" and "Flowering Judas," are set in Mexico, where Porter lived in the early 1920s.

Just as Porter had a problematic relationship with her home region, Ellison, too, moved away from the Southwest but returned to it more fondly in a series of stories set in Oklahoma and in the background of his classic novel, *Invisible Man*. Ellison lived in New York City for over fifty years, and his novel ends in an underground hole in Harlem. But Ellison always considered himself a southwesterner, and he counted his Oklahoma past as one of the most important shapers of his own character (although the National Endowment for the Humanities places the state in the Great Plains). Ellison often recalled Heraclitus's axiom that "geography is fate" and said his fate was to have been born in Oklahoma.[18] Many of Ellison's early stories were set in Oklahoma, as was much of his projected second novel, eventually published posthumously in a highly edited edition as *Juneteenth*. In his major work, *Invisible Man*, Ellison dramatized perhaps the most significant southwestern theme—"natural" freedom versus "civilized" restriction—by casting it as a young black man's struggle to find his identity in a world beset by racism and deception. Ellison often said that his experience growing up in the frontier Southwest as a black Huck Finn prepared him to resist both the vicious racism he found in the South and the subtle racism he encountered in the North.[19] Region's influence is apparent in his writing through the symbolic values held by the three primary locations where he spent his life. They provide a metaphor that permeates his work, in which the thesis and antithesis generate one overall synthesis. His southwestern frontier background provided him with freedom and possibility; the South offered restriction and limitation; and the North allowed a mature synthesis. Writing requires constant interaction with the shadow of the past—with one's geography and history—to produce the synthesis of art.

Although most of *Invisible Man* is set in Harlem, the narrative relies on frontier imagery often presented in American literature through the opposition between East and West. Ellison, growing up in Oklahoma when it was still a territory, sensed the power of a frontier world of possibility. When Ellison moved to the South, he encountered a world where the frontier ethos did not have authority, at least for an African American adult. *Invisible Man* is an American bildungsroman, in which the narrator moves from a frontier belief in freedom, simplicity, possibility, and harmony to a confrontation with the reality of restriction.

Cormac McCarthy's career demonstrates a countermovement toward the Southwest from elsewhere, rather than a movement away from it. McCarthy was born in Rhode Island but moved to Tennessee with his family when he was two years old. He attended the University of Tennessee and began writing Faulknerian novels set in the South. But in 1976 McCarthy left the South for El Paso, Texas, and he turned to the Southwest for the fiction that changed his career— *Blood Meridian* and the three novels of the Border Trilogy (*All the Pretty Horses*, *The Crossing*, and *Cities of the Plain*)—as well as for his recent novel, *No Country for Old Men*. McCarthy's genius is that he fuses the most important elements of southern literature (the power of history and a communal past)—the dominant American fiction of the first half of the twentieth century, with roots deep in the frontier myth's emphasis on individuality played out on the border between East and West. McCarthy then rotates, focusing on a North and South separation, and uses several of the major elements of the East and West frontier myth innovatively, creating a southwestern fiction that synthesizes these concerns.

In the three novels that comprise the Border Trilogy, McCarthy uses the U.S. southern border as a metaphor for an oxymoronic amalgamation of illusion and reality, individuality and community, and several similar contrasts. His border metaphor provides a complex means of knowing the world that is not simply good or evil, black or white, life or death, but is a melding of apparent dualities, such as the end and the beginning. He also employs structural patterns that emphasize journeying across such borders in order to examine the intertwining of positive and negative forces, and ultimately to present a worldview that suggests a nihilistic optimism. Although McCarthy's works present a dialectic battle between hope and despair, McCarthy stresses storytelling's ability to create synthesis.

McCarthy's world yields violence, struggle, and anguish, but it also includes powerful moments that celebrate life: John Grady Cole rides with campesinos on a flatbed truck as he escapes his hellish experience in prison, knowing that "after and for a long time to come he'd have reason to evoke the recollection of those smiles and to reflect upon the good will which provoked them for it had power to protect and to confer honor and to strengthen resolve and it had power to heal men and to bring them to safety long after all other resources were exhausted."[20] Billy Parham attempts to return the wolf to her home. A gypsy treats a stabbed horse in *The Crossing*. And John Grady Cole and Rawlins experience moments of intense friendship in *All the Pretty Horses*, just as Cole and Parham do in *Cities of the Plain*. These events are all part of the fabric of life and counter violence, sadness, and despair.

McCarthy, without a doubt, sets out to absorb the spirit of the places about which he writes. It's clear that he travels the terrain, reads the history of the region, and learns the flora, fauna, and geophysical details of the places his characters inhabit. It is a process that environmental historians like Paul Shepard and Dan Flores call "becoming native to a place."[21] Being a native does not mean the circumstance of birth; it refers to the process of amalgamating one's self with a place and achieving E. O. Wilson's consilience. And ultimately, perhaps, that is what all who work with a region do: become native to that place and time in order to do our jobs as teachers, scholars, and writers.

I've tried to become native to the various Southwests—the historical, the geographic, the geophysical, the vernacular, and the legendary, which is the one that often overwhelms the others. This mythic Southwest is a lie in the mind, denied by cattle crammed into squalid cattle yards; oil and tech busts; crack and coke hustlers on Sixth Street in Austin, Deep Ellum in Dallas, Montrose in Houston, Central Avenue in Albuquerque, Washington St. in Phoenix, and the Strip in Las Vegas; and fouled creeks, streams, and bayous. Yet it is a powerful myth that still grips the minds of supporters and attackers alike, and it reaches well beyond regional borders. The most recognized American icon internationally is the cowboy, followed closely for many years by Mickey Mouse and Elvis. So an understanding of one's region requires an understanding of the region's connection to the larger world. John Graves stated it succinctly when he said, "One river, seen right, may well be all rivers that flow to the sea."[22]

And if you know that, you will never be lost.

Notes

1. Edward O. Wilson, *Consilience: The Unity of Knowledge* (New York: Alfred A. Knopf, 1998).

2. Julie Thompson Klein, *Interdisciplinarity: History, Theory, and Practice* (Detroit: Wayne State University Press, 1991), 11.

3. Glen Lich, ed., *Regional Studies: The Interplay of Land and People* (College Station: Texas A&M University Press, 1992), 166.

4. Ayers and Onuf, *All Over the Map*, 1.

5. D. H. Lawrence, *Studies in Classic American Literature* (New York: The Viking Press, 1923), 10.

6. John Graves, *Goodbye to a River: A Narrative* (New York: Knopf, 1960), 145.

7. Yi-Fu Tuan, *Topophilia: A Study of Environmental Perception, Attitudes, and Value* (Englewood Cliffs NJ: Prentice-Hall, 1974).

8. J. Frank Dobie, *The Mustangs* (Boston: Little, Brown, 1952), 119–20.

9. Jackson, *Sense of Place*, 151.

10. Ayers and Onuf, *All Over the Map*, 1.

11. John Graves, "The American Southwest: Cradle of Literary Art," in *The American Southwest: Cradle of Literary Art*, ed. Robert W. Walts (San Marcos: Southwest Texas State University, 1981), 11.

12. As a scholar of the Southwest, I define the region and identify the qualities that appear often in southwestern history, literature, film, art, and culture; see the introduction to *The Greenwood Encyclopedia of American Regional Cultures: The Southwest*, vol. 8, ed. Mark Busby (Westport CT: Greenwood, 2004), xvii–xxviii.

13. Larry Goodwyn, "The Frontier Myth and Southwestern Literature," *Library Journal*, February 1971, 161.

14. Porter to Humphrey, October 8, 1950, quoted in Janis Stout, *Katherine Anne Porter: A Sense of the Times* (Charlottesville: University of Virginia Press, 1995), 36.

15. See Mark Busby, "Katherine Anne Porter and the Southwest: Ambivalence as Deep as the Bone," in *From Texas to the World and Back: Essays on the Journeys of Katherine Anne Porter*, ed. Mark Busby and Dick Heaberlin (Fort Worth: TCU Press, 2001), 133–47.

16. Porter quoted in Darlene Harbow Unrue, *Katherine Anne Porter: The Life of an Artist* (Jackson: University Press of Mississippi, 2005), 287.

17. Katherine Ann Porter, *The Collected Stories of Katherine Anne Porter* (New York: Harcourt, Brace and World, 1965), 324.

18. Ralph Ellison, *Going to the Territory* (New York: Random House, 1986), 189.

19. Ralph Ellison, *Shadow and Act* (New York: Random House, 1964), see esp. the introduction, xi–xvii.

20. Cormac McCarthy, *All the Pretty Horses* (New York: Random House, 1992), 219.

21. Dan Flores, *Horizontal Yellow: Nature and History in the Near Southwest* (Albuquerque: University of New Mexico Press, 1999) ix; and Paul Shepard, *Coming Home to the Pleistocene*, ed. Florence Shepard (Washington DC: Island Press, 1998), 12. See also Wes Jackson, *Becoming Native to This Place* (Lexington: University Press of Kentucky, 1994).

22. Graves, *Goodbye to a River*, 254.

4. A Border Runs through It

Looking at Regionalism through Architecture in the Southwest

MAGGIE VALENTINE

A bleached cow skull hangs on the wall next to an old poster of the El Tovar Hotel. Beneath both of them are pigskin and cedar chairs. Hand-woven rugs with red diamond patterns expose the tile floor. Next to the thick, cream-colored walls are Indian baskets, a statue of a howling coyote in profile, and an antique armoire, its wood panels cracked and dry. There is a cactus on the windowsill, and outside a *ristra* hangs drying in the sun. On the mantel, carved into the beehive corner fireplace, are dried ears of corn, a punched-tin light fixture, a figurine of Kokopelli playing a flute, small baskets, and a *molcajete* made of volcanic stone. The sounds of a Spanish guitar fill the room. Is it a stereotype or satire, a picture from a bed-and-breakfast brochure or a typical living room in Santa Fe? Or is it a stage set? All of the above.

Nearby are anonymous strip malls and big-box outlets surrounded by acres of asphalt. The neighborhoods in this part of the country are subject to the same homogenizing sprawl as the rest of America. The region is getting its fair share of boomburbs (a rapidly growing, urban-sized place in the suburbs), clustered worlds (similar houses sold to similar people at similar prices), logo buildings (golden arches), mall glut, gridlock, cul-de-sac pods, sitcom suburbs, snout houses (garage door dominating the front facade), and zoomburbs (a place growing even faster than a boomburb, such as Sun City, Arizona).[1]

These two images are contemporary. Both are southwestern; both are American. Like every region, the Southwest is simultaneously typical of the larger area and unique unto itself. Focusing on region allows us to discover how we are different and how we are similar. It helps identify who we are. Regional architecture—like regional dialects, music, and food—reveal both the past and the present in terms of values, lifestyles, and place. They are maps to where we are and how we got there.

Regionalism provides a context to understand the role that place plays in human activity and creations. Overlapping frameworks of geography, nation, state, region, community, and neighborhood operate as different lenses for examining the contexts that place provides. The term context, derived from the Latin *contexere*, means "to weave together"; each yarn, spun from many strands, has its own quality, defined by color, material, and texture. When woven with other yarns, the completed tapestry reveals a larger picture or pattern formed by the varied yarns and threads. The cultural strands that make up the yarns of region give a visual and historical context through which to explore meanings of the whole.

The tapestry of architecture is one such context. It is physical evidence of history and how people lived, formed by function and fashion. Architecture both shapes and is shaped by the way we see the world, yet it is restricted by the physical environment of climate, material, and technology. Regionalism in architecture refers to buildings and spaces that express the unique character of a geographical area— what viticulturists call *terroir* or architects refer to as *genius loci*, the spirit or essence of place—translated into three-dimensional form. The built environment is at once both art and necessity. While architects deliberately focus on the former, vernacular architecture is shaped primarily by the latter. As a result, the vernacular is often more responsive to that sense of place. It is a direct response to real needs, rather than public images made by the users (not by artists), and must deal with climatic conditions and available materials, instead of relying on manufactured solutions or promoting a political agenda. Regional vernacular architecture builds on sensory memories and combines them with cultural traditions to produce a distinctive landscape that defines and expresses a sense of place.

The boundaries of the region referred to as the Southwest depend on whether one is considering a common geography, imposed political edges, or shared cultural attributes. Since architecture is a direct result of all of these factors, the boundaries overlap. Cultural regions don't match the colors on political maps; they leak over state and national boundaries here and don't reach the edges there. While architecture responds to geography and climate, it is shaped by very specific and often contradicting cultural patterns and beliefs. The study of architecture is one of the most meaningful ways to decipher regional boundaries, because it must deal with both the physical realities of place, altered by time, and the perimeters imposed by humans through conquest and compromise. It is an intermediary between the physical sciences and the humanities, a human expression of what it means to belong to a place. Vernacular architecture especially is an expression of regionalism, because it is the result of interaction between and among these factors. It helps to define region in a unique way because it incorporates and is limited by environmental conditions, cultural norms and values, local materials, climatic responses, and the evolution of people and groups who settled in the area.

The architectural traditions of the region define the Southwest as an area extending from the Colorado River on the west, separating California from Arizona, to the Colorado River in Texas just east of San Antonio, and from the Four Corners area in the north to the northern borderlands of Mexico back up through central Texas along the Balcones Escarpment. Its core, bisected by the Continental Divide, is Arizona, New Mexico, and west Texas. Its periphery includes the southern edges of Nevada, Utah, and Colorado; north-central Mexico immediately south of the Rio Grande, extending into Sonora, Chihuahua, and Coahuila; and a swath separating west and east Texas. This definition ignores political boundaries as artificial in favor of natural conditions and cultural developments. It describes a bilingual borderland, composed of the overlapping areas of two nations, ownership of which has gone back and forth between them.

Geographically, the region is scrubland, containing cactus, chaparral, mesquite, and armadillos—what Lawrence C. Powell called "a great dry and wrinkled land."[2] Such sparseness has its own plain, stark beauty that comes from the powerful natural forms created by adaptation and survival, not from the lushness of ornament. Natural characteristics include the quality of the light created by the angle of the sun at this latitude and the arid climate due to its continentality—the lack of proximity to a coast. The dry southwestern desert can be seen, smelled, felt on the skin, heard, and even tasted. The distinctiveness of the region makes itself known immediately to the senses. The air is thinner; the sky is bigger and brighter because the light is not diffused. These qualities serve to magnify the vastness of the land and the distances between cities, resulting in a feeling of physical and cultural isolation from the rest of the United States.

Like the vegetation, the built forms might also be described as scrubland. The clichéd image of the Southwest—the howling coyote in front of a pueblo—comes from New Mexico, the heart of the American Southwest; and it is a cliché because it contains truth and is open to interpretation as romantic or chilling. The image captures the remoteness of both the physical and the political Southwest, divided by a national boundary but extended by natural features, all bathed in nostalgia and stereotypes.

Historically, three major culture groups created an identifiable building pattern in the Southwest, shaped by the physical restrictions and possibilities of the land and the human response to the land, overlaid by their own set of values and the presence of other peoples. It was in fact the harsh environment of the region that influenced every group who lived there, resulting in an architectural tradition that mixed elements of the three cultures, who separately and together developed an identifiable regionalism.

The three groups that shaped the cultural traditions were the indigenous peoples, the Hispanic settlers from Spain and Mexico, and the Anglo immigrants from the eastern United States and Europe. (In the Southwest, *Anglo* refers to anyone who isn't Indian or Hispanic.) It must be remembered that within each of these broad categories are hundreds of different cultures and subregions with similar and different beliefs, traditions, and languages. There are as many divisions among as between them, and there has always been considerable mixing.

Each group responded to the rugged conditions of the Southwest in a similar way, using organic materials with which to build and protect themselves from the harsh climate, creating patterns and motifs often copied later in industrialized materials. Like chili peppers in southwestern food, certain elements were common to the Southwest because they were there, but they were interpreted differently by each culture and in each subregion. Each group adapted native materials into forms and colors that expressed their cultural identity; and collectively, they created a southwestern architecture that belongs to the place and distinguishes itself from other regions. Building traditions reveal each group's response to nature and to the previous settlement patterns of the area, as well as the change in land ownership and the expressions of power, meaning, and identity. Later arrivals freely borrowed and mixed elements of what they found with images and skills they brought with them. The unique southwestern architecture they formed was a result of both segregation and amalgamation among these three cultures and expressed the shifting balance of power among them as well.

Southwestern culture reflects and preserves the history and the role of minorities perhaps more than most other regions of America. It is a place where ethnic foods describe regional identity and where the whole community celebrates Fiesta, Dia de los Muertos (and Halloween the night before), Juneteenth, Diez y Seise, Oktoberfest, Las Posadas, and the Fourth of July. The reasons for this are twofold. First, the area was never as desirable for agricultural development, long-term mineral extraction, or habitability as most other parts of the country. Second, none of the peoples who lived there were considered part of the mainstream American body politic. They shared a sense of not belonging to the larger group, thus their ethnicity and "outsiderness" bonded them closer to each other.

The American Southwest remained on the outskirts of civilization as a place of refuge and opportunity and never became a seat of national power, either politically or culturally. The place and the people have been peripheral. In the eighteenth century it was a Spanish bastion that required the subjugation of Native peoples as well as their support for protection against other Indians and Europeans. The early U.S. government desired to acquire the land, in part, as a buffer zone to protect itself from both external and internal threats. In the mid-nineteenth century the United States saw the area as a "Go West" escape valve and buffer zone against Mexico, in the pursuit of its Manifest Destiny. But migration patterns largely passed over it to settle the West Coast first; Arizona and New Mexico were not admitted to statehood until 1912. Surviving Native populations were forcibly assimilated into American culture by ridding them of their traditional braids, dress, and language, before being allowed to "return to" reservations, newly created confinements granted to them within what had been their land. When the Treaty of Guadalupe Hidalgo moved national boundaries in 1848, Mexican citizens suddenly found themselves living in a different country and speaking a foreign language, their loyalties questioned. Even in the twentieth century, New Mexico was seen as a wasteland and used as a site to develop and test the atomic bomb. Along with Nevada, it was where the U.S. government experimented with the possibilities of annihilating civilization. The Southwest and its relationship with Mexico is still a controversial political and economic theme—on both sides of the border.

Virtually every group of people who lived in the Southwest was *ethnic*—outsiders to the dominant national culture. They were members of minority groups who retained separate customs, languages, or social views. Immigrants who were pushed (rather than pulled) to this part of the country had strong cultural identities. Perhaps they understood that about each other. Cultures amalgamated rather than assimilated, maintaining both their separate and community identities. These southwestern subcultures included Native Americans; mestizos (i.e., those of Hispanic and Indian ancestry); Afromestizos (i.e., those of African American, Hispanic, and Indian ancestry); Tejanos (i.e., Texan nationals of Mexican ancestry); Texians (Anglo-American citizens of Coahuila and Texas during and following the Texas Revolution); Southerners, immigrants from the American East Coast, and freedmen looking for a second chance; and Euro-Americans, including Czechs, Poles, Germans, and freethinkers. It is still *El Norte* to thousands of Hispanics from Mexico and the rest of Central America as well as to South Americans. Each of these subculture groups had an architecture that expressed their community and identity, that adapted to the desert conditions of the Southwest, and that is still present.

In most places in the United States, Native American architecture was ignored or suppressed in conscious favor of European-based forms, which were deemed superior, even when inappropriate for the geography. While this also happened in the Southwest, it occurred much later in the region's history. The more dominant tradition (for people as well as forms) was amalgamation, according more respect to previous inhabitants and their solutions to the nature of the place. Anglo-European settlers evinced genocidal tendencies; but from the beginning of intercultural contact, there seemed to be more respect for the indigenous solutions to common problems—largely because they worked—and adoption of successful techniques. What is southwestern today contains elements—side by side and intermingled—of all the cultures that shaped it.

Indigenous peoples still maintain a strong cultural and architectural presence in the Southwest. Much of their architecture remains virtually unchanged, albeit made more accessible and convenient, and sits side by side with remnants of their ancestors. Indian nations in the Southwest lived in cliff dwellings, earth lodges, grass houses, tepees, and pueblos, all shelters suited to a hot, dry climate. Of these forms, the cliff dwellings and pueblos have had the most powerful impact on southwestern architectural forms, partially because the former have survived and the latter have been sustained for hundreds of years. They continue to be the dominant building patterns in small towns south of the United States–Mexico border.

Native American architecture responded to place and available materials with their limited technology and their belief systems, which emphasized integration of the human with the land in order to maintain harmony. The best examples of this in structural terms are the kiva and the hogan, two powerful forms that still resonate in southwestern architecture. Developed by the Anasazi (Ancient Ones or Ancestral Pueblans) and the Dinéh (Navajo), both forms were gifts from the gods when the tribes emerged from the center of the earth. Both were active symbols of the people's connectedness to the earth itself, marking the place where the underworld met the sky. They were sacred places, central to the organization of the community, where origins and ancestors were commemorated, children were educated, and important group decisions were made.

The kiva was made of adobe—a mixture of earth, grass, and water—and entered via a ladder emerging from the hole in the roof. The interior contained both history in wall murals and sacred space in the *sipapu*, a hole in the earth in front of the altar, which symbolized where their ancestors surfaced. The emergence from the earth was reenacted every time worshippers emerged from the kiva. Similarly, the hogan, made of horizontally stacked logs covered with mud, told of both history and divinity. Each log was a gift from a different god. The supporting pillars identified the cardinal directions. The four sides plus the sky and earth correspond to the six directions of Blessingway, the Navajo ceremonial song cycle that encapsulates many of their beliefs, praying that one is surrounded by beauty everywhere and in everything. The hogan represented the beauty of creation and the beginning of life: the door faced east, greeting the morning sun and the rebirth of the day. Both Anasazi and Dinéh structures were living entities, made of living things from the earth, and connected their peoples with the sky, earth, gods, ancestors, and descendants. *Genii loci*—the spirits of place—are literal here.

The dwellings of these first peoples evolved from pit houses to cliff houses to pueblos, all direct responses to the climate. They were built from desert sand and rock as well as from adobe; and siting and massing protected them from heat, flash floods, and extreme variations in temperature. The forms that evolved in Pueblo architecture were accordingly unique to this place, consisting of flat roofs supported by tree trunks, called *vigas* by the Spanish. The windowless organic walls reflected the colors of the desert. One entered buildings from the roof. The houses were arranged in clan communities and stacked on top of one another with setbacks for outdoor terraces and privacy. Sited to take advantage of the angle of the sunlight in both summer and winter, they utilized passive solar energy thousands of years ago. Small villages and large cities alike shared a common central core, identified by the Spanish as a *plaza*, for religious and community celebrations.

The term *pueblo* ("village") was assigned to indigenous dwellings in the sixteenth century by the Spanish, who introduced new building types, including Hispanic churches, but who built in the same materials of adobe and rubble. Despite the nineteenth-century turquoise door and window frames, house forms and layout of modern pueblos have changed very little; and certainly their meaning continues. Entrances are now on the ground floor, but kiva ladders still lean against multistoried dwellings. The houses, with their modern conveniences, remain the possession and responsibility of tribal women, who still repair the adobe surfaces by hand annually, in the tradition of the Ancient Ones.

In other parts of the United States, Native American nations were exterminated or pushed westward. In the Southwest, they maintained a strong presence. Cities such as Ácoma and Taos have survived for over one thousand years in the same site, although their land holdings have diminished considerably. Federal laws ruled the Indian reservations, and missionaries tried to "convert" their children. But the culture has survived with increasing autonomy and respect over the last half century. The imagery of the kiva, the hogan, hand-made adobe buildings, and Native American symbols such as the Zuni symbol of the sun (which is on the New Mexico state flag) have become deeply ensconced in the wider culture of the region.

The arrival of Spanish explorers and missionaries in the Southwest changed Native lifestyles drastically but had little obvious impact on their buildings. The Spanish brought wooden forms to make sun-dried adobe bricks (a technique they had learned from the Moors), making mud walls easier to build, stronger, and more manageable. They introduced other new construction techniques, including canales (water canals or runoffs on the flat roofs) and lime plaster to protect wall surfaces from wind and rain.

The Spanish wanted to acquire Native lands and save Native souls. The conversion of Indians thus necessitated the building of missions, which were at once defensive and religious structures. Each mission complex contained a church as part of an enclosed courtyard that was often protected by a nearby presidio or fort. The mission fathers brought neither blueprints nor building materials. They were not architects or stonecutters, but they knew the requisite form of a Christian church, evolved from centuries of Catholic ritual. Their Indian subjects were the construction workers for these massive projects, built of adobe brick with vigas and bell towers. Often the transept was missing, as there were not trees tall enough to span that distance. The result was a new type of church: a combination of Catholic tradition and Native technology that remained physically distinct from Catholic churches elsewhere. Although many of these churches were burned during the Pueblo Revolt of 1680, fire destroyed only the wooden beams and the Spanish icons of subjugation. New churches were built following the Reconquest of 1692, often next to or near the roofless adobe ruins.

One of the most beautiful of these types of new churches is San Francisco de Asis in Ranchos de Taos and dates from the early eighteenth century. The powerful massing and clumsy buttresses on the back side of the structure—built by hand using Native labor, materials, and methods—stand in stark contrast to the Hispanic facade with its twin bell towers, carved wooden entry, and delicate wood trim. The religion still practiced inside these hybrid churches also has traces of Native beliefs woven together with Roman Catholic practices. Interiors contain simple, bold Native symbols on whitewashed adobe walls, instead of the elaborate carved or painted *reredos* found in churches of the same era built elsewhere. Native icons and tribal forms stand next to Christian iconography, and both tell of creator gods, sacrifice, and salvation. It is an ethnic mestizo culture, an amalgamation of New World and Old World ideas, forms, practices, and people, which can only be found in this region.[3]

The Spanish asserted their power and protected their land claims by conquering Indian villages in addition to building new settlements, both before and especially following the reconquest. As the Spanish extended their presence to the north (Mexico, New Mexico), east (Texas), and west (Arizona), they established new cities, missions, and presidios. The plans for these new towns and cities were derived from the *New Laws of the Indies*, a 1542 manual intended to establish continuity and control over all Spanish colonies. It governed the political, social, and religious hierarchy of new Spanish colonies. This hierarchy was expressed in town plans centered on a square or rectangular plaza. The proportions of the plaza were determined by the size of the city. In the Southwest this ideal of a central plaza overlapped with Native concepts. While the form was similar, the interpretation differed, as the purpose of the Spanish plaza was to serve as a reminder of European conquest and social hierarchy. The communal courtyard was at once a marketplace, social gathering spot, and political statement. Its form resembled Leonardo da Vinci's drawing *Vitruvian Man*, simultaneously enclosed in a circle and a square, acting as evidence of man at the center of geometry (i.e., conquering nature in the European Renaissance tradition). The Indian plaza focused on the center as void, the intersection of man and nature. It framed the activities of man celebrating and finding his place within nature amid the sacred mountains.[4]

The requisite Spanish municipal, military, and commercial buildings surrounding the plaza were built in adobe and stone, a response to the climate and the skills of the labor force. Like the Indians, the Spanish relied on the ability of thick adobe walls to reflect heat and cold, but the Spanish also introduced colors—turquoise, pink, and yellow—that celebrated the light produced by the low angle of the sun and the landscape. Buildings bordering the plaza were protected from the harsh sun by *portales*, which created covered walkways and outlined the city center.

In addition to planned cities, the Spanish built vernacular adobe ranchos, including the fortified hacienda with its internal courtyard and the simple jacal, a structure indigenous to Mexico and still found throughout the region, especially in the northern states of Mexico and border towns, villages, and cities.[5] These modest dwellings were built by ranch hands applying native plant materials to a simple frame and roofing with yucca or other leaves and later tin.

Hispanic building types were generally grounded in the temperate climate of the Mediterranean, tempered by lessons learned in Mexico, adapted to the southwestern climate, and shaped by interactions with Native Americans. While indigenous houses adopted many Spanish characteristics, they avoided the wrap-around portico and carved lintels and corbels. These features, as well as the central courtyard that took advantage of natural cooling breezes and helped maintain privacy, distinguished Spanish adobe structures. As a result, the surviving imagery of this period of Spanish hegemony is that of the public plaza and the private courtyard (*plazuela*), surrounded by thick whitewashed adobe walls, shady portales and carved wooden doors, and canales carved into extended vigas with strings of drying chili peppers hung from them, all elements that are still present throughout the Southwest, even in new construction.

While much of the land remained part of Mexico through the mid-nineteenth century, increasing numbers of American citizens moved into the region, lured by promises of land or precious metals. Beginning in 1821 a newly independent Mexico promised American *empresarios* land grants if they would help encourage immigration into Texas. Those who responded from the American South as well as from Europe were people looking for economic opportunities. They brought with them regional traditions in building and city planning and adapted them to the new environment. Some settled permanently and some temporarily, which led to conflicts among themselves as well as with the Native Americans and Hispanics already living there.

Immigrants lower on the social scale or choosing to live a more bohemian lifestyle tended to adapt to the environment, living in dugouts, sod houses, and dogtrots, all of which were vernacular house types that put available materials in forms dictated by the climate. Dugouts and sod structures were well insulated but unstable, while the dogtrot encouraged cross-ventilation by bisecting the Yankee hall-and-parlor house with a breezeway.

New settlers also adapted regional and cultural traditions they brought with them to the southwestern environment. These included variations of ethnic American log houses and German *fachwerk* houses chinked with local Texas limestone. Other adaptations to a warmer and drier environment included outside staircases and stoves instead of open-hearth fireplaces. Rooflines were lowered, porches added, windows enlarged and their number increased. Roofs were thatched, shingled, and later covered with galvanized tin, a custom in rural Hispanic New Mexico and Arizona as well. Many houses were started in one period and added onto later, with the framework revealing the evolution of techniques. German farmers living in rural areas who went to church in town built "Sunday houses" for weekend shopping, entertaining, and attending church. Popular in the late 1800s, these one- or two-room frame or limestone houses often had sleeping lofts for the children, accessed by an exterior stairway and represented a new American building type found throughout central Texas.

Anglo immigrants from the American South and East Coast brought yet another urban pattern: the gridded township established in the United States by the Land Ordinance of 1785. Now the public square in the center of town symbolized the democratic grid and the equal opportunity afforded by education. Later this square became a park, a home for war memorials, libraries, or public socials, as well as a gathering space for political dissidents and public rallies. It was the physical embodiment of the Bill of Rights, the power of the individual over the group, addressing natural rights more than nature.

The territorial style—the most fashionable style in Anglo and Hispanic New Mexico from the 1880s, when the railroad arrived, to 1912, when statehood arrived—was the result of heavy sawmill equipment as well as finished woodwork being brought in from the East by wagon and railroad. It incorporated features from the earlier Greek revival, considered the first national (i.e., nonregional) American style. But in the Southwest the Greek revival elements were restricted to the decorative. The buildings were often still built of adobe, but they also had milled wooden trim and Victorian ornament. Finished square columns replaced chunky hewn timbers; double-hung sash windows with shutters appeared. Portales were adorned with milled blue bracket corbels, called the "New Mexican Order." Anglos created other local adaptations of regional forms in the nineteenth century. For example, the Southern Arizona ranch house developed from the single-room, flat-roofed jacales into gabled, pyramid, or hipped-roofed houses with wood-trimmed doors and windows and wooden floors, a fusion of the Spanish Mexican and American ranch traditions.[6]

Following the arrival of the railroad in the late nineteenth century and the precepts of the international style in the twentieth century, southwestern architecture followed the national trend toward homogenization. There were exceptions, however. Besides the pockets of poverty that preserved regional characteristics by default, some twentieth-century builders and architects were dedicated to incorporating both historic references and climatic realities. This approach forced architects to select features of the past, acknowledge the geographical realities of the present, and suggest a future direction for southwestern culture that connected it with its "usable" past. The results ranged from a genuine regional style to a tourist-oriented period revival to the so-called Santa Fe style.

Although coincident with literary and artistic promotion of regionalism, architectural regionalists were generally promoting aesthetics rather than politics or a philosophical rejection of modernism. Instead, they were attempting to identify the essential characteristics of the place and encourage design that acknowledged history, character, and climate. Builders and architects practicing in the Southwest accordingly began to layer and merge traditional motifs with modernist materials and techniques.

The New Mexico State Building designed by Isaac Hamilton Rapp at the 1915 Panama-Pacific International Exposition in San Francisco was a picturesque version of what was being promoted in the region as "Pueblo revival." It was a nostalgic combination of Native American and Hispanic features suitable for a variety of contemporary building types, including Rapp's 1915 Museum of Fine Arts in Santa Fe and John Gaw Meem's new and remodeled buildings at the University of New Mexico. Along with the Harvey House restaurant chain, the Atchison, Topeka, and Santa Fe Railroad commissioned a similar series of depots, trading posts, and lunchrooms along its desert route in a very conscious attempt to capitalize on the region's uniqueness for tourists.

The architect who designed many of these buildings was Minnesota-born Mary Elizabeth Jane Colter. While the railroad was interested in a tourist draw (an example of what would later be termed "commercial regionalism" or "ethnotourism"), Colter was drawn to the spirit(s) of the place.[7] She wanted an architecture that integrated site, history, and function. Instead of copying the historic elements of another culture and translating them into a stereotypical facade, as twentieth-century commercialism tended toward, she sought authenticity and respected other cultures. In *Manual for Drivers and Guides,* used for training the Harvey House conductors, she urged tour guides to understand and communicate the purpose and newness of her buildings: to disseminate knowledge of ancient craftsmanship, not to exploit that craftsmanship by selling cheap trinkets. Hers were new steel-frame buildings that made reference to the past and "should NOT be called a 'copy'; a 'replica'; a 'reproduction' or a 'restoration.' It is absolutely none of these." She preferred the term *re-creation,* as "[t]hat describes best the INTENTION of the design . . . based on fine examples of the prehistoric workman, and . . . built in the Indian spirit." She advocated copying "primitive" architects not in detail but in spirit: "each [building] differed from every other according to the character of the site, the materials that could be procured and the purpose for which [it] was intended" and never pretended to be otherwise.[8]

Promotion of the official "Santa Fe style" began with the 1912 restoration of the Governor's Palace in Santa Fe. Instead of its original 1610 appearance, the architects chose to highlight the 1770s facade with its Anglo-Hispanic corbelled colonnade. They convinced the city council that this served the city's business interests as an appropriate historical and commercial style with which to simultaneously make the city more beautiful and attract tourists. Thus the Indian-Hispanic-Anglo amalgamation of the territorial period was declared the authoritative language for new and remodeled buildings in the City's Historic District, codified and made sacrosanct in 1957. Characteristics of the style include flat, stepped roofs; walls that looked like they were made of adobe and painted in a narrow palette of warm earth tones; nonfunctioning but protruding vigas and canales; and piers with Santa Fe capitals.[9] Vernacular architecture, such as the colorful Mexican American folk dwellings that still exist throughout the Southwest, is perhaps better able to capture the region's hybrid culture.

Other attempts to create a regional modernism included art deco and New Deal interpretations from the 1920s and 1930s. Art deco became Pueblo deco, wherein historic Native symbols were substituted for the jazzy, streamlined symbols of the modern machine age. The low- and medium-rise, rough-skinned, sandy-colored buildings were ornamented with stylized Indian chevrons and turquoise sunbursts that looked like three-dimensional Indian sand paintings. New Deal–era buildings, from the outside, looked identical to those in most parts of the country: a generic modern, deco, and classical mixture termed "stripped classicism." Inside the Public Works Administration–funded and Works Progress Administration–built post offices, courthouses, and high schools were Federal Art Project murals depicting regional themes. But in the Southwest, especially in Arizona and New Mexico, there was also an increased attempt to include local materials, themes, decoration, and historical references on the outside as well as on the interior. Dozens of Native American, Hispanic, and Anglo local artists, architects, and furniture makers were employed to paint, build, and design, resulting in a number of Pueblo revival and territorial style public buildings. Architects drew on indigenous building traditions and materials for modern projects. Some buildings were even constructed of real adobe bricks and unhewn logs.[10] John Gaw Meem remodeled twenty-eight redbrick school buildings at the Santa Fe Indian School, flattening pitched roofs and adding porches and buttresses on buildings constructed between 1890 and 1928.[11] More recent reservation buildings, formerly designed under the auspices of the Bureau of Indian Affairs, are no longer instruments of assimilation into Anglo-American culture. New buildings are being designed by Native Americans and by other architects sensitive to Indian forms and symbology.

Architects from Frank Lloyd Wright to Ricardo Legerreto used geography, climate, local materials, and culture to create a regional architecture based on "organic" architectural principles rather than national styles or fads. Like earlier builders, they distilled the crucial elements of the place. They designed contemporary buildings without resorting to southwestern decorations and motifs, while drawing on the indigenous qualities of the desert, even though technology had freed them of this necessity. Wright taught architecture (and regional vernacular theory) to his students at Taliesin by instructing them to spend several nights camping in the desert. In this way, they discovered and understood, physically and intellectually, the pragmatic need for different types of shelter in the daytime and nighttime desert.

Other architects looked to the land and regional history as well. Brothers O'Neil and Lynn Ford combined the craftsmanship of German American and Mexican building traditions with the American craftsman and modernist movements, which they then applied to Texas homes and public buildings. They contrasted elegant machine-made materials with handcrafted doors and light fixtures. Ceilings featured *bovedas*, hand-laid brick vaults, done by Mexican laborers without the use of scaffolding. Americans Antoine Predock and Will Bruder and Mexican Ricardo Legoretta have similarly reintroduced ancient forms and vernacular traditions into several recent public libraries that are sensitive to local sites and cultures.

But not everyone was or is in tune with the desert. Builders and buyers considered themselves part of the nation rather than just part of a region; and by the end of the twentieth century, the Southwest was much more like the rest of America, only hotter. Retirement villages and golf courses were designed to be familiar to the snowbirds and to the increasing numbers of people moving to the Sunbelt. Like fairways, new housing tracts on cul-de-sacs with lush, green lawns belie the desert condition and the millions of gallons of water necessary to keep them lush. Phoenix and Tucson began to look like an enlarged Levittown.

Looking at regions like the Southwest through the lens of architecture avoids both the romantic regionalism of literature (due to the highly selective nature of inventing symbolic truths) and the radical regionalism of social criticism (also highly selective in order to interpret social, political, and historic trends). Architecture, while a branch of the humanities in that it explores human culture (as opposed to the natural world) and the expressive needs of the human spirit, is a practical discipline as much as an artistic one. It combines science and engineering with artistic expression and philosophical concepts of beauty in creative but pragmatic structures that must "work." Architecture is the one unavoidable art. One can ignore paintings and sculpture, but everyone must deal with architecture on both private and public levels. Architects, builders, historians, and consumers alike are confronted with the physical reality of architecture and what it reveals about beliefs and lifestyles. Architecture responds to real needs and is accessible to everyone to experience.

Thus, regionalism is in turn a valuable tool in identifying and understanding architecture. It provides a framework for categorizing and comparing. By breaking up American culture—and its architecture—into geographic subcultures, one can discover the role of place and understand the complex and intertwined roots of those subcultures. Rather than being subsumed into a larger group based on political distinctions and majority rule, a regionally based study of material culture is more specific and, therefore, more valid. It is the essence of *e pluribus unum*—the democratic ideal rather than the stereotype of the whole.

As importantly, a regional focus in the humanities generally and architecture specifically has the potential to produce better cities and places in which to live, with buildings and spaces whose meanings are tied to place and memory. Regionalism fights ubiquitous urban sprawl and the homogeneity of culture. It lends itself to the creation of a sustainable architecture, one that responds to place—physically and psychologically—incorporating available resources and returning meaning to inhabitants. Regionalism celebrates democracy, focusing on pluralities instead of the mass. The result is personal and community empowerment based on a sense of belonging to concentric groups both of people (from family to ethnicity to citizen to human) and of place (from neighborhood to city to state to nation to world). Every person has a voice and a stake in regional identity, memory, and history, which is at the core of the democratic concept of community and architecture.

Notes

1. Categories of sprawl have been identified by Dolores Hayden in *A Field Guide to Sprawl* with aerial photographs by Jim Wark (New York: W. W. Norton, 2004). More than 25 percent of the photographs illustrating her 'devil's dictionary' were taken in the Southwest.

2. Lawrence Clark Powell, introduction to *Photos of the Southwest*, by Ansel Adams (Boston: New York Graphic Society, 1976), xi.

3. With the exception of San Xavier del Bac (1776–97), south of Tucson, the Franciscan mission churches of the Sonoran and Chihuahuan deserts share characteristics distinct from those in the rest of Mexico or those in California and Texas. See Buford Pickens, ed., *The Missions of Northern Sonora: A 1935 Field Documentation* (Tucson: University of Arizona Press, 1993).

4. See Tony Anella, "Learning from the Pueblos," in *Pueblo Style and Regional Architecture*, ed. Nicholas C. Markovich, Wolfgang F. E. Preiser, and Fred G. Sturm (New York: Van Nostrand Reinhold, 1990), 31–45.

5. The missions were in essence working ranches, vaqueros being the original cowboys.

6. See Janet Ann Stewart, *Arizona Ranch Houses: Southern Territorial Styles, 1867–1900* (Tucson: University of Arizona Press and Arizona Historical Society, 1974).

7. Sylvia Rodriguez has been very critical of the economic motifs of Anglo artists and others who were drawn to the art colonies (especially in Taos) for less than altruistic reasons of preservation and celebration, but rather for exploitation of a people and a culture through the commodification of the primitive Southwest. See Rodriguez, "Art, Tourism, and Race," 143–60.

8. Quotes from Mary Jane Colter, *Manual for Drivers and Guides of the Indian Watchtower at Desert View and Its Relation, Architecturally, to the Prehistoric Ruins of the Southwest* (Grand Canyon National Park: Fred Harvey Company, 1933), 13.

9. Hispanic houses were typically still made of authentic adobe until 1900, when Anglos discovered how to fake it. See Chris Wilson, *The Myth of Santa Fe: Creating a Modern Regional Tradition* (Albuquerque: University of New Mexico Press, 1997).

10. See C. W. Short and Stanley Brown, *Public Buildings: Architecture under the Public Works Administration, 1933–1939* (Washington DC: U.S. Government Printing Office, 1939).

11. Kathryn A. Flynn and Andrew L. Connors, eds., *Treasures on New Mexico Trails: Discovery of New Deal Art and Architecture* (Santa Fe: Sunstone Press, 1994), 193.

2

Constructing Place: The Possibility of Local Representation

Ginette Aley, an agricultural historian, cites landscape theorist Donald W. Meinig's notion of vision (rather than, say, Ralph Waldo Emerson's transcendental eye) to the effect that "landscape is comprised not only by what lies before our eyes but what lies inside our head."[1] Accordingly, she employs a biographical model of history that searches for "defining moments" in internal histories of a region, moments that seem to create a new pattern in lives and landscapes. In her study of the antebellum Midwest, that defining moment comes in a Quaker woman's diary, where she records how commercial imperatives forced people with different manners to cooperate, whether for the harvest, for roads and canals, or for Indian removal.

Barbara Handy-Marchello follows up this notion of class- and gender-determined but internally produced regionalism with an exploration of urban boosterism in North Dakota. She documents the western regionalism of Linda Slaughter, a writer who published letters in the 1870s extolling the merits of the Dakota Territory. If the male booster perspective connected the land and local economy to the national urban system and market, Slaughter's letters instead connected North Dakota society to national standards of middle-class behavior, because of her focus on the work and activities of women. Slaughter's surprising depiction of polite social ritual on the frontier "proved" that such forms were so essentially part of white human nature that they could be produced by even such an uncultivated region. Their necessity was only reinforced—not eroded—by another of the region's distinctive features: encounters between Anglos and Native Americans.

Slaughter wrote at the behest of the Northern Pacific Railroad, but her letters were published in the Minnesota press, namely the *St. Paul Pioneer*. Publishers close to the frontier typically supported a "civilized" view of the West, and Slaughter's letters accordingly pictured a countryside that was socially if not topographically akin to eastern cities. As Handy-Marchello shrewdly recognizes, Slaughter deliberately adopted an aestheticized view of the landscape that distanced her from those who would view it in utilitarian terms as an agricultural commodity. Instead, her sketches were designed to attract more "disinterested" settlers, or rather, settlers whose middle- and upper-class status was marked by the possession of this aesthetic and social gaze.

Nicolas Witschi addresses similar concerns, noting that Nevadans in the 1870s practiced a kind of regional self-representation that was also rooted in how they believed outsiders viewed their region. In this realm, region becomes something of a public relations concept, as it was for Slaughter, but one wielded by locals to negotiate internal social tensions as well. As the townsfolk of Palisade, Nevada, enacted a sort of street theater or Wild West show for railroad travelers, they gained a voice by representing themselves, however stereotypically, to outsiders. At the same time, their "play" on genre expectations for violence reinforced how civilized their town was—only gullible easterners would believe that the satirical performance was reality, as a Nevada newspaper observed. Yet the dime novel's demand for all western conflicts to be limited to those between cowboys and Indians (or duels over women's honor) meant that the region's real conflicts over labor and Chinese immigration were played out in those genre terms.

Guy Reynolds carries this idea of region further in his exploration of Willa Cather. Place and regionalism in Cather's work becomes a kind of "self-fashioning," a cultural process involving marketing, advertising, and reviewing, through which she became and is considered today a regionalist or Midwest writer. A set of progressive, eastern writers found in Cather an exemplar of midwestern culture as they wished it to define the future of American culture: cosmopolitan but resistant to standardization, offering individuals the opportunity to fully realize their potential, while tying that notion of modern selfhood to an authentically American experience (the frontier). Ironically, however, as Reynolds suggests, this thoroughly mediated process of symbolic identification of a writer with a region too often resorts to the essentialist cliché of supposedly authentic features, rather than acknowledging the potentially dynamic changeability of a symbolic brand of regionalism. The result is that, if a writer or artist comes from a region, he or she is still assumed to carry it with him or her and, accordingly, his or her works must always manifest the characteristics that the region has imprinted on them.

Notes

1. Aley, "Dwelling within the Place Worth Seeking," (this volume), 97.

5. Willa Cather's Case

Region and Reputation

GUY REYNOLDS

When we talk about writers, we often think in regionalist or nationalist terms: novelists or poets explore "authentic" features of a culture, giving voice to the deep structures of a region. Writers have their "place," which they embody in writing; in marking the page with words, they also mark out a terrain. Such thinking is seductive and seems at first imbued with powerful common sense; but it also sidesteps the complexities of literary reputation, the writer's self-fashioning, and the broader cultural processes (of marketing, advertising, and reviewing) that serve to identify writer with region.[1] The Nebraskan novelist Willa Cather is a case in point. Even to deploy the epithet, "Nebraskan," is to play the regionalist game, bringing into play an army of preconceptions, myths, stereotypes. And as we play the regionalist game—at least, this crude version of regionalism— many of the subtleties that arise from the writer's relationship to her region can be swamped. Cather, for instance, is popularly known as the "Nebraskan" novelist, even though she was born and spent her early years in Virginia; and even though she is renowned for fictionalizations of Nebraska in *O Pioneers!* and *My Ántonia*, the remainder of her work explored a disparate range of regions, both in North America and in Europe.

Cather's career reached its apogee in the 1920s (she won the Pulitzer

Prize for Fiction in 1923). Increasingly, historians see this interwar period as one shaped by debates about the meaning of "region" in an age of consumerism, national markets, and standardization. Susan Hegeman argues that the 1930s saw a mapping of cultural difference through a regionalist lexicon: "from the 'domesticated' concept of culture there emerged two competing maps of cultural difference: one, based on regional difference, and the other based on class difference. Both represented idealistic attempts to make 'culture' coextensive with, and a product of, 'the real people.'"[2] I want to explore the significance of "regional difference" in the construction of Cather's identity on the national stage. How can we understand Willa Cather's work in the context of this regionalism of the marketplace? Cather's career was forged at a time when cultural production was entering a decisively new phase in the United States, as the whole institutional apparatus of the literary world (e.g., magazines, advertising, photography, reviewing) became increasingly consumerized. As a one-time managing editor of *McClure's Magazine*, Cather had gained an insider's knowledge of the complex interactions between taste, literary production, and the market. *McClure's* was a mass-market journal, but it projected a conspicuous commitment to high or serious writing. Moreover, Cather's life partner, Edith Lewis, worked for the J. Walter Thompson agency—in this very direct way, Cather was linked to the emergent world of branding, marketing, and consumerism. These two women—professionals in the varied world of literary production—were well-positioned to understand how a writer's regional identity might be fashioned within an expanding and increasingly commodified culture.

Many literary figures in early twentieth-century America wrestled with a regionalist dynamic that, as we shall see, also helped shape the reception of Cather's work. Regionalism seemed to offer a definite sense of the local and the distinctive at a time when mass or commercial culture was becoming ascendant, but a local culture might also seem inconsequentially provincial. Randolph Bourne, one of American modernism's key public intellectuals, shaped his response to Cather around this paradox. In November 1918, just before his death in the

CONSTRUCTING PLACE

postwar Spanish flu epidemic, Bourne wrote a review of *My Ánto-nia*, and he also wrote an account of Meredith Nicholson's *The Valley of Democracy*. Nicholson, reasonably well known at the time for *A Hoosier Chronicle*, was a popular Indiana writer typical of the middlebrow writing that tends to be overlooked in literary history but nonetheless tells us a good deal about the cultural zeitgeist.[3] Here we have an important critique of the Midwest by one of the era's most significant public intellectuals. Bourne's essay, "A Mirror of the Middle West," begins with an archetypal encounter between the modern traveler and the region—a vision of America's vast, interior space, glimpsed from a train window. "No Easterner, born forlornly within the sphere of New York, Boston, or Philadelphia, can pass very far beyond the Alleghenies without feeling that American civilization is here found in the full tide of believing in itself. The flat countryside looks more ordered, more farmlike; the Main Streets that flash by the car-windows somehow look more robust and communal."[4] Bourne had just read and reviewed *My Ántonia*, and his essay unconsciously echoes the beginning of that novel, where Jim Burden sits in the railway carriage as the train flashes across the landscape. Just as Jim will then encounter a kind of archetypal story from the Great Plains (Ántonia's tale), Bourne will lead us into his own critical narrative, via a reading of Nicholson. And what are the features of Bourne's analysis? First, Bourne turns his argument around an opposition between East and West, an insistent motif of his analysis. Second, there is the search for essence, or quintessence, and the sense that the region can work as a synecdoche, standing for "American civilization." Third, there is Bourne's withering critique of Nicholson's lack of analytical rigor. Bourne's project (and his work demands that term) was to create a synthesis of social theory, political critique, and cultural commentary that would equal in critical seriousness the Marxist (or "Marxian," as Bourne has it) European tradition. He also wanted to fashion a voice that would address the idiosyncratic and accelerating modernity of early twentieth-century America. In "A Mirror of the Middle West," an account of region becomes part of that project. Bourne attacks Nicholson for what he leaves out of his account of region, notably an account of the business class (he works within the shadow of Thorstein Veblen's analysis of the emergent consumer culture). Nicholson's account of folksiness is simply too folksy for Bourne.

Another point that makes Bourne such an interesting figure in the history of regionalism is that he had learned from the father of pragmatism, William James, to use a language that stresses flexibility, change, and mobility. Bourne was beginning to move toward a pragmatic vision of the dynamism and fluidity of regionalism.[5] Rather than identifying settled and unchanging essences of region, the post-Jamesian intellectual is drawn toward an account of cultural shifts; his or her local culture becomes mutable, as it organically realigns itself under the pressure of modernity. This is how I would interpret Bourne's account of Cather, written also in late 1918. Though he compared *My Ántonia* to a novel by William Allen White, *In the Heart of a Fool*, which he found to be overly moralistic and "cluttered," Bourne admired Cather's third novel for its modern artistry. Bourne praised Cather in terms that would become familiar in the reception of her work; he admired its nostalgia, for instance. But he also seems to have sensed a form of regionalist opposition between Cather's work and that of a figure like White. On the one hand, Cather heralds fluidity and grace and a post-Victorian lack of moralizing; on the other, White illustrates the persistence of the cluttered and explicitly moralistic provincial novel. This is an opposition between modernist and Victorian cultures, or between the cosmopolitan and the provincial worlds. For Bourne, as for other critics of this period such as H. L. Mencken, midwestern provincialism was to be seen as having a penchant for moralistic judgment. Cather's work seemed to escape by resisting this tendency. "Miss Cather, I think, in this book has taken herself out of the rank of provincial. . . . In her work the stiff moral molds are fortunately broken, and she writes what we can wholly understand."[6]

Critics such as Bourne placed themselves within a cultural dualism that they then applied to the Midwest and its artists. The modern critic lambastes the stuffiness, the sheer Victorianism, of William Allen White; and he finds in Cather that, thankfully, "the stiff moral molds" have been broken. Other writers at the same time came to the same conclusion. The critic Carl Van Doren, for instance, also associated Cather's region with a form of provincial extinction: "Miss Cather would not belong to her generation if she did not resent the trespasses which the world regularly commits upon pioneers and artists." According to Van Doren, Cather understood that the frontier world faced "the degradation of its wild freedom and beauty by clumsy towns, obese vulgarity, the uniform of a monotonous standardization." Thus, he concludes, the "heroic days" that Cather describes "endure but a brief period before extinction comes."[7] This is one of those classic assaults on the Midwest from the post–Great War period; it forms part of a cultural jeremiad that underpins Sinclair Lewis's *Main Street* or the commentary in Harold Stearns's quintessential collection of essays by young intellectuals, *Civilization in the United States*. In "The Small Town" from that collection, Louis Raymond Reid argued, "The civilization of America is predominantly the civilization of the small town." In this diagnosis, such "civilization" is distinctly anti-intellectual: "The basis, the underlying motive, of all cultural life in the small town is social. The intellectual never enters."[8] In these sentences, literary regionalism takes shape as a regionalist jeremiad—in particular, a critique of the Midwest as the epitome of provincialism. What is particularly interesting about this debate is that dualisms (e.g., past and present, Victorian and modern, provincial and cosmopolitan) tend to be folded into, inscribed into, a particular region. For literary intellectuals such as Bourne, the Midwest promises both a kind of futurity, a breaking of the molds, and a retreat into provincialism or (using a key word in this debate) "standardization." Cather's work sits at the heart of this argument, emerging as it does from the heart of the heart of the country, while simultaneously invoking and resisting the "provincial."

H. L. Mencken, never a critic to sit on the fence or hide his light under a bushel, produced a central instance of this dualism in his account of *My Ántonia*, where the novel is simultaneously inserted into a region, then used to attack that region, and finally seen as a transcendence of region. "Beneath the swathings of balder-dash, the surface of numskullery and illusion, the tawdry stuff of Middle Western

Kultur, she discovers human beings embattled against fate and the gods, and into her picture of their dull struggle she gets a spirit that is genuinely heroic, and a pathos that is genuinely moving." This is a now-familiar cliché of middle-American provincialism; but Mencken could see Cather as an artist who had worked with "tawdry stuff" to create "eternal tragedy." In her work, he continued, "There is not only the story of poor peasants, flung by fortune into lonely, inhospitable wilds; there is the eternal tragedy of man."[9] The structure of this argument is that of a dialectic defined then transcended. Region as provincialism; artist within region; and the artist moving beyond region to "eternal" verities.

What the commentaries by Bourne, Van Doren, and Mencken tell us, in one relatively straightforward way, is that Cather's identity as a regional writer was sponsored nationally. Accolades for her work as a regionalist emerged by means of a national literary network. Her reputation was cemented and extended through networks that were growing more national and even global in the early twentieth-century. For instance, she forged her career as a journalist in national magazines: *Century, Commonweal, Cosmopolitan, Harper's, Ladies Home Journal, McClure's, Woman's Home Companion*. She then went on to win a large number of literary prizes—the literary prize being an excellent example of how a national literary culture is institutionalized: Pulitzer (1923), Howells Medal (1930), and Gold Medal of the National Institute of Arts and Letters (1944). And she was awarded a good number of honorary degrees, from Nebraska to begin with (1917), but also from Columbia (1928), Yale (1929), and Smith (1933). In other words, Cather's reputation was amplified across a national and then an international literary scene, even though the amplification was often achieved through reading her within a regionalist lexicon (frontiers, pioneers, and the like).

Nationalized regionalism is a term that might describe the knitting together or incorporation of literary regionalisms into a larger trans-American network in the first half of the twentieth-century. Regionalist insurgencies emerged—indeed, they proliferated—but these cultural insurgencies were moderated and smoothed out to become part of a larger mosaic.[10] Such a national network has a complex but essentially dialectical function: to knit together the wider literary culture into a national culture and to celebrate and identify local, regional movements. And so, perhaps, the fundamental lesson of Cather's reputation as a regional writer is that in the twentieth century region counts only so far as it figures in the larger national story. Moreover, the notion of region became a thoroughly mediated idea, as it was framed and shaped by literary networks of publishers, literary prizes, and honorary degrees. Hence the continual, rather ironic conjunction of the words *nation* and *region*, which we find in discussions of literary localism.

For example, in 1923 Cather published her essay "Nebraska: The End of the First Cycle," which was a survey of the state's history and culture that crystallized many of her ideas about cyclical patterns of historical development and how they might apply to the regional history of Nebraska; but the essay, tellingly, was published in *The Nation*. Furthermore, it formed part of a larger series of essays in *The Nation* on the individual states. One truism about literary regionalism might be that if one spots the word *region* in a paragraph, then the word *nation* will be hovering somewhere in the vicinity. Perhaps it is only in the national consciousness that regionalism can develop in ways that are nonthreatening or nonsectional. National arenas create a space for the understanding of regionalism while offsetting the logical conclusion of regionalist thought—that there is nothing but a series of localities or regions to be understood on their own neo-separatist terms.

Is the designation of Cather as pioneer or frontier writer simply critical shorthand; or is it, by a process of the politics of naming, a distortion of her work? On the simplest level, we can say with quantitative certainty that most of her writing was set outside of Nebraska, in areas as disparate as New York, London, the varied regions of the Southwest, Virginia, and colonial-era Canada. Her last novel, begun at the time of her death, was set in medieval France. "Late" Cather, from 1927 to 1947, was undeniably a cosmopolitan and resolutely non-midwestern writer, apart from occasional diversions back to her roots (notably in *Lucy Gayheart*). In this phase of her career, the majority of it, she wrote about Canada and the South, about mesas and Mexico; and rather than moving backward toward regional origin, she was moving away geographically and culturally. Hence, the designation of a writer such as Cather by means of regionalist shorthand can act as a form of reductionism, helping to narrow and constrain the sheer imaginative diversity of her oeuvre. In fact, we might say that the career enacts one of those binary oppositions noted earlier: the regional diversity of the author's imagined worlds and the narrowed identification of the writer with a very specific region.

Why and how does this narrowing take place? One cause might be the complex patterns of institutionalization by which an author is read, criticized, placed within a university syllabus, marketed to readers, and advertised. In Cather's case there is a paradox. Her work in the late 1920s and 1930s was moving into territorial diversity, but the conception of what kind of writer Cather might be was narrowed. The terms *pioneer* and *frontier* moved to the totemic center of arguments about her work. Partly, we can blame a historian for this predicament. Cather had the fortune, or misfortune, to break through to prominence just as Frederick Jackson Turner's frontier thesis achieved real ascendancy within American historiography and, indeed, within the broader intellectual culture. As Ray Allen Billington notes, "no historian rivaled his impact on the profession during the 1910s and 1920s. . . . Textbook writers leaped on the van; every text published between 1926 and 1930 made the frontier the focal point of American history, and of the twenty-four most widely used, sixteen cited Turner by name and nineteen accepted the principle of geographic determinism as unassailable."[11] Cather was a Pulitzer Prize winner in 1923; two years later the Pulitzer Prize for History was awarded to a thoroughly Turnerian writer, Frederick L. Paxson, author of *History of the American Frontier, 1763–1893*. The 1920s had become the decade of the frontier, three decades after the actual closing of the frontier; the result would be that Cather's fiction was critically compressed in terms of its cultural signals.[12]

CONSTRUCTING PLACE

A number of early studies of Cather attempted to read her within this frontier paradigm, paradoxically narrowing the ways in which she was read even as her own creative intelligence led her away from Nebraska. One of the first extended Cather critiques to appear in book form was Lucy Lockwood Hazard's *The Frontier in American Literature*.[13] Hazard's book was symptomatic of a number of works written in the 1920s, texts that sensed that the frontier experience, in all its "Turnerian" energy and decisiveness, had become enervated and attenuated in an age of consumerism and "standardization." Commentators had begun to fret about the end of the frontier and the concomitant loss of distinctive, pioneering western individualism. Cather herself had, in an anticipation of these arguments, outlined such a thesis in her article in *The Nation* on Nebraska.[14] In Duncan Aikman's 1925 collection, *The Taming of the Frontier*, a group of writers sought out towns such as Kansas City, Cheyenne, or Portland that resisted "standardization." Aikman lamented, "the gods of individualism in both personal and community life have been thrown down to make way for the gods of standardization." "Out in the West," he continued, "where a generation or two ago the pioneer imposed his individuality upon raw and uncouth towns at the point of his six-shooter, today the group prejudices of boosters and breeders to type impose their pet conformities with gestures scarcely less ferocious."[15] The major phase of Cather's career had coincided with a crisis of representation in images of the frontier West as the memory of the old days receded, only to give way to what critics sensed was modern culture's blandness and antipathy to individualism. The recovery of a western mythos, of which the frontier was a vital component, was in part a response to the urbanization and industrialization of American society, an "escape valve" in Lee Clark Mitchell's words.[16]

Eventually, historiographical or literary-critical paradigms percolate outward into the mass culture. We can see this osmosis take place in an interesting summary of Cather in *Vanity Fair* from 1927. Titled "An American Pioneer—Willa Cather," *Vanity Fair*'s photograph of Cather has the author with her favored tie, both casual and mildly formal. It is worth quoting at length the language deployed by the editor or subeditor since this boosterish paragraph touches on many themes that then dominated Cather criticism:

> Since the publication in 1915 of *The Song of the Lark*, each new story by Willa Cather has won an increasing recognition as a picture and an evaluation of the American landscape. Today, after twenty-four years of scrupulous craftsmanship she is the heir apparent to Edith Wharton's lonely eminence among America's women novelists. Her contradictory avocations include landlord-farming in Nevada, and a one-time editorship on *McClure's Magazine*. Daughter of pioneers, graduate of a prairie farm and the University of Nebraska, her position in American letters is an absolute one by right of sheer artistic stature, beyond the categories of literary schools or *genres*. She writes in a way that seems utterly transparent and forthright but that conceals in its overtones a vast and subtle interplay of ironical intelligence. The depth and variety of her understanding is implicit in a swift, muscular style, wrought with an economy that discovers the inevitable word and the inevitable idea. No one else has so well expressed the new philosophy, the urge "to live out our potentialities," because no other novelist has so deeply felt the need of it, yet so vividly seen that such a philosophy should not mark a break with our past but an enrichment. Miss Cather's intellectual roots go deep into the soil of early America yet her spare, beautiful style has the poise and elegance inherent in the great tradition of English prose.[17]

This form of criticism is a major part, whether we like it or not, of the process of forging a literary reputation: a form of review or overview, published in a newspaper or journal, that sits on the border between literary criticism and advertising. Both middlebrow and rather archly highbrow (note the terrible overwriting of "Her contradictory avocations"!), this is the kind of blurb that does more to establish a context for reading a writer than most academic criticism. Cather is "an American pioneer," largely on the basis that she was "Daughter of pioneers, graduate of a prairie farm and the University

CONSTRUCTING PLACE

of Nebraska." This is true, in a way; but Cather's family was of long-established Virginian origin, and her father's financial business placed her in the white collar middle-class milieu that still dominates towns such as Des Moines, Iowa, or Lincoln, Nebraska. Furthermore, this "pioneer" is now an exponent of "landlord-farming in Nevada" (the Cather family had acquired property in the new state). One does not need to be a 1970s Marxist to acknowledge the economic and cultural contradictions between pioneering and landlord farming. One effect of the piece channels the professionalism of Cather and her family into being "pioneers," while masking the actual work that they did. The author states, for instance, that she had a "one-time editorship" at *McClure's*—in fact, she worked at *McClure's* for many years; and this was part of a long career as professional critic, journalist, and woman-of-letters that lasted from her late teens in Lincoln through her late thirties.

The troubled defense of women's writing in the United States (another debate that frames the reception of Cather) is seen in the statement that she is "the heir apparent to Edith Wharton's lonely eminence among America's women novelists." There is a striking disjunction between the relative simplicity of the identification of writer with region or with a singular characteristic ("American pioneer") and the ambiguity and real insight conveyed in the commentary's second half. Cather is the "American pioneer," but she is also "in the great tradition of English prose." She can be read in a broader tradition that encompasses American literature but also English and classical and French writing. Also, Cather is a "pioneer" but intellectually her "roots go deep into the soil of early America"—almost as if she were a New England author or Emerson's heir.

Then there is a sense of Cather as a true modern and the articulator of a new philosophy. What does this following sentence mean? "No one else has so well expressed the new philosophy, the urge 'to live out our potentialities,' because no other novelist has so deeply felt the need of it, yet so vividly seen that such a philosophy should not mark a break with our past but an enrichment." There was, in fact, a book published in New York in 1913, a translation of Edouard

Le Roy's text on the "new philosophy" of Henri Bergson.[18] In general, Bergson's ideas, along with those of writers he was allied with in the United States, including John Dewey and William James (and by extension, Randolph Bourne), might be thought of as establishing this "new philosophy." *Vanity Fair's* emphasis on "our potentialities" would fit with the emphasis on potential, energy, will, and the creative life that was being explored by these figures. At this point, in other words, we are getting exactly that sort of modernistic thinking seen earlier in this essay in Bourne's account of Cather. But such philosophical critique has become bracketed by a critical shorthand that erases complexity in the drive for easy categorization.

Cather's career began in the late-Victorian era, was consolidated in the early twentieth-century, and reached fruition at a decisive turning point in American culture. The postwar world witnessed the rapid spread of new media (e.g., film and radio) and a decisive shift toward consumption and consumerism. *Vanity Fair*, with its carefully calibrated appeals to sophistication and highbrow culture, was a symptom and driver of upper-class consumerism, while Cather's entry into its pages shows that her career was being strategically marketed. For, as Michael Murphy notes, *Vanity Fair* had begun to use art photographers to help create images of studied Bohemianism. The magazine was notable for "its especially skillful appraisal of and traffic in the celebrity values of the most important 'bohemian' figures, photographed stylishly by serious 'art' photographers for display in regular full-page portraits."[19] The classic image of Cather—crisp white shirt, ironic smile, tie, and discreet jewelry—is a marker of Manhattan sophistication, not earthy pioneer virtue. *Vanity Fair* had incorporated the pioneer novelist into its own imaginative realm, a hybrid composite of East Coast manners and restrained Bohemianism where "pioneers" and "frontiers" stood for authenticity and individualism. Cather, the "pioneer novelist," is an individual talent "beyond the categories of literary schools or *genres*."

The regional reputation of Cather works by a circular process of symbolic identification. Cather is a Nebraskan writer; Nebraska "is" the frontier or pioneers. This is regionalism as critical shorthand and, as such, is a familiar process in most cultures. One of the problems with thinking about a writer's regionalism is that the identification and articulation of regionalist features can come dangerously close to cliché, reductionism, and a form of essentialism that doesn't take us very far into a complex understanding of culture. A region is identified with a certain clutch of features; an author comes from a certain region; and her or his work manifests or embodies these features.

But it is possible to use regionalism as a creative critical tool, a paradigm that opens up and enriches a writer's work by providing a complex lens rather than the simplifying mirror. The reception of Cather's work provides one very good example of such regionalist enrichment, namely Dorothy Canfield Fisher's essay, "Willa Cather: Daughter of the Frontier." What is significant about Canfield Fisher's essay is that region is seen as complex and changeable and as the site of decisive social change. Rather than cultural memory, Cather's friend and fellow novelist gives us sociocultural ferment. "I offer you a hypothesis about Willa Cather's work: that the only real subject of all her books is the effect a new country—our new country—has on people transplanted to it from the old traditions of a stable, complex civilization." Cather is "the only American author who has concentrated on the only unique quality of our national life, on the one element which is present more or less in every American life and unknown and unguessable to Europeans or European colonials." That is, she writes of characters "whose inherited traits come from centuries of European or English forebears . . . set down in a new country to live a new life which is not European or English."[20] This is one of the best accounts of Cather's work, because it is so responsive to the social change mapped by her work. What Dorothy Canfield Fisher gives us is something quite rare in the early literary regionalism that shaped the reception of Cather's work. She attempts to read out the implications of the local culture that nurtured the early fiction, but she has seen local culture in terms of social change. She has mapped the local in ways that avoid cliché or the rearticulation of supposedly "authentic" features. Above all, she suggests a form of literary regionalism that is mobile and dynamic. The dreaded word, "frontier," appears again; but here it relates less to Turnerian geographical determinism than to a sense of restlessness and modernity. The frontier becomes a sociocultural border marked by endless patterns of migration—a site for cultural change rather than reified myth.

In conclusion, I want to look back from the vantage point afforded by Canfield Fisher and to relocate her essay within the discourses of region. On one hand, we see a rather static or even reified language of locality, where cultural change becomes fixed into circumscribed terminology—in Cather's case, that language of pioneers and frontiers emerges from Frederick Jackson Turner's historical writing. On the other hand, Bourne and Canfield Fisher develop the language of region as a sense of place that is nonetheless framed by keen receptivity to social and cultural movement. The irony of Cather's case is that the former language enabled her to achieve regionalist significance within the national arena, even as it reduced her oeuvre to a comforting but narrow set of thematic signals.

Notes

1. For a recent, skeptical investigation into "authenticity" see William R. Handley and Nathaniel Lewis, eds., *True West: Authenticity and the American West* (Lincoln: University of Nebraska Press, 2004). As the editors state in their introduction: "There are few terms at play in the history of this vast region that have as wide a reach and relevance, and there is no other region in America that is as haunted by the elusive appeal, legitimating power, and nostalgic pull of authenticity, whether with regard to ethnicity, cultural artifacts, or settings" (1). Handley's essay in that volume, "Willa Cather: 'The West Authentic,' the West Divided" (72–94) complements my own investigation into the construction of Cather's regionalist identity.

2. Susan Hegeman, "The Culture of the Middle: Class, Taste, and Region in the 1930s Politics of Art," in *Patterns for America: Modernism and the Concept of Culture* (Princeton: Princeton University Press, 1999), 132.

3. Warren Susman characterizes Nicholson as one kind of midwestern figure who emerged at this time, becoming the object of scorn for those liberals, leftists, and intellectuals of whom Bourne is a prime instance. Nicholson was a "conservative" for whom "the frontier had created the perfect small-town bourgeoisie: stable, reliable (i.e., Republican), uninfluenced by immigrant blocs and foreign radical ideas, the safeguard of the Republic." Warren Susman, *Culture as History: The Transformation of American Society in the Twentieth Century* (New York: Pantheon, 1984), 31.

4. Randolph Bourne, "A Mirror of the Middle West," *The Dial* 65 (November 30, 1918): 480–82. Reprinted in Randolph Bourne, *The Radical Will: Randolph Bourne, Selected Writings 1911–1918*, comp. and with an introduction by Olaf Hansen (New York: Urizen Books, 1977), 265–70, 265.

5. One reason for this might be that Bourne shared with James a suspicion of centralizing organizations and cultural conformism. Such beliefs meshed with an interest in cultural decentralization. "Bourne's own antiorganizational sentiments mirrored James's. Fearful of the conformist influence of organized groups and institutions on individual expression, he encouraged the idea of leadership as a form of engagement or political commitment working outside the 'centripetal' force of institutions." Leslie J. Vaughan, *Randolph Bourne and the Politics of Cultural Radicalism* (Lawrence: University Press of Kansas, 1997), 44.

6. Randolph Bourne, review of *My Ántonia*, by Willa Cather, *The Dial*, 65 (December 14, 1918), 557. Reprinted in John J. Murphy, ed., *Critical Essays on Willa Cather* (Boston: G. K. Hall, 1984), 145–46, 146.

7. Carl Van Doren, "Willa Cather" in *Contemporary American Novelists: 1900–1920* (New York: MacMillan, 1922). Reprinted in James Schroeter, ed., *Willa Cather and Her Critics* (Ithaca: Cornell University Press, 1967), 15.

8. Louis Raymond Reid, "The Small Town," in *Civilization in the United States: An Enquiry by Thirty Americans*, ed. Harold E. Stearns (New York: Harcourt, Brace, 1922), 285–96, 286, 289.

9. H. L. Mencken, review of *My Ántonia*, by Willa Cather, *Smart Set*, February 1919. Reprinted in Schroeter, *Willa Cather and Her Critics*, 8–9, 9.

10. My reading here perhaps adopts a more cynical (or realistic?) position on regionalism than that of Robert Dorman, while acknowledging the broad thrust of Dorman's excellent account of interwar literary provincialism. For Dorman, his study "will recount how the *region* was posed against all of these modern tendencies as the means towards a richer, freer, and more humane way of life." Dorman, *Revolt of the Provinces*, xii.

11. Ray Allen Billington, *Frederick Jackson Turner: Historian, Scholar, Teacher* (New York: Oxford University Press, 1973), 444–45.

12. Frederick L. Paxson, *History of the American Frontier 1763–1893* (Boston: Houghton Mifflin, 1924). The best account of the frontier thesis and its place in a 1920s *Kulturkampf* remains Susman, *Culture as History*, 27–38.

13. Lucy Lockwood Hazard, *The Frontier in American Literature* (New York: Thomas Y. Crowell, 1927).

14. Willa Cather, "Nebraska: The End of the First Cycle," *The Nation*, 117 (1923): 236–38.

15. Duncan Aikman, ed., *The Taming of the Frontier* (New York: Minton, Balch, 1925), xii.

16. "To wonder why cowboys were translated into such mythic status ('the Cowboy') or to ask why the Western emerged when it did is to enter into vexed historical terrain. The simplest explanation involves the collective response to industrial capitalism: the West once again as escape valve for eastern tensions and psychological pressures. . . . With the transition to an urban economy and the pressures of a newly modernized society, the allure of a more stable, agrarian working culture is not hard to imagine, perhaps especially since the frontier had come to seem irrevocably closed." Lee Clark Mitchell, *Westerns: Making the Man in Fiction and Film* (Chicago: University of Chicago Press, 1996), 26.

17. "An American Pioneer—Willa Cather," *Vanity Fair*, July 1927, 30. My thanks to Michael Schueth for bringing this piece to my attention.

18. Edouard Le Roy, *The New Philosophy of Henri Bergson*, trans. Vincent Benson (New York: Holt, 1913).

19. Michael Murphy, "'One Hundred Per Cent Bohemia': Pop Decadence and the Aestheticization of Commodity in the Rise of the Slicks," in *Marketing Modernisms: Self-Promotion, Canonization, Rereading*, ed. Kevin J. H. Dettmar and Stephen Watt (Ann Arbor: University of Michigan Press, 1996), 61–89, 62.

20. Dorothy Canfield Fisher, "Willa Cather: Daughter of the Frontier," *New York Herald-Tribune*, May 28, 1933, sec. 2.

6. Dwelling within the Place Worth Seeking

The Midwest, Regional Identity, and Internal Histories

GINETTE ALEY

Surely *place* induces poetry, and when the poet is extremely attentive to what is there, a meaning may even attach to his poem out of the spot on earth where it is spoken, and the poem signify the more because it does spring so wholly out of its place, and the sap has run up into it as into a tree.

—Eudora Welty, *The Eye of the Story*

In their introductory essay to *The American Midwest*, historians Andrew R. L. Cayton and Susan E. Gray write that "[a]mong the most important characteristics of regionality, is its contested and unfinished quality."[1] Indeed its changing relation to place, time, and generational perspective gives regionality the quality of a palimpsest, or a slate that is continually rewritten. Landscapes in this sense embody an enduring past. David Lowenthal, a geographer, observed more than twenty-five years ago that "Life is more than separate events; it in-corporates the quality of duration, of passage through time. Buffeted by change, we retain traces of our past to be sure of our enduring identity."[2] Fellow geographer D. W. Meinig has written about this as well, saying, "Life must be lived amidst that which was made before. Every landscape is an accumulation."[3] So, too, are regions. However, the dynamism and change in how regions are built, as historian Terry Barnhart points out, is also what makes it a problematic construction in its imprecision, subjectivity, irony, and relativity. Barnhart raises the question also addressed by Cayton and Gray: how then does one "read a region?"[4] I argue here that a closer examination of internal histories (i.e., historical processes, events, and people that shape a place) will help us to identify crucial turning points, or "defining moments," that appear to construct a distinctive regional identity. To Barnhart's question asking about how to read a region, my response would be: one could begin by looking for turning-point stories.

In emphasizing the human experience, the humanities afford endless possibilities for imagining and constructing potentially insightful analogies and frameworks. Even psychology's ideas about the individual may hold suggestions about theorizing regionalism. For example, one can hardly deny the fundamental importance of the "inner self" to outward appearances and behavior. Within a person's cumulative internal histories, many events trigger nothing, no response. They simply pass leaving little more than an imprint. Alternatively, certain events provoke a deep or dramatic response and are responsible for shaping the individual in a conscious new pattern or direction. These qualify as "defining," or turning-point, moments. Analogous to events in a region's history, some are positive, some are negative, and some have consequences that may be unfathomable. Individuals, like landscapes, are the accumulations of a series of defining moments.[5]

How this array of pivotal events has coalesced into the present entity or person is of crucial significance to the historian. If history, as the nineteenth-century English scholar Thomas Carlyle wrote, is the essence of innumerable biographies, then certainly the context of place and region serves as an important organizational structure that allows us to interpret the meanings, connections, and significance of those lives in both an immediate and broader collective sense. Biographies—in the sense of personal and community histories—are acted out upon the stage of *place*; and the lives historians strive to uncover and understand were rooted in a specific and unique (in time and space) landscape, which tied together all of its inhabitants. Hence, the complexity of context. Perceptively, scholars such as David Wrobel have

CONSTRUCTING PLACE

contended that places are, in effect, multidimensional. In the case of the West, for example, many "Wests" exist and have existed, and so too have there been multiple contingent and coexisting dramas therein, reflecting swings of power and competing ideologies and identities. This is obviously true of the Midwest and other regions as well.

The term *rooted* also reflects my interest in adapting feminist standpoint theory's "situated" framework to theorizing regionality and interpreting regional histories. That is, the concept of a situated framework encourages both narrative writing and interpretation about a place *from within it*, in order to create an internal perspective, grounded by the scholar's articulated (and situated) perspective and knowledge. Standpoint feminist theorists consider "the process of approximating the truth as part of a dialogical relationship among subjects who are differentially situated."[6] This avoids the problem of universalizing identities and experiences within and across regions and stimulates a paradigmatic discourse on distinctiveness. Geographer Meinig captures the interpreter's dilemma when he points out that "any landscape is comprised not only of what lies before our eyes *but what lies inside our head*."[7] What appears to be is only part of what really happened. Mentalities of the present matter to the investigation of the past. After all, geographers note, we share a history with present landscapes. They complicate historical narrative writing, requiring a judicious, inclusive balancing of narrative with counternarrative writing, as opposed to the unwieldy and pretentious metanarrative.

William Cronon's *Changes in the Land* further encourages contemplation of regional processes from *within*, in its depiction of colonists and Native Americans who linked New England ecosystems to markets in relationships resulting in dramatic new impacts upon both land and people. My own research on the Old Northwest (or early Midwest), touched on later in this essay, similarly examines the force of a commercial impulse on early-nineteenth-century westward expansion. The ensuing transformation of the landscape reflected the spread of a Euro-American hegemony based upon a commitment to commercial agriculture. Tracing this influence has revealed market connections to areas that are not usually associated with it, such as the relationship of local interests to the conduct of Indian policy and removal in the region or the surprising degree of interest in the market by early midwestern farm women.[8] Tracking this turning point requires asking how events were recorded by contemporary participants, but it also requires analyzing the changing patterns of land use in the region.

Kent Ryden thus correctly admonishes that it is the local stories inscribed upon the landscape that are imperative to grasp and interpret. In his insightful *Mapping the Invisible Landscape*, Ryden argues that the ability to "write place into being" requires historians to "listen carefully to and translate the narratives implicit in the landscape."[9] While not denying what might be termed outside influences on the Midwest, such as the large mid- to late-nineteenth-century railroads (who were responding to economic activities already in place, more than actually initiating them), midwestern landscapes and regions generally are the constructions of the people who dwell in them and of those who preceded them. To the historian in search of a regional past based on internal histories, the landscape, despite being perceptibly and imperceptibly altered with time and use, is therefore both artifact and monument. It is a living memory of the activities and reckonings of prior societies. According to novelist and Indiana-native Kurt Vonnegut, regional landscapes and geographies encapsulate a homegrown vision. "What geography can give all Middle Westerners, along with the fresh water and topsoil, if they let it," he writes, "is awe for an Edenic continent stretching forever in all directions."[10] Another internal element known intimately only by the inhabitants concerns the "spirits" of a place, or as sociologist Michael Mayerfeld Bell suggests, "the mixing of souls with spaces."[11] In other words, a localized event leaves behind not only the stories surrounding it but also an essence that is captured and spiritually rooted to the place of occurrence.

A place will give up its stories if we tap the internal vein of human drama. Based upon his own years of "looking and learning and teaching about American landscapes," geographer Peirce Lewis devised a series of axioms (with corollaries) as a guide to how insiders and outsiders

CONSTRUCTING PLACE

can "read" them. Lewis's axioms demonstrate the utility of recognizing the language of landscapes and their relationship to internal histories. Axiom number one, for example, links landscape to culture: "The man-made landscape—the ordinary run-of-the-mill things that humans have created and put upon the earth—provides strong evidence of the kind of people we are, and were, and are in the process of becoming." Axiom number seven, however, is a reminder that objects visible upon the land can designate meanings that are not immediately apparent. A landscape is not, he admonishes, "the master key to an understanding of culture." Perhaps not. But in teaching how to see a place on its own terms, Lewis points toward the construction of regional identities from within.[12]

Yet it is difficult to do that for the Midwest, a ghost among regions. *All Over the Map: Rethinking American Regions*—a collection of essays published in 1996 and written by several prominent scholars, including Edward Ayers—fails to represent the Midwest as a region. Though the field of midwestern scholarship made a tremendous move forward with the previously mentioned publication of *The American Midwest: Essays on Regional History* in 2001, book reviews of Midwest studies routinely point out the dearth of scholarship, especially of larger interpretive works. Recent reviews have labeled the region historiographically as a "forgotten province when it is not [being] denigrated," and have likened it to being the "Rodney Dangerfield of American regions."[13] So, the Midwest is not only a ghost but also one that gets no respect and, Kurt Vonnegut would add, possesses "an aggressively nasal accent."[14] The underlying problem is that historians still do not know enough about the region's history—its major and minor dramas, characters, plots, subplots, themes, and so on—and this prevents identification of those things that distinguish it from (and, conversely, connect it with) other regions. To talk about a region and its distinctiveness demands knowing its multiple internal histories and cultures, not simply its present manifestations.

As abstractor for the *Journal of Southern History*, I have read and abstracted every article appearing in it since July of 2000. Historians of the South have the strongest grasp not only on situating their studies within the context of the region's complex histories but also in examining the underlying internal processes and events that shaped their region. Like elsewhere, the South was a region of decision makers. Their example demonstrates that we need to know what brought people together or pushed them apart in these regions as well as what were the roots of these now visible manifestations of their cultural and economic activities. Groups that share the same environmental space also share common material interests (and more)—if not cultural affinities—in ways that are unique to them and link them together, despite the ongoing negotiating of competing values and situated perspectives. These dynamics are at the heart of internal histories, wherein the scholar becomes familiar with the intermingling of lives and people's intimacy with place. Understanding local activities is paramount, first, in being able to see people, in their own right, as decision makers in their immediate world and, second, in realizing a region's relationship to other regions and its role in larger national and transnational processes and histories. Allan Pred has written that "[i]t is through the medium of local activity, through the medium of place- and region-specific practices, that spatially extensive power relations are manifested." Moreover, it is in intersections with "the locally peculiar, the locally sedimented and contingent, the locally configured context, that the more global structuring processes are given their form and become perpetuated or transformed."[15] Internal histories reveal the inhabitants as actors, creators, and decision makers; thus, it is inhabitants who are responsible for defining their regions from within. In one sense, regional identity begins at home.

Within these turning-point stories lies the basis for regional distinctiveness. Eudora Welty probably would have agreed. Indeed the relationship she saw existing between the core of self and place emphasizes that each asserts an influence upon the other, like two children on a seesaw. "Place absorbs our earliest notice and attention," she wrote, "it bestows on us our original awareness. . . . It never really stops informing us, for it is forever astir, alive, changing, reflecting, like the mind of man."[16] Constructing regional identities in a manner analogous to the primacy of the internal essence upon the outward being, coupled with Welty's reminder of the reciprocal flow of influence, draws attention back to examining how the region's historical inhabitants and their personal experiences brought them to a particular point in time.

Thus, turning-point moments can be an essential organizational and interpretive tool for regionalism by offering a kind of order or hierarchy to the many stories out of a place. This is not to suggest that the only stories worth capturing are those that engendered a turning point; rather, these would serve as bold points on a dynamic and *always changing* outline of a regional discourse. Contending with another's perceived subjectivity is in fact the tension that compels scholars to rewrite historical narratives, while doing so also brings them closer to comprehending and constructing truer, more-inclusive regional identities. Indeed this echoes Cayton and Gray's characterization of regionality as "contested and unfinished"; examining and reexamining internal histories is an ongoing process.

Two nineteenth-century manuscripts—a set of letters and a diary—along with the state papers of several Indiana governors stand out as excellent examples of windows that look out upon fundamental processes touching the lives of inhabitants, even as they were in effect creating a new regional landscape. The Anna Briggs Bentley letters, housed in the Maryland Historical Society Archives, describe in rich detail what it meant for Anna, her husband Joseph, their children, and a black servant named Henry to merge themselves into the broad stream of migration in 1826. In the same year, Indiana signed treaties with the Potawatomi and Miami peoples that would ultimately remove them from their lands in order to build canals. These events, which seem to be only related by place, in fact, together reveal a key process that would determine the region's identity: commerce, and especially commercial agriculture.

The early history of the American Midwest was dominated by westward expansion that was largely motivated by economics and empire building, and which reconfigured Native American and Euro-American populations while sparking aggressive competition for land, resources, and authority. Given the steady intrusion and assumption of power by the latter group over the former, numerous events within this period could be characterized as turning-point stories, since social, economic, and physical structures, which would come to dominate and direct the region, were being erected. In and of themselves, each event and corresponding new structure represents important points of departure. However, care needs to be taken, in this context of cultural hegemony, to avoid crafting exclusively one-sided stories that mimic racist theories of essentialism. Yet to simply designate these kinds of events as merely snapshots of larger processes is to miss the significant point that local and individual decisions were made and actions taken to *adapt* such processes to serve immediate interests. These needs may themselves be familiar or common, but they were cloaked in the particular needs of a given place and its people. Failure to recognize this is to ascribe a degree of uniformity and universality of intra- and interregional development that did not exist; one need only consider, for example, how the internal improvement movement played out in the early decades of the nineteenth century to get a sense of this variety.

The Bentleys, who would help catalyze such improvements, left their Maryland home for a Quaker community on the eastern Ohio frontier and wrote regular letters to family members back home. Of the ache of leaving behind loved ones, relative comfort, and familiarity, Anna Bentley reflected, "Oh, can it be that I am so far from you? I think of it sometimes and fall to wondering how I ever could have consented to it, but still as yet I have never repented it." Of the arduous labor involved in creating a new, settled (and what would soon be commercial) agricultural place, she wrote, "The men and boys leave at daybreak and return at sundown [and] . . . are engaged in felling, grubbing, mauling, and burning and expect very shortly to have 3 or 4 acres fenced in and planted in potatoes, turnip, [etc.]." A turning point observation here is the description of the new western society that Bentley, her family, and their community were forming in Ohio, and the commercial-oriented agricultural landscape they were making. She took care to note the differences among the people and again pointed toward the emergence of a new hybrid society. "The people here," she remarked, "have a great many different kinds of preserves, puddings, pies, pickles . . . [t]hey are all Pennsylvanians or Virginians and have their manners." Bentley, a southerner accustomed to servants, was struck by how westerners used cooperative labor to achieve and survive: "They have a custom here in harvest or other busy times to collect as many neighbours as they can, and they will pay back in work."[17] Anna Bentley's letters express an awareness that their efforts were bringing about not only local but regional changes of lasting significance. This is one of the stories from within, in which some of the roots of midwestern distinctiveness are also evident.

But there are others. The process of market integration among early nineteenth-century agrarians was complex and uneven. Given conflicting scholarly interpretations of market involvement (i.e., that farm people were either generally profit-oriented or fearful of the market), a closer examination of the historical participants may yield more clarity on the subject as it relates to the emerging Midwest and so perhaps new insight. The argument that farm people of the early republic were largely ambivalent about the market is, in fact, unconvincing and is not supported to any significant degree in the accounts of early agrarian midwesterners.[18] Indeed, Bentley's writings (and others') convey nothing about market apprehension and, conversely, a considerable amount about pursuing market-minded interests. In July of 1829 the Bentley farm was three years old and beginning to produce in abundance. The real story, however, was in how well a certain neighbor was doing. "He will have a *great deal* of wheat, rye, oats, and corn *to sell*," she wrote enthusiastically to her family.[19] To her and their community this prosperity was a respectable testament to "the united labour of his wife and self. . . . They are gaining esteem everywhere." Bentley herself exhibits an ambitious, market-minded agrarianism in descriptions of her sideline in commodity production and processing of sugar and butter, which she believed "will help to extricate us from debt."[20] Her desire to use the surplus to improve the family's circumstances critically distinguishes this activity from simply meeting the demands of the household and indicates both a profit motive and a positive conception of the market. Whereas agrarian women's perspectives on market involvement are as yet understudied, tracing the commercial influence locally in Bentley's writings reveals an important connection to midwestern women as well.[21]

The Bentleys and other early midwestern farm people of the 1820s and even into the 1840s soon found that their dreams of developing profitable agricultural enterprises were stymied by poor transportation and market access. Remedying this situation would constitute a revolution in the social and economic lives of the settlers and of the native peoples who were continually displaced by such "remedies." One German immigrant farmer in Indiana wrote in 1836 that while he knew that rye and wheat "are well paid for in Indianapolis, and sell well, it is difficult to deliver them, since the roads in that direction are so terribly bad that you can't take a wagon over them."[22] Successive state administrations had grappled with how to rectify this situation beginning at least as early as 1818, two years after Indiana's statehood, when Governor Jonathan Jennings identified roads and canals as "a subject of the greatest importance [that] deserves the most serious attention." That he connected the plight of the agriculturists to the welfare of the state and region was apparent in his admonishment to his fellow legislators to take action because these "products of our soil . . . form the basis of our public and private wealth."[23]

The internal improvement movement was not simply a story about constructing an infrastructure, but it was also closely tied to Indian policy and settlement issues. The pivotal hindrance to Indiana's commercial development, statesmen and settlers came to believe, was the fact that the proposed routes for a number of the roads and canals traversed land that was still in the hands of Native Americans. Within a decade, statesmen would push federal officials hard for cession treaties that would extinguish the titles to Native American land along these routes, thus adding depth to our understanding of the motivations behind Euro-Americans' push for Indian removal. Settlers and officials harbored commercial ambitions that did not in and of themselves make them racist in their calls for these cession treaties. However, they were undeniably willing to ignore and manipulate Native American concerns and interests in favor of their own.

One of the most significant and revealing of these cession treaties, particularly when considering the complexity of motivations behind Indian removal policies in the Midwest, was the 1826 Mississinewa negotiations. Beginning as early as 1824, Indianans sought to improve their material circumstances through internal improvements. In November of that year, federal Indian agent John Tipton from the Fort Wayne Agency wrote to Lewis Cass, his supervisor, about how "[t]he people of this state are anxious for an extinguishment of Indian title to the Tract of Country through which the line of the proposed Canal will pass." Indeed, through Tipton this matter was brought before the Indiana Senate in early 1825 and resulted in the recommendation that action be taken along these lines. He, himself, was appointed as one of the three treaty commissioners in May of 1826. In the end, the treaties secured land both for settlers and for the construction of the Michigan road and the Wabash and Erie Canal, although Indianans apparently had wanted more. Yet, in their report to the Secretary of Defense, the commissioners asserted that while they never lost sight of the United States' interests, they also never forgot "that we were treating with a poor miserable people, the feeble remnant of the former owners of the country—a people who have sustained many injuries from us, and who have many claims upon our justice and humanity." They even claimed to "have allowed them a consideration more valuable than the cession they have made."[24]

Subsequently, internal improvement and settlement contributed significantly to the development of the state. While the Miamis and Potawatomis were able to deny the treaties' proposal that they remove west of the Mississippi, the direction and momentum of events were evident to all. Seeking out turning point moments for the region encourages the scholar to link together elements of a story that are typically analyzed independently, in this case the nexus of the development of commercial agriculture, the internal improvement movement, and federal Indian policy—all of which proved responsive to *internal* initiatives *and* fundamentally shaped the region uniquely.[25]

Finally, observations about the effect that the opening of midwestern canals appeared to have on the farm people and on regional development (at least from the Euro-American point of view) are captured in the diary of a young Methodist schoolteacher named Charles Titus. Titus traveled along Indiana's Wabash and Erie Canal in 1843 and noted the fertile farms and development along the recently-built canal, as well as the prices that farm produce now fetched. Such changes indicated something transformative, and he recorded that "A new day has now dawned upon the agriculturist of this region." Ironically, three years later the state's remaining Miamis would be removed on this canal, thus signifying an end to one of the region's defining-moment stories while inaugurating the beginning of another.[26]

The term *region* is perhaps most effective when it is employed, as in this analysis, simply as a cohesive device. Rather than wrangling over boundaries, such an idea of region resembles a transparent, open-ended "container" that allows the various pieces to breathe and to be seen, like a glass salad bowl. The container is there and clearly holds the stories together, while also offering different vantage points and perspectives. But it need not be anything more than that. What fills its capacity, or what is inside, is the most intriguing and satisfying part of it. Scott Sanders wrote a memorable passage about the immediacy of *place* in humanist studies and, implicitly, about considering regionality. He contends that "The truth of our existence is to be found not in some remote place or extreme condition but right-here and right-now; we already dwell in the place worth seeking. I write from within a family, a community, and a landscape, concentric rings of duty and responsibility."[27] Regional identity springs from these basic elements.

Notes

The emphasis in the epigraph is my own.

1. Cayton and Gray, "Story of the Midwest," 4.

2. David Lowenthal, "Past Time, Present Place: Landscape and Memory," *The Geographical Review* 65 (January 1975): 9.

3. Meinig, *Ordinary Landscapes*, 44. A study that considers landscapes as the product of competing ideologies is Alan R. H. Baker and Gideon Biger, eds., *Ideology and Landscape in Historical Perspective: Essays on the Meanings of Some Places in the Past* (Cambridge: Cambridge University Press, 1992).

4. Terry A. Barnhart, "'A Common Feeling': Regional Identity and Historical

Consciousness in the Old Northwest, 1820–1860," *Michigan Historical Review* 29 (Spring 2003): 39.

5. Phillip C. McGraw, *Self Matters: Creating Your Life from the Inside Out* (New York: Free Press, 2001), 103–9.

6. Marcel Stoetzler and Nira Yuval-Davis, "Standpoint Theory, Situated Knowledge and the Situated Imagination," *Feminist Theory* 3 (2002): 315. See also Virginia D. Nazarea, *Ethnoecology: Situated Knowledge, Located Lives* (Tucson: University of Arizona Press, 1999), 1–20; and Wrobel and Steiner, *Many Wests*.

7. D. W. Meinig quoted in Steiner and Wrobel, "Many Wests," 8 (emphasis added).

8. William Cronon, *Changes in the Land: Indians, Colonists, and the Ecology of New England* (New York: Hill and Wang, 1983), 167. The most recent take on Cronon's work is Dan Flores, "Twenty Years On: Thoughts on *Changes in the Land: Indians, Colonists, and the Ecology of New England*," *Agricultural History* 78 (Fall 2004): 493–96. For my look at similar changes in the Midwest, see Ginette Aley, "Bringing About the Dawn: Agriculture, Internal Improvement, Indian Policy, and Euro-American Hegemony, 1800–1840" in *The Boundaries between Us: Native and Newcomers along the Frontiers of the Old Northwest Territory, 1750–1850*, ed. Daniel P. Barr (Kent OH: Kent State University Press, 2006), 196–218; and Ginette Aley, "'Knotted Together Like Roots in the Darkness': Rural Midwestern Women and Region—A Bibliographic Guide," *Agricultural History* 77 (Summer 2003): 453–81.

9. Kent C. Ryden, *Mapping the Invisible Landscape: Folklore, Writing, and the Sense of Place* (Iowa City: University of Iowa Press, 1993), 241, 264.

10. Kurt Vonnegut, "To Be a Native Middle-Westerner," Indiana Humanities Council, http://www.indianahumanities.org/kurt.htm.

11. Michael Mayerfeld Bell, "The Ghosts of Place," *Theory and Society* 26 (1997): 813–36.

12. Peirce F. Lewis, "Axioms for Reading the Landscape: Some Guides to the American Scene," in *The Interpretation of Ordinary Landscapes*, ed., Donald W. Meinig (New York: Oxford University Press, 1979), 15, 26, 27.

13. The referenced book reviews are John E. Miller, review of *An American Colony: Regionalism and the Roots of Midwestern Culture*, by Edward Watts, *Kansas History* 26 (Spring 2003): 71, and Kent Blaser, review of *The American Midwest: Essays on Regional History*, by Andrew R. L. Cayton and Susan E. Gray, eds., *Nebraska History* 83 (Spring 2002): 52.

14. Vonnegut, "To Be A Native." Related to Vonnegut's self-deprecating comment regarding his midwestern accent, while teaching in the South, I was approached by a disgruntled student who seemed eager to point out that "you talk like you're from Wisconsin or something."

15. Allan Pred, *Making Histories and Constructing Human Geographies: The Local Transformation of Practice, Power Relations, and Consciousness* (Boulder: Westview Press, 1990), 14–15.

16. Eudora Welty, *Eye of the Story: Selected Essays and Reviews* (New York: Random House, 1977), 128.

17. Anna Briggs letters, May 22, June 14, and July 30, 1826, *American Grit: A*

Woman's Letters from the Ohio Frontier, ed. Emily Foster (Lexington: University Press of Kentucky, 2002), 26, 27, 38.

18. A major influence regarding the argument that farm people feared the market has been Christopher Clark, *The Roots of Rural Capitalism: Western Massachusetts, 1780–1860* (Ithaca: Cornell University Press, 1990), and recently, in a Midwest context, Richard F. Nation, *At Home in the Hoosier Hills: Agriculture, Politics, and Religion in Southern Indiana* (Bloomington: Indiana University Press, 2005). It is difficult to reconcile, for example, numerous instances of midwestern agrarian shrewdness with Clark's assertion that "When farmers traded more of their produce outside the region, their chief purpose was not to engage in the market economy but to satisfy the demands placed on them by the household economy" (84). In a similar vein, he portrays the market as something of a negative, magnetic force that "drew farmers" in, instead of casting farm people as positive and ambitious decision makers. With regards to profitable transactions, see Christopher Clark, "The Ohio Country in the Political Economy of Nation Building" in *The Center of a Great Empire: The Ohio Country in the Early Republic*, ed. Andrew R. L. Cayton and Stuart D. Hobbs (Athens: Ohio University Press, 2005), 146–65; an insightful account depicting Ohio's active, market-oriented agricultural economy during the early 1830s is "Diary of Aaron Miller," *Ohio Archaeological and Historical Quarterly* 33 (January 1924): 67–79.

19. Foster, *American Grit*, 98, July 26, 1829 (emphasis in original).

20. Foster, *American Grit*, 87–88, March 15, 1829. My characterization of "market-minded agrarianism" parallels Douglas Hurt's conclusion that early Ohio settlers were "a profit-minded people," in R. Douglas Hurt, *Ohio Frontier: Crucible of the Old Northwest, 1720–1830* (Bloomington: Indiana University Press, 1996), 210.

21. This whole matter is taken up in Ginette Aley, "A Republic of Farm People: Women, Families, and Market-Minded Agrarianism in Ohio, 1820s–1830s," *Ohio History* 113 (Spring 2007): 28–45.

22. Jacob Schramm to Brother-in-Law and Sister-in-Law, April 10, 1836. Reprinted in Emma S. Vonnegut, trans. and ed., *The Schramm Letters: Written by Jacob Schramm and Members of His Family From Indiana to Germany in the Year 1836* (Indianapolis: Indiana Historical Commission, 1924), 67.

23. Annual Message, December 9, 1818. Reprinted in Logan Esarey, ed., *Messages and Papers of Jonathan Jennings Ratliff Boon, William Hendricks vol. III, 1816–1825* (Indianapolis: Indiana Historical Commission, 1924), 66, 68; for the state history of Indiana, see James Madison, *The Indiana Way* (Bloomington: Indiana University Press, 1986), xiii–xiv.

24. Papers and correspondences related to the Mississinewa Treaties of 1826 used here were John Tipton to Lewis Cass, November 13, 1824; Tipton and others to John Ewing, January 1825; James Barbour to Lewis Cass and others, May 24, 1826; and Lewis Cass and others to James Barbour, October 23, 1826, in *The John Tipton Papers*, ed. Nellie Armstrong Robertson and Dorothy Riker (Indianapolis: Indiana Historical Bureau, 1942), 1:407, 441–42, 536–37, and 598–606; see also Paul Wallace Gates, introduction to *John Tipton Papers*, ed. Nellie Armstrong Robertson and Dorothy Riker (Indianapolis: Indiana Historical Bureau, 1942), 3–53, and Ginette Aley, "Westward Expansion, John Tipton, and the Emergence of the American Midwest, 1800–1839" (PhD diss., Iowa State University, 2005).

25. Proceedings, Potawatomi and Miami Treaty Negotiations, October 5, 1826, in Esarey, *Messages and Papers*, 577–92; *American State Papers*: Indian Affairs, 2:679–85.

26. The original 1843 travel journal is housed in the Huntington Library, San Marino, California, as manuscript HM 29181. It is also reprinted in part in George P. Clark, ed., "Through Indiana by Stagecoach and Canal Boat: The 1843 Travel Journal of Charles H. Titus," *Indiana Magazine of History* 85 (September 1989): 193–235. For more on the Miami removal, see Stewart Rafert, *The Miami Indians of Indiana: A Persistent People, 1654–1994* (Indianapolis: Indiana Historical Society, 1996).

27. Scott R. Sanders, *Writing from the Center* (Bloomington: Indiana University Press, 1995), 164. On the counterproductivity of boundary discussions, see Donald Worster, "New West, True West: Interpreting the Region's History," *Western Historical Quarterly* 18 (1987): 141–56.

7. Gendered Boosterism

The "Doctor's Wife" Writes from the New Northwest

BARBARA HANDY-MARCHELLO

As the Northern Pacific Railroad (NP) tracks approached the Missouri River crossing on June 3, 1873, a well-dressed woman on horseback led the crowd that rode out to meet the train at Apple Creek. She received a warm greeting from the train's passengers who recognized her as "the doctor's wife," the author of a series of letters to Minnesota newspapers boosting the region near the crossing. Writing her memoir years later, this woman, Linda Warfel Slaughter, remembered that this event brought her to tears because the railroad would finally connect her to "the world of civilization and the friends of my childhood." Sitting her horse near that puffing train, however, Linda Slaughter was the woman who had hailed the tiny military and railroad camp of Bismarck as a growing outpost of gentility and civilization in the New Northwest, where women enjoyed the respect of railroad workers, soldiers, and settlers and where, together with the gentlemen of the "city," women organized social events that mimicked in distinctly western ways the social graces of cities far to the east.[1]

This incipient city was located in the northern portion of a region that only barely existed in the imaginations of most Americans. The northern Great Plains was legally occupied by Lakota (Sioux), Arikara, Hidatsa, Mandan, and Chippewa peoples. However, as the railroad approached Bismarck, it opened a nationwide conversation about the agricultural qualities of the Northern Plains, how this region would fit into the rapidly urbanizing and industrializing United States, and whether the NP would be financially successful in such an unknown region. Linda Slaughter's letters were among the first to generate for distant newspaper readers a sense of what the northern Great Plains was like and what it would become.

Both the NP and Dakota Territory were engaged in promoting Northern Plains land claims and sales in the United States and Europe. Boosters, often paid by territorial governments or railroads, promoted "free" or inexpensive lands yearning for agricultural development. They sought economic development and often personal gain by speculating in western town sites and agricultural land. They wanted to fill the Great Plains, or at least the railroad towns and nearby farms, with people who would buy land, purchase necessities and luxuries at local mercantiles, and sell products of their labor in eastern markets accessed by railroad.

Boosterism was an important element in fostering settlement of the Great Plains, which had a suspicious history in nineteenth-century American memory as the Great American Desert. Boosterism was largely based on male-dominated commercial enterprise and interests. Typically, booster literature cited rainfall and snowfall, winter and summer temperatures, and soil type as being not only superb but just like somewhere else. Often Great Plains states and territories were compared favorably to agricultural regions in the midwestern prairie states. However, in the coyote choir of boosters' voices, the distinctive voice of Linda Slaughter, who promoted the establishment of *society* on the Northern Plains more than economic development, has been overlooked.[2]

In common with other boosters, Slaughter had a financial interest in the future of Bismarck and the region she called the New Northwest; but she had broader interests as well. She forged an argument centered on family, church, and a social network connecting the pioneers of the region to each other as well as to like-minded, middle-class readers in eastern communities. She envisioned the Northern Plains as a region that would generate communities of families supporting various commercial interests. Ironically, her female voice alone supported booster claims: if a well-bred woman with a taste for silk dresses and champagne could manage to survive—even thrive—in the New Northwest, then other women and their families could easily follow.

Slaughter's letters asserted her faith that the town and region would grow in population and sustain a substantial urban as well as a rural population. But more importantly in her booster letters, Slaughter's vision of a genteel society was organized around carefully constructed and delicately balanced gender roles that were played out against the beautiful background of northwestern scenery. It was the landscape, rather than the commodified land that Slaughter reconstructed in prose for her readers. In Slaughter's New Northwest, pioneer women were not sunburned, overworked, or socially isolated. The landscape did not diminish their femininity but enhanced it by providing beautiful surroundings and the attention of brave and courteous gentlemen. She defined it as a region where women asserted moral and political power and constructed the social order of the city in ways that supported both family and community. She adapted the social order of eastern industrial cities to the Northern Plains, infusing the region's new communities with an urban gentility that masked its frontier, male-dominated origins.[3]

Bismarck was located in central Dakota Territory, in the midst of a string of military forts constructed along the Missouri River during the 1860s and 1870s. This was Indian territory by the Treaty of 1851 and railroad land by an act of Congress. The arrival of the railroad was every settler's and speculator's dream, and Linda Slaughter's letters from the crossing reveal the activity of Bismarck's military and civilian residents in preparation for the expected expansion of population and business that the trains would bring.[4]

However, financial disaster and controversy lay in the near future. Jay Cooke's financing of the NP collapsed in September 1873, just three months after the tracks reached the Missouri River. The financial failure of the northern-most railroad, which dragged the nation into a severe economic depression, was soon followed by controversy about the climate and soil of the Northern Plains. If the New Northwest could not support agriculture and, by extension, railroad towns, the NP could not convince investors that they would see a return on their investment. Farmers had to follow the railroad, and towns had to grow up along the tracks to generate a market for rail freight and passenger traffic.[5]

A short article on the progress of the NP had appeared in *The Nation* on August 22, 1872. In great sweeping phrases that placed the NP on the world historical stage, the unacknowledged author wrote, "The entire aspect of the far Northwest is undergoing a rapid change in consequence of the construction of the Northern Pacific Railroad. For the first time in the world's history the awful solitudes of that remote and hitherto almost totally unknown region resound to the busy hum of industry and advancing civilization." The author also states that freighting throughout the region had increased and that immigrants were flocking to the railroad lands, which were fertile and well watered. The article depicts climate as "genial and the soil [as] admirably adapted for the cultivation of grain." Then, amazingly, the author reports that the NP was a model of conciliation in its relations with Indians that "has so far prevented all difficulties." The company's kindness and "equity" had converted "savages" from "enemies into friends." The NP wildly claimed to have settled "at once and forever the Indian question on the most difficult and threatening portion of our frontier."[6]

Assuming that the writer was employed by the NP and that this notice was part of Cooke's vast advertising campaign to sell railroad bonds, this piece is a typical booster mixture of lies and facts with a focus on soil and climate. Reference to Indians as possibly troublesome was unusual for booster literature. Though the author made an effort to convince readers that Indians were no longer a threat to the success of the railroad, anyone who read a daily newspaper would know that the statement was boldly false.[7]

In 1872 the NP was constructing its tracks from the Red River valley of the North across the drift prairie of northern Dakota Territory toward the Missouri River. Of necessity, the location of the river crossing would also be the site of an important regional urban center for further railroad construction as well as for rapid transport of people and freight. River transport, upon which the community and the military posts had long depended, was limited to seasons of navigation; horse- or oxen-drawn overland transport was unreliable and dangerous. The railroad represented not only permanent settlement for most towns along the track but also the potential for regional economic growth in the form of farms and towns. Wealth would follow railroad construction, especially for those engaged in economic activity before the influx of newcomers raised land values.

When, on August 17, 1872, the chief engineer of the construction crew hired Linda Slaughter to compose letters to eastern newspapers describing the community and prospects for settlers at "the crossing," he must have known she was an unusual choice as a booster. She was an army officer's wife, accustomed to having servants, attending dances, and dressing well. She was not (at that time) a farmer and had shown little interest in agriculture. Indeed, her interest in Dakota's future was fairly new. She signed the NP contract just three weeks after her husband, an army lieutenant and physician, B. Frank Slaughter, returned from an expedition to locate a fort (later named Fort Abraham Lincoln) to protect railroad construction crews, bringing with him a wholly new opinion of the project. He and other officers stationed at forts along the Missouri River had previously announced that Dakota would not be settled and that the railroad would not be completed, because those were "the days when 'it never rained in Dakota.'" However, he had been swayed by the promotional energy of the engineers, so the Slaughters decided to quit army life and become residents of the little community that was growing at the crossing.[8]

Slaughter later wrote that she took the job, not for the four city lots (of questionable title) that the NP gave her in exchange for her letters and that she staked out carrying the surveyor's chain from one corner to another by herself, but because she "honestly believed the railroad would be built and the country could support settlers." She could "conscientiously undertake" writing letters to eastern papers encouraging migration to the Northern Plains because she and her husband had made that commitment themselves.[9]

Slaughter was an experienced writer. She had published a book of poems and two memoirs about teaching in Kentucky freedmen's schools after the Civil War. If the railroad was looking for someone to promote the crossing and the community growing around it, it would have had few choices among the small population of local residents. Those who were literate were busy building stores, houses, and hotels; freighting goods to military posts; and guarding their own land claims. A college-educated woman who loved to write and had the leisure to pursue the project was the perfect prospect for the job.[10]

Slaughter jumped right into her assignment. Her first letter was dated August 17 and was published in the *St. Paul Pioneer* on August 23. The title was "Descriptions of an Embryotic City—Business—Climate—Game—The Soldiers' Camp—Yellowstone Expedition—Personal, etc." It was written for those who "may contemplate emigration to the frontier," and it promised to "have the merit of impartiality." This first letter fits the booster type. In her words, the "city" of Bismarck stands on a "level plateau, hemmed in by a semi-circle of gently rolling hills." The "soil is alluvial and its fertility cannot be surpassed. Water is abundant and of the purest quality . . . the wells . . . yielding an apparently inexhaustable [sic] supply." In this letter she encourages farmers to forget lingering doubts about the Great Plains and its long reputation as the Great American Desert. By the 1870s the central Great Plains had been reconstructed as part of the bountiful garden that had blessed the republic. Slaughter enfolds the Northern Plains into the garden with her descriptions of the bountiful landscape and its agricultural value.[11]

After presenting the basic booster chorus on soil, climate, and water, Slaughter then, in the thinnest prose, begins to foreshadow her own twist on booster literature. She describes the military camp that protects the crossing and lies within the growing town. The soldiers of Camp Hancock are brave gentlemen, of course, but also surprisingly cultured. Slaughter noted that one is brother to well-known writer Grace Greenwood. The railroad engineers and executives are courteous and thoughtful. This "embryotic city" was not a rough and wild frontier town. It was a place where a lady felt safe and highly regarded, and where she was in no danger of losing touch with the refinements of her class. Slaughter was not the sole person with an interest in establishing genteel society in early Bismarck; there were in the predominantly male population several young professionals and merchants who shared her anticipation of a socially conscious middle-class dominating Bismarck society. As a railroad booster, Linda Slaughter secures for herself and her family a position among the emerging elite of Bismarck society.[12]

In subsequent letters, Slaughter broadens her departure from the booster genre and from the official line of railroad advertising. Lacking the tedium of recitations about soil and climate and track-laying progress, the letters she writes are engaging, filled with bits of information about local events, and present a woman's view of the New Northwest. Her gendered viewpoint is also steeped in the culture of class expectations. She was the daughter of a well-to-do Ohio merchant and miller; her husband came from a wealthy Kentucky family. Both had grown up in material comfort and had better than average education. Though life at a frontier army post was less than comfortable, they enjoyed the constant round of social events common to officers' families as well as servants to manage the manual labor of daily life. Slaughter was a frontier woman who had never scrubbed laundry on a washboard nor squinted into the horizon longing for company.[13]

Slaughter's feminine voice emerges in the second letter of the nine-part series. The tepid and timid language of the first letter is replaced by forthright political opinions and detailed descriptions of social events. She is boosting the region in so far as she draws delightful pictures of the countryside, but she does so with few references to agricultural potential or commercial development. Her prose tends to be descriptive and poetic. In the second letter, she writes, "Far as the eye can reach, a charming prospect greets it. A wide sweep of plain and meadow, bounded on the far horizon with a rim of low rolling hills, stretches away to the south. On the west stand heavy clumps of forest trees, bordered by a soft fringe of willows, between whose thread-like foliage the river shines like a silver line of light." She briefly mentions the NP, noting only the presence of its steamboat, the *Ida Stockdale*, on the river and the company's concerns about land titles. She proceeds, however, to describe the river as "low" and marred by sandbars. This is a scene not intended to encourage yeoman farmers and urban entrepreneurs, but one "worthy of the raptures of an artist."[14]

On the tour that prompted this description, Slaughter and her companions discover an ancient earthen fortification above the Missouri littered with potsherds and other artifacts of an Indian village. She recounts, but dismisses, the Arikara explanation of a battle at the site. She concludes instead that this site contains the remnants of a "superior race who inhabited the continent years before." Though her assessment exposes her ignorance of Northern Plains ancient history and civilizations, and ultimately proved inaccurate, Slaughter generates a public discussion of prehistoric Indian cultures in the region. Her interest in the ancient battle site also suggests that because the region was, in the past, home to people who were superior to the "savages" she had met on the Northern Plains, it could again become the center of a highly civilized society. With her sense of history and the historic moment, she gives the region a past as well as a future.[15]

Slaughter soon dispels the NP's claim to have settled the "Indian question." In this and subsequent letters, she describes Indian hostility toward the army, the railroad, and its work crews. She names the dangers that existed for settlers, soldiers, and railroad crews whenever they ventured out of the crossing community. Though she asserts that the residents of Bismarck were safe with the presence of soldiers at Camp Hancock, in four of the nine articles in the series, she describes events in which Indians attack soldiers, civilians, or railroad crews. In her experience as an army wife, the Indian question would not be resolved with "equity" and fair trade. She unapologetically calls for a short, decisive war that would send "half the thieving nation's wards to the happy hunting grounds." Slaughter notes that hostile Indians had been pampered by the federal government and treated to tours of Washington and meetings with government officials, while on the Northern Plains their kin attacked pioneers, soldiers, and railroad workers. Tribal annuities included weapons of war with which they committed "murders of men women and children, and other crimes, that make humanity to blush." She was harshly critical of the Grant administration's Peace Policy and of easterners who could not understand the realities of western life because they had no personal experience with Indians.[16]

The warring nations she writes about were primarily Sioux tribes. The peaceful, "gaily dressed" Arikara appear in these letters as loyal scouts for the army and as victims of the Sioux. Slaughter explains these distinctions with a story about an idyllic picnic that had brought her to the hills north of Bismarck with her baby daughter, her kind elderly neighbor and pioneering mentor named Mrs. Anthony, and several men. They are bent on duck hunting and wild plum gathering in the "aquatic paradise" of Burnt Creek, while they make grand plans for many fine feasts to follow. The men carry rifles in addition to their shotguns—in case an elk or antelope should appear, the women are told. They top a hill and suddenly encounter a camp of Indians. Both parties draw their guns, and the men tell the women to run for cover in nearby bushes. When the Arikara identify themselves and explain that they intend no harm to the picnic party, they all exchange handshakes. Linda Slaughter could barely tolerate the expression of peace and friendship extended by the Arikara when "every black, dirty villian [sic] thrust out his big greasy paw" to shake hands with the members of her party. The revelers give up their plans and travel with the Arikara back to Bismarck. They are all concerned about the possibility that the Sioux will soon attack.[17]

The tone of this piece is humorous and light. Mrs. Anthony is a wonderful companion, who, Slaughter tells us, has taught her much about pioneering life. The men are brave and well prepared for emergencies; the Arikara, peaceful. It is clear that the New Northwest continues to offer pioneers a chance to prove their hardiness and fitness for spreading American progress over the landscape. Slaughter enjoys the excitement of the encounter with Indians but displays fear suitable and expected in a refined woman. In her imagination, she sees her "cherished ringlets dangling at some chieftain's belt." Though Slaughter, in her many autobiographical pieces, revealed herself as a determined, tough woman who soon became accustomed to the presence and even the friendship of Indians during her years in Bismarck, the fear she relates in this article appears to be part of her construction of gender roles for the Northern Plains, which heightens the masculinity of her husband and other male settlers.[18]

Slaughter appropriates for the village of Bismarck the title of "city" in expectation of its grand future. The reader learns that the town has a brickyard that, she explains with forthright honesty, expects to acquire brick-making machinery soon. There is a sandstone quarry to provide stone for building. Bismarck has a telegraph office, a Sunday school (which meets in a tent), saloons, and a drug store. "Streets are rapidly extending to every side," she asserts. The town is occupied by a number of middle-class professionals, including two doctors, several engineers, and many merchants, all apparently living and working in log houses, the two-story hotel, or military tents.[19]

The little town was also the site of numerous social events. Upon the completion of the Edwinton Hotel, "a fine entertainment" was held there to display the "generosity and good taste of the proprietors." On the Slaughters' fourth wedding anniversary, "the ladies and gentlemen of the city gave a charming little entertainment in [their] honor, at the principal hotel of the place." That the Edwinton Hotel had not yet been completed on the date of this party—and the "principal hotel" was the Anthonys' log cabin—is a detail that Slaughter neglects to mention. However primitive their surroundings, on such occasions the Slaughters and their friends enjoyed fine suppers of wild game and fruits with wine or champagne.[20]

In two of her letters, Slaughter assumes the voice of a character she names Dolly Varden, after the Victorian gown festooned with ruffles and loops of excess flower-printed fabric. Dolly Varden gives Slaughter an alternative voice, ultra-feminine and domestic, which she uses to rebuke men for failing to live up to their middle-class obligation to protect and pamper women. Mrs. Dolly, who is an obedient wife but an unhappy pioneer, complains about living in a tent, which burns, and subsequently a log cabin, which is not properly daubed with mud to keep out the wind and snow. When Mrs. Dolly becomes quite gloomy about her state of affairs, she writes about women's rights, which she believes are not suitable for a genteel woman. While claiming to be a "good soldier" and subordinate wife, she uses her newspaper column to chastise her husband for being selfish about his hunting clothes, which, to his dismay, she has cut into small strips and stuffed into the spaces between the logs. He expresses his displeasure. She counters by writing of a celebrated murder trial, in which the infamous Laura Fair, accused of murdering her married lover, was acquitted by a jury of men who were swayed by her beauty. Mrs. Dolly is quite certain that a jury of the woman's peers—a jury of women—would not have been so easily distracted. Slaughter is not boldly suggesting an expansion of civil rights for women. The New Northwest would not offer women expanded civil rights. She is claiming, however, the public moral right and responsibility to restore proper social order in private and public spaces if men were corrupted by illicit pleasures and irresponsible behavior, so often characteristic of western pioneer cities.[21]

The railroad boosters of the Northern Plains met a controversial naysayer in General W. B. Hazen. Commanding officer of Fort Buford, Hazen wrote to the *New York Tribune* early in 1874 a letter filled with charts containing data of rainfall and temperatures, which he claimed proved that NP railroad lands could not support agriculture. A number of writers challenged his observations. The most significant of these was Colonel George Armstrong Custer, who by 1874 was commanding officer at Fort Lincoln across the Missouri River from Bismarck. In a lengthy letter to the *Minneapolis Tribune*, he described the great value of the Northern Plains. He cited as proof his notes from his 1873 expedition to the Yellowstone River. Hazen responded with another letter, published in the *North American Review*, and later with a book. His data, gathered at Fort Buford and other posts, showed that 1873 was an exceptionally wet year on the Northern Plains, so Custer's encounter with the land and climate was skewed by this aberration. Hazen briefly mentions and gently dismisses Slaughter's letters—noting that 1872, when she was writing to the *St. Paul Pioneer*, was another unusually wet year. Hazen refers to Slaughter (his respected friend) as the "best letter-writer of the press," an acknowledgment of her role as a booster for the New Northwest; but he criticizes her for fostering

CONSTRUCTING PLACE

the idea that the West would support farmers, even though she barely addresses agriculture in her letters.[22]

Though Slaughter addressed the controversy briefly in these letters and in subsequent writing, her voice was weak. Climate and soil were really not topics of interest to her, and she had not established the appropriate credentials to enter the discussion. Booster literature about railroad construction and land promotion was fundamentally economic, promoting individualism, early arrival, and personal gain. However, Slaughter's approach to promotion was social in focus and portrayed the Northern Plains as a region that nurtured familiar social organization and supported middle-class moral standards, gender relations, and aestheticism. No data appear, no lists of amazing resources, no recitations of wondrous or discouraging events of climate, no claim to scientific proof. Slaughter wanted to build a permanent community, rather than scattered farms, where individual gain was secondary to family and communal interests. Her letters offered encouragement to settlers who would enjoy the beauty of the landscape; would seek warm companionship of other pioneers; had faith that the land would produce and the cities would grow to support churches, schools, and businesses; and were willing to let their experience as pioneers of the New Northwest reconstruct their politics. She introduced women and their interests to the discourse about the Northern Plains, thereby suggesting that women would find in Bismarck interesting and prosperous gentlemen; proper, cultivated women; and familiar social institutions such as Sunday schools. The message to men was just as plain: if they were to follow the railroad to Bismarck, they had better bring their manners.[23]

Linda Slaughter's booster letters are gendered and social rather than economic or scientific. They alert readers to the nature of frontier gender relations, to constructions of masculinity and femininity, and to the ways in which the New Northwest demanded renegotiation of sex roles in a western but genteel manner. Rather than writing about women who reached for a rifle when danger threatened or who clambered over their log cabins with buckets of mud for chinking, she primped and pouted. She indulged in little romances in which the landscape provided a scenic pastoral setting for a gentle adventure with peaceful, if dirty, Indians, starring her husband as the brave hero. Her image of the New Northwest seemed to require women to embrace a stereotypical femininity that served to enhance the masculinity of soldiers and pioneers and to preserve middle-class notions of gender roles.

However, Slaughter also writes of a region where women could not afford to let men assert control over politics. It was women who were left to weep for young men killed by Indians; and it was women, therefore, who must demand of Congress a stronger, more-punishing policy for Indian removal from or extermination in the Northern Plains. The woman who wept over her leaky log cabin is the same woman who called for a war of extermination against the Indians. She demands that politicians listen to westerners, both men and women, who had to live with the results of a confusing and unworkable Indian policy. Slaughter's New Northwest is a place of high contrasts and complex human beings who would be neither impoverished nor prosperous servants to the land and climate, as Hazen and Custer might have viewed them, but who were powerful agents advancing U.S. civilization and social order.[24]

Slaughter did not retire from the business of boosting the New Northwest when she completed her work for the NP. In 1874 she wrote a pamphlet for the Burleigh County Pioneers' Association, in which she quoted Hazen's article at length. She then dismissed his concerns for agricultural production by stating that soldiers gardened as part of their "fatigue duty" and were not disposed to "a judicious system of farming," which would obviously be far more productive. Once again, she resorted to human factors rather than to such uncontrollable and impersonal forces as soil and climate in her assessment of the New Northwest.[25]

The Slaughters stayed in Bismarck, and Linda eventually claimed farm land. In 1892 she published a series of articles about pioneer days in Bismarck. By then she considered herself a historian. Freed from the pressures of her contemporaries' interests and of the NP's interests, she revisited her booster letters. Safely established in a growing city that was now the capital of North Dakota—with a social order so neatly drawn from the eastern model that she, as an aging pioneer and divorced woman, had been relegated to the margins of the middle class—she was proud of the role she had played in creating a stable community out of the tents and log houses at the crossing. Slaughter's letters created an identity for the New Northwest out of a handful of tents and log cabins in a land whose value had yet to be determined. This region was not "just like Iowa" or anywhere else. It had a distinct landscape, a mixture of cultures, and a history that provided the perfect environment for the establishment of middle-class social organization; but at the same time, it would also reshape men's and women's lives and relationships in many ways.[26]

The boosters' imagining of the Great Plains was a powerful antidote to the limitations of the grasslands and the fear that westward migration might break the nation into disparate pieces. But if the "plunge and grab" image of the West, which Elliott West has described, best fit the growing industrial interests of the post–Civil War United States, it must be understood as a masculine image that neglected the perspective of genteel women who sought stable homes, reliable husbands, good neighbors, a beautiful and safe environment, well-stocked stores, and public spaces where they could entertain their friends. Linda Slaughter's New Northwest invited middle-class men and women of "social and literary tastes," who viewed the grasslands with an "artist's rapture" and who would remain tied to a new community, not by the possibly vacant potential for wealth in land or business but by the establishment of such solid middle-class institutions as schools, churches, dinner parties, neighbors, and picnics on late summer afternoons. It was, both in her booster letters and her memoir, a region where families and society would prosper even if vegetables could not.[27]

Notes

1. Linda Warfel Slaughter, *Fortress to Farm; or, Twenty-three Years on the Frontier*, ed. Hazel Eastman (New York: Exposition Press, 1972), 143–44. Slaughter originally wrote her memoirs for publication in the *Bismarck Tribune* in 1892. Bismarck, for many months known simply as "the crossing," was originally called Edwinton until soon after the NP tracks arrived. I refer to it as Bismarck to avoid confusion.

Slaughter refers to the region as the New Northwest. Today it is more familiarly called the northern Great Plains.

2. Elwyn B. Robinson, *History of North Dakota* (Lincoln: University of Nebraska Press, 1966), 131–32; Richard White, *It's Your Misfortune, Ain't None of My Own: A New History of the American West* (Norman: University of Oklahoma Press, 1991), 153, 417; Allan G. Bogue, "An Agricultural Empire" in *The Oxford History of the American West*, ed. Clyde A. Milner, Carol A. O'Connor, and Martha Sandweiss (New York: Oxford University Press, 1994), 285–87. On boosterism, see David M. Emmons, *Garden in the Grasslands: Boomer Literature of the Central Great Plains* (Lincoln: University of Nebraska Press, 1971); David M. Wrobel, *Promised Lands: Promotion, Memory, and the Creation of the American West* (Lawrence: The University of Kansas Press, 2002); B. H. Baltensperger, "Plains Boomers and the Creation of the Great American Desert Myth," *Journal of Historical Geography* 18 (January 1992): 59–73; Edgar I. Stewart, ed., *Penny-an-Acre Empire in the West* (Norman: University of Oklahoma Press, 1968); Elliott West, "Golden Dreams: Colorado, California, and the Re-imagining of America," *Montana* 49, no. 3 (Autumn 1999): 2–11. Slaughter was not the only woman to write booster literature. Among others, Lucy Larcom wrote a booster poem to encourage migration to Kansas during the era of popular sovereignty. But her poem, which won a fifty-dollar prize, is directed to men who would farm with their sons in a state dedicated to free men and liberty. The political nature of the booster piece is evident here but does not promote women's interests in Kansas's future. Lucy Larcom, "A Call to Kansas!" (1855), Poetry of Kansas, http://skyways.lib.ks.us/poetry/llcall.html.

3. Slaughter, *Fortress to Farm*, 98–99; Slaughter Family Papers, Archives, State Historical Society of North Dakota, Bismarck. On Linda W. Slaughter, see also Edna Waldo, *Dakota* (Caxton ID: Caxton Printers, 1936), 96–133. On emerging middle-class standards, see Mary P. Ryan, *Cradle of the Middle Class: The Family in Oneida County, New York 1790–1865* (New York: Cambridge University Press, 1983). Julie Roy Jeffrey argues that women brought class standards and gender roles to the West when they emigrated, in *Frontier Women: The Trans-Mississippi West, 1840–1880* (New York: Hill and Wang, 1998). On genteel middle-class womanhood on the rural Great Plains, see Andrea G. Radke, "Refining Rural Spaces: Women and Vernacular Gentility in the Great Plains, 1880–1920" *Great Plains Quarterly* 24 (Fall 2004): 227–48. In Timothy R. Mahoney, *Provincial Lives: Middle-Class Experience in the Antebellum Middle West* (New York: Cambridge University Press, 1999), the author argues that boosterism was closely linked to the establishment of genteel society and that middle-class men (who dominated the frontier) boosted their regions to see economic growth and stability whereas women lacked the public venue to promote genteel values.

4. Slaughter, *Fortress to Farm*, 113.

5. Robinson, *History of North Dakota*, 127.

6. "Progress of the Northern Pacific Railroad," *The Nation*, August 22, 1872, 74. *The Nation* credited the *New York Daily Bulletin* as their source for the article.

7. For further discussion of booster (boomer) literature, see David Emmons, *Garden in the Grasslands*, and Baltensperger, "Plains Boomers."

8. Slaughter, *Fortress to Farm*, 56, 69, 99. About ten years later, Linda Slaughter claimed two sections of land and hired the labor while she taught school nearby.

9. Slaughter, *Fortress to Farm*, 99.

10. Linda Warfel, *Early Efforts* (Philadelphia: J. W. Daughady, 1868); Linda Warfel, *Summerings in the South* (n.p., n.d.); Linda Warfel, *Freedmen of the South* (New York: Kraus Reprint Company, 1969). First published in 1869.

11. Henry Nash Smith, *Virgin Land: The American West as Symbol and Myth* (Cambridge MA: Harvard University Press, 1970), 176–79.

12. Mahoney, *Provincial Lives*, 3, 113, 213, 261. Grace Greenwood (born Sarah Jane Clarke, 1823–1904) was a popular and widely published poet, essayist, and newspaper journalist.

13. Hazel Eastman, introduction to *Fortress to Farm; or, Twenty-three Years on the Frontier*, by Linda Warfel Slaughter, ed. Hazel Eastman (New York: Exposition Press, 1972), 9–13. Eastman states that Linda Slaughter graduated from Oberlin College; but Oberlin records indicate that she did not graduate, though she attended for a few years. W. E. Bigglestone to Charles B. Wallace, Oberlin, Ohio, January 5, 1979. Copy in author's possession. On officers' wives' activities and obligations, see Patricia Y. Stallard, *Glittering Misery: Dependents of the Indian Fighting Army* (Norman: University of Oklahoma Press, 1978). Anne Bruner Eales discusses the class and gender expectations for officers' wives in *Army Wives of the American Frontier: Living by the Bugles* (Boulder CO: Johnson Books, 1996). See also Shirley Anne Leckie, ed. *The Colonel's Lady on the Western Frontier: The Correspondence of Alice Kirk Grierson* (Lincoln: University of Nebraska Press, 1989).

14. Linda Warfel Slaughter [CWS], "From the Missouri River Crossing of the Northern Pacific Railway," *St. Paul Pioneer*, September 11, 1872. Though Slaughter's letters were typically signed with her initials (LWS), this letter, dated August 21, 1872, was misprinted as CWS.

15. Slaughter, August 21, 1872. This site is known today as Double Ditch and is undergoing excavation under the supervision of the State Historical Society of North Dakota.

16. Linda Warfel Slaughter [LWS], "From the Missouri River. Crossing of the Northern Pacific. Highly Interesting Letters—Scouts Killed and Scalped by Indians—Condemnation of the Peace Policy—Military Whiskey Raid—Wonderful Progress of the Northern Pacific. Etc., Etc., Etc.," *St. Paul Pioneer*, October 4, 1872, letter dated August 29, 1872; Linda Warfel Slaughter [LWS], "From the Missouri. Letter from Edwinton. Return of the Yellowstone Expedition. Conflicts with the Indians," *St. Paul Pioneer*, November 28, 1872, letter dated October 27, 1872. Slaughter, a former abolitionist, departed from the abolitionist view of Indians when she called for wars of extermination. Her views on Indians are complex and significantly variant throughout her lifetime. See also Linda K. Kerber, "The Abolitionist Perception of the Indian," *Journal of American History* 62 (September 1975): 271–95.

17. Linda Warfel Slaughter [CWS], "From the Missouri River. Northern Pacific Railroad Crossing. Interesting Sketches of Life at a Frontier Post," *St. Paul Pioneer*, October 25, 1872, letter dated October 1, 1872.

18. Slaughter, October 1, 1872. Slaughter's autobiographical pieces include two

novellas for newspapers, "The Amazonian Corps: A Romance of the Army," *Bismarck Tribune*, December 2, 1874, to May 19, 1875, and "The Portfolio of a Western Postmaster: A Tale of Civilian Life," *Yankton Herald*, January 12, 1878, to March 30, 1878; a series of articles for territorial newspapers, written during her residence in Washington DC in the mid-1880s; and "Leaves from Northwestern History," *Collections of the State Historical Society of North Dakota* 1 (1906): 200–92.

19. Slaughter, October 4, 1872.

20. Slaughter, October 4, 1872; Slaughter, September 11, 1872. See also Slaughter, *Fortress to Farm*, 100–1.

21. Linda Warfel Slaughter [LWS], "Letter from a Woman. Her Pioneering Experiences. Her Little Log Cabin. And Her Poetical Musings," *St. Paul Pioneer*, December 1, 1872, letter dated October 20, 1872; Linda Warfel Slaughter [LWS], "A Woman's Letter. From the Far Western Frontier. Laura Fair and Josie Mansfield. What a True Woman Thinks of Woman's Rights and Woman's Wrongs," *St. Paul Pioneer*, November 24, 1872, letter dated November 18, 1872. On Laura Fair, see Dee Brown, *Gentle Tamers: Women of the Old West* (New York: Bantam Pathfinder Editions, 1958), 234–36.

22. W. B. Hazen, "The Northern Pacific Railroad Country. Views of Major-General Hazen," *New York Tribune*, February 27, 1874; Major General G. A. Custer, letter to the editor, *Minneapolis Tribune*, April 17, 1874; both articles are also published in Stewart, *Penny-an-Acre Empire*. W. B. Hazen, "The Great Middle Region of the United States, and Its Limited Space of Arable Land," *North American Review* 120 (January 1875): 29. Hazen does not mention Slaughter by name, but the reference is clear. They were good friends and accepted their disagreement. See also W. B. Hazen, *Our Barren Lands: The Interior of the United States West of the 100th Meridian and East of the Sierra Nevadas* (Cincinnati: R. Clarke, 1875). Fort Buford is located north and west of Bismarck on the Missouri River.

23. Susan Rosowski asserts that "gender assigns authors to genre, and we are unaccustomed to recognizing epic seriousness in women." Susan J. Rosowski, *Birthing a Nation: Gender, Creativity, and the West in American Literature* (Lincoln: University of Nebraska Press, 1999), x.

24. Slaughter's thinking on Indian removal is clearly within the well-established framework of the ideology of Manifest Destiny. See Anders Stephanson, *Manifest Destiny: American Expansion and the Empire of Right* (New York: Hill and Wang, 1995), 3–27.

25. Linda W. Slaughter, *The New Northwest: A Pamphlet Stating Briefly the Advantages of Bismarck and Vicinity* (Bismarck: Burleigh County Pioneers' Association, 1874; repr., New Haven CT: Yale University Press, 1956).

26. Slaughter, *Fortress to Farm*, 56, 68, 69. The Slaughters divorced twice and married three times.

27. Elliott West, "Golden Dreams," 11; Slaughter, September 11, 1872; Slaughter, *Fortress to Farm*, 119.

8. "With Powder Smoke and Profanity"

Genre Conventions, Regional Identity, and the Palisade Gunfight Hoax

NICOLAS S. WITSCHI

Accor ding to legend, when late-nineteenth-century travelers on the Central Pacific Railroad's overland limited route stopped in the little Nevada town of Palisade on their way to Virginia City or even San Francisco, they found themselves, as often as not, in the middle of a gunfight. Drunken cowboys were calling each other out in the street to redress the tainted honor of a woman; Indians were either wreaking havoc with their scalping knives or being chased down and tied up; and freshly spilled blood could be seen all over the streets and railroad platform. However, what the westward-bound tourists usually did not know was that these gunfights were elaborately staged hoaxes put on by the townspeople (who eventually formed a Thespian Society to handle the logistics of the show). Evidently, these fake gunfights were designed to frighten travelers by exploiting their ingrained assumptions about the wild, wild West. As a newspaper reporter at the time put it, the excessive and grandiose frontier lawlessness evident in Palisade "would shame the author of a dime novel."[1] The sham or mock gunfights were also reportedly intended as entertainment for the people of Palisade, designed to provide the community with moments of tension- and anxiety-releasing laughter, in what was otherwise a typically arduous mining and ore-processing existence. These performances succeeded in granting to Palisade, for a time, the reputation

of being the toughest town in the West; for those in the know, the repeated hoax made Palisade the funniest town in the West.[2]

The conventional imagery of the Wild West deployed in the Palisade
gunfights is highly suggestive of the sort of frontier reenactments that,
in more recent times, take place almost daily in every corner of the
United States, from present-day Tombstone, Arizona, to Wild West
City in Netcong, New Jersey (a mere forty-five miles west of midtown
Manhattan), to the supersized theme parks of both Florida and California.[3] However, the events in Palisade reportedly first occurred in
the fall of 1876. This date indicates that less than a decade after the
completion of the transcontinental railroad, which is to say, just as the
great era of railroad tourism in the American West was getting underway, so, too, were dime novels and other popular genre forms already
having their effect, particularly in how they defined the realness of a
region and a historical period for both locals and visitors.[4]

A governing tautology that is implicit in many assumptions about
representation and reality maintains that if a thing is going to represent something, that thing had better have some degree of resemblance to that which it represents. Very often, elements of the American
West—such as objects, places, or people—are recognized as typically
belonging to that region because they look "western." Thus, items
such as the cactus, the dusty cowboy, the feathered headdress–wearing Indian, and the expansive vistas of the desert Southwest become
signifiers of a certain historical authenticity. Alex Nemerov, in writing about the visual arts of the late nineteenth century, observes that
"any analysis of the image of the West must begin with the base of its
ideological power: its accreted claims to realism. People from Reming-
ton's time to our own have taken his paintings and those of his contemporaries as the facts about the American West."[5] The same can be
said of an appeal to realism that is endemic to a wide range of representations related to the West.[6] Indeed, the complex negotiations of
fact, genre, fiction, and authenticity that characterize both locals' and
tourists' assumptions about the frontier have prompted Louis S. Warren to identify the postbellum, nineteenth-century West as "not just
a region, or a place, but a subject in which fact and fiction had been

CONSTRUCTING PLACE

so thoroughly mixed that the very idea of the Far West suggested deception, some of it entertaining."[7] In this world, hoaxes and historical facts ride side-by-side.

Thus, the Palisade fake gunfights, with their deliberate deployment of the now-familiar icons of the Wild West, present an opportunity in the study of western American (self-)representation to explore the intersections of ostensibly realistic genre codes with community identity formation at a time when these codes were first coming into the national (and regional) lexicon. Bonnie Christensen's analysis of the history of Red Lodge, Montana, demonstrates compellingly how a western community can easily find itself both at the mercy of and socially and economically reliant on its own successful deployment of conventional codes that are widely perceived to be realistically western.[8] In the case of Palisade, the apparent efforts undertaken by its citizens to put one over on passing tourists affords a glimpse at how one late-nineteenth-century western community adapted to and exploited, for its own sake, the tendency for violence ascribed to it by popular culture. As will become evident below, the people of Palisade may very well have used these gunfights as a means of negotiating otherwise unacknowledged tensions within their own community, tensions only marginally related to the town's status as "western."

Moreover, given that the Palisade gunfight story has become one that more recent Nevadans enjoy telling about themselves and their past, its status as a folkloric reminiscence also tells us something about contemporary desires to construct and imagine that wild, wild West. If in fact the doings in 1876 Palisade really did take place, then they stand as material history; and in any case, they matter vitally at a discursive and cultural level.[9] In short, a look at what has been *described*, while conditionally giving the benefit of the doubt to a brief newspaper item from 1876, affords the opportunity to pose a number of vital questions concerning the relationship between assumptions based on popular genre forms and regional self-determination. As the case of Palisade demonstrates, the role of popular genres cannot be easily overlooked when assessing the confluence of regional culture, collective identity, and history. Popular genre codes function both as a shorthand for identifying a regional culture's most saleable character-istics and, for those who live within a region so defined, as the means by which to resist further cooptation through satirical exploitation. That is, the performance of the West as a wild space that reeks of gun-powder gives the eastern tourist exactly what he or she wants, and it also affords the western town the chance, for better or for worse, to manage its understanding of its own identity.[10]

The following newspaper account, published in the *Eureka Senti-nel* on October 17, 1876, and included here in its entirety, relates how things generally proceeded once the Central Pacific overland limited pulled in for water, fuel, and rest:

> A correspondent of the Virginia *Enterprise*, writing from Palisade, says: "The credulity of western bound emigrants has passed into a proverb, and, when business was dull, a hundred pranks were per-petrated at their expense and for their especial benefit. For example, a half a dozen Piutes [*sic*], for a reasonable compensation, would submit to being bound hand and foot and laid on the platform dur-ing the stay of the train, and around their prostrate bodies a guard of citizens, armed with immense revolvers, long rifles and blood-thirsty looking bowie knives, would march with martial mein [*sic*], meanwhile entertaining the gaping, open mouthed greenhorns with blood curdling tales of border warfare with the noble red men that would shame the author of a dime novel. In the absence of the nec-essary Piute, shot-guns and revolvers were loaded with powder—ball omitted—and, as soon as the platform was filled with emigrants seeking exercise and information, a desperate rencontre, provoked by some drunken ruffian, would commence and in a moment the air would reek with powder smoke and profanity, and blood (pre-viously procured from the slaughterhouse) besprinkled the platform as plentifully as water. As the fire arms were exhausted, sympathetic friends carried off the dead and wounded to some neighboring sa-loon, there to recuperate from the exertions of the fray, while the frightened and bewildered emigrants crawled from under seats and behind cars, their blanched faces and trembling limbs attesting their belief in the genuineness of the fight.[11]

CONSTRUCTING PLACE

A popular-press history entitled *Lost Legends of the Silver State*, compiled and written a century later by Gerald B. Higgs, adds further details explaining that the hoax often involved a verbal challenge offered to one Alvin Kittleby by a man appropriately named Frank West, who would reportedly shout, "'There ya are, ya low-down polecat. Ah bin waitin' fer ya. Ah'm goin' to kill ya b'cause of what ya did ta mah sister."[12]

Judging by this small but highly suggestive piece of evidence, one can certainly appreciate that the community of Palisade had a perfectly clear understanding of how its region, broadly and amorphously known as the Wild West, appeared to outside eyes. In this regard, a number of salient generic details are worth noting: for one, the Palisade gun battles promoted the very familiar western image of the smoke-filled frontier town governed by blazing pistols. To be sure, this image was not exclusive to the Far West; a series of hoax letters sent from Georgia and published in the *London Times* in 1856 reported that all of America's small towns were known for their lawlessness and for bodies piled up amidst the stench of burnt gunpowder.[13] However, by the mid-1870s, this stereotype had become firmly fixed as a distinctly western phenomenon. A traveler named Henry Davies, writing in 1872 about a hunting trip he had taken the previous summer with William F. "Buffalo Bill" Cody, observed that tourists on the western plains fully expected to meet "the typical desperado of the West, bristling with knives and pistols."[14] Thus, the "credulity of western bound emigrants" passing through Palisade had by 1876 been very much conditioned to expect a frontier setting filled with the outlaws and gun smoke that were rapidly becoming the standard generic codes for the formula western. Moreover, just as this brief piece of a newspaper story describes Palisade's attempt to exploit the rail tourist's potential misunderstandings about the ostensibly real basis of Wild West genre codes already in place by 1876, so too does it rely on the reader understanding these same codes. From the very first, the reporter confirms the distance between the victims of the hoax and its perpetrators as one founded on the recognition of the speciousness of certain "dime novel" genre codes.

In other words, readers of the news story are let in on the joke. And if there's any one place where a newspaper reader in 1870s Nevada might have found him- or herself, it would have been somewhere in relation to a printed joke or hoax. During the heyday of silver mining in western Nevada, Virginia City's *Territorial Enterprise* served as the proving ground for a number of western humorists, not the least among them being Samuel Clemens.[15] In 1863 Clemens published, as Mark Twain, a scandalous hoax now known as "A Bloody Massacre," in which a crazed miner reportedly murders his whole family in response to his having lost money in a San Francisco water company stock swindle.[16] In the art of journalistic hoaxing, however, Twain was hardly alone. As Lawrence I. Berkove has shown, Nevada's so-called sagebrush school of journalism and literature made ample use of hoaxes, jokes, and other such misrepresentations to liven up what might otherwise have been a fairly distressing cultural milieu of mining, speculation, and boom-to-bust existence.[17] For instance, an editor and speculator named James W. H. Townsend, quite possibly the model for Bret Harte's "Truthful James," was known far and wide for creating an entirely fictional mining town, complete with colorful characters and local scandals and the like, for which he published an occasional newspaper, all for the sake of duping investors in England. Mark Twain's mentor at the *Territorial Enterprise*, William Wright, who wrote under the name Dan De Quille, was perhaps the region's most accomplished hoaxer. One tale of De Quille's about a group of moving rocks attracted the curiosity of P. T. Barnum and the skeptical attention of newspapers around the globe. After confessing to the tale's fabrications, De Quille came clean by writing the "true" story of these rocks, thereby perpetuating the hoax by ostensibly clearing up any misrepresentations. Needless to say, there were never any such rocks to begin with.[18]

In the fall of 1876, at roughly the same time as the start of the Palisade hoax, De Quille published in Hartford, Connecticut (with the help of Twain's business connections and editorial suggestions), his monumental history of silver mining on the Comstock Lode, *The Big Bonanza*.[19] Modeled in part on *Roughing It*, Twain's own 1872 collection of humorous, partially autobiographical and partially tall tales set mostly in Virginia City, *The Big Bonanza* allowed De Quille to combine two publishing ambitions. Urged on by Virginia City's silver barons to create a celebratory pamphlet about the Comstock, De Quille also sought an outlet for his creative sketches about Nevada. *The Big Bonanza*, in its final form, allowed a measure of both; and the balancing act De Quille performs offers an exemplary instance of the manner in which distinctions between western fact and fiction could easily be blurred (very much in the manner identified by Warren). For instance, De Quille's account of "Pancake," Comstock's famous discovery of Nevada silver, is immediately preceded by an early iteration of the moving stones hoax.[20] At the very least, the publication of this volume by a locally known Nevada journalist no doubt contributed in areas such as Palisade to a general feeling that the status of the Far West, as far as Nevadans could sense, was becoming culturally significant on a national scale. With the wide availability of humorous texts such Twain's *Roughing It* and De Quille's *The Big Bonanza*, the "credulity of western bound emigrants" had by October 1876 been conditioned even further by the genre of the hoax-prone western tall tale that offered exaggeratedly familiar representations of cowboys, Indians, and bloodshed.[21]

As far as salient generic details are concerned, however, none signify as extensively as does the performed encounter between Natives and Anglo-European settlers or laborers. More pointedly, to both rail travelers and newspaper readers in October 1876, the sight of Indians swooping down to attack and being subdued by gun-wielding white men would have resonated quite keenly with the knowledge of what had transpired fewer than four months earlier at the Little Big Horn. This image alone could almost certainly be counted on to create a genuine measure of discomfort and fear. Other versions of the oft-told Palisade story even have Indians invading the town and leaving most of the local men for dead.[22] In this regard, the Palisade hoaxes participated in a well-established practice of using the image of a "savage" Indian to frighten specific groups of white people, with humor or otherwise.

In 1866, for example, while overseeing the construction of the Union Pacific Railroad (which would soon link up with the Central Pacific Railroad to form the first transcontinental railroad), Silas Seymour witnessed a "sham Indian fight" between some Pawnees in the employ of the railroad company and a group of fellow Pawnees dressed as Sioux. The fight had been arranged by the railroad company, ostensibly to frighten but ultimately to entertain the workers on the railroad. According to Seymour, a crucial part of the entertainment involved the audience's marveling over the Indians' greed for the "several hundred dollars' worth of presents" that were doled out in payment for their participation in the joke.[23] In his 1879 autobiography, William F. Cody also describes a hoax attack that he and some Indian companions had arranged in 1871, just prior to the advent of his theatrical career, for the members of a hunting party he was leading on the plains (the aforementioned Henry Davies was a member of this party, but not the subject of the hoax).[24]

However, not all Euro-American efforts at "playing Indian," to use Philip Deloria's phrase, were undertaken with lighthearted or generally benign entertainment in mind. In examining the release of social tension made possible by a community's use of performed humor, Timothy R. Mahoney has documented how men in recently settled frontier towns employed a variety of satires, mock meetings, and jokes, including dressing up like Indians to frighten away weak-kneed tourists, all for the purpose of establishing and regulating a class hierarchy.[25] And of course, the members of the Mormon Church who, in 1857, perpetrated the Mountain Meadows Massacre remain the most notorious example of Euro-Americans' use of the Indian figure as a shield for questionable or reprehensible actions. Thus, the *Enterprise* reporter's reference to reasonable compensation and necessary Paiutes, similar to Silas Seymour's comment about the Pawnees' interest in remuneration, raises the matter of the Native Americans' willing participation in the spectacle. A question for further consideration, but beyond the scope of this present essay, remains the extent to which the joking around with self-representation (evident in the Palisade story) involves Native Americans and their own sense of

CONSTRUCTING PLACE

how they were perceived as elements in and of the West.[26] How did they particularly react to what Rosemarie Bank refers to as the frontier concept's "simultaneously taking in and rubbing out Indian and frontier cultures alike"?[27]

One final piece of cultural context for the Palisade gunfights that deserves investigation is the performative or theatrical context of the hoax. By the mid-1870s, the West had become what Bank calls a "space of representation," a place in which cultures clash in strongly theatrical terms over the complex interactions of ideals and realities.[28] Notably, the *Enterprise* reporter's use of "rencontre," an archaic version of an equally strange and formal word for duel, "rencounter," draws attention to the staged quality of the Palisade shootout, a flavor picked up and amplified one hundred years later by Higgs's fragments of hackneyed dialogue. But even more directly, by the time the Palisade gunfights were getting underway, the frontier West was already a well-established setting and topic in theaters across the nation. "Buffalo Bill" Cody, for instance, was in 1876 a regular performer on the New York stage. Although he would not mount his first "Wild West Show" until 1882, he first hit the boards in December of 1872 in a Chicago performance of a Ned Buntline blood-and-thunder melodrama that co-starred fellow scouts Buntline and Texas Jack Omohundro. For most of the early to mid-1870s, Cody alternated between scouting on the Plains during the summers and "reenacting" his adventures on the stage during the off-season. As Roger A. Hall has documented, by the fall of 1876, the Wild West of dime-novel fame was also well established as a theatrical spectacle.[29] This point is further emphasized by the fact that within a mere seven weeks of Custer's defeat at Little Big Horn, audiences in New York were already attending typically melodramatic and racist re-creations of Custer's Last Stand in Bowery and Brooklyn theaters.[30] And though the reporter from the *Enterprise* makes no explicit mention of it, more recent accounts of the hoax note that a group called "The Palisades Thespian Players" was established for the purpose of better managing the complex logistics of the ongoing performances.[31]

The linchpin to the hoax ultimately lies in the *Enterprise* reporter's choice of framing assertions, beginning with "the credulity of western bound immigrants" and ending with these same travelers' "belief in the genuineness" of the event. In other words, as noted earlier, any representation of the West requires a certain degree of fidelity to already existing, genre-derived impressions (such as those identified in 1872 by Henry Davies). The performers in Palisade relied upon this principle just as much as did the tourists who fell victim to the hoax. Another way to make this point is to consider the problem inherent in a current, oft-employed definition of popular culture, specifically the one that asserts, "In popular culture the text is a cultural resource to be plundered or used in ways that are determined by the social interests of the reader/user not by the structure of the text itself, nor by the intentions (however we may discern them) of its author."[32] This definition allows quite broadly for the many interpretations of popular culture that have consumer-creators resisting and subversively reconfiguring the dominant paradigm.

In one respect, this is very much a useful way of looking at what the people of Palisade have done: for their own apparent entertainment and edification, they have taken it upon themselves to give the eastern tourist exactly what he or she expects—a bloody West in which cowboys (and sometimes Indians) shoot it out endlessly for the honor of the land. In the process of doing so, the townsfolk of Palisade presumably preserve a measure of regional autonomy, dignity, and self-determination by making a buck while putting on a show. The central problem with the above definition and the conclusion about Palisade that it leads to, however, is that this connection conveniently elides any consideration of the broader fields of media and cultural production (the question often raised about more contemporary popular culture concerns is how does watching TV enable one to resist and defy consumerist media?).[33] In the case of the Palisade gunfights, the broader fields of production surrounding the event include the vital fact that every single "performer" in the hoax gunfights was, in all likelihood, also a miner or teamster or in some measure related economically to the work of the town. Aside from the hoaxes, Palisade is also reportedly famous for the extent to which one man, "Nick of the Woods"

Pritchard, held an absolute monopoly on the mule and wagon trains responsible for hauling ore out of and supplies into the mines.[34] The locals may have been putting on a show, but by doing so they were also contributing to the cultural side of an economy that derived its profits from the processing of western material. That is, by theatrically confirming a view of the American frontier West that rail passengers may have come to town with, the people of Palisade were agreeing to perform on yet another level the role chosen for them, namely that of provider of resources for other parts of the culture. Nonwestern consumers were eager for silver ore and quintessentially western impressions alike, and the Palisade performers who in their daily roles brought forth the former also amply provided the latter.

Thus, the question remains: why might the residents of Palisade have chosen to devote their energies to the elaborate production required of such a large-scale hoax? The suggestion that nothing more than the legendary status of eastern touristic credulity had prompted "a hundred pranks," as attractive as it may be, simply does not satisfy. A more compelling reason, however, can be found in the figure, once again, of those "necessary Piutes." Judging by a number of contemporaneous accounts, Palisade was simply a working town with too much time on its hands. On September 3, 1876, a reporter for the nearby *Weekly Elko Independent* describes a visit to Palisade that prompts him to comment favorably on the town's various industrial activities and hospitality services but also to conclude that "The town is unusually dull, but still those who are in business don't growl. They simply pray for better times."[35] Printed a little over a month prior to the *Enterprise* account of the fake gunfights, this prehoax notice may very well lead a reader who knows what is coming to assume that local ingenuity was about to answer those prayers. However, a reporter for the *Eureka Daily Sentinel*, the same paper that carried the October 17 notice about the gunfights, writes on November 5, 1876, that Palisade "is a pleasant little village whose inhabitants all appear contented and prosperous." This second reporter comments favorably, again, on the industry and hospitality; but he concludes somewhat curiously that "Some other matters about Palisade should doubtless receive notice, but we negligently failed to make notes, and can not therefore give from memory as full details as we could desire. It only remains to be said that the place has a milder climate than Eureka, and is inhabited by as hospitable a people as ever dwelt together anywhere under the sun."[36] Does the phrase "some other matters" refer to the otherwise unmentioned gunfights, or is it simply a way for the reporter to wind down his piece by alluding to details genuinely too trivial to warrant mention?

Aside from the item about "Western Deviltry" reprinted from the *Territorial Enterprise*, no contemporaneous mention of the gunfights has thus far been located in local newspapers or in more broadly regional or national publications. In short, initial appearances suggest that the gunfights made less of a stir than more recent recapitulations might have us believe. To be sure, the second *Daily Sentinel* piece quoted above, in which the people of Palisade are praised for their hospitality, could potentially be seen as a smokescreen designed to assure readers in the immediate vicinity that Palisade has not gone completely and criminally insane. However, all that can truly be concluded with any confidence is that the town has gone from "dull" to "contented," which may simply be attributed to two different reporters' stated opinions.

Neither newspaper, however, gives any hint at a brewing racial problem in Palisade, one involving not Native Americans but rather the Chinese. Laborers who had emigrated from China to California and then worked eastward as they built the railroad were, by the mid-1870s, settling in the communities they had helped to connect by rail. This situation led to a great many regional tensions, a spate of racist exclusionary laws passed by the Nevada state legislature, and not a few violent encounters.[37] Indeed, the *New York Times* for July 29, 1877, less than a year after the reported start of the hoax (and presumably right in the middle of its heyday), published a dispatch from Palisade that reports how "a crowd assembled this afternoon and held an indignation meeting, expressing themselves bitterly opposed to the Chinese population." Clearly the residents of Palisade were wrestling with what they perceived to be an intrusion by nonwhite foreigners

CONSTRUCTING PLACE

into their community and, as did a great many other Nevada towns, resorted to the threat of violence. According to the *Times*, "Several fires started, but were speedily extinguished."[38] If, as some more recent commentators would have it, officials with the Central Pacific actively helped to create and maintain the hoax gunfights, then the railroad company certainly would also have been interested in protecting its investment.[39] Even though law enforcement officers were able to avert a riot, "The Central Pacific Railroad Company is keeping its engines fired up all along the line and on the side tracks so that they can speedily be moved if necessary, and not allowing any to be put in the roundhouses."[40]

Herein lies the crux of the matter: as noted above, Palisade was fundamentally a company town, and racial violence does not do the company any good. The hoax, rather than simply offering workers a chance for a topsy-turvy appropriation of authoritative discourse, in all likelihood afforded them an opportunity to blow off steam, to release tensions related to the racial situation in town by displacing it from the Chinese laborer to the more generically appropriate, indeed, "necessary" Paiute. Violence against Indians had, by 1876, become a central generic fact of the so-called American West, especially in the wake of Custer's defeat at Little Big Horn. In crafting a series of performances that trafficked in and catered to assumptions about this "space of representation," it simply made more sense to attack the Indians for fun than to attack the Chinese for fun. Tourists would not have expected the latter, and so Native Americans became, in one context, surrogate targets for ill feelings prompted by the Chinese.[41] In this respect, there is some measure of the carnivalesque or topsy-turvy to the enterprise, in that local control has reframed existing social tensions as a manageable and ultimately "harmless" set of performances. Racial violence displaced as theater is not nearly as threatening as the real thing. However, as this essay has attempted to demonstrate, genre conventions associated with how the region of the West is viewed from without have dictated that the terms of any oppositional performance are necessarily limited or constrained.

John Dorst argues in *Looking West* that "the ways of looking" consistent with the so-called first world of "advanced consumer culture take on a heightened visibility in the American West as they are enacted in its regional display sites and institutions."[42] Dorst's class- and production-aware analysis of popular culture takes in reconstructions of frontier camps, a museum in Wyoming located within a defunct prison in which Butch Cassidy was once incarcerated, and the cultural and political arguments over Devils Tower. However, his terms for analysis are perfectly appropriate for what was probably happening in Palisade. Deciding to put on a show, something that would be *seen* and hence *consumed* by outsiders, the locals based their performance on what tourists expected to see when they got there. The extent to which this show confirms existing stereotypes; the extent to which it masks the network of economic relations by which much of the West is made possible; and the extent to which it expresses tremendous race-based anxieties about the presence of minorities on the frontier—such issues are easily overlooked if the people of Palisade are thought of simply as clever self-representers.

Although the scholarship on tourism, popular culture, and the creation of the American frontier West is extensive, relatively little research has been done to assess the relationship of generic assumptions about the region to people already in residence in that region.[43] By offering a thumbnail examination of such local phenomena as the Palisade hoaxes, this essay attempts to raise the question of what it means for people to live in a region overdetermined by genre conventions imposed, as often as not, by those looking at it from the outside. Judging by a singular *Enterprise* report reprinted in the *Eureka Daily Sentinel*, people in central Nevada in 1876 fully understood how their region was being viewed from the outside (in dime novels, for one) and, perhaps, staged for themselves a series of productions designed both to exploit those genre conventions and to allow themselves a measure of control over their own self-representation, even if it ultimately involved the displacement of racial animus onto a group that did not pose as significant a threat to the labor pool. This is to say, in attempting to play out their identity as westerners, the people of Palisade appear to have found that their roles were already created for them. The upshot? The example of Palisade, Nevada, raises the possibility that regional self-representation is largely made tenable by the assumptions thrust upon a region from without. We would be well served to look even more closely at the role of genre conventions in this, or any similar, process of regional individuation and identification through self-representation.

Notes

1. "Western Deviltry," *The Eureka (NV) Daily Sentinel*, October 17, 1876.

2. Gerald B. Higgs, *Lost Legends of the Silver State* (Salt Lake City UT: Western Epics, 1976), 53.

3. For a particularly illuminating analysis of how the West is defined in contemporary theme parks, see Hsuan L. Hsu, "Authentic Re-Creations: Ideology, Practice, and Regional History along Buena Park's Entertainment Corridor," in *True West: Authenticity and the American West*, ed. William R. Handley and Nathaniel Lewis (Lincoln: University of Nebraska Press, 2004), 304–27.

4. On railroad tourism, see Anne Farrar Hyde, *An American Vision: Far Western Landscape and National Culture, 1820–1920* (New York: New York University Press, 1990), 107–46. On the effects of genre productions on the reception and understanding of the late-nineteenth-century West, see the first two chapters of Christine Bold, *Selling the Wild West: Popular Western Fiction, 1860–1960* (Bloomington: Indiana University Press, 1987), 1–75.

5. Alex Nemerov, "Doing the 'Old America': The Image of the American West, 1880–1920," in *The West as America: Reinterpreting Images of the Frontier, 1820–1920*, ed. William H. Truettner (Washington DC: Smithsonian Institution Press, 1991), 289.

6. See William R. Handley and Nathaniel Lewis, introduction to *True West: Authenticity and the American West*, ed. William R. Handley and Nathaniel Lewis (Lincoln: University of Nebraska Press, 2004), 1–17. For a thorough rundown of the ways in which the western mythos as it was understood in the 1870s and onward has accrued meaning in American culture, see Richard Slotkin, *The Fatal Environment: The Myth of the Frontier in the Age of Industrialization* (Middletown CT: Wesleyan University Press, 1985); and Richard Slotkin, *Gunfighter Nation: The Myth of the Frontier in Twentieth-Century America* (New York: Harper Perennial, 1993).

7. Louis S. Warren, *Buffalo Bill's America: William Cody and the Wild West Show* (New York: Knopf, 2005), 71.

8. Bonnie Christensen, *Red Lodge and the Mythic West: Coal Miners to Cowboys* (Lawrence: University Press of Kansas, 2002). See also Hal Rothman, *Devil's Bargains: Tourism in the Twentieth-Century American West* (Lawrence: University Press of Kansas, 1998). For an instance of performance and community formation not related to the frontier West, see Steven D. Hoelscher's analysis of New Glarus, Wisconsin, in *Heritage on Stage: The Invention of Ethnic Place in America's Little Switzerland* (Madison: University of Wisconsin Press, 1998).

9. The historical verifiability of the Palisade gunfights is not really at issue here. In both its contemporaneous and more recent forms, exemplified respectively by the *Enterprise* newspaper excerpt and the recountings of those such as Higgs, the story of the hoaxes stands as a genre-informed narrative that points to a desire to reproduce, for whatever reason, the idea of a West filled with gun smoke. It is the sources and ramifications of those reproductions that concern this essay.

10. In addition to benefiting tremendously from Christensen's work, the theoretical framework for the present analysis also relies on the work of Edward M. Bruner and Barbara Kirshenblatt-Gimblett, who have analyzed from a performance studies perspective the complex negotiations of history, self-identity, and tourist expectations undertaken by the Maasai tribe in Kenya. See in particular Bruner and Kirshenblatt-Gimblett, "Maasai on the Lawn: Tourist Realism in East Africa," *Cultural Anthropology* 9, no. 4 (1994): 435–70.

11. "Western Deviltry."

12. Higgs, *Lost Legends*, 50–51.

13. Fred Fedler, "Reinforcing a Stereotype: Railways and Revolvers in Georgia," in *Media Hoaxes* (Ames: Iowa State University Press, 1989), 69–96.

14. Henry E. Davies, *Ten Days on the Plains* (1872), quoted in Joy S. Kasson, *Buffalo Bill's Wild West: Celebrity, Memory, and Popular History* (New York: Hill and Wang, 2000), 16.

15. Jake Highton, *Nevada Newspaper Days: A History of Journalism in the Silver State* (Stockton CA: Heritage West Books, 1990), 7–28, passim. On Clemens in Nevada, see Edgar Marquess Branch, *The Literary Apprenticeship of Mark Twain* (Urbana: University of Illinois Press, 1950); Henry Nash Smith, ed., *Mark Twain of the Enterprise: Newspaper Articles and Other Documents 1862–1864* (Berkeley: University of California Press, 1957); Paul Fatout, *Mark Twain in Virginia City* (Bloomington: Indiana University Press, 1964).

16. Mark Twain, "A Bloody Massacre Near Carson," *Virginia City (NV) Territorial Enterprise*, October 28, 1863. Reprinted in Mark Twain, *Early Tales and Sketches: Volume 1 (1851–1864)*, ed. Edgar Marquess Branch, Robert H. Hirst, and Harriet Elinor Smith (Berkeley: University of California Press, 1979), 320–26.

17. Lawrence I. Berkove, "The Sagebrush School Revived," in *A Companion to the Regional Literatures of America*, ed. Charles L. Crow (Malden MA: Blackwell, 2003), 324–43. See also Highton, *Nevada Newspaper Days*, 49–58. Oscar Lewis documents the humorous journalism that characterized the territory's second-most-famous paper (after the *Enterprise*) in *The Town That Died Laughing: The Story of Austin, Nevada, Rambunctious Early-Day Mining Camp, and of Its Renowned Newspaper, the Reese River Reveille* (Reno: University of Nevada Press, 1986). On the broader history of media and newspaper hoaxes in the United States, see Fred Fedler, *Media Hoaxes*.

18. For a full account of the life of this hoax, see Lawrence I. Berkove, ed., *The Fighting Horse of the Stanislaus: Stories and Essays by Dan De Quille* (Iowa City: University of Iowa Press, 1990), 9–13.

19. Dan De Quille, *The Big Bonanza: An Authentic Account of the Discovery, History, and Working of the World-Renowned Comstock Lode of Nevada* (New York: Knopf, 1947).

20. De Quille, *Big Bonanza*, 18–33.

21. Given the *Virginia City Territorial Enterprise*'s history with hoaxing and otherwise false reportage, it is certainly not beyond the realm of possibility to suggest that the *Enterprise* staff of 1876 (perhaps even De Quille himself) have reached through time to pull one over on popular publications and historically minded scholars alike. Perhaps the *Enterprise*'s description of a small town out along the Central Pacific rails signifies little more than another frontier fabrication (a further clue may very well be the use of the past tense—"when business *was* dull," "revolvers *were* loaded," and so forth). This particular news story as reprinted in the *Eureka Daily Sentinel*, however, does not share the identifying characteristics of other *Enterprise* hoaxes, in that the joke is not on the readers; it only describes a joke played on others and, as such, maintains a measure of legitimacy.

22. See Thomas C. Wilson Advertising Agency, *Pioneer Nevada* (Reno NV: Harold's Club, 1951); Higgs, *Lost Legends*, 52; John H. Harrison, "Bloodbath at Palisade," *Las Vegas Review-Journal* June 17, 1979; Norm Nielson, "The Deadly Massacre at Palisades," in *Tales of Nevada* (Reno NV: Tales of Nevada, 1990), 2:176–77.

23. Silas Seymour, *Incidents of a Trip through the Great Platte Valley, to the Rocky Mountains and Laramie Plains, in the Fall of 1866, with a Synoptical Statement of the Various Pacific Railroads, and an Account of the Great Union Pacific Railroad Excursion to the One Hundreth Meridian of Longitude* (New York: D. Van Nostrand, 1867), 88–89. Thanks to Timothy Mahoney for alerting me to this source.

24. William F. Cody, *The Life of Hon. William F. Cody, Known as Buffalo Bill, the Famous Hunter, Scout, and Guide: An Autobiography* (1879; repr., with a foreword by Don Russell, Lincoln: University of Nebraska Press, 1978), 290–92.

25. Mahoney, *Provincial Lives*, 83–112.

26. For an overview of the history of Native American participation in their own theatrical representations, see the essays in Hanay Geiogamah and Jaye T. Darby, eds., *American Indian Theater in Performance: A Reader* (Los Angeles: UCLA American Indian Studies Center, 2000). See also Roger A. Hall, *Performing the American Frontier, 1870–1906* (New York: Cambridge University Press, 2001). On the history of Euro-Americans' fondness for "playing Indian," see Philip Joseph Deloria, *Playing Indian* (New Haven CT: Yale University Press, 1998).

27. Rosemarie K. Bank, *Theatre Culture in America, 1825–1860* (New York: Cambridge University Press, 1997), 73.

28. Bank devotes an entire chapter to illustrating this concept. For her discussion specific to what she identifies as "the frontier," see Bank, *Theatre Culture in America*, 59–72.

29. Hall, *Performing the American Frontier*, 1, 50–67. See also Kasson, *Buffalo Bill's Wild West*; and Bank, *Theatre Culture in America*, 59–72; and Don B. Wilmeth, "Noble or Ruthless Savage? The American Indian on Stage and in the Drama," in Geiogamah and Darby, *American Indian Theater*, 127–56.

30. Custer was defeated on June 25, 1876; a play called *Sitting Bull; or, Custer's Last Charge* opened at Wood's Theatre on August 14. See Hall, *Performing the American Frontier*, 86.

31. Higgs, *Lost Legends*, 52. The theatrical element is also alluded to by Harrison,

"Bloodbath at Palisade"; Nielson, "Deadly Massacre at Palisades," 2:177; and Richard Moreno, *Roadside History of Nevada* (Missoula MT: Mountain Press, 2000), 37.

32. John Fiske, "Popular Culture," in *Critical Terms for Literary Study*, ed. Frank Lentricchia and Thomas McLaughlin (Chicago: University of Chicago Press, 1995), 331. Of course, this is not the definitive statement of this theoretical premise, only a succinct and effective version of it. See also John Fiske, *Understanding Popular Culture* (Boston: Unwin Hyman, 1989). For an example of this idea in practice, see Janice A. Radway, *Reading the Romance: Women, Patriarchy, and Popular Literature* (Chapel Hill: University of North Carolina Press, 1984).

33. A recent and concise critique of this sort is offered by Patrick Brantlinger, *Who Killed Shakespeare? What's Happened to English since the Radical Sixties* (New York: Routledge, 2001), 125–49.

34. See Don Ashbaugh, *Nevada's Turbulent Yesterday: A Study in Ghost Towns* (Los Angeles: Westernlore, 1963), 263.

35. "Palisade Items," *Weekly Elko (NV) Independent*, September 3, 1876.

36. "Palisade," *Eureka (NV) Daily Sentinel*, November 5, 1876.

37. Russell R. Elliott and William D. Rowley, *History of Nevada*, 2nd ed. (Lincoln: University of Nebraska Press, 1987), 166–69.

38. "On the Pacific Slope," *New York Times*, July 29, 1877.

39. See Higgs, *Lost Legends*, 50; and Nielson, "Deadly Massacre at Palisades," 2:176.

40. "On the Pacific Slope."

41. For a suggestive, corollary argument on the use of Native Americans as surrogate scapegoats for African Americans in antebellum Southern literature, see Alan Henry Rose, *Demonic Visions: Racial Fantasy and Southern Fiction* (Hamden CT: Archon Books, 1976). On the use of Native Americans in racial surrogacy as a factor in the performance of regional identity, see Joseph Roach, *Cities of the Dead: Circum-Atlantic Performance* (New York: Columbia University Press, 1996), 179–211, passim.

42. John Dorst, *Looking West* (Philadelphia: University of Pennsylvania Press, 1999), 9.

43. Notable exceptions are Christensen and Rothman. See also Wrobel, *Promised Lands*.

3

*Place Is a Relationship: Regionalism,
Nationalism, and Transnationalism*

In part 2 Barbara Handy-Marchello and Guy Reynolds demonstrated that markets impose limits on the possibilities of regional self-representation for authors: Linda Slaughter wrote for a Midwest publication in terms that characterized the Northern Plains as an enclave for genteel eastern Anglos; Willa Cather wrote for eastern publishers about the same Plains in terms that characterized it instead as an immigrant frontier. Their respective willingness to picture the Midwest as a region whose hallmarks were and were not gentility were conditioned by these markets, as Edward Watts convincingly demonstrates in his analysis in this section of midwestern regionalism as the manifestation of a colonial culture. While Watts does not try to equate white settlers in new territories with the experience of the subaltern, he argues that "colony" is a better term than "region," because it more clearly points to the asymmetrical and nonreciprocal relations between a center and a periphery. That asymmetry is made evident in the center's view of various regions as closer to nature and so possessing an authenticity that the center has lost. Midwestern literature in Watts's account is thus postcolonial literature at times, because in certain instances, it posed a real challenge to the domination of eastern markets and the control of eastern publishers by expressing local needs, albeit always within the larger construct of the nation and claims to nationality.[1]

As Douglas Powell asserts, "region is always a relational term." Unlike a home, a community, a city, a state, or a nation, he observes, a region doesn't refer to a specific site or have a flag or an army to enforce its boundaries; instead, it is always part of a larger network of sites. Even when definitions of region are used to isolate just such a network, that very process of finding definitions is done in relation— whether temporal, spatial, or material—to broader patterns of history or politics or culture. To study the unique and isolated in a way that clarifies how it is interconnected with other places is, Powell says, to practice regionalism.[2] Watts and the other essayists in this section deal specifically with the idea that regionalism is hardly a "local" phenomenon but is instead something produced by a central market or government as a way of managing difference and opposition. Watts, writing about the nineteenth century and often about sections of the country not yet incorporated into the Union, sees this process or relationship as an essentially colonial form of production; but literary historians who tackle the twentieth century frame it in different terms, particularly ones that emphasize the author's independent self-creation and marketing.

Larry Moore offers the example of Vachel Lindsay, a middle-class midwesterner whose experiences in Springfield, Illinois, would shape the social engagements of his verse, particularly its racial and class attitudes. In Moore's account, Lindsay internalized the tensions of his home city (becoming a kind of literal embodiment of region) and thus carried it with him wherever he went in his wide-ranging travels across the United States. His poetry attempted to grasp the nature of the "larger" America but relied on a regionalist style to transmute or market that knowledge to a popular national audience.

Mark Robison asserts, quoting Richard Johnston, that humanists need to avoid "reified regional frameworks" imbued with essentialist characteristics, because the substance of region lies not in a "static collection of local details, but in an interaction between people and place, a dynamic process."[3] Robison's focus on the dynamic economic processes in Willa Cather's novels does indeed work to diminish regional divisions constructed on harder topographical, geographical, or ecological differences. His argument points instead to the importance of class, rather than topography, in how regionalism is produced: Cather's middle-class females are not confined to any one realm but exist in both the city and the country, and they experience the shift between the two as an empowering connection rather than a destructive barrier, unlike the naturalist fiction of her peers. Rather than being part of nature, raw products who get consumed by the culture of the male city, Cather's protagonists possess the "masculine" ability to objectify nature as landscape AND commodity, a skill requisite for their success in both agricultural Red Cloud and urban Chicago. Their region is a horizontal and vertical community of mutual exchanges between rural and urban that defies conventional or "natural" definitions or boundaries.

As Robison is aware, Cather's view of the Midwest is not a Populist one. For her, the market economy that encompasses and shapes the built environment of small town, farm, and city is one of benign mutuality, not exploitation; and it is those economic exchanges that in fact diminish the topographical divisions of the region. The region becomes a middle-class space and a kind of "second nature," which owes its existence to human creation and over which nature exerts less independent power.[4] Cather heroines such as Thea Kronberg succeed because this economic nature—their region—allows them to distance themselves from genteel versions of women's relationship to nature and culture. Kronberg turns her gaze from the moldy lions outside the Chicago Art Institute, symbols of the old guard, to the lumber ships on Lake Michigan. Her gaze does not reject city for country, so much as it disregards the cosmopolitan and aestheticized view of the world that had limited women's roles in the middle and upper classes to art objects, in favor of a view that allows those women to participate in the fabrication of regional culture instead.

Like Robison, literary historian Stephen Behrendt argues that humanists must resist reification of region. He focuses on a tension within academia that is the inheritance of the eighteenth-century Enlightenment

PLACE IS A RELATIONSHIP

scholar's encyclopedic contempt for the local antiquarian. Every time a researcher is encouraged to show the relevance of his or her choice of an anecdote, example, case, instance, fact, or particularity, he or she is being instructed to make those particulars relevant according to the standards of the humanities' professional discourses and disciplines, which privilege the universal rather than the local. The tension then between general and specific is, in effect, one created by the very project of the humanities, the aim of creating a total map of human life. And as Behrendt wisely observes, it cannot be resolved without abandoning that project or even the humanities themselves.

Notes

1. Watts, "The Midwest as a Colony," (this issue), 170–71.
2. Powell, *Critical Regionalism*, 4–5.
3. Robison, "Transcending the Urban-Rural Divide," (this issue), 196.
4. Robison, "Transcending the Urban-Rural Divide," (this issue), 198–99.

9. Regionalism and the Realities of Naming

STEPHEN C. BEHRENDT

Complications seem inevitably to arise whenever one tries to define either *regionalism* in general or any specific region like the South or the Great Plains or to categorize the art and artifacts that come from or relate to that area by means of such language. Commentators occasionally try to take the easy way out of these taxonomic difficulties by simply declaring that "writing is writing," by which reductive expression they apparently mean that all writing is "universal" in nature (the local manifestation of some "universal language") and that, therefore, all that varies from "region" to "region" is the *inflection. Inflection* is a convenient word because it seems to delimit linguistic variation (or other variations) less strictly than words like *dialect* or *idiom*. A less immediately diagnostic term, *inflection* appears to permit a far greater range of localisms within the discourse in question. Even so, it is not convincing that what we usually think of as "regionalisms" (whether in literature, the arts, culture, society, class, or economics) actually amount to little more than differing inflections upon some universal or general language or discourse that is itself associated with a larger and more heterogeneous geographical or cultural entity like a nation, continent, or socioeconomic class. Consequently, this essay represents an attempt to articulate a slightly different perspective upon the matter of regionalism and its slippery definitions. This attempt comes with a significant disclaimer: it does not so much *resolve* the difficulties as suggest a different and perhaps more constructive way of regarding them.

The cultural geographer Yi-Fu Tuan—native of Tientsin, China, graduate of Oxford, longtime resident of Madison, Wisconsin, and author of ten books and dozens of remarkable articles on geography and human perception and cognition—has often expressed his belief that all of us carry with us throughout our adult life the landscape in which we lived our early lives. Wherever we find ourselves, our real "home" lies in this internal landscape that informs our sense of who we are and that makes us "whole" in ways that can scarcely be imagined by those persons whose fragmented view of the world (and themselves) reflects the rootlessness inseparable from the peripatetic nature of modern life.[1] People tend to identify with their earliest experiences and the places in which those experiences transpired, perhaps because those residual places and experiences provide a security that rootless adulthood usually denies us. Indeed, it is often the particularly and peculiarly local aspects of those early experiences that most clearly associate them with notions of "home." This idea of being intuitively rooted in a particular place—a geographical and cultural origin—is of course one distinguishing characteristic of what academic discourse usually identifies as *regional*. The more apparent the evidence of this rooting is in the local and the particular in any artifact of culture, the reasoning seems to go, the more powerfully regional are those artifacts.

One consequence of such thinking is an inevitable privileging of natives. If one is born in a particular place and then stays there, what that person produces is especially likely to be defined as directly reflective of that person's region. This formulation assumes an intensive and longstanding personal interaction between the individual self and the external (and to some extent the internal) environment. It also assumes that a native person is able to know more—and better—the cultural minutiae of a region than the immigrant, the late-arriving artist or observer, who is assumed to be less capable of producing a genuine regionalism in the locale precisely because she or he is a late-comer, an "outsider," a "foreigner." Faced with this prospect, the individual (or social unit) characterized by mobility rather than rootedness must compensate by privileging some other quality. Expanding one's locational and cultural horizons in this fashion is therefore typically regarded as "bettering" oneself or one's society. More than two centuries ago, Immanuel Kant advocated at the close of the European Enlightenment what he called a "universal cosmopolitan existence," which would help humanity overcome its seemingly instinctive parochialism.[2] Recent social theory in the modern age of the global community has increasingly preached the desirability of this sort of cosmopolitanism, precisely because it seems at once to transcend "the seemingly exhausted nation-state model" and "to mediate actions and ideals oriented both to the universal and the particular, the global and the local."[3] In fact, and especially when we are talking about regionalism, the reality is that the usual outcome is not really transcendence but avoidance—a glossing-over of real irreconcilabilities by rhetorical contrivances; the "mediations" typically prove, upon closer inspection, to be remarkably shaky unions held together by semantic Band-Aids. Ivan Turgenev's mid-nineteenth-century rejoinder to the European call for cosmopolitanism was right on target: "The cosmopolitan is a nonentity—worse than a nonentity; without nationality is no art, nor truth, nor life, nor anything."[4]

Turgenev's objection is an important one for the present discussion of regionalism. For every push in cultural debate, something pushes back, whether we are talking about regions, which we typically think of as relatively local in nature, or whether we have in mind larger entities, perhaps national or even international. Much of the critical and cultural theory that drove scholarship in all fields at the beginning of the twenty-first century arises from the impulse to embrace and endorse cosmopolitanism as a somehow more-inclusive way of representing the world. But that representation brings with it a very real danger of leveling and erasure that one early modern Irish nationalist—William Butler Yeats—particularly feared. Like Turgenev in Russia, Yeats pushed back. He worried that in becoming British, his country's literature risked losing that which made it most vital: its thoroughgoing *Irishness*. To sacrifice that which is distinctively *national*, Yeats argued, to cede it to a larger and more cosmopolitan entity bearing the label "British," is to abandon the Irish altogether and become complicitous in the cultural colonization that would subsume that historical nationhood within a larger but nevertheless foreign and indeed alien entity.

Moreover, some scholars see in the fashionable embrace of the cosmopolitan a disturbing elitism that situates the standard of cosmopolitanism directly within the limited cultural circumstances and attitudes of the very individual or group that claims to espouse a more global perspective. Seen in this way, as a gesture that makes one's own limited perspective the measure of a so-called universalist one, such cosmopolitanism may be seen, paradoxically, as even more parochial than the perspective that it claims to be transcending. As Timothy Brennan puts it, this sort of self-centered cosmopolitanism "is a discourse of the universal that is inherently local—a locality that's always surreptitiously imperial."[5]

The current debate over the advantages and disadvantages of a cosmopolitan perspective is therefore directly related to a longstanding one about the nature and function of regionalism within characterizations of national cultural phenomena. In many respects, therefore, the issue of regionalism with which I am concerned here proceeds from the conflicting impulses inherent in cultural and critical nomenclature alike toward generalization and cultural consensus on one hand and the particularization and local variants on the other. Let me approach these broad issues first by way of personal experience, framing them "from the inside out," as it were, to highlight some of the key difficulties that are integral to conceptualizing regionalism. My own experiences are by no means unique; indeed, they may suggest comparable experiences and perceptions that many of us share. I am a writer and scholar who has spent twenty-plus years in Nebraska, which is routinely identified as part of the Great Plains; as a matter of fact, the University of Nebraska is home to an interdisciplinary academic program called Great Plains Studies, featuring the Center for Great Plains Studies. Nevertheless, I definitely do not think of myself as a Great Plains writer. My scholarly work is grounded in British literature, but I also teach and publish on southern writers like Flannery O'Connor. Furthermore, though I am a publishing poet whose subject matter may sometimes reflect the Great Plains, there is no question that my roots (and my vision) are still firmly tied to my northern Wisconsin origin. Even so, I hesitate to define myself according to any region, for various reasons. According to the formal definitions of regions adopted, published, and promulgated by the National Endowment for the Humanities, I ought to call myself an "Upper Mississippi Valley" writer. But that term sounds so patently phony that I cannot imagine myself (or any other earlier or contemporary writers from that part of the country—August Derleth, Edna Meudt, Michael Dennis Brown) actually subscribing to such a moniker. Indeed, the term itself is symptomatic of the problem that lies at the heart of all discussions of regionalism: it is a neologism coined because it was bureaucratically necessary to label various parts of the country in order to paint the entire map, leaving no gaps.

Academic discussions of regionalism (and regional writing) are typically hampered both by the absence of workable definitions—or by artificially imposed ones that do not in fact work—and by the further complications inherent in academic structures and curricula. Colleges and universities routinely offer courses in southern American literature, for instance; and the University of Nebraska (where I teach) offers a course on Great Plains literature. But it also offers a course on Canadian literature, which both is and is *not* literature of the Great Plains (think of a writer from Nova Scotia or Quebec), just as Great Plains literature may or may not be literature of Canada (both Louis Real and John Neihardt were Great Plains writers though only Real was Canadian). Since southern literature is a more familiar curricular category, I illustrate some of the difficulties of nomenclature by asking what we do with a writer like Flannery O'Connor. Where— *in terms of curricular categories*—do we put her? Does she go into "Literature of the South" or "Women's Literature"? What about Alice Walker: "Southern"? "Woman"? "African American"? Note that nowhere here have I even addressed religion, economic class, political party, or other possible delimiters. Paradoxically, in a national and institutional culture now preoccupied with issues of diversity and inclusiveness, the taxonomy that governs the varieties of human experience (especially as reflected in academic curricula) seems ever more insistently bound up in distinctions and discriminations, not in unifiers and levelers. The more we claim to be inclusive, the more we end up reinforcing labels and stereotypes by naming and categorizing features of difference (or otherness) that we profess to be ignoring or repudiating.

Nor is the problem unique to literary studies. The curricular plans and course catalogues of history departments, for example, are replete with courses in American history bearing geographical delimiters like "Southern" or "Western," while their offerings in world history routinely divide along comparable lines of region. This geographical pie-slicing is, of course, not unlike the chronological divisions that partition the vast continuum of historical time in terms of periods defined by sociopolitical phenomena (e.g., Reconstruction or the Depression in American history and the Napoleonic Age or the Age of Industrialism and Imperialism in world history) or—perhaps worse—by dates that are often as arbitrary as they are misleading (e.g., nineteenth-century American history or eighteenth-century Europe). When we look again into literary studies, we inevitably encounter the never-ending dispute about what constitutes just about any literary-historical period. The absurdity of the situation is aptly illustrated by longstanding debates about the appropriate dating of "the eighteenth century," which has usually been understood among traditional British literature scholars to include 1660–1789 and which dating patently confutes any rational conception of what constitutes a century. The very fact that discussions and definitions of regionalism are rooted in the academy and its reductive intellectual and curricular structures may offer the most telling evidence of how discussion of the subject has come to be characterized by its frequently blinkered, impractical, and piecemeal nature.

One approach to defining regionalism in literary and cultural studies is sometimes to focus upon characteristic themes and subjects that are identifiably tied to the particular region in question. Indeed, this is probably the most familiar paradigm. But what if the artist is not *from* that region? Is it still regional art? I have often fancied, for example, writing a detective novel centered on the British Romantic artist and poet William Blake and set in Blake's London of 1800. I have studied the period, the culture, and the author for most of my adult life; and yet if I were to write my novel, it would never occur to me to call myself a British writer, my subject matter notwithstanding. America is a big country, both geographically and culturally; and so one can reasonably think about identifiable geographical, linguistic, and cultural regions. But even a small nation like Britain still subdivides; one still thinks, for instance, of Lake District poets or of Liverpudlian writers or of Scots philosophers. Perhaps the really key issue here is not that of nativity—of whether one is native-born to the region in which her or his art is grounded—so much as it is a matter of the presence (or absence) in that art of some particularly intense transaction that occurs between artists and their particular locales. This would mean that regionalists might reasonably be defined as artists and thinkers who simply include an unusual—and unusually *central*—specificity of place (and time) in their efforts to understand and interpret life, self, and reality. I shall return to this point shortly, but I want to get there by considering first the matter of definitions in greater detail.

In wrestling with my subject in the first place, I tried going for help to that most regional of projects: the *Dictionary of American Regional English*. The Web site for the *Dictionary of American Regional English* tells me that the project is neither prescriptive nor even precisely descriptive but that its task is "to document the varieties of English that are not found everywhere in the United States" and that "are part of our oral rather than our written culture."[6] The first print volume of this remarkable work tells us that the editors regard as *regional* "any word or phrase whose form is not used generally throughout the United States but only in part (or parts) of it, or by a particular social group," or "any word or phrase whose form or meaning is distinctively a folk usage (regardless of region)."[7] The editors point out that one of the difficulties they encountered from the start in their own

PLACE IS A RELATIONSHIP

work on the *Dictionary of American Regional English* lay in the fact that geographical regionality and linguistic regionality often conflict and that there are peculiar artificial examples of seeming universality. The language of seamen, to take an obvious example, often reflects the individual regions from which the sailors come, as in the case of New England commercial fishermen. But crews in the United States Navy, on the other hand, are drawn from all regions of the nation and therefore represent a linguistic melting pot. Even so, that heterodox language inevitably also includes variations that are grounded in the particular vernaculars of the individual sailors' own diverse cultural heritages. Moreover, that mixed language gradually acquires additional elements that reflect language practices local to the sailors' worldwide ports of call. The same might be said of the language of soldiers—or, for that matter, of that of student (and faculty) communities at relatively cosmopolitan colleges and universities.

Standard dictionary definitions are not especially helpful either when it comes to addressing the taxonomy of regionalism. My research there revealed some predictable references to political or ideological divisions of geographical areas, as well as to more modern geopolitical inflections that involve *loyalty* to the interests of a region (or a nation) in relation to those of other regions or to policies that define a nation's interests in terms of particular countries or regions—NAFTA (North American Free Trade Agreement), for instance, or NATO (North Atlantic Treaty Organization). Such usages turn out to be especially common in *oppositional* rhetoric, as becomes evident in public discourse when a particular regional entity sees its interests and identity threatened by some leveling and homogenizing larger structure or entity.

Especially intriguing, however, is the way in which *regionalism* is used as a term among literary critics and art historians, for its usage in these contexts points to a larger issue concerning the culturally ambiguous relationship of regions to national or global wholes. In art history, for example, *regionalism* usually refers to the work of "a number of rural artists, mostly from the Midwest," working in the 1930s: Thomas Hart Benton, John Steuart Curry, and Grant Wood in particular. One academic Web site describes these regionalists as "idiosyncratic" artists who shared "a humble, antimodernist style and a fondness for depicting everyday life."[8] Another Internet source informs us that the regionalists "wanted to paint the American scene—away from the New York area—in a clear, simple way that could be understood and enjoyed by everyone."[9] These definitions subtly advertise both the fundamental anti-intellectualism and the distrust of urban life that has always figured prominently in the "country" half of city-country dualisms in the cultural life of the Western world.

Moreover, when we add into the equation what literary scholars have to say about regionalism in literature, this split gets inflected still further. One academic Web site unquestioningly equates "regional literature" with "local color" in its focus on features "particular to a specific region." This same Web site reports that prominent among what it calls weaknesses of regional literature are "nostalgia or sentimentality."[10] Like the art historical descriptions noted above, this one reflects an inherently condescending treatment of that which is defined as regional and which seems typically to be presented in such formulations as a defensive, protectionist retreat from that which is supposedly complex, sophisticated, and modern. Indeed, equating *regional* art with *local* color involves an implicit semantic gesture that renders the regional even smaller, even more localized and cloistered.

This is, of course, precisely the attitude one discovers in a great deal of cultural discussion about that which is regional. While it is often regarded by professional critics and connoisseurs as "interesting," "quaint," or "eclectic," the regional artifact (or artistic feature) is nevertheless often relegated to the status of a "merely" (I use the word deliberately) interesting—even engaging—*curiosity*, rather than being regarded as something that belongs to, participates in, and contributes meaningfully to the cultural mainstream. It is an us-against-them mentality on both sides. And from such polarized thinking there is little to be gained—on *either* side.

When *The Hudson Valley Regional Review* was begun in 1999, it featured a fascinating lead article by David Pierce and Richard Wiles that attempted to come to grips with people's seemingly endless fascination with trying to resolve the distinctions between regionalism and what we might now call globalism, or what earlier in this essay I referred to as cosmopolitanism.[11] Pierce and Wiles trace at least some of the interest in regionalism back to our own contemporary resistance—in an increasingly globalized, postindustrial world—to the sort of socioeconomic leveling that produced the European Economic Community and then the European Union and its dubious euro, for example. For any such process also implies a leveling of national and cultural distinctions: the elimination of national *political* boundaries implied by the EU passport suggests a comparable blurring of national *cultural* boundaries and the consequent erasure of longstanding *cultural* features that often transcend the artificial boundaries set up by political entities. Further propelling this leveling process is the growth in communication technologies that has yielded phenomena like the Internet and the real-time cable television coverage of the start of the war in Iraq, led by the United States in March 2003.

Pierce and Wiles suggest that the widespread modern view that the world is shrinking is only partly correct. They cite the paradox of the Western world on the eve of the French Revolution: a world at once almost incalculably vast and yet small and localized for most of its inhabitants. Against this paradox, they posit the paradox of the modern world. Our world is unquestionably larger still, in population, in inhabited spaces, in knowledge. At the same time, it is smaller because of the miracles of transport and technology that seem to place it all literally at our fingertips. Two years ago, for example, I coedited a complex electronic collection of texts and scholarship on Scottish women poets, which included more than sixty volumes of poetry along with critical essays on the individual poets written expressly for the project by several dozen scholars scattered around the world.[12] We did our work entirely in electronic fashion, submitting, revising, editing, and assembling our various contributions via e-mail and then publishing them electronically in a CD-ROM format that can be accessed virtually anywhere in the world. Undertaking an ambitious project of that sort—which we completed in less than two years from start to finish—would have been unthinkable twenty years ago when every aspect of it would have required depending upon the regular postal system and employing conventional print technologies.

My point is simply that with all this instantaneous communication and the seamless, borderless, global community that exists, at least in some hypothetical (or "virtual") form comes a very real sense that we are being stripped of all that distinguishes us, one from another. Our unique, individual characteristics vanish just as surely as our idiosyncratic handwriting vanishes into the fonts of our e-mail programs. Oddly, this often results in our having a clearer picture of that which is distant—even remote—from us than we have of that which actually surrounds us and, more importantly, of that which has shaped us and made us what we are, each and individually. What is eroded is our sense of place, our sense of our lives as both a function and a reflection of specifically and irresistibly local phenomena. Shakespeare understood this fully when he had Duke Theseus say in *A Midsummer Night's Dream*,

> the poet's pen
> . . . gives to airy nothing
> A local habitation and a name.[13]

Even in the technologically advanced twenty-first century, we do not live in an abstract world of "airy nothing" but rather in a world of tactile realities. The tension between the abstract and the tactile—between "airy nothings" and "local habitations"—is analogous to that which exists between the global and the regional. Nearly two centuries ago, writing about the fundamental nature of life and being, Percy Shelley said this of the individual intellect: "Each is at once the centre and the circumference; the point to which all things are referred, and the line in which all things are contained."[14] Center and circumference, in culture as in physics, are each absolutely necessary to the integrity—indeed to the very existence—of the other. The trick is to be able to do what Shelley's great, Romantic visionary predecessor William Blake urged us to do:

> To see a World in a Grain of Sand
> And a Heaven in a Wild Flower[;]
> Hold Infinity in the palm of your hand
> And Eternity in an hour[.][15]

If it is possible to envision a seamless global community, it is nevertheless the lived reality of the paradigm, which is provided by the local, that makes that vision possible. At the same time, it is the existence of the global whole (Blake's "World" or Shelley's "circumference") that assures us of the existence also of the local and particular (Blake's "Grain of Sand" or Shelley's "center").

Ironically, in writing about what they mean by regionalism in the context of the Hudson Valley, Pierce and Wiles cited as a perfect example of regionalism—of all things—Mari Sandoz's writings about her native Sand Hills and her *Love Song to the Plains* in particular. In that work, they argue, Sandoz creates a sense of place that transcends mere "local color" by virtue of its wholly "non-self-conscious treatment of and feeling for a region."[16] And yet they are careful to observe that one does not need to be a native to possess—or at least to experience—just such a sense of place. "Effective regional writing," Pierce and Wiles point out, "often is an intensely personal response to a physical place—but not so personal that a reader or viewer cannot identify with [it] at least to a small extent."[17] This is intriguing and may help account for what I believe as a writer to be a number of identifiable verbal and stylistic features in my own poetry that I consider to have evolved in response to the natural features and environment of Nebraska, where I have now lived for more than two decades. And it may mean, too, that I may yet get around to my London novel.

More to the point, what Pierce and Wiles are talking about is a sense of place—of *region*—that inheres not just in a physical locale but rather in the creative interaction that transpires between the consciousness of an observer, participant, or artist and that particular place. It is neither exclusively one nor the other—internal consciousness nor external locale—nor is it precisely the sum of both. Rather, regionalism manifests itself as a *transaction* that is rooted in a most complex fashion in a very particular time and place and that involves both the observing and recording artist and her or his audience. For a sense of region to be manifested for the reader or viewer, she or he must already have some personal point of reference against which to measure and assess what the artist records. In short, even in the most seemingly globalized world—whether it be literary, artistic, or geopolitical—it is the active and envisageable presence of the particular that gives fullest meaning to the general. The logical, intellectual movement toward abstract principles is activated and propelled by the active existence of the particulars, which are themselves preserved by a comparable logical pursuit of the discrete data upon which the generalization rests. These tensions cannot be resolved. Their proper relationship is suggested by William Blake's shrewd observation that "Opposition is True Friendship," and that "Without Contraries is no progression."[18] In a sense, the regional and the national (or global) constitute such contraries, and it is the friendly and creative opposition that inheres between them that energizes both.

Moreover, every age—and every region—likes to puff itself up by deflating that to which it compares itself: witness both the longstanding and the more recent rivalries between any university's football team (and its fans) and the teams (and the fans) of its traditional opponents. On the Great Plains, for example, it is no coincidence that rivalries—and hot ones, at that—exist between Nebraska (by which Nebraskans mean both a football team and a region or state) and traditional opponents like Oklahoma or Colorado (which likewise designate both football teams and state or cultural identities). It is also no coincidence that rivalries of this sort do *not* exist between Nebraska and, say, McNeese State or Middle Tennessee State, teams of demonstrably inferior talent and status that appear once to fill out a football schedule and provide what is essentially a paid-admission scrimmage and then are seen no more. Furthermore, it is only logical that disparaging comments about such athletic teams spill over to—or, more properly, reflect—an attitude toward the teams' institutions and their geographical and cultural status that is equally disparaging, if not simply condescending. Rather than simply representing an analogy that may strike some as both excessively local and relatively inconsequential, I would argue that this analogy of football and culture speaks directly to the issues I have been examining here. That is, it emphasizes the fiercely partisan nature of local or regional cultural phenomena and reminds us that for the majority of citizens it is precisely these local or regional contests for "bragging rights" that define and reinforce local or regional identities in the face of broader and culturally leveling forces involved in any national or global perspective. This is where regional identities are forged and preserved; and if ours is a culture that seems to value sporting events out of all proportion, then we will do well to recognize the fierce pride and loyalty that are involved in such local and regional identities. For this is also where we all encounter within a localized group culture the identities that we claim without hesitation to be, literally, our own.

Why is this? For the sort of opposition that Blake calls "true friendship" to evolve, the opposing parties must be more or less evenly paired and must have comparably compelling cases for their claim to supremacy—and therefore to dignity (or "respect," as athletes increasingly like to style it). And yet I would argue that all regional identities are themselves both shaped and informed by "larger" identities and histories, whether at the level of competing athletic teams (and traditions, regional identities, and bowl games) or at the level of competing nations (and traditions, identities, and wars). Competing with strong opponents makes us appear strong; it may even *make* us strong.

Certainly it enables us to wrap ourselves in a blanket of dignity—even of heroism—that everyday experience seldom affords. Regions are inherently smaller than nations; in a culture (like America's) that regards underdogs with affection, this is no small matter, whether the issue is engaged on the athletic field or in the discourse of a cosmopolitan culture that aspires to apply (its own) "global" criteria to the assessment of cultural phenomena.

My conclusion necessarily returns to the issue with which I started: the difficulty of defining regionalism in an increasingly globalized world. There are separate and perhaps contradictory—and certainly contesting—impulses implicit in the National Endowment for the Humanities's own language about the nature and mission of the Regional Humanities Centers that were established under that organization's auspices in the final decade of the twentieth century. That language reminds us that the various regions defined by the National Endowment for the Humanities are grounded in their own discrete "regional culture, regional memory and regional identity" as defined by "history, language, landscape and architecture—that is, by the things we know as the humanities."[19] *Humanities* is an inherently inclusive and expansive term that implies an almost neoclassical impulse toward incorporation and consensus. *Regional*, on the other hand, is fundamentally romantic in its insistence on the integrity of the local and the particular. And yet, paradoxically, both neoclassical and romantic thought have historically aimed at accessing and articulating much the same ideal values, principles, and truths, albeit by different avenues and from alternative perspectives. Blake's statement that "Opposition is True Friendship," then, serves us well as a reminder that perhaps our greatest challenge in all discussions about regionalism and the humanities is to resist the desire for consensus and closure, opting instead to delight in the very irreconcilability of those things that most distinguish us one from another. For, in the greatest paradox of all, those may be the very things that reveal to us just how much alike we actually are, as persons, as regions, and as national entities.

Notes

1. See, for example, Yi-Fu Tuan, *Topophilia: A Study of Environmental Perception, Attitudes, and Values* (New York: Columbia University Press, 1990); and, more recently, Yi-Fu Tuan, *Space and Place*.

2. Immanuel Kant, "Idea for a Universal History with a Cosmopolitan Purpose," in *Kant: Political Writings*, trans. H. B. Nisbet, ed. Hans Reiss (Cambridge: Cambridge University Press, 1970), 51.

3. Steven Vertovic and Robin Cohen, eds. *Conceiving Cosmopolitanism: Theory, Context, and Practice* (Oxford: Oxford University Press, 2002), x.

4. Ivan Turgenev, *Rudin*, trans. Constance Garnett (London: William Heinemann, 1894), 222, quoted in Mark Story, introduction to *Poetry and Ireland Since 1800: A Source Book*, ed. Mark Story (London: Routledge, 1988), 5.

5. Timothy Brennan, "Cosmopolitanism and Internationalism," in *Debating Cosmopolitics*, ed. Daniele Archibugi (London: Verso, 2003), 40–51, 45.

6. *Dictionary of American Regional English*, ed. Joan Houston Hall, http://polyglot.lss.wisc.edu/dare/ (accessed April 19, 2008). Here and elsewhere in this essay, I have turned both to traditional print materials and to electronic ones like Web sites, in part because these two vehicles themselves epitomize the contesting impulses toward globalization and locality. Any conventional printed book or journal is tied to a particular place (and time) in a way that the infinitely portable and placeless World Wide Web is not, just as the former is usually the product of some formal, often academic, process of peer review while the latter is for the most part entirely open ground,

without formal rules for vetting what may be posted there by anyone with access to the Internet.

7. *Dictionary of American Regional English*, vol. 1, *Introduction and A–C*, ed. Frederic G. Cassidy (Cambridge MA: Harvard University Press, 1985), xvi.

8. John Malyon, "Artists by Movement: American Regionalism, 1930s," ArtCyclopedia, http://www.artcyclopedia.com/history/regionalism.html. Because of its virtually universal currency and easy accessibility, the World Wide Web exerts an unusual shaping influence upon discourse, an influence that interestingly *preserves* differences and distinctions of the kind involved in the taxonomy of regionalism—even as it tends to level those distinctions—by presenting all of them together, "unsorted" and therefore unprivileged, as happens when one conducts an Internet search. For this reason, I have deliberately included numerous Internet sources for examples in the present discussion.

9. Michael Delahunt, "Regionalism or regionalism," ArtLex: Art Dictionary, http://www.artlex.com/ArtLex/r/regionalism.html.

10. Donna M. Campbell, "Regionalism and Local Color Fiction, 1865–1895," Washington State University, s.v., "Literary Movements," http://www.wsu.edu/~campbelld/amlit/lcolor.html (accessed April 19, 2008).

11. David C. Pierce and Richard C. Wiles, "A Place for Regionalism?" *The Hudson Valley Regional Review: A Journal of Regional Studies*, Bard College, http://www.hudsonrivervalley.net/hrvr/essays/regional.php (accessed April 19, 2008).

12. *Scottish Women Poets of the Romantic Period*, ed. Stephen C. Behrendt and Nancy J. Kushigian (Alexandria VA: Alexander Street Press, 2002).

13. William Shakespeare, *A Midsummer Night's Dream*, ed. R. A. Foakes (Cambridge: Cambridge University Press, 2003), act 5, scene 1, lines 15–17.

14. Percy Bysshe Shelley, "On Life," in *Shelley's Poetry and Prose*, ed. Donald H. Reiman and Neil Fraistat, 2nd ed. (New York: W. W. Norton, 2002), 507. Shelley's essay was first published in 1819.

15. William Blake, "Auguries of Innocence," in *The Complete Poetry and Prose of William Blake*, ed. David V. Erdman, rev. ed. (New York: Doubleday, 1988), 490.

16. Pierce and Wiles, "A Place for Regionalism?"

17. Pierce and Wiles, "A Place for Regionalism?"

18. William Blake, *The Marriage of Heaven and Hell*, in *Complete Poetry and Prose*, 42, 34, plates 20, 3. *The Marriage of Heaven and Hell* was created ca. 1790–1794.

19. "NEH Launches Initiative to Develop 10 Regional Humanities Centers throughout the Nation," May 10, 1999, http://www.neh.gov/news/archive/19990510.html.

10. The Midwest as a Colony

Transnational Regionalism

EDWARD WATTS

This essay undertakes a very general redefinition of midwestern regional culture as colonial, understood within the context of the global European diaspora of the nineteenth century. The region's cultural identity might be understood not only in conjunction with other American regions, particularly the East, but also among the colonies of the British Empire that were settled by whites during the same decades: Canada, New Zealand, Australia, and South Africa—the Dominions. This line of thinking is not intended to supersede other ways of thinking about region. Rather, it represents a way to understand the Midwest in and of itself and its relationship to other regions that also allows "region" to contribute to the scholarly exploration of American subjectivities in the wake of the civil rights movements. This in turn might contribute to the revitalization of this important but underexamined and undertheorized field in American studies, bringing the United States into global, transnational conversations about place, history, and culture.

American cultural studies have too often excluded themselves from such conversations, citing the outdated notion of American exceptionalism. That is, region has been largely omitted from the ongoing scholarly project to diversify the study of U.S. history and culture. While there have been signs of life, regionalism has garnered nowhere near the attention of other important sources of pluralization, such as race, class, and gender. In 1998 Charles Reagan Wilson conceded that "Postmodernism has not developed a regional theory. . . . Postmodernists are a specific global group, a global class that is borderless and without region or sense of any meaningful place. The capitalist market swamps local traditions. Places survive only as collectibles."[1] While Wilson's impulse to contextualize region in terms of internationalist or global perspectives is encouraging, it overlooks the fact that, while higher forms of art have explored postmodernity, politics and economics have become increasingly local and vernacular. In the post–cold war era, *region* has acquired a new transnational meaning, while still retaining its older, intranational definition. Throughout the former outposts of the British, Soviet, and other European empires, region has reemerged as a vital force, shaping international events in the postimperial world. Bosnia was once a region; now it's a nation. More recently, regions that stretched over more than one nation— Kurdistan, Chechnya, and Kashmir, for example—have entered the global conversation as regions that problematize the boundaries of nations. Therefore, postcolonialism—rather than postmodernism— might be deployed as a way of reformulating the relation of American regions to the American nation, or, some would say, the American empire.

As such, this line of thought is meant to work in conjunction with the most important recent work in American regionalism: Tom Lutz's *Cosmopolitan Vistas: American Regionalism and Literary Value.* Lutz appropriates Zitkala-Ša's term *crossroads*—used by the Indian author to describe her interstitial position between assimilated boarding school experience and tribal identity—to define regionalism's place between the cosmopolitan and the local. Invoking Edward Said, Gayatri Spivak, and a number of other postcolonial theorists, Lutz tracks American literary history between 1870 and 1930 as a negotiation between these oppositions involving race, class, gender, and finally place.[2] Postcolonialism—especially that strain of it that studies the Dominions—addresses parallel narratives on their in-between nature throughout the European diaspora. Looking at the same period addressed by Lutz, my intent is to widen his argument in regard to both geographic scope and extraliterary forms of nationalist and regionalist self-definition.

Region has been largely overlooked as a field of scholarly enquiry because of the emphasis on non–place specific subjectivities favored by a sequence of academic generations: from humanists of the 1950s to the multiculturalists of the 1990s, the conversation has been national or postnational in scope. Such exceptionalist exclusions have left American studies offstage in regard to international scholarly developments that might help us better understand the United States as a nation with a strikingly complex international legacy and presence. For example, despite the fact that postcolonial studies has pushed the word "colonial" beyond its chronological origins, the colonial era still ends for the United States with 1776, although only a small percentage of the territory that would become the nation was decolonized at that moment. Such a national(-ist) narrative positions the East's regional culture as *the* national culture, a position from which it then pursued the political and cultural colonization of the rest of what would become the nation.

In the wake of the transnationalization of both "colony" and "region," scholars of American regions could profit by examining the limits of their own fields. This conversation has already started: historians of British Dominion are already looking at American regions as cognates to their own. In 2003, historians of and from the Dominions attended a conference on the spread of "Angloworld" in the long nineteenth century. My paper was on the influence of James Fenimore Cooper on literary nationalism in the Dominions. I feared being accused of suggesting that the Dominions were simply mini-Americas, de facto colonies of the United States, that my paper would be viewed as implicitly celebrating "Coca-colonization"—the pervasiveness of American corporate ubiquity.[3]

James Belich, chair of the Department of History at the University of Auckland and one of the most prominent scholars of New Zealand history, gave the keynote.[4] He addressed the emergence of hypercolonies between 1800 and 1850 around the world. Such colonies were

PLACE IS A RELATIONSHIP

characterized by the removal or marginalization of indigenous populations, the simultaneous development of urban and rural spaces, industrial and agrarian economies operating in tandem, and a diverse and fast-growing white immigrant population. Last, each had an Anglo-based, elitist ruling class with close personal, financial, and political ties to the empire's center. In these colonies, systems of centralized control instilled patterns of economic, political, and cultural dependence to assure the loyalty of the settlers (and the resources they controlled) to the empire. The *hyper-* in *hypercolonies* is in reference to speed: what needed 120 years in Boston or Charleston took 20 in Sydney, Toronto, Wellington, Johannesburg, or Cincinnati, Belich added without skipping a beat. Belich portrayed the American Midwest as part of the same pattern of hypercolonization and used data from Ontario in Canada, Otago in New Zealand, and Ohio in the United States interchangeably. In brief, he had arrived at a conclusion similar to mine: the Midwest didn't belong only in conversations about the history of American regions. Rather its history was part of larger international processes involving the mechanisms of imperialism, the globalization of capitalism, the commercialization and industrialization of agricultural production, and the diaspora of European populations. American regionalism has usually been discussed as a largely intranational affair, with the occasional inclusion of bits of Canada or Mexico excused as reflecting the arbitrary nature of map-making in the nineteenth century.[5]

On a smaller scale than Belich, over the last fifty years, midwestern historians Richard Wade, John Mack Faragher, Jon Gjerde, Andrew R. L. Cayton, Eric Hindraker, and Susan Gray have all borrowed from the language of colonial studies to describe regional experience.[6] In their detachment of midwestern regional history from the triumphalist narrative of the nationalist school, they create a context for internationalizing their subject. That is, they point to the difficulties, diversities, and divergences of regional experience throughout the nineteenth century, suggesting a far more complex process than the narrative of democratization and assimilation rooted in Frederick Jackson Turner's famous "Frontier" thesis. The narrative of national cultural consolidation is an incomplete reading that overlooks Turner's defense of "section" throughout the latter half of his career. As a context for work on the Midwest, it is fifty years old: in *Planting Cornbelt Culture* (1953), Richard Lyle Power used "Yankee Cultural Imperialism" to describe the deliberate effort of New England culture to rein over the non-Anglo, non-Protestant, and noncommercial agriculturally oriented folks they found in Indiana.[7]

Such language has been sporadically employed by midwesternists ranging from literary critic James Hurt to urban historian Jon C. Teaford.[8] The understanding of the Midwest as a colony—or at least as a region subject to many of the same asymmetries and misrepresentations typical of colonial experience—should not be mistaken for placement of it in what has become known as subaltern studies. Students of British imperialism draw a sharp line between understanding the administration and exploitation of West Africa or India and their occupation and settlement of Australia or Upper Canada. White settlers—Anglo or otherwise—experienced nothing like the oppression and victimization suffered by nonwhite populations in those places. In fact, white settlers might be said to become "colonial" (as opposed to "colonizer") when they perceive themselves as simultaneously victimizer of indigenous populations and as victims (to a lesser degree) of colonial, second-class citizenship in the empire. Further west, in *Legacy of Conquest*, Patricia Nelson Limerick has disparaged such "would-be" "disgruntled colonials" for misappropriating the term.[9] Yet Limerick's subjects are the landholders and ranchers; the plains and mountainous West, in regard to class, never developed the critical mass of small farmers and urban working-class populations that characterize midwestern agriculture, even though those farmers were often bankrupted and forced to migrate by predatory speculators and the workers were systemically displaced and exploited by national and international corporate entities. However, it has been suggested that colonial whites who claim no nativist hegemony and who seek to lessen and come to terms with the legacies of white conquest can be called *colonials*, so long as they are still distinguished from the *colonized* indigenes.[10] For example, the overreaction of the federal

PLACE IS A RELATIONSHIP

government to intraregional conflicts in the Midwest—such as the Whiskey Rebellion of 1794, the Black Hawk War of 1832, or the Populist Movement of the 1890s—evidences a national fear that the settlers were either too immature to handle their own affairs or that they might not need the protection offered by the nation. Either way, a more narrowly defined national identity was imposed to police the challenges to empire offered by both nonwhite subject peoples *and* the peripheral whites.

Finally, many historians of the British Dominions often refer retroactively to the separate areas they study as "regions" of the empire. In such a taxonomy, former colonies such as Australia and Canada become regions under an assumption that, through the leveling ideology of Commonwealth policy, they have achieved equality—cultural and sociological as well as political and economic—with England in the British Empire. However, their cultures are more often described as postcolonial—characterized by their complex and entangled relationship to the mother country that sent settlers into lands taken from a removed indigenous population. Postcolonial cultures assume a former (if not perpetual) condition of marginality, of being behind or peripheral, in comparison to the imperial home. As such, despite hopes of being defined as regions from the early twentieth century forward, most historians still acknowledge that having been a colony is an inescapable and defining characteristic in the self-conscious identity of the former Dominions.

Such an effort—to relabel colonies as regions—brings three terms into question: nation, colony, and region. The variety of ways in which these terms now overlap opens new understandings of the relationships of different American regions to each other and, more significantly, extends the study of regionalism beyond the borders of nation. Specifically, by defining the Midwest as a colony of the East Coast–based nation, especially during the nineteenth century, its characteristic traits can be reconsidered not only in regard to its role in the nation, but it can also more generally be revalued as part of the nineteenth-century global diaspora of European populations, as opposed to its current image—the nation's agrarian heartland. The identification of the Midwest's relation to the nation as colonial in particular draws attention to the asymmetrical and nonreciprocal relation of the region to the nation, since region connotes difference based on geographical space rather than on cultural coercions and imbalances.

Arguments like these have been long in coming, and their role is to flesh out and more fully apply the transnational and global approach to midwestern regionalism and American expansionism they imply. But let's not dismiss Turner's concept of regionalism too abruptly. His 1909 foundational essay, "The Ohio Valley in American History," basically defined the Midwest as a cultural region distinct from the colonialist political entity of the Old Northwest.[11] In his essay, Turner boasts that, with the addition of the Ohio Valley, "A new strain was added to the American nation, a new element was fused into the combination which we call the United States, a new flavor was given to the American spirit."[12] These emergent notions of diversification of American identity—keeping in mind the composite and singular ideal at the core of the more famous 1893 "frontier" thesis—represent a growing sympathy in Turner's thought toward a more supple and horizontal idea of the nation and its places and populations. Given the open imperialism of the post–Spanish American War era in which Turner was writing, his sympathy with the anti-imperialist energies unleashed by that war might clearly be linked to his reconsideration of the relation of region and nation.

The version of nationalism more dominant in Turner's era was that of his friend Theodore Roosevelt. Moreover, Roosevelt's central definition of the American race shares assumptions with a later British counterpart, Winston Churchill: the first chapter of Roosevelt's 1894 *The Winning of the West* is "The Spread of English-Speaking Peoples." In 1955 Churchill would turn this phrase into the title for his own series of like-minded imperial historiography, *History of the English Speaking Peoples*, reflecting that moment's cold war–era version of empire building around the American superpower to which Britain wished to attach itself. Each usage suggests a link between language, race, and a grand master narrative of the expansion of a single civilization, one based in common values of culture, behavior, and, inevitably, superiority. Roosevelt's wielding of these concepts, however, was far less subtle than both the early Turner and the later Churchill. Nonetheless, the bully pulpit he assumed for himself as a politician informed his identity as a historian as well; the "pulpit"—also a place where ministers give sermons—ascended by Roosevelt in his history of the conquest of the American frontier by English-speaking whites is worked out as a divinely ordained morality tale, one whose central premise is the expansion of interregional sameness, not intercultural exchange or dissemination that germinates regional divergence. It should be noted that Roosevelt drew profound parallels throughout *The Winning of the West* between Dominion and American western experiences, but his effort was to prove the consolidation of racial expansion; my project has more to do with its diversification.

Roosevelt laid out his vision of national and racial unity in that opening chapter. In regard to settlement, he writes, "Some latter-day writers deplore the enormous immigration to our shores as making us a heterogeneous instead of an homogeneous people; but as a matter of fact we are less heterogeneous at the present day than we were at the outbreak of the Revolution. Our blood was as much mixed a century ago as it is now." In his narrative, America provides a site for reuniting strains of Germanic blood from throughout northern Europe: "But we were being rapidly fused into one people. As the Celt from Cornwall and the Saxon of Wessex are now alike Englishmen, so in 1775 Hollander and Huguenot, whether in New York or South Carolina, had become Americans, undistinguishable from the New Englanders and Virginians. . . . When the great western movement began we were already a people by ourselves."[13] Roosevelt's tribal nation is morphed into Manifest Destiny, and he retells the same story of conquest over the next thousand pages. Unlike Turner, who saw Ohio as the genesis of an elastic national identity based on exchange or dialogue, Roosevelt is concerned only with transcription and imposition. There is no region in Roosevelt's America, only nation.

Roosevelt is more usefully read now—one hundred years later—as a primary rather than a secondary source. A product of his times, his work is demonstrative of the growing need in the English-speaking world at the turn of the century to reformulate the relationships of hypercolonies to the national metropolises, reflecting a defensive impulse within the eastern establishment. Just as the Midwest was experiencing its own growing pains—the literary success of midwestern writers and the Chicago World's Fair's anxious cosmopolitanism coincided with mass farm bankruptcies, the Dawes Act's forcible acculturation of Indian tribes, and the rise of the Ku Klux Klan in Indiana—similar growing pains in other settler-colonies catalyzed similar recurring patterns of exclusion and violence, impeding continued development. Once and for all, a decision was needed: should their rapid trajectory of growth lead them to independent nationhood, or should more horizontal arrangements allow them to stay attached to their parent nations?

In brief, the late nineteenth century found the hypercolonies feeling thwarted and frustrated as to issues of identity, centrality, and inclusion—patterns that characterize, among other things, the literature of each from the period. Authors of tales of agrarian failure in the colonies, once the boom was over, found their villains in the financial centers of the imperial cores: Henry Lawson in Australia, Olive Schreiner in South Africa, William Satchell in New Zealand, Alexander Begg in Canada, and Hamlin Garland in the Midwest tell versions of the same story. Throughout, they reflect an important disillusionment on the part of colonials when they found that their place in the empire was not what they had been led to believe it was, as visions like Roosevelt's erased them from national or imperial narratives.

Shifts in both institutional policy and imperial culture between 1890 and 1914 show how the next step in the relations of both the Dominions to the empire and the Midwest to the nation was informed by parallel dialogues between the metropolitan parent and the colonial child, in a manner of speaking. Even though the individual British Dominions moved toward nationhood while the Midwest must still be viewed as a region, the distinction increasingly mattered and mattered very little. My point is not that the Midwest is a colony only in some vague, theoretical sense but that it shares some very specific characteristics with the Dominions more precisely. These patterns were established not only in the processes and moment of the settlement era, but also through a cultivated awareness of their marginality and similar responses to it—culturally and politically—in the decades before the First World War.

Coming into the 1890s, both the British Empire and the United States feared history. With the models of the American Revolution, the War of 1812, and the Civil War, some hard choices were needed to avoid repeating those patterns of violence and division within a set of Anglophone, white-based communities, all tinged with regional or colonial complications.[14] On one end, unilateral nationalists such as Roosevelt reflect an unwavering fear of division, losing one's colonies or regions, and so implicitly endorse a tighter rein on potential sources of divergence or diversity. A literary analogue might be William Dean Howells, whose calls for American writing resonate over his long and public editorial and authorial careers. For example, in *Criticism and Fiction*, Howells writes, "It is the difference of the American novelist's ideals from those of the Englishman's that gives him his advantage and seems to promise him the future." Roosevelt's and Howells's shared assumption that "American" is white, Anglophone, and superior reflect the same impulse toward national singularity, even as Howells encouraged "local color" in his contributors' writing.[15]

This way of thinking inevitably accedes a hierarchy of regions, with all roads leading east. A British counterpart might be Rudyard Kipling, raised in the colonies just as Howells was from Ohio (colonials are often complicit or more in the patterns of their colonization). Kipling's narratives likewise describe a superior British Empire never at fault for the wars that disrupt its harmony (though Kipling at least admitted the ubiquity of violence), with all ships sailing back to London.[16] Furthermore, each constructs his national or imperial narrative not only in opposition to the inferior others but also in opposition to English-speaking populations who allowed themselves to be distracted and forget the millennial and racial underpinnings of their mission as universalizing civilizers.

For example, in each imperial nation, the development of oppositional local nationalisms, manifest as sectionalism, was rejected. Roosevelt's,

Churchill's, Howells's, and Kipling's implicit Anglo-Saxonism points to a convergence in their definitions of nations and empires as well. In British imperialist discourse, the bête noire is the American Revolution; in the equally monocultural, American narrative of Roosevelt or Howells, it is the Civil War. As defined by Howard W. Odum and Henry Estill Moore in 1938, sectionalism is oppositional and reactionary and, therefore, inadequate for expressing or developing place-specific policy or culture that is reflective of distinctive local characteristics.[17] It should be noted then that both imperial nationalists and colonial regionalists equally and appropriately rejected sectionalism as a vehicle for local resistance to the metropolitan model. Even as he opposed Kipling's England-centered imperial model, British colonial theoretician Richard Jebb in 1905, while applauding the restraint of Canadian nationalism, colored the American Revolution as sectionalist at its core: "Indeed it may be said that Canadian nationalism was founded upon a repugnance to American nationalism."[18] Likewise, in *Crumbling Idols*, Hamlin Garland decried Southern "provincialism" as nearly as dangerous as the reactionary antisectionalism that catalyzed Roosevelt's monolithic nationalism.[19]

Despite their differences—Roosevelt and Kipling on the one side and Jebb and Garland on the other—all feared sectionalism, but each side for its own reasons. For the imperialists, of course, sectionalism is divisive and contrary to their goals. More importantly, for localists in both the United States and the Dominions, sectionalism discourages genuine localism by coloring all local self-expression as undifferentiated otherness—an oppositional thinking that had created three wars they viewed as internecine and avoidable. Sectionalism is reactionary and reductive, a barrier to true local self-exploration because the local is defined exclusively as the antimetropolitan. As such, sectionalism must be avoided at all costs.

Nonetheless, the specter of sectionalism could be and was used by imperial nationalists to discourage and squelch regionalist or localist impulses, by insisting on understanding the collective identity of the nation or empire as constructed on a set of opposed binaries: self or other, white or savage, civilization or anarchy, order or chaos. By contrast, regionalism and colonial nationalism commonly explore a middle ground, a way of expressing local needs and achieving local goals within the construct of nation or empire. However, this demands not only an interventionist yet reasonable definition of regionalism but also a more diverse definition of nation in theory and supple definition of nationalism in practice.

Back to the main story: by 1890 or so, the former hypercolonies had come to be as prosperous and as populated as other nations around the world, and so some type of accommodation was needed. One solution, discussed above in regard to Roosevelt and Kipling, was a more stringent integration of the region into the imperial nation. But there was another option. In the United States the answer was regionalism; and in Britain Jebb coined the oxymoronic phrase "colonial nationalism," a concept not unlike that of Garland's demand for regional self-identification. Outside the rituals of politics, these two terms mean nearly the same thing. Starting with the United States, in the late nineteenth century, there was an increasing recognition of the inevitable entanglement of the nation's regions with their need to be balanced against the nation as a whole in the national imaginary, keeping in check the excesses of each—the potential of each to distort local needs by monopolizing the terms of discussion. Neither is secessionist.[20] Of the East and the Midwest, each simply desires to be dealt with by the other symmetrically and reciprocally. In reference to the 1890s, the painter Grant Wood in 1935 disparaged midwesterners for their lasting "colonial subservience" to New York, while more directly offering a working definition of regionalism: "[Regionalism] has been a revolt against cultural nationalism—that is, the tendency of artists to ignore or deny the fact that there are important differences, psychologically and otherwise, between the different regions of America. But this does not mean that Regionalism, in turn, advocates a concentration on local peculiarities; such an approach results in anecdotalism and local color."[21] What Wood and other 1930s regionalists had in mind was essentially a redefined nationalism—one that was horizontal rather than vertical. Thus, in a more scholarly way, Walter Prescott Webb's *Divided We Stand: The Crisis of a Frontierless Democracy* extended Turner's later ideas about regionalism's necessary policing of nationalism's monolithic aspirations.[22] Updating the terminology inherited from the nineteenth century, Wood's and Webb's view is not sectional in that it is not oppositional. Resistance to and affiliation with nationalizing institutions are entangled, and simultaneous efforts are needed to find the balance appropriate to the physical and cultural space of the region.

During the last twenty years, regionalism has been underrepresented in the ongoing reformulation of American studies as a field of inquiry in the postmodern age. Discussions of the current understanding of nationalism in American studies usually invoke the multicultural, basing the plurality on race, class, and gender. As a result, scholarly conversations have been guided more by inductive rather than reductive reasonings, a methodological pluralization suited to the complexity of its subjects. To these, regionalists would add place and insist that to exclude regional difference from our discussion of the cultural plurality in the United States would be as absurd as the exclusion of any of the other three. And just as advocacy of the other three is rooted in a rejection of oppressive historical hierarchies, so too is regionalism. But all four represent a process, not an arrival: through each is achieved the engagement of a fairer balance between the historically included and the historically marginalized.[23] The civil rights movement did not end racial discrimination but rather initiated a greater awareness of it, a trajectory that must be perpetually policed.

Likewise, regionalism was and is not only a means of correcting historical imbalances, but it is also a tool for the diagnosis and prevention of ongoing patterns of inappropriate cultural or imperial nationalism. However, this modus operandi can be neither uniformly reactionary nor uncritically localist. A more constructive and appropriate strategy must instead be based on moments of interregional exchange. In certain cases, cultural nationalism can and must be viewed as a positive good. However, when cultural nationalism comes at the cost of regional integrity, some form of resistance must be brought forth to restore balance and reciprocity. Andrew Cayton and Susan Gray's collection of reflective essays by scholars of the Midwest, *The*

American Midwest: Essays on Regional History, articulates the revitalized and diverse ways in which midwestern history is largely a narrative of a continual tension between the dual allegiances of midwesterners to both their region and their nation.

Richard Jebb's "colonial nationalism," a concept likewise defined by incessant contestations of the local and the imperial, has survived a century, and it might now be reconsidered as a paradigm for regionalism in the age of globalization. First, Jebb used the terms *colony* and *region* interchangeably, observing that, in the age of steam travel as transportation technology evolved from sail and wagon to steam and rail, the physical or spatial separation of the Dominions and colonies from the imperial core mattered less and less. Second, this passage from *Studies in Colonial Nationalism* describes a pattern of partial detachment from empire that sounds a lot like Wood's articulation of midwestern regionalism: "So far from repressing any national diversification otherwise possible, the British Empire is proving itself the fruitful parent of new nationalities; not only safeguarding their infant growth, but offering them, as they reach maturity, a career of national utility in imperial partnership, as an alternative to the barren impotence of self-centred isolation."[24] That is, Jebb rewrites imperial history in the settlement colonies as a march toward a degree of local autonomy that rejects sectionalism or secessionism. He views the colonies' relationship to the imperial center as one that was negotiated on both sides. And with the exception of South Africa and the ethnic and class-based peculiarities of the Boer War, the commonwealth was created following Jebb's theories of negotiated nationhood.

In 1988 John Eddy and Deryck Schreuder did for the Dominions what Cayton and Gray did for the Midwest.[25] In *The Rise of Colonial Nationalism*, they used Jebb to bring together the leading historians of the colonies in question and asked them to relate their work to the larger issue of the "dual inscription" of the settlement colony—their loyalty to both the local and the national, or imperial. Their introduction defines their project: "The ideological thrust of colonial nationalism here at issue expressed a different outlook to that adopted by the revolutionary leaders of the great American rebellion and war of independence. Significantly, it was closer to those of some of the Loyalist leaders who departed the America of 1776 for British North America—not because they rejected a reform of British policy towards the Thirteen Colonies, but rather because they refused to separate from the Crown to do so. The colonial nationalists of this book pursued a path of 'independence' which was reformist rather than revolutionary, gradualist rather than confrontationalist."[26] Oliver McDonagh, Keith Sinclair, and others responded with essays not unlike those edited by Cayton and Gray: narratives of regional and colonial history informed by a constant interchange between the empire and the colony. Just like midwestern regionalist scholars, they rely not only upon the development of local self-awareness in the colonies but also on the development of a form of nationalism in the metropolis that is less rigidly hierarchical and jealous of losing its ascendant position in the imperial nation. The historians of both books conclude, of course, that neither process is or ever will be complete. Yet they share a recognition that, ever since the 1890s, the local—in the English-speaking world, that is—has been somehow more empowered to compete with the national or the imperial than it had been before either American regionalism or Dominion-based colonial nationalism created an intellectual framework for deconstructing and challenging the images and economies that had left them on the margins of each respective imperial nation.

The last two decades have witnessed two groups of historians working in virtual isolation from one another. Just as Commonwealth historians have been working to redefine what a "settlement colony" is to the empire, so have Americanists been struggling with the relationship of regions to the nation. Read together, however, their work shows unmistakable parallels. No longer must we view terms like *colony*, *region*, *nation*, and *empire* as entities existing on different sides of the planet or in other places: the United States had colonies and the British Empire had regions. Turn-of-the-century figures like Jebb and Garland were crucial to creating a space for cultural localization in the age of steam-based transportation and print-based mass media. The issues of distance and the ability of cultural nationalists to

PLACE IS A RELATIONSHIP

monitor and police local divergence, however, made the premises of their arguments all the more tenable. In today's age of accelerated globalization, do the same arguments work? Can a balance between the national and global and the local and regional still be maintained? And is such surveillance on the part of regionalists still needed? Under the paradigms of balance set forth by Jebb and Garland, regionalism and colonial nationalism are not only still needed but have, in fact, successfully responded to new forms of delocalization engendered by the postmodern age.

To focus this discussion, I pose one last rhetorical question: does the Midwest serve the same function in current American culture as the Dominions do in British culture? Few talk these days of culture in either without adding an "s." A leftover from the days of Roosevelt and Kipling (really Matthew Arnold), the notion of a nondiversified national (or human) culture has been mostly put out to pasture. Nonetheless, such pluralization, ironically, has usually been limited to the metropolises, and the peripheralization of the former colonies and regions has been perpetuated by the denial of their participation in the globalization of metropolitan cultures. Other developments further complicate the issue—much has changed since the premises of both regionalism and colonial nationalism were laid out a century ago. Global superpower has swung from Britain to the United States; early-twenty-first-century electronic media often transgress, transpose, or simply ignore international borders.

Still, Grant Wood's old notion of "cultural nationalism"—as a means of culling what matters and what is current from what is trivial and out-of-date—is still in the air in the wake of the fall of the iron curtain and 9/11. As such, a continuing parallelism is yet appropriate. Using the Midwest's media representation in American books, television, and cinema and Australia's representation on these platforms in Britain, a case can be made for continuing to cultivate regionalism, colonial nationalism, or any other locally based means of cultural self-identification. The threats of homogenization and placeless sameness in the era of multinational franchising cannot be understood simply in terms of resistance to an overaggressive federal government or in the reactionary celebration of the local at the expense of the global. Rather, the contemporary question of localist study has to do with making conscious choices—and teaching our students and readers to make conscious choices. Wal-Mart cannot and should not be banned or blamed for its drain on local small businesses, but local consumers might learn the consequences to their local community if they choose to shop there.

By reminding them of other options, regionalist scholars, authors, painters, performers, and others can educate their communities about the importance of their own role in either the perpetuation or mitigation of the forces that threaten to make their place just like any other place. For most Americans, *colonial* accurately describes only the era before 1776, because they assume colonialism is both external and oppressive, something that must be cast off in a process of self-liberation. On the other hand, *region* just recalls cold geography. The interventionist mission of regionalist studies is aided by *colony* precisely because it brings with it all the connotations and implications needed to bring their thinking about geography back to life. At the same time, it asks scholars themselves to rethink the local circumstances and conditions they study—to study the local has become trivial. To study the local as manifestations of larger and longer stories about empires and races, however, is to seek out and find broader audiences.

Cultural nationalism in the United States has always had two uses for the Midwest: as a museum-piece source of preindustrial virtue and as an undifferentiated hinterland that might be either populated by harmless laughingstocks or dangerous psychopaths, or both.[27] The first—the *Field of Dreams* approach—is thoroughly culturally nationalist: the sophisticated and jaded postindustrial coasts can be cleansed by the Midwest's peacefully democratic values. Aside from issues of accuracy, this writes regional history into national history, appropriating and misrepresenting the region only so far as it serves a national need for a living memory of a unified and unifying past. Shouldn't it have been a bloodied Black Hawk, or broken farmer, or mixed-race *voyageur* walking out of the corn?

The innocence of the *Field of Dreams* approach is very close to the laughingstock image—for example, Woody Boyd of *Cheers* fame is a hayseed whose long history goes way back to the eighteenth century. Moreover, on October 2, 2003, a Gannett News Service story about a new ABC-TV sitcom—"Married to the Kellys"—juxtaposed a sophisticated New York novelist against his lunkheaded, suburban–Kansas City in-laws. To Gannett's credit, the headline was "ABC's Midwest Does Not Exist."[28] Nonetheless, it does exist in the minds of the show's producers, cultural nationalists who see the nation's culture as a single entity with every community measured against an apogee of coastal sophistication. The last image—oddly enough personified by the same actor as the lunkhead—is *Natural Born Killers'* psychopathic killer Mickey (trailed, coincidentally, by an Australian tabloid TV reporter), the leftover legacy of James Hall's Indian Hater. The white, backwoods killer—though more commonly an Appalachian image, it is also represented in Bruce Springsteen's song "Nebraska" and Martin Sheen's film *Badlands*, both of which are based on Charley Starkweather—is the most damaging of the colonizing images generated by cultural nationalists since it suggests that the violence of the frontier period had never truly ended, even a century after Turner had announced the frontier's geographical demise.[29]

In response, do contemporary regionalists rebut these images without venturing into sectionalism's xenophobia? In music, the Midwest can boast the blues of Chicago and Detroit and the alt-country movement of the Ohio basin as ways in which the Midwest acts on a global stage without the mediating supervision of the coasts. Since electronic media rely so heavily on coastal funding, let's look at literature. Right now, there's a strong regionalist ethos in midwestern writing. Many good books are being written that don't just set their stories in the Midwest but rather use the peculiarities of regional history, language, tradition, and demographics to tell stories that could be set in no other place. Toni Morrison's *Song of Solomon* or *Sula*, Richard Powers's *The Goldbug Variations*, Louise Erdrich's entire oeuvre, David Foster Wallace's *Infinite Jest*, and many others—not to mention Garrison Keillor—offer serious considerations of place in their complex fictions. Many of these writers are nonwhite and none of them is rural. Their

Midwest is multiracial, historically turgid, and not centered around agriculture. While this image reflects certain metropolitan and cosmopolitan presences in the region, each author blends those presences with locally distinctive characteristics and quirks and does not measure their place in comparison with the monolithic scale of cultural nationalism. It's not more or less sophisticated; it's just different. Regionalism and nationalism—particularism and universalism in the literary sense—are still in contention in their books; and that's a good thing, as now even the Gannett News Service recognizes the absurdity of the usual stereotypes and the damage they do.

Can the same be said of the colonial nations? To establish a manageable scale, I'll focus on Australia's self-representations that Britain embraces and buys. Televising nineteenth-century drama is popular in Britain. However, when they show their own, they're as complicated as Hardy or Dickens. When they rebroadcast Australian stories like *The Thorn Birds* or *The Man from Snowy River*, they are antipodal children's shows that could be compared to "Little House on the Prairie"—preindustrial and based in a closer, uncorrupted, and fictitious intimate relation to nature, an authenticity supposedly lost in the jaded metropolises. Next, the clown resonates in Paul Hogan, the Melbourne construction worker who became Crocodile Dundee, selling the rest of the world the image of Australia as a nineteenth-century backwoods rather than the complex immigrant- and urban-based culture it became in the second half of the twentieth century. Although he's the victorious trickster, his "mates" are classic colonial "larrikins."[30] Lastly, for dangerous backwoodsmen, there are the Mad Max films.

While these are not the only Australian movies to succeed overseas, each reflects what Ross Gibson, following Peter Fuller's lead, calls an "antipodean" (as opposed to Australian) aesthetic: "By definition the orientation of an antipodean aesthetic must locate England as the principal reference point in the program."[31] Much of Australian culture then is still antipodean and thus provincial—defined more by what it is not, than what it is, just as midwestern culture is often defined by being everything the coasts are *not*. Colonial whites who embrace antipodean culture accept themselves as displaced Britons, extending the empire, and not much concerned with local distinctiveness beyond its ability to serve the need for cultural hierarchy in the empire. Elsewhere, I differentiate "literature in the Midwest" from "midwestern literature."[32] On the level of theory, the point is the same: just because a cultural product is generated in a certain region, it does not necessarily serve or reflect that region's needs. Only the careful interpretation of the roles of place and cultural politics in any given work can reveal its role in either perpetuating empire or articulating region.

In further reference to Australia, Richard Nile has brought together scholars in a book debating this issue called *The Australian Legend and Its Discontents*. David Carter in particular stands out. After describing current conflicts over Australian identity, Carter writes, "the more inclusive, pluralist, open-ended ways of defining Australia have moved firmly onto the agenda, and have done so not only in official domains or on large-scale national occasions but also in mundane and popular forms." And he continues, "The English heritage is gently displaced from a normative position while 'Australian' is defined as something other than an ethnic identity."[33] What's left is place, and Australia has writers like Sam Watson, David Malouf, Peter Carey, Thea Astley, and Tim Winton who narrativize an Australian place where continuity (or lack thereof) with empire is just one of many stories. The events in 1988 surrounding the bicentennial of the first fleet provided Australians with a watershed opportunity to reflect publicly on issues such as these, the conflicts between different camps of Australian historians. More recently, the public debates over 1993's *Mabo* ruling, recognizing the land rights of indigenous people, and the work of Kenneth Windschuttle (*The Killing of History*) have forced Australians to think hard about their history and their simultaneous complicity in and resistance to British imperialism.[34]

Perhaps that level of self-awareness, rooted in the premise of nationalism and the occasional referenda on becoming a "republic"—as opposed to constitutional monarchies within the commonwealth—will cause the erstwhile settlement colonies to diverge from the Midwest.

The prospect of nationalism gives them a degree or a premise of autonomy that regionalism cannot match. At the same time, the Coca-colonization of the world by global multinationals offers new challenges, for which the older taxonomies may be inadequate in formulating strategies for defining and maintaining local self-determination and self-expression. Yet thinking of themselves as regions might help the former colonies understand their position better now, just as thinking of themselves as colonials might help regionalists understand their own situation.

As long ago as 1957, in his groundbreaking essay "If Turner Had Looked at Canada, Australia, and New Zealand When He Wrote about the West," A. L. Burt—reflecting the general underreading of Turner's later, more supple work—summarized his ideas about why the study of regions must transcend nation: "Here we touch upon what is perhaps the most serious criticism that can be leveled at the Turner school. It is that they have studied and written as national historians without realizing the besetting sin of national history, in this as in every other country, is too exclusive a concern with what has happened within its own borders."[35] Regional historians, that is, would do better to remember that nations and empires are overrepresented on a global scale in the processes of the formation and evolution of regional identities. Asian and Mexican cultures surely inform the development of Californian culture as much as does being politically part of the United States; Asia informs Queensland. Nation and empire are only two components of many feeding into more complex local identities, including international presences that transcend the national.

Burt's recommendation has been heard: the historians represented in *The American Midwest* and *The Rise of Colonial Nationalism* continue the conversations started by Jebb, Garland, Wood, Burt, and others about the inter- and intranational patterns of regional development—political, economic, and cultural. Likewise, Australian historians such as Russell Ward have contemplated Turner's role in their own colonial histories as they look to places other than London for sources of their distinctive experiences and needs.[36] My argument turns more on the scholarly redefinition of what a colony is (and what its relationship to its metropolis is) than on whether the Midwest was ever a colony to the East the same way Massachusetts was a colony of the British Empire in 1776. A colony in the eighteenth century was one thing; in the nineteenth, another. And the Midwest can and should be studied alongside not just the other regions with whom it shares a nation, but also alongside the other colonies with whom it shared a century.

Notes

1. Wilson, *New Regionalism*, xiv–xv.

2. Tom Lutz, *Cosmopolitan Vistas: Regionalism and Literary Value* (Ithaca NY: Cornell University Press, 2004).

3. The most recent use of this term is in Steven Flusty, *De-Coca-Colonization: Making the Globe from the Inside Out* (New York: Routledge, 2003).

4. The first volume in James Belich's comprehensive history of New Zealand (Aotearoa) has been released in the United States as *Making Peoples: A History of New Zealanders from Polynesian Settlement to the End of the Nineteenth Century* (Honolulu: University of Hawaii Press, 2001).

5. See for example the most recent work in historical regionalism: Dorman, *Revolt of the Provinces*; or Wilson, *New Regionalism*. Only Wilson's introduction briefly connects the book's contents to international patterns. With regard to literary studies, only Stephanie Foote, *Regional Fictions: Culture and Identity in Nineteenth-Century American Literature* (Madison: University of Wisconsin Press, 2001) engages, however briefly, the global contexts of regional self-identification in the United States.

6. Starting with Richard Wade, *The Urban Frontier: The Rise of Western Cities, 1790–1830* (Urbana: University of Illinois Press, 1957); and Richard Lyle Powers, *Planting Corn Belt Culture: The Impress of the Upland Southerner and Yankee in the Old Northwest* (Indianapolis: Indiana Historical Society, 1953), historians of the Midwest have resisted the Turnerian myth of agrarian democratization and national cultural consolidation. Their work has been carried on in John Mack Faragher, *Sugar Creek: Life on the Illinois Prairie* (New Haven CT: Yale University Press, 1986); Jon Gjerde, *Minds of the West: Ethnocultural Evolution in the Rural Midwest, 1830–1917* (Chapel Hill: University of North Carolina Press, 1997); Andrew R. L. Cayton, *Frontier Indiana* (Bloomington: Indiana University Press, 1998) (though Cayton's impact extends beyond this work, it is his most notable contribution); and Susan E. Gray, *The Yankee West: Community Life on the Michigan Frontier* (Chapel Hill: University of North Carolina Press, 1996). See also Gray and Cayton, eds., *The American Midwest* (Bloomington: Indiana University Press, 1991), to which most of the important scholars working in these areas contributed.

7. See James Hurt, *Writing Illinois: The Prairie, Lincoln, and Chicago* (Urbana: University of Illinois Press, 1992); and Jon C. Teaford, *Cities in the Heartland: the Rise and Fall of the Industrial Midwest* (Bloomington: Indiana University Press, 1994).

8. On Powers's impact, see Edward Watts, *An American Colony: Regionalism and the Roots of Midwestern Culture* (Athens: Ohio University Press, 2002). Michael Steiner's two seminal articles on Turner have reshaped my thinking on that historian: "From Frontier to Region: Frederick Jackson Turner and the New Western History," *Pacific History Review* 64, no. 4 (November 1995): 479–501; and "The Significance of Turner's Sectional Thesis," *The Western Historical Quarterly* 10, no. 4 (October 1979): 437–66.

9. See Patricia Nelson Limerick, *The Legacy of Conquest: The Unbroken Past of the American West* (New York: W. W. Norton, 1987), 48–50.

10. See W. H. New's "Colonial Literatures," 102–19 in *New National and Post-Colonial Literatures*, ed. Bruce King (New York: Oxford University Press, 1996).

11. Frederick Jackson Turner, "The Ohio Valley in American History," in *The Frontier in American History* (1920; repr. Tucson: University of Arizona Press, 1986), 157–76.

12. Turner, "The Ohio Valley," 166.

13. Theodore Roosevelt, *The Winning of the West*, vol. 1, *From the Alleghenies to the Mississippi, 1769–1776* (New York: Putnam, 1894). References are to the Bison Books reprint (Lincoln: University of Nebraska Press, 1995), 20–21.

14. While the American Civil War might seem an odd fit for a discussion of the anxieties surrounding the separation of colonies from the mother country, turn-of-the-century British and Dominion historians discussed it as such, even if American historians find the parallel difficult. See, for example, Norman Pollock, "Metropolitan and Colonial Economies in the Nineteenth Century" in *Studies in Overseas Settlement and Population*, ed. Anthony Lemon and Norman Pollak (New York: Longman, 1980), 31–48; and Anthony Lemon, "Social and Political Development of Colonies in the Nineteenth Century" in that same collection (49–80). Each anticipates Belich's argument but never addresses the Midwest specifically, focusing instead on "regions" within the United States more generally and the effect of the Civil War in crafting a more monolithic, unilateral definition of nation.

15. William Dean Howells, *Criticism and Fiction*, in *Anthology of American Literature*, vol. 2, *Realism to the Present*, ed. George McMichael and others (New York: Macmillan, 1993). First published 1891.

16. For a discussion of Kipling and empire, see Martin Green, *Dreams of Adventure, Deeds of Empire* (New York: Basic, 1979), 264–96.

17. Howard W. Odum and Harry Estill Moore, *American Regionalism: A Cultural-Historical Approach to National Integration* (New York: Henry Holt, 1938).

18. See Richard Jebb, *Studies in Colonial Nationalism* (London: Arnold, 1905), 5.

19. My references to Garland are from his *Crumbling Idols: Twelve Essays on Art Dealing Chiefly with Literature, Painting and the Drama* (1893; repr., ed. Jane Johnson, Cambridge MA: Harvard University Press, 1960).

20. See Watts, *American Colony*, 185–201.

21. Woods is quoted and discussed at length in E. Bradford Burns, *Kinship with the Land: Regionalist Thought in Iowa, 1894–1942* (Iowa City: University of Iowa Press, 1996), 148–61.

22. Walter Prescott Webb, *Divided We Stand: The Crisis of a Frontierless Democracy* (New York: Farrar, 1937).

23. I have borrowed the concept of *process not arrival* here from Canadian postcolonial theorist Helen Tiffin. See Tiffin, "Post-Colonial Literature and Counter-Discourse," in *The Post-Colonial Studies Reader*, ed. Bill Ashcroft, Gareth Griffiths, and Helen Tiffin (London: Routledge, 1994), 95–98.

24. Jebb, *Studies in Colonial Nationalism*, 102.

25. John Eddy and Deryck Schreuder, *The Rise of Colonial Nationalism: Australia, New Zealand, Canada, and South Africa, 1880–1914* (Sydney: Allen and Unwin, 1988).

26. Eddy and Schreuder, *Rise of Colonial Nationalism*, 7.

27. The best discussion of this cultural role is in James Shortridge, *The Middle West: Its Meaning in American Culture* (Lawrence: University of Kansas Press, 1989), 27–38.

28. *Field of Dreams*, directed by Phil Alden Robinson (Universal City CA: Universal Pictures, 1989); *Cheers*, NBCTV, 1982–1993; "ABC's Midwest Does Not Exist," *Lansing State Journal*, October 10, 2003. The story was copyrighted to the Gannet News Service.

29. *Natural Born Killers*, directed by Oliver Stone (Burbank CA: Warner Brothers Pictures International, 1994); James Hall, *Sketches of History, Life and Manners in the West* (Philadelphia: H. Hall, 1835); Bruce Springsteen, "Nebraska," on *Nebraska* (Columbia Records, 1984); *Badlands*, directed by Terrence Malick (Burbank CA: Warner Brothers Pictures International, 1974).

30. See Russel Ward, *The Australian Legend* (Melbourne: Oxford University Press, 1958). Americanists might compare this with R. W. B. Lewis, *The American Adam: Innocence and Tragedy in the Nineteenth Century* (Chicago: University of Chicago Press, 1955) as a founding text in nationalist interdisciplinary scholarship.

31. Ross Gibson, *South of the West: Postcolonialism and the Narrative Construction of Australia* (Bloomington: Indiana University Press, 1992), 216. Many of my comments on Australian film are drawn from Gibson. Gibson cites Peter Fuller, *The Australian Scapegoat* (Perth: University of Western Australia Press, 1986).

32. Edward Watts, "Midwestern Literature before 1860," in *The Midwest*, ed. Judith Yaross Lee and Joseph Slade (New York: Greenwood Press, 2004), 59–71.

33. David Carter, "Past and Future," in *The Australian Legend and Its Discontents*, ed. Richard Nile (St. Lucia: University of Queensland Press, 2000), 59–80, 70–71. I recommend this book to anyone seeking a brief introduction to Australian studies.

34. Keith Windschuttle, *The Killing of History: How Literary Critics and Social Theorists are Murdering Our Past* (Sydney: Encounter, 1996).

35. A. L. Burt, "If Turner Had Looked at Canada, Australia, and New Zealand When He Wrote about the West," in *The Frontier in Perspective*, ed. Walker D. Wyman and Clifton Kroeber (Madison: University of Wisconsin Press, 1957), 59–78.

36. See Ward, *Australian Legend*, 13–29.

11. Transcending the Urban-Rural Divide

Willa Cather's Thea Kronborg Goes to Chicago

MARK A. ROBISON

Two young women are traveling by train to Chicago—country girls off to the big city. Caroline Meeber leaves Columbia City, Wisconsin, carrying a box lunch, a small trunk, a fake alligator-skin satchel, and "a yellow leather snap purse," which holds her ticket, her sister's Chicago address, and four dollars.[1] Thea Kronborg leaves Moonstone, Colorado, carrying a trunk, a telescoping canvas suitcase, and a large handbag, which holds "her trunk-key and all of her money that was not in an envelope pinned to her chemise."[2] In going to Chicago, both of these travelers cross a divide that separates their rural roots from their urban futures. Carrie Meeber, eighteen years old, does not return to Wisconsin. Thea Kronborg, sixteen, sees Moonstone only once more before leaving for good. Both women eventually quit Chicago to attain success on New York City stages. Carrie, with a modicum of talent and much luck, rises from chorus girl to headliner on Broadway while Thea, with burgeoning artistry and a modicum of luck, triumphs with the Metropolitan Opera Company. Before realizing such success, however, both meet adversity on the streets of Chicago.

Indeed, the dissonance created by a rural character's arrival in a large city propels more than a few novels of the early twentieth century. Upton Sinclair gives this fundamental conflict one of its rawest depictions in his 1906 novel, *The Jungle*; his protagonist Jurgis

Rudkus epitomizes the rural newcomer to the city, having come to Chicago from "half a dozen acres of cleared land in the midst of a wilderness."[3] This eastern European immigrant's penetration of the city, especially his ability to sustain employment, is made even more difficult by barriers of language and culture. Though Jurgis survives Chicago's urban jungle, many of his compatriots cannot escape Darwinian forces that batter and destroy them. But not every city novel is so darkly junglelike. In Willa Cather's hands, Chicago is much more benignant toward her protagonist Thea Kronborg than that city is toward Jurgis Rudkus or even Carrie Meeber. Through her depiction of the relative ease with which Thea transfers to the city, Cather reduces conceptual distance between rural and urban spaces and, in so doing, bids readers to reconfigure concepts of region.

The protagonist of Theodore Dreiser's 1900 novel *Sister Carrie* finds the city economically inhospitable to an unskilled female laborer. Her low-paying job in a shoe factory barely pays her rent, inadequately supplies clothing, and affords none of the city's alluring pleasures. Without a coat to protect her, Carrie soon becomes ill, loses her position, and despairs of finding another. Faced with imminent return to her rural hometown, Carrie "rapidly assumes the cosmopolitan standard of virtue," parlaying her beauty into a situation as mistress to a traveling salesman.[4] It is only by abandoning a rural-based morality and surrendering herself to male economic protection that Carrie remains in Chicago to enjoy its attractions, and she partakes of these largely on terms dictated by her lovers. Susan J. Rosowski finds in Willa Cather's treatment of cities a dual binary of "male/city versus female/country," noting that "whereas the classic city novel grants full development to a male protagonist . . . Cather divides experience by gender," writing "of country and city as two opposing movements, like the diastolic/systolic rhythm of a heartbeat."[5] Varying the classic pattern only slightly, Dreiser presents a female protagonist beholden to an unfettered male—Carrie waits idly in her urban apartment while her lover Charles Drouet mediates seamlessly between city supplier and country retailer.

On the other hand, Willa Cather, in her 1915 novel *The Song of the*

Lark, constructs a cityscape that is considerably friendlier to her female protagonist, creating what Rosowski calls "Cather's fullest and most positive version of the female city novel."[6] While Thea Kronborg at first finds a bewildering urban bleakness in Chicago, she experiences much less difficulty than does Carrie Meeber in situating herself within Chicago's urban economy. She soon secures employment as a musician, an arrangement that gives Thea the financial foundation to remain in the metropolis. To be sure, Thea's socioeconomic footing is decidedly middle class, and her foray into urban spaces is substantially supported by males. Performing for her minister-father's congregation, Thea develops marketable musical skills. Thea's Chicago venture is bankrolled by a male admirer's life insurance payout. Her first employer in Chicago is a clergyman friend of her father. Her physician friend Dr. Archie accompanies her to Chicago, and he stays long enough to see that Thea is securely employed and safely housed. Once ensconced in the city, however, Thea single-handedly manages her life and career, fending off would-be suitors, arranging more suitable housing, switching music teachers, negotiating patronage, and discovering ties to the metropolis.

As Thea first surveys Chicago, her acutely perceptive eye discovers a remarkable degree of familiarity within the city. Rosowski observes that "in going to the city, Thea has entered as foreign a place as the empty plains were to Cather's immigrants." This observation notwithstanding, one is struck by the way in which Thea minimizes urban foreignness by seeking out the city's recognizable aspects, by identifying connections to her rural childhood within its environs. Arriving in Chicago, Thea expresses "a wish to see two places: Montgomery Ward and Company's big mail-order store, and the packing-houses, to which all the hogs and cattle that went through Moonstone were bound." Soon after settling in, Thea lays eyes on both.[7]

When a young man takes Thea to see the slaughterhouses at Packingtown, he is disappointed that she "neither grew faint nor clung to the arm he kept offering her" but "asked innumerable questions and was impatient because he knew so little." Clearly, Thea carries more than a passing interest in the Chicago stockyards, finding there an

PLACE IS A RELATIONSHIP

urban nexus to her rural hometown. Taking in the meatpacking operation with her keen eye for detail enables Thea to write her father "a brief but clear account of what she had seen." What Thea sees on her tour of Packingtown—the disassembling of animal carcasses into cuts of meat and numerous byproducts—is not for the faint of heart. Upton Sinclair calls the operation "a very river of death," and when his characters encounter the gore, they do so with far less equanimity than does Thea. "Now and then a visitor wept," Sinclair tells his readers, "but this slaughtering machine ran on, visitors or no visitors."[8] For Thea, the stockyards provide a link between small-town Moonstone and metropolitan Chicago that is comforting in its familiarity.

Thea's interest in the meat industry manifests in other pastimes as well. While playing with her piano instructor's children in their Chicago home, Thea helps them construct a model of commercial transportation. Using a toy train set and a Noah's ark village, "they worked out their shipment so realistically that when Andor put the two little reindeer into the stock car, Tanya snatched them out and began to cry, saying she wasn't going to have all their animals killed." Isn't it odd that a budding musician chooses to begin her urban experience with a visit to Packingtown? This is especially notable when contrasted with the experience of Cather herself, who first visited Chicago to immerse herself in five grand opera performances.[9] Thea's interest in the stockyards of South Chicago signals her acute awareness of (and need for) close ties between the metropolis and her rural home.

"A contrast between country and city, as fundamental ways of life, reaches back into classical times," writes Raymond Williams in *The Country and the City*, his critical study of English literature.[10] Any number of voices might serve to establish how deeply the opposition between city and country lies ingrained in American letters as well. For instance, in his analysis of Chicago novels (including *The Song of the Lark*) Sidney H. Bremer writes of how "the confrontation between a lone newcomer and the material, challenging city provides the basis for Americans' continuing Romantic antipathy toward urban artifice."[11] Morton and Lucia White have shown in "The American Intellectual versus the American City" that antiurban sentiment permeates American thought: "The urbanist must face the fact that the anti-urbanist . . . lives in the mind and heart of America."[12] Williams reminds his readers that antipathy cuts both ways: "Powerful hostile associations have also developed: on the city as a place of noise, worldliness and ambition; on the country as a place of backwardness, ignorance, limitation."[13] Hostility and partisanship may turn out to be less noteworthy than the creative sparks that ignite when authors visit the intersection of difference.

Late-nineteenth- and early-twentieth-century American novelists have leaned toward engaging rural-urban oppositions as an engine that drives their fiction. Dwight W. Hoover, for example, points out that for "Dreiser and Crane there are visions of a vigorous and exciting life in the city. The city crushes its victims, to be sure, but life is that way."[14] Given Cather's affinity for Virgilian pastoral (Cather selected an epigraph from the *Georgics* for *My Ántonia*), we might expect her to fall in line with the antiurbanists.[15] Yet in Willa Cather's 1904 story "A Wagner Matinee" it is not the city itself but "the inconceivable silence of the plains" that crushes the central character. This character's encounter with the vigorous cultural life of Boston, where she finds herself "stepping suddenly into the world to which she had been dead for a quarter of a century," fuels Cather's plot.[16] And Cather finds no use for simplistic caricatures of city slicker and country bumpkin. In *The Song of the Lark* Thea Kronborg's rusticity receives matter-of-fact rather than comic treatment and acts not so much as a barrier but as creative energy source within the Chicago artistic community.

In *The Song of the Lark* and its predecessor *O Pioneers!*, Cather conceives a permeable boundary between the urban and the rural that prefigures historian William Cronon's analysis of Chicago's relationship of mutuality with its rural hinterland that appears in his 1991 book *Nature's Metropolis: Chicago and the Great West*. Cronon's thesis— that the metropolis of Chicago and its outlying agricultural hinterlands are created reciprocally—provides an intriguing historical paradigm that moderates the rigidity of an urban-rural binary. Steeped in binary thinking, readers too often slip into the notion that city and country fundamentally oppose each other, presuming it unnatural to think of the urban and the rural collaborating as a single entity. City-country binaries are not inevitably false; in fact, as Rosowski's linking of an urban-rural binary to gendered oppositions shows us, consideration of such binaries gives birth to valuable analysis. Still, underscoring opposition and detachment may obscure the fundamentally vital connections that bind the urban to the rural, blurring one's understanding of Cather's fiction—and of regional boundaries.[17]

William Cronon posits that "the central story of the nineteenth-century West is that of an expanding metropolitan economy creating ever more elaborate and intimate linkages between city and country." At its core, this argument demands that we acknowledge "the symbiotic relationship between cities and their surrounding countrysides," that we visualize urban and rural landscapes as "not two places but one," as codependents that "created each other," that "transformed each other's environments and economies."[18] Not all historians subscribe to this viewpoint, some seeing the rural-urban relationship as less benign and far from mutual. Robert D. Johnston of the University of Illinois at Chicago takes Cronon to task for "his detailed, almost loving, attention to market processes." Johnston faults him for "naturalizing capitalism," for celebrating "the market's own illusory promise of a timeless abundance shared by all," for pointing "to systematic exploitation of nature alone" while maintaining "an untenable denial of exploitation" of people. Johnston asks for greater notice of "the city's exploitation of the country" in which "farmers with mortgages constantly felt they were being squeezed in a vise." Cronon (and Cather, we might well add) "gives little indication that a protest movement of major proportions, Populism, was mobilizing in the hinterland."[19]

Johnston's remarks on Cronon appear within the larger framework of a critique of New Western historians—Patricia Nelson Limerick, Donald Worster, Cronon, and Richard White—whom he admonishes for depending "upon the formulation of a 'West' that has consistent, often ahistorical, and indeed exceptional, characteristics." Johnston's contention with New Western historians involves a longstanding tussle among American historians over how to deal with the frontier thesis of Frederick Jackson Turner, "the previous grand narrative of western history" so influential that an "anti-Turnerian myth required the birth of a New West." Johnston writes, "In creating a 'West' with such essentialist characteristics, however, the New Western historians have helped to freeze out of western history far too large a portion of human experience." The political arena particularly interests Johnston, who calls for an orientation of western history "with less emphasis on distinctive characteristics and exceptionalism; more flexible geographical categories; and greater attention to contingency, change over time, alternative social movements, and—most substantively—politics."[20] In emphasizing the political gaps in the New Western historians' analysis, Johnston, who decries the creation of "reified regional frameworks" and believes "that regional identities are becoming increasingly attenuated," neglects the fluidity that emerges in Cronon's concept of regional interaction.[21] As David Jordan has written, "The nebulous 'substance' of regionalism does not reside in a static collection of local details, but in *an interaction between people and place, a dynamic process* that will inevitably elude the author whose gaze is fixed exclusively on external phenomena" such as topographical features that "contribute to a shared *sense of place*."[22] A focus on economic processes—human dynamics that tie the urban to the rural and tie West to East—works to diminish regional divisions constructed on geographical, topographical, ecological, and architectural difference. Regional fluidity deemphasizes boundaries to underscore human connectivity. Regional fluidity focuses on how Americans have cooperatively interacted across formidable distances and among contrasting spaces.

In light of regional fluidity, the city-country binary collapses, as *either-or* becomes *both-and*. Willa Cather affirms this perspective when she plants images of rural-urban connectivity within her novels. In *The Song of the Lark* Cather merges rural settings with city settings in ways that leave no doubt that the novelist is deeply aware of the matrix of urban-rural economic connections. By the novel's end, Cather has laid out a clear picture of transportation and commerce between country and city, has supplied a strong sense of urban hierarchies and hinterlands, has provided a look at Chicago's emergence as the Midwest's gateway metropolis, and has lengthened the list of rural products to include cultural raw materials. Specifically, Thea Kronborg's rise to artistic success—from the flats of Colorado through Chicago to New York—traces a path that closely resembles that of prairie agricultural products making their way to eastern markets.

In contrast, the predominantly rural setting of *O Pioneers!*, at first glance, seems immune to urban influence. For instance, the novel's opening description of windblown Hanover, Nebraska, emphasizes the tenuousness of human habitation: "The main street was a deeply rutted road, now frozen hard, which ran from the squat red railway station and the grain 'elevator' at the north end of the town to the lumber yard and the horse pond at the south end. On either side of this road straggled two uneven rows of wooden buildings; the general merchandise stores, the two banks, the drug store, the feed store, the saloon, the post-office."[23] Reread this passage with regional fluidity in mind, though, and distinct markers of the close connection between rural Nebraska and urban Chicago begin to emerge from Cather's frontier landscape. Even while establishing a motif of human insubstantiality, Cather embeds a countermelody, a recital of commercial activity—rail station, elevator, lumber yard, stores, banks, post office—whose presence signals an emerging prosperity that belies the sense of isolation that Cather's description of Hanover evokes. A rail station indicates Hanover is served by train, a fact that would prompt John R. Stilgoe to include the hamlet in what he identifies as *metropolitan corridor* because "no traditional spatial term, not *urban*, *suburban*, or *rural*, not *cityscape* or *landscape*, adequately identifies" this sort of space. Stilgoe writes, "Metropolitan Corridor designates the portion of the American built environment that evolved along railroad rights-of-way in the years between 1880 and 1935."[24] While Stilgoe emphasizes the structures that emerge in proximity to rail lines, regional fluidity looks to the economic connections that each of those structures represents.

An elevator beside the railway station indicates Hanover's surrounding farmers convert crops into cash and goods by sending grain east by rail to market. Rail cars do not arrive here empty; instead, they stock the lumber yard at the south end of town and supply merchandise to retailers. From Cather's description we learn that Hanover supports more than one general store, two banks, as well as specialty stores in feed and pharmaceuticals. "The hierarchy of urban settlements," writes Cronon, "is also a hierarchy of markets." A small town such as Hanover was "quintessentially a *retail* place, and counted for its customers on the rural residents who lived in its immediate vicinity." Fulfilling its position as a retail center, essentially a conduit of goods to its own hinterland, meant that a small town could not remain isolated—neither from its own rural surroundings nor from its supplying metropolis. Rather, the town's very existence depended on its connection to the city, particularly to Chicago. Cather demonstrates this rural-urban umbilical by including a cigar-chomping traveling man in her opening chapter, a clothing salesman drumming up business for his Chicago wholesale house in this seemingly out-of-the-way spot. Cronon describes how "Chicago wholesale merchants became famous—some said notorious—for their use of 'drummers,'" who "scoured the western landscape, using every conceivable hard-sell technique in their efforts to gain orders for themselves and their firms."[25] Rail lines fanned out from Chicago like veins and arteries connecting farm and town to Chicago with goods that only a metropolis could supply, as Cather well knew. Arranging her cousin's wedding breakfast in February 1896, Cather "went to the extravagance of ordering strawberries, fresh tomatoes, and watercress from Chicago" to be delivered to the Red Cloud, Nebraska, train depot.[26]

In Cather's story of Nebraska farming, the urban and the rural coalesce in a mythology that rewrites the landscape in terms of human usage. Roland Barthes noted that "myth is constituted by the loss of the historical quality of things: in it, things lose the memory that they once were made."[27] While Barthes's semiological interpretation deals with myth as metalanguage, Cronon's analysis of human-built structures within American landscapes—he calls these accretions "second nature"—functions quite similarly to Barthean myth. Through the

PLACE IS A RELATIONSHIP

concept of second nature, Cronon explains how rural-urban links become so embedded in people's consciousness that such links become invisible. Cronon states, "The emergence of the city required that a new human order be superimposed on nature until the two became completely entangled. The result was a hybrid system, at least as artificial as it was natural, that became second nature to those who lived within it." Or, as Barthes puts it, "A conjuring trick has taken place; it has turned reality inside out, it has emptied it of history and has filled it with nature."[28] With the advent of improvements such as canals, dredged and sheltered lake harbors, roads, railroads, and, we might well add, plowed sections and half sections, a "kind of 'second nature,' designed by people and 'improved' toward human ends, gradually emerged atop the original landscape that nature—'first nature'—had created as such an inconvenient jumble."[29]

In Part II of O Pioneers!, the novelist revisits the landscape around Hanover after a lapse of sixteen years. In effect, Cather describes an urbanized prairie when "from the Norwegian graveyard one looks out over a vast checker-board, marked off in squares of wheat and corn." Adding that "telephone wires hum along the white roads, which always run at right angles," Cather completes a picture of prairie as grid, a grid that not only eases the tasks of surveying ownership and planting straight crop lines, but also mirrors the lattice of Chicago streets and avenues that stretch west from Lake Michigan. In the novel's portrayal of a reconfigured prairie divide, human struggle is past. Because the land has been transfigured from first to second nature, human interaction now appears integral to the landscape. A single evocative sentence shows the extent to which human activity has become naturalized within Cather's narrative: "There are few scenes more gratifying than a spring plowing in that country, where the furrows of a single field often lie a mile in length, and the brown earth, with such a strong, clean smell, and such a power of growth and fertility in it, yields itself eagerly to the plow; rolls away from the shear, not even dimming the brightness of the metal, with a soft, deep sigh of happiness."[30] Such intimacy between soil and plow signals that the landscape of Alexandra Bergson's divide has become as urban as it is rural. In a consummation of the rural-urban alliance, western soil ecstatically yields to eastern or metropolitan manufactured steel plow.

Rural-urban connections make Cather's imagery possible in several ways. Rail transportation, making possible the exchange of agricultural produce for manufactured goods, is perhaps the most obvious. Less obvious is that urban demand for produce and commerce provides impetus for plowing and planting. Cather's protagonist plants a checkerboard of corn and wheat because city markets demand corn and wheat. "As the human inhabitants of Chicago's hinterland responded to the siren song of its markets, they simplified local ecosystems in the direction of monocultures," writes Cronon.[31] Thus, it is not just what will grow on the divide that gets planted, it is what will sell in Chicago's markets.

By 1859 Chicago's grain trade was all but established because of the emergence of three components: "the elevator warehouse, the grading system, and, linking them, the privately regulated central market governed by the Board of Trade."[32] Telegraph and newspapers quickly disseminated market information to the hinterland, and discerning farmers paid heed. From the very opening of the novel we can see that Alexandra has access to market prices. In the first chapter of *O Pioneers!*, readers may note that the telegraph pole, from which young Emil Bergson's kitten is rescued, holds a wire that carries vital market information; and even before her father's death in the novel's second chapter, Alexandra has earned a reputation for studying the market. She not only knows grain prices but can predict the value of meat commodities: "It was Alexandra who read the papers and followed the markets, and who learned by the mistakes of their neighbors." The newspapers in which Alexandra follows the market may come from as far away as Chicago. In 1884 the Burlington railroad regularly carried mail and newspapers from Chicago to Council Bluffs, Iowa, in fewer than sixteen hours.[33] In a demonstration of her market astuteness, Alexandra sells off cattle and corn to raise the cash necessary to purchase a neighboring homestead. But because selling will raise a sum still insufficient for Alexandra's land-buying strategy, she also mortgages the Bergson property to "raise every dollar we can, and buy every acre we can."[34]

PLACE IS A RELATIONSHIP

From whom does she borrow? Hanover has two banks, and Alexandra apparently goes to both of them—"I was always squeezing and borrowing until I was ashamed to show my face in the banks," she tells Carl Linstrum. But these banks do not function in rural isolation as Cather, whose father ran a real estate and farm loan business in Red Cloud, was undoubtedly aware. Banks throughout the nation depended on one another for crucial services and financial backing: "No matter where in the country they were located, banks low in the nineteenth-century urban hierarchy had to establish 'correspondent' relations with larger metropolitan banks in order to redeem banknotes, process out-of- town checks, gain access to credit, and perform any number of other financial functions."[35] Alexandra's credit dependency ties her in yet another way to the urban East and to Chicago in particular. Cronon's study of debt patterns establishes that "Chicago's financial hinterland in 1881 extended from Cleveland in the east to Denver in the west." The finances that Alexandra requires to assemble her "vast checker-board" derive heavily from urban markets and sources of capital lying to the east.[36]

Even Alexandra's agricultural experimentation, a major component of her success, demonstrates convergence of the urban and the rural. Some ideas for innovation, such as raising hogs on fresh fodder in a clean enclosure, come from Ivar, the most rural of the novel's characters, while two significant innovations—planting alfalfa to rejuvenate the soil and storing silage in a silo—come from an urban source, the university. Students such as Alexandra's brother Emil travel from the countryside to the land-grant University of Nebraska in Lincoln to be trained in ideas and methods that reshape the outlying prairie landscape. It is easy to miss these connections between the urban and the rural because they lie buried like so many seeds in Cather's text. William Barillas observes, "On the one hand, Cather's Nebraska novels celebrate the hard work and foresight needed to succeed on a small farm. . . . At the same time, Cather characterizes her protagonists as Romantic visionaries who appreciate their home places not only as productive but also as beautiful, meaningful, and numinous."[37] The numinous atmosphere with which Cather imbues the emergence of

Alexandra's prosperous relationship to the soil tends to disguise the more probable, if mundane, ingredients to her success: market savvy, creative debt management, crop experimentation, and, controlling these, a pervasive urban influence delivered by rail.

In 1912, between her first two novels *Alexander's Bridge* and *O Pioneers!*, Cather published "Behind the Singer Tower," a short story that mulls a growing dissatisfaction with purely urban spaces. Observing New York's skyline from the harbor, Cather's narrator gazes at "those incredible towers of stone and steel . . . grouped confusedly together, as if they were confronting each other with a question." The narrator concludes, "One might fancy that the city was protesting, was asserting its helplessness, its irresponsibility for its physical conformation, for the direction it had taken. It was an irregular parallelogram pressed between two hemispheres, and, like any other solid squeezed in a vise, it shot upward."[38] Cather's narrator, bridling at the constraints imposed by unidirectional progress, is appalled that "our whole scheme of life and progress and profit was perpendicular," that "there was nothing for us but height."[39] Whereas visual artists such as Alfred Stieglitz and Florine Stettheimer were able to aestheticize the New York skyline, writers such as Cather and Henry James found the jumble of buildings overwhelming.[40] Morton and Lucia White state that "to Henry Adams, New York symbolized the spiritual confusion of America at the end of the nineteenth century," and write that Henry James "spoke of the city's chaos" and that the city's skyline "insulted his very expressively complex sensibilities."[41] Stephen Crane's New York is comprised of "a multitude of buildings, of pitiless hues and sternly high." To the nameless protagonist of "An Experiment in Misery" the skyline is "emblematic of a nation forcing its regal head into the clouds, throwing no downward glances; in the sublimity of its aspirations ignoring the wretches who may flounder at its feet."[42] In a similar vein Arthur Feiler, who visited from Germany in 1920, observes that "the Manhattan skyline seems to loom above the arriving ship like a citadel raised on high by the cyclops," the city's "amazing agglomeration of iron and cement" representing "capitalism turned into stone."[43] While Crane's and Feiler's skyscrapers

PLACE IS A RELATIONSHIP

signal looming economic dominance, Cather's perturbation appears more psychic in nature.

In "Behind the Singer Tower" Cather describes a trap she hopes to evade. The novelist resists becoming a victim of verticality by turning away from the city settings of *Alexander's Bridge* and "Behind the Singer Tower" toward the western horizons of *O Pioneers!*. But this turning should not be construed as a mere veering from city confinement to prairie openness; for in her subsequent novel *The Song of the Lark*, Cather begins on the plains and travels to the city of Chicago and beyond, only to return to rural Moonstone in her epilogue. By fusing the rural to the urban in her fiction, the author avoids being crushed viselike between urban and rural hemispheres. The vehemence with which Cather recoils from that "parallelogram pressed between two hemispheres" leads one to believe that Cather holds the brain's hemispheres in mind; what one sees here is an author striving to transcend a confining mindset. In *O Pioneers!* and *The Song of the Lark*, Cather turns away from the constraints of writing unidirectionally; that is, she escapes polarity by reimagining the landscape as one large community that is as horizontal as it is vertical.[44]

Not all binaries are diametrically opposed: significant difference exists between a single *up-down* axis and a dual *vertical-horizontal* axis. The perpendicular involves a 90-degree turn, not a 180-degree reversal. Outlining a model of perpendicularity, William Cronon's thesis reminds us that only by reaching out horizontally to its rural hinterlands does Chicago rise vertically. In *The Song of the Lark* Cather recalls this rising when she depicts a metropolis in the process of growing out of slough and marsh.[45] Furthermore, Willa Cather transcends the limitations of an urban-rural binary by incorporating both urban verticality and rural horizontality within her depiction of Chicago. Thea arrives from the rural horizon wishing to visit the Montgomery Ward Building, which, in contrast to the violent verticality of the Singer Tower, sprouts upward from the shores of Lake Michigan like prairie tallgrass or a stalk of corn.

Chicago merchandising reached out to rural towns like Thea's after 1872 through the innovative mail-order methods of Aaron Montgomery

Ward, whose company featured large volumes of goods and direct sales to the final customer: "By the end of the 1880s, Ward's catalog . . . offered over 24,000 items to its readers."[46] The Montgomery Ward Building so impresses Cather's young musician that, in comparison, the Chicago Art Institute is at first only "the place with the big lions out in front" that she saw "when [she] went to Montgomery Ward's." When Montgomery Ward and Company moved into its new headquarters in 1898, the modern building on Michigan Avenue sported the highest tower in the city. A cutaway illustration on the cover to the 1900 catalog shows the rural customer "A Busy Bee-Hive" in which the building's twenty floors teem with clerks and cashiers and shippers working to complete his or her mail order.[47] The Montgomery Ward Building's verticality is nourished by its rootedness in the prairie expanse, its connections stretching beyond the horizon to towns such as Moonstone and Hanover.

When Robert Johnston criticizes Cronon for allowing the "homey image" of a Ward's mail-order catalog "sitting on the kitchen table . . . with its promise of cheap and abundant goods" to take precedence over a deeper consideration of the often grim realities of grain markets and farm mortgages, he might well take aim at Cather for valorizing railway operations and services in *The Song of the Lark* while she turns a blind eye to Populist furor over rail tariffs.[48] Yet to do so may be tantamount to wishing Cather had written *The Octopus* instead of the novel she gives us. Cather writes from her own experience, not that of Frank Norris; and from her experience, Cather knew that regional boundaries could readily be crossed. Cather's geographical relocations within her own life—from backwoods Virginia to frontier Nebraska to increasingly more urban settings in Red Cloud, Lincoln, Pittsburgh, and ultimately New York City—taught her to value rail transportation as a conduit among various spaces. Even in childhood Cather knew that trains brought entertainment troupes from larger culture centers to Red Cloud. Trains carried Cather from Red Cloud to study at the university in Lincoln, and from Lincoln she rode the train to enjoy opera in Chicago. Afterward, she rode by rail to take up new jobs—as editor and teacher in Pittsburgh, as editor and

　　　　　　　　　PLACE IS A RELATIONSHIP

writer in New York. Trains carried her back for extended visits to Nebraska's farmlands and beyond to the deserts of the American Southwest that inspired some of her greatest work. Connectivity provided by rail gave cultural and artistic lifeblood to Cather. These connections were as important to the author as they are to her characters. In *O Pioneers!* Alexandra Bergson, as Rosowski points out, "creates a great farm that resembles a communal village, its parts joined in a web-like design."[49] In extending our conception of how inextricably Alexandra's web-like design connects her enterprise to Chicago, we ought also to acknowledge how Cather's artistic trajectory transcends regional boundaries. As the novelist was drawn eastward to pursue and perfect her art in urban centers, she mediated between city and country, cultivating close connections to those rural roots out of which she grew her fiction. Is it any wonder that in Thea Kronborg the novelist inscribes an artist and protagonist who also learns to negotiate the urban-rural divide?

Tracing the same eastward route as that of cattle, hogs, and grain traveling to market, Thea enters the metropolis by rail, like so much raw material waiting to be converted into a finished product. As a manufacturing center, Chicago created wealth by assembling raw materials into finished products—McCormick Reapers, for example. Similarly, cattle arrived at Chicago stockyards to be disassembled into cuts of beef whose added value (their marketable size and shape) allowed them to flow eastward in refrigerated cars as viable commodities. Thea arrives as cultural raw material that is transformed into a finished product in the urban environs of Chicago. In Chicago the prairie girl with natural but as yet unfocused gifts encounters the Midwest's most respected teachers and rubs shoulders with influential patrons of the arts who have sensibilities to appreciate her artistic promise. This interaction with her urban environment helps to refine Thea's nascent rural force into a powerful musical skill that propels her beyond Chicago.[50]

That this flow of cultural goods represents something other than a simply extractive economy becomes clear when we notice the reciprocal complexity of cultural commerce as revealed by Cather. For instance, urban refinement is rejuvenated by an influx of the young musician's rurality. The novelist emphasizes Thea's unfinished appearance as the girl interviews for her first Chicago job, "sitting on the lounge, her knees far apart . . . like a country girl." Later, Thea tells her piano instructor, "I come of rough people"; and while her teacher Harsanyi agrees, viewing Thea as "a fine young savage, a book with nothing written in it," he also recognizes an intrinsic artistic value. When Thea sings for him the first time "like a wild bird that had flown into his studio," Harsanyi welcomes the infusion of rural vigor. Cather writes, "After Miss Kronborg left him, he often lay down in his studio for an hour before dinner, with his head full of musical ideas, with an effervescence in his brain which he had sometimes lost for weeks together under the grind of teaching. He had never got so much back for himself from any pupil as he did from Miss Kronborg." Theirs is an interaction marked by reciprocity in which both rural student and urban teacher profit from their time together. Even as Thea herself (and subsequently her East Coast and European audiences) benefits from her transformation into polished artist, her hometown savors eastern culture that streams westward. Back in Moonstone, Thea's Aunt Tillie subscribes to a New York newspaper, whose notices and reviews bring vicarious participation in Thea's artistic success, and when the Metropolitan Opera Company becomes accessible to her during a Kansas City engagement, Tillie attends as Thea's guest. So the urban flows into the rural, enhancing life on the plains, effacing the painful division between cultured East and roughshod West that Cather renders so acutely in "A Wagner Matinee."[51]

In Cather's fiction, city entwines countryside. *The Song of the Lark*, whose setting proceeds from rural to urban only to revisit the rural, unmasks country-city connections, clearly showing the mutual dependence of these settings. In featuring a rural landscape in *O Pioneers!*, Cather presents a setting that subtly folds the urban into the rural, creating a second nature to which her readers intuitively respond. Cather's treatment of these relationships between city and countryside neither renders the rural urban nor makes the urban rural. Her fiction, while maintaining geographical distinctions, collapses psychic

PLACE IS A RELATIONSHIP

distance, urging readers to rethink the mental barriers that we erect when we insist on thinking of the urban in opposition to the rural. In so responding, we find fresh conceptions of regionalism emerging. Robert Johnston's call for "more flexible geographical categories" may have been anticipated by Cather, whose novels not only reveal intraregional community but also invite readers to discover *interre-gional* connectivity.

Chicago's rail connections and its location on Lake Michigan made "a city located in one of the nation's most treeless landscapes, the greatest lumber center in the world," according to Cronon. The lake, "a natural corridor between two ecosystems," extended north into forest regions, to those "who had more trees than they knew what to do with," while rail lines extended west toward "prairie people desperately short of trees." Lumber flowed from the forests through the wholesale yards of Chicago and out to the tree-starved prairies to be fashioned into fences, barns, and houses. This brief explanation of interregional trade brings one back to the remarkable eye of Thea Kronborg, who, sitting in a restaurant in the Pullman Building on Michigan Avenue, looks out over the Chicago Art Institute with its "green lions, dripping in the rain," gazing at, of all things, a "lumber boat, with two very tall masts, . . . emerging gaunt and black out of the fog." A country girl in the heart of the metropolis notices a trail of commerce. Her perceptive gaze not only connects region to region; but also in that one reflective moment, Thea's urban present and rural past merge with her artistic future.[52] What are you thinking, Thea? What draws your eye to that ship just beyond the art museum? Are you imagining that boat docking at the great lumber wharves along the Chicago River's South Branch? Do you see the lumber being sorted and stacked and loaded onto train cars? Is that lumber shipping home to Moonstone?

Notes

1. Theodore Dreiser, *Sister Carrie* (1900; repr., New York: Signet Classics, 2000), 1.

2. Willa Cather, *The Song of the Lark* (1915; repr., New York: Vintage Books, 1999), 142.

3. Upton Sinclair, *The Jungle* (1906; repr., New York: Barnes and Noble, 1995), 22.

4. Dreiser, 1. Carrie Meeber's relationship to Charles Drouet is described in subsequent chapters.

5. Susan J. Rosowski, "Willa Cather as a City Novelist," in *Writing the City: Eden, Babylon, and the New Jerusalem*, ed. Peter Preston and Paul Simpson-Housley (London: Routledge, 1994), 149–70, 156.

6. Rosowski, "Willa Cather as a City Novelist," 159.

7. Rosowski, "Willa Cather as a City Novelist," 159; Cather, *Lark*, 179.

8. Cather, *Lark*, 180; Sinclair, *Jungle*, 35, 37.

9. Cather, *Lark*, 167; James Woodress, *Willa Cather: A Literary Life* (Lincoln: University of Nebraska Press, 1987), 102.

10. Raymond Williams, *The Country and the City* (New York: Oxford University Press, 1973), 1.

11. Sidney H. Bremer, "Lost Continuities: Alternative Urban Visions in Chicago Novels, 1890–1915," *Soundings* 64, no. 1 (1981): 30.

12. Morton White and Lucia White, "The American Intellectual versus the American City," in *American Urban History: An Interpretive Reader with Commentaries*, ed. Alexander B. Callow Jr. (New York: Oxford University Press, 1969), 353–63, 353. Previously published in *Daedalus*, Winter 1961, 166–79. Citing Thomas Jefferson, Ralph Waldo Emerson, William James, John Dewey, Henry James, Henry Adams, and Frank Lloyd Wright—"our greatest political thinker, our greatest essayist, our greatest philosopher, our greatest theorist of education, our greatest novelist, our greatest autobiographer, and our greatest architect"—the Whites write that "it is impossible to produce a list of *pro*-urban American thinkers who remotely approach this collection in distinction and intellectual influence" (361).

13. Williams, *Country and the City*, 1.

14. Dwight W. Hoover, *A Teacher's Guide to American Urban History* (Chicago: Quadrangle Books, 1971), 251.

15. See also Susan J. Rosowski's discussion of parallels between *O Pioneers!* and Virgil's *Eclogues* in *The Voyage Perilous: Willa Cather's Romanticism* (Lincoln: University of Nebraska Press, 1986), 46–49, 60–61.

16. Willa Cather, "A Wagner Matinee," in *Willa Cather's Collected Short Fiction, 1892–1912*, ed. Virginia Faulkner (Lincoln: University of Nebraska Press, 1970), 235–42, 238–39. Previously published in *Everybody's Magazine*, February 1904.

17. Marcus Cunliffe writes that "Willa Cather refuses to be saddled with the orthodox polarities of supposed East-West behavior," observing that Cather "was not committed, as Turner and some of her contemporaries were, to the attractive yet oversimplified East-West polarity." He also notes that for Cather, "frontier and civilization were not so much opposites as co-ordinates" and that "The true human being . . . at home in all environments, . . . a respecter both of persons and of places" and the "false human being, . . . a hater and spoiler, both of persons and of places[, t]hose are Willa Cather's opposites." "The Two or More Worlds of Willa Cather" in *The Art of Willa Cather*, ed. Bernice Slote and Virginia Faulkner (Lincoln: University of Nebraska Press, 1974), 21–42, 39–40.

18. William Cronon, *Nature's Metropolis: Chicago and the Great West* (New York: W. W. Norton, 1991), xv, 34, 348.

19. Robert D. Johnston, "Beyond 'The West': Regionalism, Liberalism, and the Evasion of Politics in the New Western History," *Rethinking History* 2 (1998): 252–55. Cather gives a nod to Populism in *O Pioneers!* when she includes a conversation between Alexandra's brother Lou and her friend Carl Linstrum, who just returned from the east coast: "'Well, what do folks in New York think of William Jennings Bryan?' Lou began to bluster, as he always did when he talked politics. 'We gave Wall Street a scare in ninety-six, all right, and we're fixing another to hand them. Silver wasn't the only issue,' he nodded mysteriously. 'There's a good many things got to be changed. The West is going to make itself heard.'" Willa Cather, *O Pioneers!*, ed. Susan J. Rosowski and Charles W. Mignon with Kathleen Danker, Willa Cather Scholarly Edition (1913; repr., Lincoln: University of Nebraska Press, 1992), 104. Cather addressed the divisiveness of Populist politics more directly in her 1931 story "Two Friends," which depicts the fracturing of a long-time friendship over the Bryan-McKinley presidential contest and its free-silver debate. Willa Cather, "Two Friends," in *Obscure Destinies*, ed. Susan J. Rosowski, Kari Ronning, Frederick M. Link, and Mark Kamrath, Willa Cather Scholarly Edition (1932; repr., Lincoln: University of Nebraska Press, 1998), 161–91.

20. Johnston, "Beyond 'The West,'" 240–41.

21. Johnston, "Beyond 'The West,'" 251, 263.

22. David Jordan, "Representing Regionalism," *Canadian Review of American Studies* 23, no. 2 (1993): 106 (emphasis added).

23. Cather, *O Pioneers!*, 11–12.

24. John R. Stilgoe, *Metropolitan Corridor: Railroads and the American Scene* (New Haven CT: Yale University Press, 1983), 3.

25. Cronon, *Nature's Metropolis*, 280, 329.

26. Woodress, *Willa Cather*, 105.

27. Roland Barthes, *Mythologies*, trans. Annette Lavers (New York: Hill and Wang, 1972), 142.

28. Cronon, *Nature's Metropolis*, 264; Barthes, *Mythologies*, 142.

29. Cronon, *Nature's Metropolis*, 56.

30. Cather, *O Pioneers!*, 73, 74.

31. Cronon, *Nature's Metropolis*, 267.

32. Cronon, *Nature's Metropolis*, 120.

33. Cather, *O Pioneers!*, 28; Richard C. Overton, *Burlington Route: A History of the Burlington Lines* (New York: Knopf, 1965), 201.

34. Cather, *O Pioneers!*, 64.

35. Cather, *O Pioneers!*, 108; Woodress, *Willa Cather*, 43.

36. Cronon, *Nature's Metropolis*, 305.

37. William Barrillas, "Jim Harrison, Willa Cather, and the Revision of Midwestern Pastoral," *MidAmerica* 26 (1999): 172.

38. Willa Cather, "Behind the Singer Tower," in *Willa Cather's Collected Short Fiction, 1892–1912*, ed. Virginia Faulkner (Lincoln: University of Nebraska Press, 1970), 43–54, 44. Previously published in *Collier's*, May 1912.

39. Cather, "Behind the Singer Tower," 46.

40. Describing Stettheimer's *Family Portrait, II*, Cécile Whiting writes about how the artist "transformed the city into an extravagant feminine fantasy, complete with delicate white skyscrapers which, defined by a fluid line, rhyme with the billowing cellophane curtain, the ornate crystal chandelier, and Carrie's flowing gown." "Decorating with Stettheimer and the Boys," *American Art* 14 (2000): 25–49, 44. In addition to Alfred Stieglitz's iconic 1903 "Flatiron Building," see his "Spring Showers, New York," taken in 1902, and his brooding 1915 nightscape, "From the Back Window, 291."

41. White and White, "American Intellectual," 357.

42. Stephen Crane, "An Experiment in Misery," in *Great Short Works of Stephen Crane* (1894; repr., New York: Harper and Row, 1965), 248–58, 257–58. Crane's story originally appeared in the *New York Press*, April 22, 1894.

43. Arthur Feiler, "Skyscrapers and Ethnic Settlements," in *The City in American History*, ed. Blake McKelvey (London: George Allen and Unwin, 1969), 187–89, 187–88. Feiler's remarks appeared originally in *America Seen through German Eyes*, trans. Margaret L. Goldsmith (New York: New Republic, 1928).

44. In the early 1920s Cather revisited the New York City skyline in her fiction with a more tranquil eye. When Claude Wheeler, the prairie-bred protagonist of Cather's Pulitzer Prize–winning *One of Ours*, peers at the cityscape from the deck of a troopship, it is as if he gazes into a mist-filled Stieglitz image: "The tall buildings, of which he had heard so much, looked unsubstantial and illusionary,—mere shadows of grey and pink and blue that might dissolve with the mist and fade away in it. . . . Which of those pale giants was the Singer Building?" (1922; repr., New York: Vintage Books, 1991), 220.

45. Thea Kronborg's first employer in Chicago is the minister of the Swedish Reform Church, located "in a sloughy, weedy district, near a group of factories." Cather, *Lark*, 150.

46. Cronon, *Nature's Metropolis*, 336.

47. Cather, *Lark*, 180; Cronon, *Nature's Metropolis*, 336–37.

48. Johnston, "Beyond 'The West,'" 253.

49. Rosowski, "Willa Cather as a City Novelist," 154–55.

50. To be sure, the indispensable musical training that Thea receives in Chicago is not the sole factor in her becoming an artist. Indeed, she leaves the city disheartened, feeling that "her two years in Chicago had not resulted in anything" (Cather, *Lark*, 272). Only after Thea travels to the desert Southwest and discovers a vital musical idea to complement her training ("In singing, one made a vessel of one's throat and nostrils and held it on one's breath, caught the stream in a scale of natural intervals" [Cather, *Lark*, 279].) is she able fully to enter her art.

51. Cather, *Lark*, 151, 195, 188, 173, 175.

52. Cronon, *Nature's Metropolis*, 183, 153; Cather, *Lark*, 265.

12. Preaching the Gospel of Higher Vaudeville

Vachel Lindsay's Poetic Journey from Springfield, Illinois, across America, and Back

LARRY W. MOORE

Booth led boldly on his big bass drum—
(Are you washed in the blood of the Lamb?)
The Saints smiled gravely and they said: "He's come."
(Are you washed in the blood of the Lamb?)
  —Vachel Lindsay, "General William Booth Enters into Heaven,"

THEN I SAW THE CONGO, CREEPING THROUGH THE BLACK,
CUTTING THROUGH THE FOREST WITH A GOLDEN TRACK.
  —Vachel Lindsay, "The Congo,"

Music of the mob am I,
Circus day's tremendous cry:—
I am the Kallyope, Kallyope, Kallyope!
Hoot toot, hoot toot, hoot toot, hoot toot,
Willy willy willy wah HOO!
Sizz, fizz. . . .
  —Vachel Lindsay, "The Kallyope Yell"

For a time in the first quarter of the twentieth century, the man who first gave voice to these lines was perhaps the best-known poet in America: Vachel Lindsay. Wildly original and eccentric, Lindsay blazed a poetic trail across the expanse of the United States like no one before him; and not even among those who followed—often unknowingly—in his footsteps, from the Beat poets to today's poetry-slam performers, has there been another writer to capture the public imagination quite as he did. No American writer was ever more physically engaged with the vastness of this nation and her peoples or any more dedicated to the task of creating a uniquely American poetry. But his was also a moral crusade, a "gospel of beauty" incorporating his triune values of religion, beauty, and equality, intended to rebuild the nation to the blueprint of his vision of an American New Jerusalem.[1]

Within the context of this volume, my intention in examining Lindsay's life and work is a practical exploration of one issue of regionalism: the tension between the limitations of region—pejoratively termed provincialism—and the effort to produce a national expression that embraces and is embraced by Americans from all regions. This tension arises from the very existence of regional identity (as distinct from national identity)—the aggregate and unique experience of the generations who have peopled a shared space, the "accidents of history and cultural values" that define a region as much as if not more than mere geography.[2]

Once these regional distinctions—or at least our perception of such—come into being, they tend to be conserved through our natural disposition to define ourselves in terms of similarities and differences, or us and them; and in the worst case, they harden over time into stereotypes and prejudices. By contrast with regional identity, a national identity is a far more rarified thing. Even given our modern pace of travel and communications, it is difficult to be from an entire nation, especially one of such continental expanse as the United States. Despite over two centuries of appeal to our supposed common citizenship, the fractured—and fractious—nature of our polity remains evident in the United States. Regionalism, it seems, is still very much alive as a principle of American experience.

Lindsay's life and work are the story of that tension between the regional and the national; his effort was not so much to transcend the boundaries of his region as it was to make his vision of his region the model for all America. As such, his ultimate failure was predictable. Both history and contemporary experience teach that Americans resist the imposition of any one regional vision or set of cultural values and experiences on the nation as a whole. Lindsay's artistic failures may be attributed in some degree to the limitations of the regionalism he embraced.

Still, however tragic its end, Lindsay's story is not exclusively one of failure. At his height, for a few years at least, he achieved national acclaim and popularity. Where he succeeded, he did with an appeal to common humanity, a childlike sense of wonder and beauty, a fluency in the language of our national folklore, and most of all with an embodiment of one of our most fundamental national myths, the boundless energy and optimism and inventiveness of America. In the process of doing so, he did transcend his region and became himself a truly American original. Lindsay's former fame has faded to such an extent that he has practically vanished from our literary canon, and it is time for a reappraisal of his place in our letters.

Lindsay was very much attached to his home, however far afield his life and work may have taken him; and this regional attachment shaped and, to some degree, limited his artistic development. He himself was very much aware of regional issues. He developed his own—typically idiosyncratic—vision of America's regions and their respective contributions to the national character; and he believed that a harmonious whole could be assembled out of those parts, rather than by any one region subsuming the others (though I contend that he did use his region as a model for his vision of the ideal society).

What was Lindsay's region? Fellow poet Amy Lowell once described—or perhaps dismissed—Lindsay as a "Midwesterner of the Middle Class," a phrase that at first appears to tell us more about her Boston prejudice than it does about Lindsay himself; but it is in fact as good a start as any at situating Lindsay in terms of geography and society.[3] Nicholas Vachel Lindsay was born November 10, 1879, in Springfield, Illinois. His father, Vachel Thomas Lindsay, was a doctor and, like a great contingent of Springfield and southern Illinois generally, a transplanted Kentuckian.[4] The father's slaveholding family had been ruined by the Civil War; and despite settling in the city that had been home to the great Union president, Thomas Lindsay was no fan of Lincoln's. As the son later recalled, "If there were ever two things my father wanted me to do they were to hate Lincoln and the Republican Party."[5]

Lindsay's father also wanted his son to follow him into the medical profession and to gain a respectable position in society. For a time the boy attempted to stay to that course; but his temperament was far more influenced by the cultural and spiritual inclinations of his mother. Esther Catherine Frazee was born on a prosperous farm in Rush County, Indiana, her forebears also having abandoned the slaveholding state of Kentucky. A well-educated woman for her day, she taught mathematics and art in women's colleges, which brought her to Lexington, Kentucky, and into a friendship with fellow teacher Eudora Lindsay, sister of Vachel Thomas, through which connection the poet's parents met and married. She was also a devout member of the Disciples of Christ, which provided the foundation for her son's religious beliefs. "Lindsay, then, was the product of Springfield, Illinois, but of a Springfield and an Illinois with deep roots in the pioneer west of Kentucky. As he wrote in "My Fathers Came from Kentucky," being born in Illinois might mean he had "Northern words, / And thoughts, / And ways," but his great-grandfathers' mythic (Daniel Boone) origins meant no drop of his blood was from north of the Mason-Dixon Line. In fact, Lindsay often commented that the Mason-Dixon Line ran through the middle of his living room, and his city as well was politically and culturally separated by that line even decades after the Civil War.[6]

As Nicole Etcheson has observed in her study of the role of upland Southerners in the development of the Old Northwest, Kentuckians played a prominent part in the settlement of the region and, along with other Southerners, exerted strong influence on the evolution of the emerging midwestern regional character. Aristocratic settlers from Kentucky brought with them the Southern values of manliness and honor, defended when necessary by force.[7] The integration of these

Southern values with the Northern emphasis on virtue and common good helped forge a common political language for the new region. In the years that followed, Etcheson writes, "an emerging sense of Westernness increasingly subsumed sectional identities, encompassing them within a Western identity. Ultimately this Western, or Midwestern identity, became the nation's identity." Perhaps, but in the Lindsay household, as in the region generally, remnants of the old North-South tensions remained.[8]

Part of the tension resulted from unresolved issues regarding race and slavery. Many of the Kentuckians who settled in Illinois came, like Lindsay's father, from slaveholding families; and while most of these eventually became strong Unionists, they did so out of opposition to what they saw as Southern arrogance, not from any objection to slavery per se. Of course, the majority of the settlers who moved into the Old Northwest from Kentucky and elsewhere in the South were never slaveholders themselves. Of these, some—including Lindsay's mother's family—left Kentucky because of moral objection to life in a slave state. More typically, however, the objection to slavery by these transplanted Southerners was based on economics, not morality. They believed that slavery degraded the wages and status of white workingmen, farmers, and laborers, forcing them to seek better opportunities afforded in the Free States to the north. But whatever their attitude toward slavery, they tended to be "unambivalent" with regard to free blacks, demonstrating a "visceral and powerful" racial prejudice. As Etcheson notes, "Southerners carried racism into the Midwest."[9] This had serious consequences for Lindsay's life and work.

In many respects, Lindsay was inextricably linked with his hometown, which makes understanding the character of Springfield all the more critical to understanding that of the poet. Springfield was no stereotypical small town on the prairie, bucolic and agrarian. It was a railroad hub and a center of mining and manufacturing. The arrival of the railroads, mines, and factories led to the development of a small "oligarchic elite," a subset of the conservative leading merchants, or "old middle class," who became the true financial and political power in the community, often almost a "shadow government."[10] The power of the elite was reinforced by the fact that Springfield was the state capital. The presence of state government insulated Springfield from the economic pressures that affect, and sometimes undermine, the livelihood of other small cities.[11] Springfield boosters well understood the crucial role of the capital in their midst and rallied against occasional efforts to relocate the seat of government.[12] For Lindsay, this assured that he grew up surrounded by the trappings and transactions of government (the state executive mansion being literally across the street from his house). Lindsay would lash out at this elite time and again.

This booster elite was challenged by the arrival of waves of Irish and other peoples—mostly working-class with a variety of religious, economic, and social beliefs. On the streets of Springfield, among its more than forty thousand inhabitants, the young Lindsay would encounter Swedenborgians and Socialists, "Single-Taxers" and the Anti-Saloon League, along with Northerners and Southerners, Democrats and Republicans, blacks and whites, laborers and businessmen. If we define Lindsay's region as Springfield, then we can also view Springfield as representing in microcosm that constellation of demographic, political, and economic forces that shaped the development of its region.[13]

Lastly, Springfield was foremost the city of Abraham Lincoln. However much Lindsay's father may have despised the martyred president, his presence in the community was pervasive and inescapable. Indeed, the Lindsay house had once been home to a sister of Mary Todd Lincoln, and Lincoln himself had been a frequent visitor. The Lincoln house was only a few blocks away, and Lindsay visited it often as a child, even before it was turned into a national shrine. In time, this Lincoln stamp on Springfield was officially embraced by the city promoters as a way to claim a distinct identity for their community in the face of the economic and cultural juggernaut of Chicago. As Illinois historian Richard J. Jensen has observed, yet another tension existed within the state: between Chicago, the "second city" of the nation, and "downstate." In reaction to the wealth and intellectual and artistic attainments (and Democratic politics) of their northern

PLACE IS A RELATIONSHIP

neighbor, central and southern Illinois communities preferred instead "practical, lower-middle-class art, useful colleges, nostalgic memorials, and Republican machines." Specifically, "Springfield developed a Lincoln legend to guide downstate back to a rustic heritage of the sort Carl Sandburg celebrated so well."[14] Lindsay certainly imbibed this legend at the source, and Lincoln was a powerful and recurring presence in his poetry.

For Lindsay, the Springfield of his imagination was just such an ideal, and much of his political and social ideology was indeed developed out of his experience in this hybrid space falling somewhere between the rural and the urban.[15] Lindsay's political consciousness, and conscience, were thus formed early and on a distinctly midwestern model.

Lindsay, then, was indeed as Amy Lowell declared, the quintessential product of the middle class in the "uniquely American region" of the Midwest, and more specifically the quintessential product of the small midwestern city of Springfield, embodying all of the historical and cultural tensions of that time and place.[16] But most of all, he was an artist, and that set in motion the greatest tension of all.

After an abortive try at college, Lindsay wanted to make a career as an illustrator and to this end studied art in Chicago and New York; but he had also begun writing at an early age. In 1905 he read a poem to one of his art instructors, Robert Henri, who immediately advised Lindsay to pursue a career as a writer. While anyone else might have found such advice discouraging, Lindsay was instead heartened by this reception. Thereafter, he pursued writing as his primary means of creative expression, though he always considered himself a visual artist.

He first expressed his literary program in a letter of that year:

> I have invented a formula—but I don't write that kind of verse. The formula—two thirds Kipling, one third W. J. Bryan. It might not be poetry?
>
> . . . I am amazed to realize for the first time what Europeans mean

by American Hurry, American restlessness, brashness, lack of tradition, omnivorous industrialism. Things go at a hotter clip every minute. Of course there is poetry in this. But can I respond to it? And ought I? Can I stride the steam engine and go puffing over the prairies?

There is a whole lot that Whitman did not put in. It is the Metallic roar, the terrible overhead railroads, the harshness of it all, that dulls every fine sensibility for the greater part of every day. What little time is left for the soul to live is so little a man cannot read a poem twice. . . . The only way to make him read a poem twice is to construct a jingle haunting as a popular tune, a jingle that can almost be whistled.[17]

So much of Lindsay's eventual style and subject matter is anticipated in this early letter because much of his self-appointed literary mission was formed in reaction to his experiences in Chicago and New York. The essential restlessness and brash energy of the biggest cities resonated with him as a citizen of the Midwest, where the puffing of the steam engine across the prairie formed the connecting tissue of his region with the wider nation. But the darker side of the frantic pace, the roar, the focus on business and wealth and the crowding out of culture, threatened his values of beauty and spirit; and he felt drawn to defend them through some means that would enlist the common man.

Unsuccessful at selling his poems for publication, he turned to hawking his works on the streets. This life as a beggar-poet took on a new dimension in 1906, when Lindsay undertook the first of his tramps across America. After he and a companion sailed from New York to Florida, they began a six hundred–mile walk across Georgia, North Carolina, Tennessee, and Kentucky, destined for Lindsay's home in Springfield. Lindsay planned to trade readings and copies of his poetry for food and lodging along the way, thus forming (and depending upon) a very direct connection with the common folk of the land. Writing of this, he anticipated, "We will probably have a great many adventures of a disagreeable or sordid kind, but we have made up our minds to stand the racket. We will have no money when we reach

Florida. We will be armed with several letters of introduction and carry one clean shirt and collar, for use in emergencies. Otherwise the open road and the hand-out for ours."[18] Lindsay's companion dropped out early in the trek, and the poet's own stamina flagged just short of his goal, ending his walk at his Aunt Eudora's home in Kentucky. His "disagreeable and sordid" adventures were eventually romanticized in the book *A Handy Guide for Beggars*.[19]

Lindsay made two more great walking tours in the years that followed: In 1908 he made his first trek from New York City to his home across New Jersey, Pennsylvania, and Ohio. Then in 1912—after some years back home in Springfield—he began his second trek, in which he planned to walk from Springfield to the Pacific and back. He made it only as far as New Mexico, borrowing train fare from his father to complete the trip to Los Angeles before returning to Springfield that fall. In writing of his travels, he admitted, "I have America—East and South pretty well in my hand. I have lectured all over New England and begged in most of the other states. . . . And if I walk over the West—if I have nothing else—I will have a certain grip on America—and matter to think on, that will keep me years in fathoming."[20]

Lindsay planned for his 1912 walk to preach his "gospel of beauty," and he took along copies of his *Rhymes to Be Traded for Bread*. As he prepared to set out on this last effort to get his arms around the entire expanse of his country, he was, as he put it to another correspondent, "haunted always by a vision of a splendid America. . . . I picture a type of vigorous Americanism born from our six feet deep black soil—a passionate and hardy race—able to conquer and master our tremendous physical resources without being smothered by them. . . ."[21] Lindsay's conception of his life as a national mission had clearly taken shape by 1912.

He eventually published a memoir of this trip, too, *Adventures While Preaching the Gospel of Beauty*.[22] But there was a more immediately important result. While in California, he composed the verse that made him famous. Oddly enough, the theme came not from his experience of the great expanse of America but from a death thousands of miles away: the passing of William Booth, founder of the Salvation Army.

Still, Lindsay eulogized the old general with all the fire and fervor of a revival camp meeting back in his ancestral Kentucky; and he did it with a device that set his poem apart: parenthetical instructions to sing the poem to a gospel tune, and for musical accompaniment by bass drums, banjos, flutes, and tambourines.

By 1912 Lindsay had already achieved some minor publishing success, and the story of his "trading rhymes for bread" had attracted the attention of Harriet Monroe, who was then launching *Poetry: A Magazine of Verse* in Chicago. She invited him to submit some work, and he responded with "General William Booth Enters into Heaven." On the basis of this poem, Lindsay received a one hundred–dollar award, the first solid indication (or deception) that he might make a living from his writing. His work began to appear more frequently, prompting both critical acclaim and an audience for readings.[23]

Within a year he was tired of reciting "General William Booth Enters into Heaven," allegedly till his jaws ached, "4444 times." He hoped the public would take to a recently published piece, "The Kallyope Yell" and "forget General Booth awhile." He had also embarked on another poem that would soon eclipse both of these, and ultimately curse him with its success. As he described it, "I am working on a Congo piece that will make the Kallyope look like thirty cents. . . . I am doubtful whether this stuff is poetry. But I discover a lot of it in me."[24]

"The Congo," a notoriously racist poem, is Lindsay's most famous—or infamous—work. It was known by people who knew nothing else about him: witness the patron who requested Lindsay to read "the poem about Negroes whose name Mrs. Schwartz does not recall"![25] Small wonder, for it was a gripping performance piece, if not what it purported to be, "A Study of the Negro Race."[26] As Lindsay's son Nicholas notes, the poem "is not anthropology or sociology. It is a memorial to an African missionary."[27] Specifically, it commemorates Ray Eldred, a Disciples of Christ missionary in the Congo, as Lindsay tells us in his endnote to the poem; and it celebrates the triumph of the Christian faith over "Mumbo-Jumbo, God of the Congo."[28]

This poem originated from one of the most disturbing experiences of Lindsay's life. In August 1908 a race war erupted in Springfield; and Lindsay was there to witness it, living alone in the family home while his parents were in Europe. For three days a white mob rampaged, destroying black-owned businesses, burning black neighborhoods, and lynching two black men, one an elderly neighbor of the Lindsay's.[29] The event was in no way unique to Springfield, being played out in other cities across the southern Midwest in response to the economic and social pressures created by black migration from the South after the Civil War. The virulent racism introduced into the Midwest by Southern settlers was only exacerbated when working-class whites felt their opportunities threatened by competition with a growing new labor pool. To this was added the deep suspicion by the conservative, small-city business elites against the tide of modernism in the first years of the new century, a "simmering anger and resentment against modern immorality, diversity, and labor." The general sentiment was for a preservation of the old order, reinforcing or attempting to reinstitute traditional gender, class, and racial structures.[30]

While Lindsay was himself disturbed by some of the elements of modernity, in his case this was not accompanied by a reactionary retreat to past order or to racism. Lindsay was horrified by the race riot, though not especially surprised. To a correspondent who was shocked that such an event could have taken place in the home of Lincoln, he observed, "You ask me how Lincoln's name counts in this town. He is of course a convenient climax for sermons on civic righteousness, but none of them have been much heeded. The negro is as heartedly [*sic*] hated here as anywhere by the general populace. As far as the sober can see, we are as likely to have ten riots as one."[31]

Lindsay reacted to the riots in his writing. In the story "The Golden-Faced People," he attempted to put white Springfield in the shoes of their black neighbors by portraying a future in which white people had only recently been liberated from the oppression of a Chinese master race. Such a progressive work on race relations by a white writer was rare enough to draw the attention of W. E. B. DuBois, who reprinted it in 1914 in *The Crisis*.[32]

But positive reviews of his racial writings were not to last. In 1916

Lindsay complained to J. G. Spingarn, the head of the NAACP (himself a white man), that he had recently been "skinned" by DuBois in *The Crisis*: "My 'Congo' and 'Booker T. Washington Trilogy' have both been denounced by the colored people for reasons that I cannot fathom. As far as I can see, they have not taken the trouble to read them through." Lindsay believed that his portrayal of blacks was both positive and hopeful, since he had envisioned them redeemed from superstition and "basic savagery." Spingarn responded, "No colored man doubts your good intentions, but many of them doubt your understanding of their hopes. You look about you and see a black world full of a strange beauty different from that of the white world; they look about them and see other men with exactly the same feelings and desires who refuse to recognize the resemblance." The problem, he felt, was that Lindsay treated black humanity differently from white humanity.[33]

Missing from this white critique of black sentiment was any recognition that Lindsay's descriptions might have been misrepresentative and naive at best, demeaning and hurtful at worst. The obvious and intentional stylistic connection of "The Congo" with blackface minstrelsy only exacerbated an old wound in terms of white conception of black behavior. The smug satisfaction taken in the redemption of the "primitive" (however exotic) natives by the missionaries simply restated the "white man's burden."

Following the line of Spingarn's response, Lindsay's racial consciousness seems to consider other races as romantically different, but equal.[34] While his was certainly not a racialism of hatred, he was criticized for being too "New England," too "Harriet-Beecher-Stowe," in his treatment of African Americans in his writing. Lindsay did spend much time in his youth with the black waiters and staff in Springfield hotels, and wrote affectionately of a black lawyer in Springfield, who was a model for "The Congo." But he was uninformed in many ways regarding race and other nationalities. "The Congo" had nothing to do with the real Africa or real black experience.[35] Yet it is also clear that Lindsay's attitudes toward race were signally different from the norm for his community and his time.

Perhaps for this very reason, "The Congo" was a sensation. In one of Lindsay's first public performances, W. B. Yeats was present and congratulated Lindsay on his achievement. Calls for performances came in from around the country, especially after it appeared in book form.[36] "Performance" is better than reading; for with "The Congo," Lindsay began the practice he called "Higher Vaudeville," presenting his work in a highly stylized manner of both gesture and voice, often employing whoops, whispers, and yells as well as musical instruments and sound effects. His performances both made his reputation and doomed him to endless repetition. Although he contended that only about 10 percent of his poetry fell into the category of higher vaudeville, these were the poems that his audience demanded.

To the extent that Lindsay was recognized and celebrated for the form of his presentation, he ultimately failed in his mission; for his adoption of this higher-vaudeville style was intended only to provide a means of conveying his message to the masses. As his first biographer Albert Trombly recounts, "Mr. Lindsay had observed how vaudeville actors, with a seemingly informal presentation—they sang, spoke, acted, danced, as mood or role or expediency dictated—established a certain intimacy with their audience, and this appealed to him as democratic if not as art. Something like it, then, would perhaps afford the best possible medium for his democratic gospel of beauty."[37]

Lindsay's connection to vaudeville has been explored by his grandson, Nicholas (Nick) Lindsay Jr., a filmmaker in New York City. One of the younger Lindsay's key insights is that his grandfather's audiences did not find his performance style in any way unusual, since it accorded with popular tastes and expectations—it was only the "literary types" who were surprised by it.[38] He further suggests that his grandfather's performance character continued a frontier-theater tradition of the "Kentuckian" as a rustic folkloric figure. Whether consciously or not, Lindsay, in crafting his stage persona, was recalling a "natural primitive" antecedent from his Kentucky ancestry, thus reinforcing the regional nature of his style.[39]

On one hand, higher vaudeville was the basis for whatever financial success Lindsay gained from his poetry. Nick Lindsay Jr. simply states that his grandfather "was in show business" and this made it possible for him to publish his books and otherwise pursue his artistic mission.[40] He made his money on the road, crisscrossing the country by train for years on end, reading at colleges and high schools, ladies' clubs and chambers of commerce, anywhere a paying audience could be found, "sure of flattery and fried chicken in every town."[41] He claimed to have read in all forty-eight states. On the other hand, it was physically and emotionally draining ("like digging ditches," as his grandson remarked). It destroyed his love for the road, which had been a source of energy and inspiration in his younger years. It consumed his time for writing; and in any case, he found that his audiences only wanted to hear the same few poems, most especially and endlessly "The Congo." Increasingly, his new books met with critical and commercial disappointment. Finally, exhausted, his future dark, Lindsay turned again to Springfield.

He had gone back to Springfield once before, in 1908, a man in his late twenties still under his parents' roof, to stay for the next four years. While certainly aware that his neighbors saw him as a failure, Lindsay viewed his homecoming as a mission. He had experienced both the great cities of Chicago and New York and the small towns of the South and the Midwest, and he was back in Springfield to reform not to retreat. Noting that most of his high school classmates had abandoned the city to "the fools, the villains and the weak," he determined, "These people need a vision of a possible Springfield." And with that he declared war on everything he found wrong and wanting in his community in a series of bulletins he published at his own expense.[42]

Most of his *War Bulletins* were directed against "Mammon," the capitalism, commercialism, and materialism that had conquered the country in the years following the Civil War, and which was specifically embodied in the oligarchic elite of Springfield. As he later caricatured his opposition, "The gentleman who incarnates this dream lives in the north, is therefore a Republican. He is quite sure the Emancipation Proclamation meant that millionaires are exempt from criticism, except from other millionaires. . . . He is quite sure that every large bank account is automatically moral, that every small one is almost moral, and the one crime is to be without money. He is quite convinced that Abraham Lincoln died to establish such ideals more firmly in the Republican Party.[43]

Lindsay instead envisioned a nation of "Happy Healthy Beauty Producing Human Beings," and his prescription to achieve this was a "New Localism," a rejection of the large, commercial cities in favor of life organized around the "village" as a democratic and spiritual center of craft and culture existing in harmony, supporting and supported by, the surrounding countryside. Note, though, that in choosing the term "village" for his ideal community, Lindsay was not suggesting it must be small in size, recalling that Springfield was his model. Nor was Lindsay suggesting by this term a return to some imagined halcyon preindustrial past. Instead, the New Localism reveals Lindsay at his most active engagement with regionalism and his attempt to amalgamate the aesthetic and functional merits he attributed to the various regions of America, while accommodating his belief in unchanging spiritual values to a constantly changing material world, at the only level where this appeared possible, the local community.[44]

Lindsay had already constructed an idealized Springfield as his model for civic religion by the time he began to achieve fame for his poetry; and to the disappointment of his admirers then and now, he devoted the bulk of his writing in the next few years to his purest and most baffling expression of that ideal, *The Golden Book of Springfield*. His encounter with the West had made his crusade a national one: "I am not yet an American citizen," he wrote in 1917, "and it seems to me this book is my first chance to be one." In doing so he had no illusions about the influence of poets on world affairs, noting in the same letter, "As a body, critics and poets . . . are one faction, about as well known as the Christadelphians or the No-Necktie holiness faction of the Mennonites, and we have about as much political and social leadership."[45] Nevertheless he seriously intended this book to begin a slow process of societal transformation, and his letters in the years leading up to its publication in 1920 reveal the intensity of his effort.

A strange utopian novel—part political allegory, part religious vision, and often an opaque idiosyncrasy—*The Golden Book of Springfield* defies brief synopsis, though to give just a suggestion: It begins in the contemporary Springfield of 1920, as a disparate group of Springfield residents share their visions of their city in the far future of 2018, all of which involve a mysterious "Golden Book" that appears variously mystical or mundane to those to whom it is revealed. Lindsay is then reborn in that future Springfield, finding himself in the guise of various citizens as well as in his own body, thus witnessing from several vantages the political and cultural events of that time. His guide and companion is Avenal Boone, an Amazon warrior descended from Daniel Boone.

In many respects Springfield is much transformed, having become almost a medieval city with a prominent cathedral and gated city walls; while the appearance of numerous glass-walled skyscrapers set in parks suggests a modernist architectural revolution inspired by Frank Lloyd Wright.[46] Human nature has not much changed, however; and we witness intrigues and assassinations as the faction of "buried gold and alcohol" (the oligarchic elite of Lindsay's Springfield) continues to wield corrupt power in city hall. Clouding over all of this is the specter of approaching war between a vaguely defined "World Government" (of which the United States is voluntarily a part) and an Asian coalition led by Singapore in allegiance to the "Cocaine Buddha" of wealth and self-indulgence. This war at last breaks out and Avenal leads her army of Springfield warriors into battle.

The final chapters take place in the years after the defeat of Singapore and consist of revelations from the golden book and a final mystical vision, in which Lindsay and Avenal sail through the jungles of heaven—depopulated when the angels surrendered themselves to crucifixion on a million "suns and stars and planets" in order to put an end to war. They find that the author of the golden book was Hunter Kelly, the pioneer founder of Springfield, later reborn as St. Scribe of the Shrines who sought to unite all of the religions of the world. As Avenal realizes that Kelly is again "pioneering for our little city in the little earth," she returns to join in the task, and Lindsay finds

PLACE IS A RELATIONSHIP

himself back in the Springfield of 1920, wondering what the next day's weather will be.[47]

Unfortunately for Lindsay—and not surprisingly given even this sketchy synopsis—his *Golden Book* confounded most readers and found little audience outside of Springfield itself. By the time of publication, he described it as "the poorest thing I ever wrote," lamenting, "All I really want is a bunch of about fifty severe but carefully written reviews of the Golden Book. I have not as yet one review of any kind of that volume. It has not even been mentioned or roasted. It has been *absolutely ignored*."[48] In more recent years, some critics have taken on the *Golden Book*. For example, Ann Massa suggests that "the selective imagination which enabled him to be accurately selective of trends which could for good or ill prevail had worked overtime, and could not stop working. The clarity of what could have been an impressively prosaic delineation of the future was clouded by his emotional preoccupation with man's blindness to things divine and America's failure to follow her best traditions."[49] More succinctly, Lindsay could imagine the future of his beloved Springfield but was typically impractical in prescribing the means to achieve it. His New Springfield, like the New Jerusalem, was a construct of religious faith.

Thus, Lindsay's metaphorical journey to an idealized Springfield ended in failure. His connection to the real city was also strained. He spent much of his time traveling the country on speaking tours, largely out of financial necessity, but still with his sense of mission intact. As he declared after canceling the rest of a 1923 tour due to exhaustion, "I wanted to break like a wave on the Rock of the United States." He was still in love with America and claimed a pride of place as a result of his first-hand encounters with so many of her people. Identifying himself with the country so much, he lamented, "those who hate 'Americanism' rejoice exceedingly and say I have written myself out." His new verse did not suit the mood of the postwar nation, and he found himself increasingly marginalized as a regional writer, in demand only for his higher vaudeville works.[50]

He had once declared that he felt safe only when he was on the road or in his own room in Springfield. Tragically, when he needed solace *from* the road, he was temporarily cut off from Springfield because his family home had been leased after the death of his parents. For some years, he settled in Spokane, Washington, where his expenses were underwritten by local boosters who felt the presence of a nationally famous poet would promote the cultural reputation of their city. He finally married there at the age of forty-five, to a teacher twenty years younger, and fathered two children with her. But he was, he wrote in 1927, "always in imagination in the streets of Springfield." He lashed out at the very business interests that had lured him to Spokane, just as he had their counterparts in Springfield in his earlier years.[51]

Finally, in April 1929 he moved his family back into his old Springfield house. But he was still forced to travel for his livelihood; and writing after a reading in May 1931, he despaired that the bulk of his poems "are all *merely incidental* to my audiences because they are audiences three times the size of the Old ones, and have learned only catch-words about me, and the thing promises to grow into a maelstrom, of people who know nothing about me except a Stunt Artist who 'DOES' the Congo."

At the age of fifty-one, he was an "agonized prisoner" of a poem written when he was thirty-four. This despair finally led him to consume a bottle of Lysol on December 5, 1931, ending his life where it had begun, in his Springfield home.[52]

To know how a region can give birth to a national voice, look to Lindsay. His life and work were devoted to the attempt to transcend the limits of regionalism. Lindsay made a conscious effort to achieve "a certain grip on America" through first-hand experience of her land and people. To become an American citizen, he felt he needed to transmute that knowledge into a vision for the nation, assimilating the virtues of all regions into a "New Localism," rooted in his gospel of beauty. In creating his "Higher Vaudeville" presentation style, he drew on the conventions of a national vernacular theater and (perhaps unconsciously) reintroduced a regional "type" as a latter-day folkloric rustic, all with the aim of reaching a mass audience. To a great extent, his physical failure may be attributed to the very vastness of the nation he attempted to encompass, while his artistic failure was

PLACE IS A RELATIONSHIP

as much or more a product of the idiosyncratic nature of his creative vision as it was his regional affiliation.

He was a pure, if exotic, distillation of the Springfield, Illinois, of his day, supremely aware of the myriad contending ideas and ideals surrounding him, consciously working and reworking these themes in his verse and his prose. On the streets of Springfield, and in the words of her poet, great national themes of the frontier, of the bitter and not yet healed wounds of Civil War, of the still unresolved question of race, of Populism and the agrarian ideal, of the struggle for the dignity of labor against the rising tide of industrialism and capitalism, of new West against old East, were all woven into a grand regional, midwestern chorale. Whitman may have heard America singing, but Lindsay went forth to teach that melody to all America and to lead a great national choir.

Notes

I wish especially to thank Jennie Battles, site administrator of the Vachel Lindsay Home in Springfield, Illinois, for her hospitality and assistance with the original version of this paper at the Regionalism and Humanities Conference of the Consortium of Regional Humanities Centers in November 2003 and for inviting me back to Springfield to participate in the celebration of the 125th anniversary of Vachel Lindsay's birth in November 2004, where I had the great fortune to meet the poet's son and grandson, Nicholas Cave Lindsay and Nicholas Cave Lindsay Jr., to both of whom I also express my gratitude for their insights and encouragement.

Much of the appeal and legacy of Lindsay's poetry is derived from his style of presentation. Interested readers should seek out the recordings Lindsay made a few months before his death in 1931 (although the contemporary assessment was that Lindsay was well past his prime performance style by the time of these recordings). Originally released on 78 rpm records by the National Council of Teachers of English, they have recently been made available by the University of Pennsylvania at http://writing.upenn.edu/ pennsound/x/Lindsay.html. The recordings were later released on LP by Caedmon Publishers under the title *Vachel Lindsay Reading "The Congo," "Chinese Nightingale" and Other Poems*, Caedmon TC 1941; and some have appeared in other formats over the years from other publishers. Caedmon also released an LP of Lindsay works read by the poet's son, Nicholas Cave Lindsay, in his father's style (*Vachel Lindsay Poetry*, TC 1216).

1. For general biographical reference see Albert Edmund Trombly, *Vachel Lindsay, Adventurer* (Columbia MO: Lucas Brothers, 1929), the only biography published during the poet's lifetime; Edgar Lee Masters, *Vachel Lindsay: A Poet in America* (New York: Charles Scribner's Sons, 1935); Eleanor Ruggles, *The West-Going Heart: A Life of Vachel Lindsay* (New York: W. W. Norton, 1959); and a semifictionalized account

of his life in Mark Harris, *City of Discontent: An Interpretive Biography of Vachel Lindsay, Being Also the Story of Springfield, Illinois, USA, and the Love of the Poet for That City, That State and That Nation* (Indianapolis: Bobbs-Merrill, 1952). Critical works discussing Lindsay's mission as well as his art include Michael Yatron, *America's Literary Revolt* (New York: Philosophical Library, 1959); Ann Massa, *Vachel Lindsay: Fieldworker for the American Dream* (Bloomington: Indiana University Press, 1970); and Ron Sakolsky, introduction to *The Golden Book of Springfield*, by Vachel Lindsay (Chicago: Charles H. Kerr, 1999). There is also an excellent Lindsay Web site, Mark W. Van Wienen, "Vachel Lindsay (1879–1931)," *Modern American Poetry*, University of Illinois at Urbana–Champaign, www.english.uiuc.edu/maps/poets/g_l/lindsay/lindsay.htm.

2. Etcheson, *Emerging Midwest*, xi.

3. As evidence that Lowell was not voicing a mere personal stereotype, Nicole Etcheson notes that "In the decades after the Civil War, Midwesterners and most Americans came to see the Midwest as a uniquely American region typified by the dominance of the middle class and its business culture." Etcheson, *Emerging Midwest*, 143.

4. Etcheson includes much discussion of the role and influence of Kentuckians in the settlement and later political development of Illinois among the other states of the Old Northwest.

5. Vachel Lindsay to R. W. Gilder, November 6, 1908, in *Letters of Vachel Lindsay*, ed. Marc Chénetier (New York: Burt Franklin, 1979), 29.

6. Sakolsky observes that the Mason-Dixon Line, if extended, would indeed have almost literally divided the town of Springfield. Lindsay, *Golden Book*, xl.

7. Stephen A. Douglas discovered early in his political career that being a member of an "old Kentucky family" was the strongest possible recommendation for public office in southern Illinois. Etcheson, *Emerging Midwest*, 4, 8.

8. Etcheson, *Emerging Midwest*, 39, 141.

9. Etcheson, *Emerging Midwest*, 67–68, 94.

10. Timothy R. Mahoney, "The Small City in American History," *Indiana Magazine of History* 99, no. 4 (December 2003), 323–27.

11. Mahoney, "Small City in American History," 323.

12. There were also downsides to being the state capital, as noted by Robert P. Howard, *Illinois: A History of the Prairie State* (Grand Rapids: William B. Eerdemans, 1972), 330.

13. Among several discussions of Springfield in Lindsay's time in the references I have cited, see Sakolsky, *Golden Book*, xl–xlii. For the influence of the development of the railroads on the region, see James E. Davis, *Frontier Illinois* (Bloomington: Indiana University Press, 1998), 364–81.

14. Richard T. Jensen, *Illinois: A Bicentennial History* (New York: W. W. Norton, 1978), 100–1.

15. Mahoney, "Small City in American History," 315, 319–21. See also Massa, *Vachel Lindsay*, 110–14, which discusses the Springfield survey conducted by the Russell Sage Foundation beginning in 1914, which found Springfield to be an "unusually American city" and a prototype for reform. This survey played a particularly important

role in Lindsay's conception of the future that Springfield portrayed in Vachel Lindsay, *The Golden Book of Springfield* (1920; facsimile, Chicago: Charles H. Kerr, 1999).

16. Etcheson, *Emerging Midwest*, 143.

17. Vachel Lindsay to Susan Wilcox, May 1, 1905, in *Letters*, 7–8.

18. Vachel Lindsay to Susan Wilcox, February 28, 1906, in *Letters*, 19.

19. Vachel Lindsay, *A Handy Guide for Beggars, Especially Those of the Poetic Fraternity* (New York: Macmillan, 1916).

20. Vachel Lindsay to Witter Brynner, February 28, 1912, in *Letters*, 53.

21. Vachel Lindsay to Professor Paul, February 19, 1912, in *Letters*, 56.

22. Vachel Lindsay, *Adventures: Rhymes and Designs* (New York: Eakins Press, 1968).

23. Vachel Lindsay to Harriet Moore, September 18, 1912, in *Letters*, 61–62. For a study of Monroe and *Poetry* including her relationship with Lindsay, see Ellen Williams, *Harriet Monroe and the Poetry Renaissance: The First Ten Years of Poetry, 1912–22* (Urbana: University of Illinois Press, 1977).

24. Vachel Lindsay to Arthur Davidson Ficke, November 11, 1913, in *Letters*, 81.

25. Cited in Massa, *Vachel Lindsay*, 13.

26. Vachel Lindsay, *The Poetry of Vachel Lindsay*, ed. Dennis Camp, 3 vols. (Granite Falls MN: Spoon River Poetry Press, 1984), 1:174–78.

27. Nicholas C. Lindsay, liner note to *Vachel Lindsay Poetry*, read by Nicholas Cave Lindsay, Caedmon TC 1216, (P) and (C) 1967.

28. Lindsay, *Poetry of Vachel Lindsay*, 1:175.

29. For a readily accessible account of the Springfield riot, see Roberta Senechal, "The Springfield Race Riot of 1908," *Illinois History Teacher* (1996), also available at "Illinois Periodicals Online," http://www.lib.niu.edu/ipo/1996/iht329622.html. See also Sakolsky's discussion in Lindsay, *Golden Book*, xii–xxi.

30. Mahoney, "Small City in American History," 327.

31. Vachel Lindsay to R. W. Gilder, November 6, 1908, in *Letters*, 28.

32. Sakolsky in Lindsay, *Golden Book*, xvi–xix.

33. Vachel Lindsay to J. G. Spingarn, November 16, 1916, quoted in Massa, *Vachel Lindsay*, 168–70.

34. For one discussion of Lindsay's views on race, see Massa, *Vachel Lindsay*, 162–70.

35. Vachel Lindsay, in *Letters*, 179, 188, 364–65. See also Lindsay, *Letters*, 74n3 for Lindsay's similar confusion over Asian peoples and cultures.

36. Vachel Lindsay's book *The Congo and Other Poems* (New York: MacMillan, 1914) featured an introduction by Harriet Monroe praising the aural effect of the poem, which Lindsay blatantly encouraged so as to build demand for his appearances. Vachel Lindsay to Harriet Monroe, May 12, 1914, in *Letters*, 96–97.

37. Trombly, *Vachel Lindsay, Adventurer*, 116–17. Investigating this same theme, Massa contends that Lindsay found that vaudeville "had relevance for his propaganda," owing both to the cross section of society that comprised its audience and to the fact that its audience could be "mesmerized by art." Since Lindsay was determined

"to keep it to a real art," as he stated, he coined the term "Higher Vaudeville" to distinguish his loftier purpose. Massa, *Vachel Lindsay*, 231–33.

38. Nicholas Lindsay Jr., "Vachel Lindsay's *The Art of the Motion Picture*" (lecture, Springfield, Illinois, November 6, 2004).

39. Nicholas Lindsay Jr., e-mail message to author, November 15, 2004.

40. Nicholas Lindsay Jr., e-mail message to author, November 22, 2004.

41. Vachel Lindsay to Elizabeth Mann Wills, June 9, 1923, in *Letters*, 288.

42. Vachel Lindsay to R. W. Gilder, October 4, 1908, in *Letters*, 27; Vachel Lindsay, *Collected Poems*, rev. and ill. ed. (New York: Macmillan, 1927), xxxv.

43. Lindsay, *Golden Book*, 11–12.

44. Vachel Lindsay to Witter Bynner, February 18, 1912, in *Letters*, 51; Sakolsky in Lindsay, *Golden Book*, lxxi–lxxiii; Massa, *Vachel Lindsay*, 37–42. Massa treats Lindsay's conception of regionalism, and in particular his idiosyncratic but occasionally prescient assignment of particular characteristics to specific regions of his own device, in a separate chapter (176–93).

45. Vachel Lindsay to Louis Untermeyer, December 21, 1917, in *Letters*, 157–59.

46. Wright's landmark Dana-Thomas house remains, not incidentally, one of the leading attractions in present-day Springfield.

47. The facsimile edition of *The Golden Book* cited here was issued in 1999, after having been out of print and largely forgotten for decades, by the Charles H. Kerr Publishing Company under the aegis of their "Lost Utopias Series." Sakolsky's introduction to that volume contains an extensive, if sometimes debatable, analysis; there is also an extended discussion of the work in Massa, *Vachel Lindsay*, 109–50.

48. Vachel Lindsay to Stephen and Rose Graham, July 25, 1922, in *Letters*, 242; Vachel Lindsay to Harriet Monroe, March 28, 1923, in *Letters*, 214.

49. Massa, *Vachel Lindsay*, 147–48.

50. Vachel Lindsay to Witter Bynner, February 1, 1923, in *Letters*, 274; Vachel Lindsay to Harriet Monroe, March 28, 1923, in *Letters*, 285.

51. Vachel Lindsay to Harriet Moody, December 2, 1914, in *Letters*, 110; Vachel Lindsay to George Greenwood, May 11, 1925, in *Letters*, 358–59; Vachel Lindsay to Marguerite Wilkinson, July 4, 1927, in *Letters*, 405; Vachel Lindsay to William Webster Ellsworth, March 2, 1928, in *Letters*, 424. For a collection of Lindsay's writings published in Spokane newspapers while he was in residence there, see Vachel Lindsay, *Troubadour in "The Wild Flower City,"* ed. Shaun O'L. Higgins (Spokane: New Media Ventures, 1999).

52. Vachel Lindsay to Elizabeth Conner Lindsay, February 22, 1929, in *Letters*, 442; Vachel Lindsay to Margaret Conklin, March 20, 1931, in *Letters*, 453.

4

Place is Political:
Creating Regional Cultures

Michael Saffle and Patrick Lucas offer case studies of what Edward Watts in the previous section might term colonized regional culture, focusing respectively on music in the Southeast and architecture in the Midwest. Whereas Watts discusses the potential for pluralization in regional analysis, akin to models of cultural study that employ race and gender, both Saffle and Lucas find in their studies of regional culture a unifying character, though not one that is derived from nature in any direct sense. Saffle argues that the music of the South Atlantic, which includes Puerto Rico and the U.S. Virgin Islands according to the National Endowment for the Humanities, is characteristically private, implying racial exclusivity's impact in the social organization of the region and the region's consequent historically undeveloped public sphere and market.

Patrick Lucas, in turn, sees settlers hailing from both the North and the South who, upon arriving in the trans-Appalachian West, turned to Greek revival architecture as a way of staking their claim to represent a national model for culture. Where historians have more often noted the survival of sectional differences in the antebellum frontier, Lucas points out that elites consciously deployed this nationally and internationally popular architecture as a "visual rhetoric" for the landscape, in order to create a common idea of democracy that in its

Grecian simplicity was "natural" to the West. Unlike Saffle's argument that private music making dominated cultivated as well as folk practices, however, Lucas does not analyze vernacular architecture, leaving open the question of how widely the democratic meanings of the Greek revival style were understood or shared.[1]

Kurt Kinbacher's essay on the Nebraska Territory similarly argues that this later frontier was a region that was consciously constructed—invented—over time. He demonstrates that how western territories were visually and verbally imagined in the 1850s met very different regional goals than those met by even similar descriptions from "regional" writers like Cather. Alternating visions of the Plains as desert, garden, or transportation corridor served those who desired in it either a replication of yeoman liberties (settlers who retained a conservative culture) or a modern cash economy (railroad investors who fueled the market). Kinbacher cites the territorial seal, on which the farmer and the businessman are hand in hand. Physically and economically bound by the market, together they illustrate the Midwest's regional distinctiveness, which is the result of the diverging and converging goals of those who sought to economically exploit the Plains.

The idea of regionalism being produced by the newly arrived represents a long-standing problem for those who look for "determining" origins for regional identity in the physical rather than the human nature of a place. The problem is that in the classic pattern, one evoked by several essayists in this volume, most regionalists had to leave the region in order to find their regional voice. An alternate narrative poses the regionalist as an outsider who arrives in a region and immerses him- or herself in it, going native and thus becoming authentically of the place. One or the other of these stories is necessary for regionalist writers and artists to separate themselves from the shallow sort who produce local color or, worse, from the tourist, both of whom presumably aim at a home market located elsewhere. The frequency of regionalists as outsiders, however, reinforces the difficulty of finding a region's internal histories, since the kind of distance necessary to observe a break in a pattern or to observe a characteristic regional pattern at all, is not often the product of an insider. Kinbacher, Saffle,

Lucas, and Cheryl Glotfelty resolve the problem by emphasizing that a regional expression is produced to serve particular social and political purposes, whatever its cultural or geographic origins.

Thus, where Valentine leaves Las Vegas out of her story of authentic southwestern architecture, the city's fantasies of Venice and New York are important to Glotfelty as evidence that the desert's influence is less relevant than the political and legal realm are for regional identity. The distinctive features of Nevada literature and regional representation—its ranch novels that undermine the mythic cowboy as well as its divorces, casinos, and prizefighting—were produced not by the landscape but by state laws. An argument might be made that the harsh environment led to an absence of women and so to laws that were distant and different from those controlling genteel eastern society, but Glotfelty's point is well taken: the region's distinctive features and rapid population growth have little to do with the desert and much more to do with state laws. Or more generally, following the theme of this section, regional identity is about political boundaries and political purposes more than the angle of the sun's light.

Notes

1. Patrick Lucas, "Architecture Crosses Region: Building in the Grecian Style," (this volume), 284. The literature on vernacular architecture in this region is extensive; for a still influential model of how to approach it, see Fred Kniffen, "Folk Housing: Key to Diffusion," *Annals of the Association of American Geographers* 55, no. 4 (1965): 549–77.

13. State Pieces in the U.S. Regions Puzzle

Nevada and the Problem of Fit

CHERYLL GLOTFELTY

The 1961 classic film *The Misfits*, starring Marilyn Monroe and Clark Gable, was shot in Nevada and features cowboys who are out of place in the modern West. Picking up on the theme of misfit and using Nevada as a case study, this essay explores the notion that individual U.S. states constitute meaningful cultural subregions whose distinctiveness is brought into relief when viewed in a larger regional context. Nevada's placement in the Southwest—one of the regions designated by the National Endowment for the Humanities in 2001, when it established nine Regional Humanities Centers across the United States—develops this point. According to this model, the Southwest consists of Texas, New Mexico, Arizona, and Nevada. This essay begins by comparing Nevada to a broad range of southwestern cultural paradigms. Then it will survey Nevada's literary tradition, noting how it is and is not southwestern. Nevada's problematic fit in the southwestern cultural mold highlights the tricky nature of any regional designation and calls, finally, for a flexible, multilayered, even ad hoc understanding of region.

Browsing through airport gift shops throughout the Southwest reveals quite a bit about popular conceptions of region. In the airports of cities that are paradigmatically southwestern—Tucson, Phoenix, Albuquerque, and El Paso—gift shops display strings of red chili peppers and abound in kitschy coyote imagery, the acme of which is a silhou-etted coyote, clad in sombrero and bandana, haunches on a mesa, howling at the moon. Shoppers can expect saguaro cactus–shaped salt and pepper shakers, woven Indian rug placemats, turquoise and silver jewelry, pottery in earth tones, Kokopelli coasters, and gour-met salsas. Now, for comparison, check out the Reno and Las Vegas airports, whose terminals jangle with shiny chrome slot machines. You'll find tacky shot glasses and ash trays imprinted with city lo-gos in gold leaf, books on how to beat the house, fluffy pairs of dice to hang from your rearview mirror, decks of cards, automobile mo-tifs from the 1950s and 1960s, some Lake Tahoe sweatshirts and ski themes, Hard Rock Cafe T-shirts, sagebrush-scented hand cream, and corny maps identifying the location of whore houses. Admittedly, such curio shops register only a superficial understanding of region; still, these artifacts are rooted in deeper realities about a region's history: how people live there, what economies sustain the area, and what plants and animals share the place. Southwestern curios emphasize the region's long history of human habitation; the enduring presence of Native American peoples and art; the influence of Mexican fash-ion and foods; and strong cultural ties to the desert and its signature plant, the saguaro. In contrast, Nevada curios, rather than cashing in on continuities with an ancient past, celebrate life in the moment—carpe diem!—reflecting an economy based heavily on tourism, gam-bling, and adult entertainment.

Looking beyond popular consumer culture, we find that traditional cultural indices reinforce the sense that Nevada's fit within the South-west is somewhat anomalous. For example, southwestern architec-ture tends to be Spanish-influenced, maintains ties with the past, is often expressed in adobe, and is typified in Santa Fe. Nevada archi-tecture, in dramatic contrast, screams neon! new! ritzy! More sign than substance, it is postmodern, celebrated by the gala implosions of yesterday's edifices to make way for the newest erections in Las Vegas—the Bellagio, New York–New York, the Mirage, the Strato-sphere, the Luxor. Popular southwestern cuisine is Mexican or Tex-Mex, whereas Nevada's famous casino-food deals boast $14.99 all-you-can-eat buffets with shrimp, live Maine lobster, and steak, while Nevada's celebrated ethnic cuisine is Basque, featuring mutton and lamb dishes served family style. These food ways correspond to dominant ethnicities—Hispanic in the Southwest, Basque in Nevada. In religion, the Southwest is historically Catholic, while Nevada shows a strong Mormon influence.

Geographically, Nevada shares the aridity characteristic of the Southwest generally, although the Southwest is dominated by the Sonoran Desert, while most of Nevada belongs to the Great Basin Desert and, in the south, the Mojave. The Great Basin is a high-elevation desert, with warm days, cool nights, and cold winters. Sagebrush is the dominant plant in the Great Basin, a region also known as "the sagebrush ocean." To the south, the Mojave is lower-elevation and much hotter, with summer temperatures soaring well over a hundred degrees Fahrenheit. Joshua trees and mesquite are native to the Mojave landscape. Comparing a map of the United States to the National Endowment for the Humanities–defined regions shows that about 55 percent of Nevada's border is shared with states in the Pacific Region; 35 percent borders the Rocky Mountain Region; while a mere 10 percent borders the Southwest Region.

Although Nevada is indisputably in the American West, most of Nevada is *north* of the geographic midpoint of the continental United States, making *South*west an odd designation.

Nevada is the most arid, the most mountainous, and the fastest-growing state in the nation. It has the highest percentage of federally owned land of any state (at 85 percent), whereas Texas has among the lowest percentages (at 1.4 percent). Demographically, Nevada is one of the most urban states in America, with the vast majority of its citizens living in the Las Vegas and Reno–Sparks–Carson City metropolitan areas, while most counties in Nevada could be classified frontier, averaging less than two people per square mile. Nevada's economy relies heavily on mining and tourism, while the economies of the rest of the Southwest are more diverse. Perhaps most tellingly for Nevada's culture, the state has sanctioned activities that are illegal elsewhere: historically, the state was known for prize fighting and easy divorce;

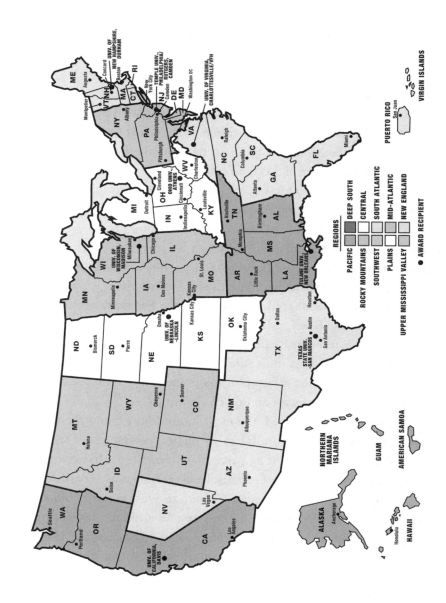

FIG. 1: NEH Regional Humanities Centers. *Source:* Southwest Regional Humanities Center.

and today, it has added gambling, prostitution, and hassle-free marriage. Finally, Nevada is where America tests its nuclear bombs and plans to dump its nuclear waste.[1]

Not to belabor this argument, but Nevada has many profound differences from the Southwest, perhaps fitting better in the Pacific or Rocky Mountain regions. If, however, one were to compare Nevada to those regions, important differences would also emerge. Indeed, it may be argued that culturally Nevada is a region unto itself, influenced by the cultures of neighboring regions and states certainly, but so overwhelmingly tied to the gaming industry and tourism that its culture has evolved along a path that diverges from the larger regions that contain it.

The Nevada exceptionalism discussed in the foregoing examples holds true in literature as well. Before elucidating the ways in which Nevada's literary tradition diverges from the southwestern mainstream, it's worth acknowledging that considering Nevada as part of the Southwest helps demonstrate striking commonalties among the literatures of this region, notably long-standing and quite similar Native American and ranch writing traditions as well as abundant—albeit self-consciously distinct—desert nature writing. Southwestern literature often portrays Native American experience, which in part accounts for the flowering of contemporary Native American literature. Nevada shares in this general pattern, producing one of the nation's earliest Native writers—Sarah Winnemucca Hopkins, who in 1883 wrote *Life Among the Piutes*, believed to be the first book written by a Native American woman. Present-day Paiute poets Adrian C. Louis and nila northSun write with anger and humor about reservation life, while essayist Joe Ely weaves together traditional stories with modern-day environmental concerns. Shoshone elder Corbin Harney is a leading antinuclear activist, and several Native Americans from Nevada have authored tribal histories.

Another commonality between the literature of Nevada and the other southwestern states is literary treatments of ranching, which abound, receiving refined treatment in the novels of Nevada's Walter Van Tilburg Clark in *The Ox-Bow Incident* (1940) and *The Track of the Cat* (1949).[2] Much Nevada ranch writing strives to show ranching as it really is, replacing the mythic cowboy of popular westerns with realistic depictions of working cowboys, including the impact of federal land management policies on their lives. Ranch writing includes the thriving folk genre of cowboy poetry, Nevada's best-known cowboy poets being Waddie Mitchell, Rod McQueary, Jack Walther, and Georgie Connell Sicking, each of whom has been featured in documentaries and included in anthologies of cowboy poetry. Waddie Mitchell, who is instantly recognizable for his hallmark handlebar mustache, has become such a successful writer and performer that in contrast to most cowboy poets he is no longer a working cowboy. A full-time performer with several albums and books, he has played to Carnegie Hall and in Europe, sharing the wit, the grit, and the wisdom of life on the range with audiences throughout the world. The renaissance of cowboy poetry throughout the West began in Elko, Nevada, in 1985 with the stunningly popular Cowboy Poetry Gathering, an annual event that draws nearly ten thousand people every January to this wintry little town in the middle of nowhere.

Southwestern literature frequently describes desert living, with John C. Van Dyke's 1901 *The Desert* setting a pattern of appreciation for the beauty of desert landscapes. As Ann Ronald's scholarly essay "Why Don't They Write About Nevada?" argues, Nevada deserts have not enjoyed the literary attention that the more charismatic Sonoran deserts of Arizona, Utah, and New Mexico have received by writers such as John Wesley Powell, Edward Abbey, Ann Zwinger, Charles Bowden, Rob Schulteis, Gary Nabhan, and others.[3] Although turn-of-the-century Nevada author and desert lover Idah Meacham Strobridge—a friend of Mary Austin—is an early exception, having published *In Miner's Mirage-Land* in 1904 and *The Land of Purple Shadows* in 1909, in general it has taken writers until the late twentieth century to articulate the beauty of the vast, dry ocean of sage gray; the empty white playas; and the endless scrappy mountain ranges of Nevada. But the literary storm has arrived to this parched land; and Nevada wilderness calendars sell like hotcakes, complemented by a fecund selection of finely wrought tributes to the Great Basin desert by numerous contemporary writers.[4] Nevada, in fact, is well represented in the recent anthology *Getting Over the Color Green: Contemporary Environmental Literature of the Southwest.*[5] While it takes aesthetic education to "get over the color green," to learn to see beauty in desert browns and tans, it requires an even more finely honed sensibility to be a connoisseur of the still subtler, drab gray Great Basin.

Southwestern literature has predominantly concerned itself with the Mexican American experience and borderland issues, but these central literary preoccupations of the Southwest are entirely absent in Nevada's literature. Unlike the other three states in the Southwest Region, Nevada shares no border with Mexico, and its literature almost never presents Mexican American central characters or issues. Although there are Nevada writers who are originally from Colombia (German Santanilla) or Chile (Emma Sepúlveda-Pulvirenti), one would be hard-pressed to name a single author who traces his or her lineage to Mexico. When ethnicity is engaged in Nevada literature, the subject is most likely to be the Basque American experience, most beautifully expressed in the two dozen works of Robert Laxalt, whose book *Sweet Promised Land*, a memoir of his father's immigration to America to become a sheepherder, received national attention when it appeared in 1957 and has never gone out of print. *Sweet Promised Land* is the book that inspired the annual Basque festivals now held throughout the northern American West. Robert Laxalt was also instrumental in establishing a world-renowned Basque Studies Program at the University of Nevada, Reno, and for launching the Basque book series at the University of Nevada Press.[6]

What Nevada literature lacks in Mexican American and borderland themes, it makes up for in handling themes that Southwestern literature rarely touches—notably divorce, gambling, the Mob, and nuclear testing, each of which has generated distinctive literary traditions. The Reno divorce novel flourished between the 1920s and 1960s, years when Reno's liberal divorce laws and promotional campaigns in major newspapers on the East Coast made it famous as the divorce capital of the world. Authors who contributed to this genre were typically themselves temporary Reno residents and graduates of the "divorce mill." These literary works furnished for the authors therapy, diversion, and cash.[7] After the 1960s, Nevada's literary epicenter shifted south, corresponding to a shift in thematic preoccupation from divorce to gambling and the Mob. Names and titles are almost too numerous to mention, but among the best are Hunter S. Thompson's *Fear and Loathing in Las Vegas* (1971), John Gregory Dunne's *A Memoir of a Dark Season* (1974), Mario Puzo's *Fools Die* (1978), Susan Berman's *Easy Street* (1981), John O'Brien's *Leaving Las Vegas* (1990), Nicolas Pileggi's *Casino* (1995), Michael Ventura's *The Death of Frank Sinatra* (1996), John H. Irsfeld's *Radio Elvis and Other Stories* (2002), and H. Lee Barnes's *The Lucky* (2003). Most of Nevada's works that center around the mob or gambling are set in Las Vegas—"Sin City"—a place so unlike any other that it constitutes a region unto itself even within Nevada, possessing a unique, colorful literary tradition of its own.[8]

Several southwestern states were involved in the development and early testing of atomic weapons, and the nuclear shadow thus falls on the Southwest Region as a whole; however, atomic testing moved permanently and exclusively to Nevada in 1951, spawning a powerful tradition of protest literature, recently given new impetus by the federal campaign to site the nation's only high-level nuclear waste dump at Yucca Mountain, Nevada.[9] While the literature of divorce, gambling, and nuclear radiation is to an extent distinctively Nevadan, it also speaks to the human condition, exploring complexities, desires, fears, and compulsions that characterize modern life. In the last half of the twentieth century, Nevada became a crucible of American social and military experimentation and, some might say, transgression.

Finally, perhaps because truth in Nevada is so often stranger than fiction, the state has spawned an unusually vibrant literary tradition of journalism and travel literature that dates back to the days of the Comstock Lode, when Mark Twain made a name for himself working for the *Territorial Enterprise* in Virginia City; other sterling frontier newspapermen include Dan De Quille (in the *Territorial Enterprise*), J. Ross Browne (in *Harper's Monthly*), Alfred Doten (in the *Gold Hill News*), Samuel Davis (in the *Morning Appeal*), Fred Hart (in the *Reese River Reveille*). This trend continues into modern times with the lively columns of A. J. Liebling (in the *New Yorker*), Hank Greenspun (in the *Las Vegas Sun*), John L. Smith (in the *Las Vegas Review-Journal*), Rollan Melton (in the *Reno Gazette-Journal*), Jim Sloan (in the *Reno Gazette-Journal*), and Jon Christensen (in *High Country News*).

While the Southwest in general is a popular tourist destination that generates a corresponding amount of travel writing, Nevada is perhaps exceptional in attracting a horde of literary detractors. I've explored this phenomenon elsewhere in an essay on place bashing, but let me here share just two representative examples, the first from rambling naturalist John Muir and the second from former president Harry S. Truman.[10] Hiking into Nevada from his beloved Sierra Nevada mountains, Muir writes, "From the very noblest forests in the world [the traveler] emerges into . . . dead alkaline lake-levels. Mountains are seen beyond, rising in bewildering abundance, range beyond range. But . . . these always present a singularly barren aspect, appearing gray and forbidding and shadeless, like heaps of ashes dumped from the blazing sky."[11] Viewing Nevada from an airplane, then-president Truman pens these impressions: "We came to the great gambling and marriage destruction hell, known as Nevada. To look at it from the air it is just that—hell on earth. There are tiny green specks on the landscape where dice, roulette, light-o-loves, crooked poker and gambling thugs thrive. Such places should be abolished and so should Nevada. It never should have been made a State."[12]

After his initial aesthetic disorientation, Muir acquired a taste for Nevada. Treading 1,800 miles on foot in the Silver State to study its geology and natural history, he concluded that "Nevada is beautiful in her wildness."[13] With all due respect, the nearly one million people who have moved to Nevada in the last decade might disagree with Truman; to wit, Nevada has been the fastest growing state in the nation for two decades running. This giant population influx means that a hefty percentage of Nevadans are relative newcomers. Many within the niche of literary studies share the National Endowment for the Humanities Regional Humanities Centers' goal of helping these and other people cultivate a sense of place for where they live. The purpose of a forthcoming anthology of the literature of Nevada, similar in concept and scope to Montana's *The Last Best Place: A Montana Anthology*, is to introduce to new Nevadans, while preserving for longtime residents, the stories of the place in order to enrich their experience of living in the Silver State and to help them to feel at home, with a stake in Nevada's future. A similar effort is currently being undertaken by Nevada Humanities, which is developing the Nevada Online Encyclopedia to "provide reliable, up-to-date information, . . . [which] will make it possible for all students, whether in urban or rural areas, to have equal access to resources necessary for the study and appreciation of Nevada history."[14]

People identify with states. When you ask someone, where are you from? do you expect to hear *I'm from the South Atlantic* or *I'm from the Plains*? No, the response is more likely to be *I'm from Virginia* or *I'm from Kansas*. Conference name badges identify participants by state universities. Upon moving out of state, one of the first rituals is to apply for license plates; and when we slap those new plates onto our car we feel—with joy or regret—the change in identity that they signify. Bumper stickers announce, "Colorado Native"; "Don't Mess with Texas"; "Nevada Is Not a Wasteland." When driving cross-country, one road sign thanks us for visiting the state receding in the rearview mirror, while another sign welcomes us to the state beckoning through the windshield. Sometimes even the quality of the road surface changes at state lines. Each state has its state bird, state mammal, state flower, state flag, state song, state motto. The U.S. Postal Service issued a fifty-state "lick 'em" stamp series that was so popular that it was reissued in a "peel off" sheet after stamp prices increased. Soon each state will have a commemorative quarter. States are real to people and are closely tied to public policy issues because of the institution of state governments and laws.

It would make an interesting study to determine how many other states are misfits in larger regional puzzles. Geographical regions may be analogous to literary canons. Like a region, a canon is a mental construct that helps us discern and describe patterns and traditions; but

PLACE IS POLITICAL

when any one literary work is held up against canonical norms, the work invariably asserts its difference and individuality, its *departure* from the general pattern. Indeed, the very formation of a canon—the grouping of a selection of works together—helps us notice the diversity within it. The so-called canon wars have led literary scholars to revise and redefine canons, necessitating new editions of anthologies to reflect changing values. Perhaps regional humanities scholars will likewise periodically redraw the boundaries of regional maps. Regional revisionists might ask which cultural elements are state-specific and which ones hold true for larger regions. Can a regional cultural theory be developed that takes scale into account? We should consider the history, economy, and laws of the individual states within a region. Where these factors vary dramatically from state to state, it is likely that striking cultural differences will as well, differences that will in some cases overshadow geographical and biophysical similarities.

In other words, individual states have been and continue to be meaningful regions, closely tied to culture and to people's sense of place. Any theory of regionalism and the humanities that fails to consider the salience of American states as possibly distinctive cultural regions ignores artifactual data, political and institutional reality, and lived experience. At the same time, however, any theory of regionalism that considers only states is likewise incomplete. What is needed is an understanding of the ways that regions are comprised of distinctive subregions, which may overlap and themselves be subdivided into still smaller regions. While it is an important insight that culture is regional and that identification with place can reaffirm common bonds among an otherwise diverse public, we should also keep in mind that people identify with a variety of different regions for different purposes. To some people states are salient regions for some purposes. At other times, for other purposes, giant areas—the West, for example—are regions. For still other kinds of endeavors, local microregions—the Truckee Meadows or the Vegas Valley—constitute practicable regions. And, for still other purposes, bioregions or ecoregions hold their own significance in regional theory. Milkweed Editions, for example, has established a Web site entitled "The World as

FIG. 2: The World as Home Ecoregions. *Source*: Milkweed Editions
and the World as Home program, www.milkweed.org.
Sara St. Antoine and Gary Nabhan.

Home," which maps "literary writing about the natural world." In
that map, all of Nevada, all of Arizona, and the western half of New
Mexico fall into the Western Deserts and Plateaus Ecoregion, while
Texas spans five ecoregions.

Such a division of America into ecoregions delineated by habitat and
climatic zones encourages Americans to think beyond state boundaries to natural properties of the land itself and to ponder the relation
between nature and culture.

Designating regions can be a tool for perception by throwing certain patterns and features into vivid relief while obscuring others.

Regional taxonomies create a sense of order, but any taxonomy—
even a taxonomy of naturalistic ecoregions—is an artificial construct.
If nothing else, Nevada's problem of fit should caution against making
too-easy regional assumptions and should encourage continuous engagement in the self-reflexive, theoretical practice of pondering both
regions and regionalism.

Notes

1. Historian Elizabeth Raymond ably characterizes Nevada's geographic, demo-
graphic, and economic distinctiveness from the broader American West in her essay
"When the Desert Won't Bloom: Environmental Limitation and the Great Basin," in
Many Wests: Place, Culture, and Regional Identity, ed. David M. Wrobel and Michael
C. Steiner, making a case for subregional diversity within a larger region. Taking a cue
from that book, an alternate title for my essay could be "Many Southwests."

2. Other important Nevada ranch writers are Will James (*Lone Cowboy*, 1930),
Owen Ulph (*The Fiddleback: Lore of the Line Camp*, 1981), Molly Flagg Knudtsen
(*Under the Mountain*, 1982), R. Guild Gray (*The Treble V: The Legacy of a Cattle
Baron of the Old West*, 1986), and Carolyn Dufurrena (*Fifty Miles from Home: Rid-
ing the Long Circle on a Nevada Family Ranch*, 2002).

3. Ann Ronald, "Why Don't They Write About Nevada?" *Western American Literature* 24, no. 3 (November 1989): 213–24.

4. Examples of this more contemporary literature include Sessions S. Wheeler (*The
Nevada Desert*, 1971), John McPhee (*Basin and Range*, 1981), Stephen Trimble (*The
Sagebrush Ocean*, 1989), Bernard Schopen (*The Desert Look*, 1989), Rebecca Sol-
nit (*Savage Dreams*, 1994), Shaun T. Griffin (*Snowmelt*, 1994), Ann Ronald (*Earth-
tones*, 1995), Gary Short (*Flying over Sonny Liston*, 1996), Kirk Robertson (*Just Past
Labor Day: Selected and New Poems, 1969–1995*, 1996), Mary Webb (*A Doubtful
River*, 2000), Jon Christensen (*Nevada*, 2001), William L. Fox (*Reading Sand: Se-
lected Desert Poems, 1976–2000*, 2002), and Richard V. Francaviglia (*Believing in
Place*, 2003).

5. Scott Slovic, ed., *Getting over the Color Green: Contemporary Environmental
Literature of the Southwest* (Tucson: University of Arizona Press, 2001).

6. Other Nevada writers who explore the Basque American experience include
Jean McElrath (*Aged in Sage*, 1964), Monique Urza (*The Deep Blue Memory*, 1993),
Frank Bergon (*Wild Game*, 1995), Gregory Martin (*Mountain City*, 2000), Michael A.
Thomas (*Ostrich*, 2000), and Carolyn Dufurrena (*Fifty Miles From Home*, 2002).

7. They include Cornelius Vanderbilt Jr. (*Reno*, 1929), John Hamlin (*Whirlpool
of Reno*, 1931), Dorothy Walworth Carman (*Reno Fever*, 1932), Clare Booth Luce
(*The Women*, 1937), Faith Baldwin (*Temporary Address: Reno*, 1941), Jill Stern (*Not
in Our Stars*, 1957), Arthur Miller (*The Misfits*, 1961), and Jane Rule (*Desert of the
Heart*, 1964).

8. For more on charting Las Vegas's unique literary tradition, see Mike Tronnes,
Literary Las Vegas: The Best Writing about America's Most Fabulous City (New

York: Henry Holt, 1995); and Richard Logsdon, Todd Moffett, and Tina D. Eliopulos, eds., *In the Shadow of the Strip: Las Vegas Stories* (Reno: University of Nevada Press, 2003).

9. Authors who have borne witness to the bombing and radioactive waste dumping in Nevada include William Kittredge ("In My Backyard," 1988), Terry Tempest Williams ("The Clan of One-Breasted Women," 1991), Adrian C. Louis ("Nevada Red Blues," 1992), Carole Gallagher (*American Ground Zero*, 1993), Frank Bergon (*The Temptations of St. Ed and Brother S*, 1993), Rebecca Solnit (*Savage Dreams*, 1994), Robert Vasquez ("Early Morning Test Light over Nevada, 1955," 1995), Corbin Harney (*The Way It Is*, 1995), Gary Short ("Tidings," 1996), Tracy Daugherty (*What Falls Away*, 1996), Shaun T. Griffin ("Nevada No Longer," 1999), James Conrad (*Making Love to the Minor Poets of Chicago*, 2000), and Nicole Krauss (*Man Walks into a Room*, 2002).

10. Cheryll Glotfelty, "Literary Place Bashing, Test Site Nevada," in *Beyond Nature Writing: Expanding the Boundaries of Ecocriticism*, ed. Karla Armbruster and Kathleen R. Wallace (Charlottesville: University Press of Virginia, 2001), 233–47.

11. John Muir, *Steep Trails: California, Utah, Nevada, Washington, Oregon, The Grand Canyon* (Boston: Houghton Mifflin, 1918), 164.

12. Harry S. Truman, *Off the Record: The Private Papers of Harry S. Truman*, ed. Robert H. Ferrell (New York: Harper and Row, 1980), 317.

13. Muir, *Steep Trails*, 162.

14. Cheryll Glotfelty, ed., *Literary Nevada: From Native America to the Nuclear Age* (Reno: University of Nevada Press, forthcoming); and *Nevada Online Encyclopedia*, Nevada Humanities, http://www.nevadahumanities.org/encyclopedia/ (accessed July 11, 2006).

14. Imagining Place

Nebraska Territory, 1854–1867

KURT E. KINBACHER

Nebraska Territory became a legal entity on May 30, 1854. Politically connected to Kansas Territory by a desperate maneuver to settle the national sectional debate, it emerged as a new field of opportunity for a vibrant and mobile population. The Americans who massed on the Iowa border waiting to take possession of the latest open property had little first-hand (or even accurate second-hand) information on the land they were about to claim. Despite this geographic challenge, many believed their fortunes awaited them. As an early statesman, Merrill H. Clark noted, "No one can comprehend the vast wealth of Nebraska, or realize the proud position she is destined to occupy in the history of the world."[1]

When considering region, historian Dan Flores suggests that "specific human cultures and specific landscapes" often intertwine to create distinctive places.[2] With this in mind, human imagination and development in early Nebraska were dominated by two symbiotic forces. The territory was shaped, in part, by mid-nineteenth-century farmers and town builders who adapted their imported cultures to fit the demands of a vast grassland. Simultaneously, the same players reenvisioned and then altered these prairies to meet familiar sensibilities. In both cases, settlers "conceived of their whole history of westward migration as one of continual progress," a concept immortalized on the great Territorial Seal and reiterated by early legislators who praised the "industrious and enterprising pioneers" who came to "better their condition."[3] In doing so—in large part by establishing market economies and reproducing familiar social structures—they brought Nebraska to statehood in just over a dozen years, a feat accomplished only by Kansas, Oregon, and Nevada during the 1860s.

The Great Plains—home of Buffalo Bill, Crazy Horse, and the long cattle drive—emerged in the American consciousness as the very heart of the West during the late nineteenth century. Fin de siècle scholars, most notably historian Frederick Jackson Turner, even celebrated the Plains as the last frontier. Revolutionizing his field of study, Turner envisioned American movement across the continent as the force that separated the United States "from the influence of Europe." Farmers— the main players in a grand process—grappled with and then settled the "wilderness." Their movements from civilization into barbarism and back again endowed noble American citizens with the traits of "individualism, democracy, and nationalism."[4]

Four decades later, Walter Prescott Webb extended this argument by suggesting that the "Great Plains have bent and molded Anglo-American life, have destroyed traditions, and have influenced institutions." The environment was the mechanism of this change as the flat, sub-humid, and treeless Plains created an institutional fault line. As American agriculturists entered the region, they were forced to construct new establishments in accordance with physical conditions.[5]

Enthralled with the myth of the American yeoman, Turner and Webb assumed that agriculture and rural landholding were the basis of development on the Great Plains. Writing barely a generation after Webb, James C. Malin argued that the "actual settler" running the "family size farm" was part of a social myth "more closely associated with propaganda than with history." He suggested that by 1854 a "machine civilization broke down local self sufficiency" and brought Plains farmers into a world economy.[6] By the late twentieth century, many influential scholars contended that because outlets for farm produce were vital to growth, "nucleated settlements at the edge of the frontier on or near the best routes of transportation,"

PLACE IS POLITICAL

were the true engines of economic growth.[7] In many instances, cities preceded farms and became "the principle colonizing agent of the western landscape."[8]

Despite changing interpretations and ample criticisms, the works of Turner and Webb remain remarkably influential, as scholars alternately condemn their theses or dedicate their own work in their memory. Still, most agree that their emphasis on place at the expense of culture was grossly overstated. Currently, scholars attempt to find balance between environmental and cultural forces. Geographer Edward Soja, for instance, argues that "our actions and thoughts shape the spaces around us," but at the same time, "spaces and places within which we live also shape our actions and thoughts."[9] The options for utilizing a particular place have limits, however, as human imagination is not always pliant. Frequently, "material and mental barriers limit the capacity for change." As a result, culture and environment are often at odds.[10]

Still, human imagination in Nebraska was often elastic among the Euro-Americans who established themselves on the Great Plains before it even had that name. Indeed, American statesmen and explorers had already assigned conflicted meanings to these grasslands years prior to the establishment of Nebraska Territory. Additionally, farmers, boosters, speculators, town builders, and politicians continuously reconsidered Nebraska's significance after it was opened for settlement. Visions of farmsteads, town sites, landscapes, and political structures continued to shift throughout the territorial era and beyond. Such representations of Nebraska demonstrate that cultural imagination is rarely static. Though known and occupied by Indigenous peoples centuries before "discovery," Americans prior to 1854 imagined the entire region alternately as an agrarian Garden of Eden, the Great American Desert, or a transportation corridor.

Joining the nation as part of the Louisiana Purchase, greater Nebraska—the original territory included the present state of Nebraska, the Dakotas west of the Missouri, most of Montana, three-quarters of Wyoming, and one-third of Colorado—was declared to be the "garden of the world" by then-president Thomas Jefferson.[11] In this Virginian's worldview, the newfound land was the ideal place for yeoman farmers to build an empire of liberty—an area free both of slavery and of the pitfalls of mercantile America. To secure this vision, Jefferson dispatched the Corps of Discovery to explore, catalogue, and claim vast tracts of unknown real estate. Sympathetic to their commander in chief's view, Lewis and Clark were overwhelmed by the beauty and economic potential of the long and wide Missouri Valley and largely supported the garden view in their journals. Interestingly, this rosy depiction of the region lasted less than a generation.

Explorers who ventured past the Missouri's wooded riparian corridor, beginning with Zebulon Pike, confronted a different reality. Indeed, most of those traveling west along alternate routes had little to recommend about the surrounding environment. In 1819 the Stephen Long expedition traversed up the Platte and down the Arkansas. In the only surviving report of this expedition, Dr. Edwin James described both river valleys and the entire region as "an inescapable obstacle in the way of settling the country," and he labeled it the "Great American Desert." This vision dominated textbooks by 1824 and clouded the minds of cartographers and, consequently, citizens through the 1860s.[12]

Jeffersonian visions of the region were forgotten for several decades following the Long report. The national discussion regarding the trans-Missouri West focused on the resettlement of Native Americans, who were perceived to be inhibiting progress. In 1834 the Indian Trade and Intercourse Act was passed and the federal government began to assign new homelands to many Native nations. For the time being, the tribes confined to the future Nebraska—Omahas, Otoes and Missourias, and Pawnees—were already at home in their prescribed ranges.[13] For the next twenty years, entry onto the Great Plains required the permission of the Department of War. With land available in Oregon, California, and Utah, this edict was frequently ignored as fifty thousand American migrants turned the Platte River valley into a transportation corridor each season. (The numbers spiked dramatically when gold was discovered in the Sacramento River region.)

PLACE IS POLITICAL

Reports of Nebraska during the overland era were notably divergent. Soldiers garrisoned along the wagon roads described the region as "lonely and desolate."[14] Concurrently, a small but vocal cadre of boosters insisted that it was "the empire of the future."[15] The latter group's voice became more and more noticeable as the best lands in the Far West were claimed and populated. As Americans looked back at the region they had crossed over, even the broad Plains seemed smaller. Nebraska, by this time, was part of a worldview that encouraged encroachment on Indian territory and the expansion of "civilization" to the Pacific. Sectional concerns thwarted Congressional attempts to open the region several times during the 1840s, but despite these difficulties, settlement seemed inevitable. Ultimately, the federal government negotiated a series of treaties that curtailed the territory of the Indians in the Missouri and Platte river valleys. By early 1854, Americans were ready to weave Nebraska into the national fabric.[16]

Yet, on the eve of settlement, the new territory was still "a poorly understood land for most white Americans."[17] Vast tracts were still the sovereign countries of untreated tribes; some of these areas would remain outside the pale of American settlement even after Nebraska achieved statehood in 1867. Additionally, the term "unexplored" was used with some frequency north of the Platte.[18] None of this uncertainty stopped Nebraska boosters from claiming "these prairies will be peopled from the great river to the mountains. This is a mighty and majestic future to which we look." According to this worldview, the territory's wide open spaces were a blessing that provided settlers "an immense field wheron [sic] we may expend our energy."[19]

Although Nebraska was not consistently defined as a "garden" in 1854, in the American imagination, farming brought all lands to their highest calling.[20] It was also "a tradition-oriented occupation" that was not necessarily readily adaptable. Agriculturists, according to historian Peter Boag, imported a "performed culture" comprising a set of "assumptions" and remembered "physical features" that served as the blueprint for farmers in newly opened lands for at least a generation. As a result, they often unknowingly limited their own options

FIG. 3: Great Seal of Nebraska Territory. *Centennial Handbook: Nebraska Territory, 1854–1954* (Lincoln: Nebraska Territorial Centennial Commission, 1954). Courtesy of the Nebraska State Historical Society.

for growth, a tendency that was exacerbated by a headlong collision with a unique physical environment.[21]

Still, the agriculturist—seen at the left on the Territorial Seal—was presented as one of the chief agents of "Progress," which was one of the territory's mottoes on the seal, along with "Popular Sovereignty" and "The Constitution."

With his long rifle, long pants, thigh-length jacket, and wide brimmed hat, the farmer-frontiersman with his plow and orchard would allow the territory to blossom. Not surprisingly, most of the earliest settlers were farmers. Of the 743 heads of household reporting an occupation in the 1854 census, 471 claimed to be farmers. The majority gave way

PLACE IS POLITICAL

to a plurality by 1860 when the census found 40 percent of the population engaged in farming or farm labor, but many people claiming other occupations serviced this agricultural population.[22]

To most new arrivals—generally Caucasian, native-born, and hailing from the Old Northwest or Central Atlantic states—the grasslands of eastern Nebraska seemed "a land of uniformity and monotony." The proclivity for forested environments had roots stretching back into European societies. Consequently, these nascent Nebraskans avoided fertile loess hills because they were blanketed by unfamiliar tall grass prairies, flocking instead to the wooded western bank of the Missouri River before trickling into the well-traveled Platte River valley and then the flood plains of the Loup, Nemaha, Elkhorn, and Big Blue rivers that dissected the prairies. The width of these later valleys varied from one hundred feet to ten miles. These relatively familiar environments allowed settlers to maintain aspects of their farming culture developed prior to migration.[23]

Indeed, it would be almost two generations before farming in Nebraska was transformed into "a commercial enterprise that disregarded topography."[24] The equally indifferent grid that currently crisscrosses the Great Plains, creating a land of mile roads that converge in right angles, developed slowly. Facilitated by the Public Land Survey System inaugurated by the Land Ordinance of 1785, the survey of Nebraska Territory began on November 11, 1854. Surveying the Plains, however, proved difficult for surveyors accustomed to marking corners with trees. The survey reached 140 miles west of the Missouri by 1860, and by statehood it remained only three-eighths completed.[25]

More about land distribution than ecology or human community, the survey and the grid facilitated the "cheap and simple" transfer of title from the federal government to private interests.[26] Accordingly, some territorial communities developed unique solutions to sharing river access, and occasionally they even skewed the typical American grid to accommodate demand for water and wood. In the Elkhorn Valley, quarter sections were elongated to assure that all members of a fledgling German colony would have access to water and timber.[27] Even those obtaining surveyed land were particular about this aspect of their homesteads. A. R. Hagerman's farmstead was intentionally situated along the Big Blue River for close proximity to fresh water and fuel, but also because settlers believed the flood plain was the only fertile land. Hagerman recalled that "they didn't think the table land would produce good crops."[28] This view was shared by the territory's executive officers, who also imagined that Nebraska's development would occur in the vicinity of "the Platte, the Loup, the Elkhorn, the Nemaha, the Niobrara, and other streams."[29]

Despite such confinement, agriculture in Nebraska generated its own brand of boosterism. The buildup of the territory as a garden began even before it was opened. A year prior to the Organic Act, the *St. Joseph Gazette* in Missouri proclaimed, "This beautiful country now in the possession of the Indians is destined soon to belong to the white man, and made to blossom like the rose."[30] Each session of the territorial legislature touted Nebraska's potential. Governor Samuel Black, for instance, proclaimed that the "soil was so rich and prolific" that "God has written his decree of her prosperity deep in the earth." Although he was not a farmer and hailed from Pennsylvania, he noted the "almost miraculous production of corn, potatoes, melons, pumpkins, sweet potatoes, wheat, rye, oats, barley, and Chinese sugar cane, and every other garden vegetable common to a temperate climate." In a few years he anticipated "peaches, apples, pears, plums and grapes" would join the list. Yet despite such prophesies, the ghosts of the past haunted the territory. Black found he was also forced to argue that "Nebraska should be vindicated" from the persistent national impression that it was part of the Great American Desert.[31]

Even with the spirit of local government behind them, farmers generally found they had little knowledge of how to bring this new Garden of Eden into profitable production. To help, the *Bellevue Gazette* (near Omaha) published a weekly column on the latest developments in agriculture. The series of articles was taken from sources such as *The Ohio Farmer*. Fruit crops, hops, Concord grapes, Tarter sheep, shade trees, and Chinese sugar cane were all featured in these columns.[32] These tips were probably of little use to farmers as few of these crops proved viable in the Great Plains climate.

Even modern Nebraskan staples presented difficulties. One settler in Gage County described his first plantings of corn in 1857 as "experiments." He also recalled that the "early settlers had the idea that wheat would not do well here." Others reportedly adopted strains of corn they obtained from the Pawnees because they were more appropriate for flour making. There were also stories of failures. Theron Nye recalled her family pressing their harvest of sorghum in hopes of producing a sweet syrup. They ended up with a substance closer to vinegar.[33]

Ultimately, the type of commercial farming favored by the territorial government did not develop overnight. Even where farmers had amassed surplus corn prior to 1858, it took two years of the Colorado gold rush to bring the price up enough to make it profitable. Still, by the time Colorado Territory was formed in 1861, the "cash based economy conquered all but a few remnants of the older agricultural economy."[34] Indeed, the yeoman ideal of the Jeffersonian era was largely abandoned on the Great Plains. At the same time, the potential of modern farming helped bring "a calm and healthy confidence" to Nebraska even in difficult economic times.[35] Merrill Clark of the territorial assembly hoped to market crop surpluses as far away as Denver and to create an agricultural empire within the Platte River region.[36]

Despite the importance of farming, another agent of "Progress" was also present in Nebraska and represented on the Great Seal: the town builder–businessman, wearing a top hat, waistcoat, vest, and knee-high pants. Under his auspices, technologically advanced and capital-intensive business ventures—as denoted by the steamboat and the locomotive—would stimulate Nebraska's growth. Nebraska—as depicted by both farmer and capitalist—was envisioned as part of an integrated West where market forces "bound city and country" together and "forever altered human relationships with the American land."[37] In such a world, urban and rural spaces in the territory became symbiotic components of an economy that required both agricultural surpluses and urban entrepôts to distribute them.

Consequently, speculation and transportation were the key components of the commercial imagination. Although the contract between farmers and businessmen theoretically benefited a greater common-wealth, many of the territory's immigrants preferred get-rich-quick schemes to long-term investment. Cashing in on the rapid expansion of the national industrial and agricultural economies, the specula-tive spirit in Nebraska peaked between 1854 and 1858. Not actually wishing to remain on this new frontier, they hoped to turn a profit on an investment and then get out. As an early settler noted, "Every fel-low was on the speculate, designing to make their pile, then go home to 'America.'"[38]

To facilitate speculative investment, the establishment of political entities far outpaced the influx of settlers. The territory's eight orig-inal counties divided into ten in 1855, expanded to fifteen in 1858, and reached thirty-four by 1860, when growth was curtailed by south-ern secession. Town builders were at work in each of these counties. Hoping to better themselves by getting out of farming and into other professions, these boosters and entrepreneurs were part of the "ur-ban drift" common in antebellum America. While this movement ac-counted for less than 5 percent of the population in the "old" America, the interior West, with its great prospects of becoming a transporta-tion hub, was imagined as a series of thriving towns. As a result, Ne-braska experienced intense competition among cities attempting to place themselves in strategic locations in order to take advantage of anticipated wealth.[39]

Abandoning some pretexts of Jeffersonian policy, Congress passed the Federal Township Act in 1844. This statute allowed speculators and town builders to preempt 320 acres in order to stake out new communities.[40] In typical fashion, new city sites in Nebraska were pro-moted as prosperous centers in the middle of the agrarian garden. In reality, territorial squalor was more often the initial result. Dr. George Miller, for instance, arrived in Omaha in 1854 and described the na-scent metropolis as "320 acres subdivided into townlots" by "numer-ous white stakes." Miller, an esteemed member of a community where physicians were scarce, described his first lodgings as a "hovel" that "consisted of a single room perhaps twelve by fourteen feet in an area walled in by cottonwood boards which were decorated on the inside by one coat of what was called plaster, which was mostly clay."[41] Another early settler from the east remarked, "Necessities in Buffalo are luxuries in Omaha."[42]

While Omaha did rapidly develop into a conduit for river and overland travel, other communities founded as would-be competitors struggled. Florence—now a neighborhood in Omaha—was once a contender for territorial dominance. In 1858 the town dignitaries even enticed dissatisfied members of the legislature—which met at the territorial capital in Omaha—to hold rogue sessions in their fair community. They boasted of their rapid development which included a steam flour mill, two saw mills, a four story hotel, an Odd Fellows Hall, and a Masonic Lodge. The local editor trumpeted that the "city continues to improve with unexampled rapidity."[43]

Florence was not alone in its endeavors. Twenty-seven cities were incorporated between March 1855 and January 1857. Situated on the known routes of travel, eighty-four incorporated communities were listed at the beginning of 1860—many of them existing only on paper. They were promoted, but never realized. In Dakota County, for instance, Omadi, Logan, St. John's, Pacific City, Franklin City, Blyburg, Verona, Randolph, and Lodi were plotted to service a population that, in 1860, amounted to 819 individuals. Not surprisingly, all these communities disappeared prior to statehood. After statehood, atrophy continued. Of the sixty-two towns successfully founded during the territorial period, only thirty-eight survived into the twenty-first century.[44]

To finance all real and fictitious cities, farms, and other endeavors, ten banks were chartered by the territorial legislature by 1858. Each of these "wild cat" institutions printed its own paper money that was generally not backed by hard currency. Patrons recalled exchanging the script from one bank for that of another and never seeing anything issued by the United States Treasury. From 1855 through 1857, "money was plentiful and almost without value." That changed with the Panic of 1857 when the banks "had gone into their holes, and had apparently pulled their holes around them." For the next several years, the measure of value was cottonwood lumber.[45]

Ultimately, speculation had serious consequences as the national financial crisis "swept away" much of the territory's wealth. The Nebraska territorial legislature experienced substantial shortfalls in revenue in the last years of the 1850s. Omaha was reportedly "practically destroyed and depopulated."[46] To make matters worse, gold was discovered in Colorado in 1858; and young Nebraska men—who outnumbered women two to one—went west in droves to try their luck. Even though the gold fields were technically in Nebraska, the rush initially failed to bring back optimistic outlooks.

Transportation empires helped Nebraska's economy rebound. Indeed, the territory's location in the center of the continent was still imagined as one of its greatest strengths. It was generally assumed that the Platte River valley would be the ideal route for the proposed transcontinental railroad. With this in mind, when acting Governor Thomas B. Cuming addressed the First Territorial Legislature in 1855, he stressed the territory's importance in connecting "the shores of both oceans," even to "India, China, and the Pacific Islands." Governor Alvin Saunders echoed his predecessor's words by touting Nebraska's unique position between the "Old and New Worlds."[47]

Historian James R. Shortridge maintains that these nineteenth-century preconceptions were largely correct, as "[t]ransportation drives growth."[48] Even before the railroad, the Great Territorial Road, which was developed in 1855 to smooth out the old migrant route to the Pacific, ran between Omaha and Fort Kearny. Not to be left out, residents south of the Platte—this treacherous river impeded commerce, transportation, and political unity—developed the Nebraska City cutoff that joined the main trail at Fort Kearny. These highways were the conduits for the 100,000 men who marched across the prairies during the Colorado gold rush. Pioneer Nebraska was intrinsically tied to its overland trails, and these corridors became its salvation.

A vibrant overland freighting industry developed, especially in Omaha and Nebraska City. Located on the banks of the Missouri River, merchants in these communities enjoyed access to goods shipped via steamboat and, consequently, profited more from the gold fields than the average Colorado miner. They outfitted the migrants and then shipped them supplies once they were in camp. As many as one hundred firms ran freight from the Missouri to the gold mines. The most famous outfit was, undoubtedly, Russell, Majors, and Waddell, who owned and operated six to eight thousand wagons pulled by forty thousand oxen and manned by several thousand bullwhackers.[49]

By the time statehood was achieved on March 1, 1867, the population had increased to just over 120,000—double the statutory requirement for achieving that status. Most Nebraskans had Euro-American origins, and a sizable minority were European immigrants. The region's original inhabitants were confined to reservations and systematically excluded from economic or political participation. African Americans—whose official status within the United States improved dramatically by the end of the territorial era—were few in number and not particularly welcome.

The racial composition in the vast spaces of Nebraska Territory was in many ways shaped by the first tenet listed on the Great Seal— "Popular Sovereignty." This doctrine was championed by Stephen A. Douglas, U.S. senator of Illinois, who authored the Kansas-Nebraska Act in order to impress on Americans that "expansion and liberty were indistinguishable." Additionally, he maintained that the creation of the two territories would soothe sectional schisms regarding the extension of slavery by giving residents the agency to decide the issue themselves.[50] Consequently, popular sovereignty served the interests of the *United* States, indicated by the two men on the seal holding the Constitution and pointing to the American flag.

Although civil rights were never an issue in either territory, turmoil wracked Kansas in the 1850s, while Nebraska remained relatively tranquil, as it was never imagined suitable for slavery. As historian Joan E. Lampton observed, "the two territories were created that one might be slave—the other not." This suggestion was supported by Nebraska territorial governor Mark Izard, a native of Arkansas, who in 1856 urged his constituents to bury the "regional hatchet."[51] While southern migrants would later sympathize with the Confederacy, most had no problems with Governor Samuel Black's later appraisal of the issue. Citing climate and the general predisposition of the population, he averred, "No sane person for a moment, supposes that Nebraska is in the slightest possible danger of being either a slave territory or a slave state."[52]

In many respects, popular sovereignty took "white men's political rights" to the extreme, while producing a Nebraska that was unable to tolerate nonwhite residents. The mere presence of other racial groups was believed to degrade the prospects of mainstream American settlers. Consequently, although few early Nebraskans were enslaved, African Americans were commonly marginalized. The territorial legislature even considered—but did not pass—bills to exclude all blacks from the territory in 1859 and 1860.[53]

No one supposed that Native Americans would participate in Nebraska's government or economy either. After Otoes, Missourias, Omahas, and Pawnees moved to reservations, their collective presence became an "annoyance" to Nebraska's new owners who had no intention of sharing the land.[54] Indeed, pioneers along the Missouri River noted that the region's original inhabitants were impoverished and often "came begging for things."[55] Similarly, in the Platte Valley settlements of Fremont and Columbus, Pawnees—still four thousand strong—were commonly decried by settlers such as Theron Nye, who believed "stealing was their forté."[56]

Solutions to the "Indian problem" ranged from accommodation to exclusion. Governor Izard noted that settlers were generally relieved of their concerns of attack by Omahas and Otoes after reasonable annuity payments improved conditions on their reservations in 1857.[57] Conversely, to protect growing white populations, Pawnees were moved further west along the Loup River in 1859 and out of the state altogether in 1876. As Euro-American settlement expanded the territory westward in the 1860s, more Indian nations were confronted. Convinced of white superiority, the territorial legislature of 1864 asserted that the Sioux, Cheyennes, Arapahoes, Kiowas, and Comanches could ultimately be defeated, even if they united.[58]

During the Civil War, migration into Nebraska slowed to a trickle, and the departure of soldiers to fight in the war actually shrank the population. To compensate, the Nebraska legislature financed (in 1865) and then organized a territorial Board of Immigration in 1866.[59] The board promoted the "healthfulness of climate, character of soil, mineral resources, and superior facilities" in the territory. Fluent in German and at least one Scandinavian language, board members organized recruitment from other western states, New York, and foreign countries "from which we already have the largest representations in our population."[60] As part of the strategy, maps were printed of available homestead sites. While the Nebraska board was short lived, a number of Germans, English, and Irish joined their fellow countrymen who were already in the state.

The prevailing attitude of most residents of Nebraska Territory—native-born and immigrant alike—insisted that American civilization should be free to conquer "savagery," exclude blacks, and make the territory safe for the expansion of the white body politic. Despite the state's motto—"Equality before the Law"—Nebraska was imagined as a racially specific place. Euro-Americans and most Europeans were welcome. African Americans, though present in small numbers, were not particularly welcomed. Native Americans were marginalized and removed in order to further the "progress" of American settlement.

Together, Nebraska Territory's racial predisposition, agrarian impulses, and urban-centered business preferences enabled it to emerge as a successful economic and political entity. The citizens of the territory and then the state adapted commercial farming, town building, boosterism, and speculation to a relatively unfamiliar environment. In the process, the emerging body politic imagined and then reimagined the landscape it settled upon and the business possibilities it allowed.

In many respects, developments in Nebraska were state or territory specific only in the way the forces of "progress" manifested themselves on its prairies. Similar "systemic changes" were implemented across the many territories of the trans-Missouri West.[61] But because advancement was influenced by both cultural and environmental factors, Oregon, Kansas, and Nevada territories were imagined in different lights than Nebrasaka and consequently achieved statehood in distinct manners. Interestingly, established territories in Utah and New Mexico were deemed unready for statehood for decades.

Kansas, like Nebraska, was opened as a territory in 1854. Named after the Kansa tribe and admitted to the Union as a state in 1861, it, too, was promoted as a farming paradise and as a corridor connecting the established East with the burgeoning Pacific West. Kansans and Nebraskans both imagined their territories as a collection of urban-based business ventures. Many early boosters and speculators in both areas staked out communities that had no real chance of survival. Despite boosterism, more towns in Nebraska and Kansas territories failed than succeeded. The entrepôts that did survive were connected to cash crops, transportation systems, and national commerce.[62]

Agrarian and political variances, however, made development in the neighboring territories remarkably dissimilar. Early Euro-American settlement focused on the "elbow region" around the intersection of the Kansas and Missouri rivers. Imagined as a continuation of Missouri's hemp belt, these rich bottomlands appeared appropriate for plantation (slave) agriculture. Nebraska—which lacked navigable inland waterways and a long growing season—did not. This view of the latter territory was vindicated after experiments yielded saleable crops that precluded profitable slave labor. Kansas, on the other hand, endured years of political turmoil before an influx of northern immigration quietly solved the problem of slavery.[63] Advocates of free soil and of slavery in both territories saw the fates of African Americans as incidental to debates about the land's suitability for race-based slavery.

Farming was deemed the highest calling of the land not only on the Great Plains, but in the Pacific Northwest as well; and settlers in Oregon Territory—like those in Nebraska and Kansas—viewed landscapes of native floras as unimproved spaces.[64] Most Euro-Americans in the Oregon Territory—officially organized in 1848 but opened nearly a decade earlier—trekked through Nebraska and subsequent western districts before entering a country they imagined as a new Garden of Eden. Congregating in and around the Willamette River valley, the

　　　　　PLACE IS POLITICAL

first settlers claimed forested foothills, cleared the timber, and promoted pastoral settlement rather than attempting to manipulate low-lying prairies that were prized by Indians. As on the Great Plains, it took several generations before these fertile but formerly unfamiliar landscapes were transformed into profitable breadbaskets.[65]

Ultimately, despite different environments, Oregon, Nebraska, and Kansas were "the cultural creations" of Euro-Americans.[66] As such, the confinement of Native Americans in Oregon began prior to statehood in 1859 and continued until most Indigenous territory was occupied. Though unquestionably a land of free soil, the exclusion of African Americans in Oregon was more or less a given until after the Civil War. Indeed, racial equality was never an assumption in the agrarian West. In several instances, exclusionary prejudices even kept western territories from becoming states. New Mexico and Utah—both imagined and constructed as farming regions—were prominent cases in point. Although New Mexicans were largely neutral about slavery, their territorial era lasted from 1850 until 1912 largely because they "remained stubbornly and overwhelmingly Spanish-American in culture."[67] Although this culture was first established in 1598, the territory's inclusion into the United States stirred a discussion about its citizens' "racial character and their 'fitness' for democracy," reminiscent of Nebraska's dialogues involving blacks and Indians.[68] Ultimately, statehood was delayed until an Anglo-American majority was established in the twentieth century. Similarly, Utah became a territory in 1850 and a state in 1896. Despite its enterprising white populations, Mormon doctrines created unique cultural and political institutions and consequently tensions during the territorial period.[69]

Uniquely, Utah Territory's non-Mormon fringes on the east and on the west were detached and successfully integrated into the Union long before its populated, agrarian heartland. Arid Nevada, for instance, became a territory in 1861, two years after the Comstock Lode was discovered. Nevada Territory's economy had more in common with California's mining district than with western agricultural regions. The "great majority" of the earliest citizens in both districts "came in hopes that they could quickly plunder" the landscape of its "treasure and return to their homes."[70] While this sort of speculative spirit existed in territorial Nebraska, no commodity was available to take it on a similar course. Indeed, the weight of the mineral district brought Nevada to statehood in three short years, despite its small population of fewer than forty thousand citizens—sixty thousand was the usual requirement.[71]

As a general rule, advancement from territory to state in the 1850s and 1860s required racial and cultural harmony and the ability and desire to enter an integrated market economy. Accepting these preconditions, Nebraska became part of a relatively elite group by entering the Union as a full partner in just thirteen years. This success was predicated, in part, on the flexible worldviews of citizens willing to try new forms of production in hope of profit and rapidly move on to other experiments if they failed or became obsolete. In this manner, Nebraska Territory as a place emerged in an unfamiliar environment that was slowly modified as "the result of specific social practices."[72] By 1867, farmsteads and urban centers began to look permanent as the new state's identity as a prosperous agrarian region was sealed. Nebraska was ready to attract new migrations of Americans and Europeans.

Notes

1. Nebraska Territorial Legislature, *House Journal of the Legislative Assembly of the Territory of Nebraska*, 7th sess. (Nebraska City: Thomas Morton, 1861), 251.

2. Dan Flores, *The Natural West: Environmental History in the Great Plains and the Rocky Mountains* (Norman: University of Oklahoma Press, 2001), 94.

3. Peter G. Boag, *Environment and Experience: Settlement Culture in Nineteenth-Century Oregon* (Berkeley: University of California Press, 1992), 141. Mr. Jones, quoted in Nebraska Territorial Legislature, *Journal of the Council, at the Second Session of the General Assembly of the Territory of Nebraska* (Omaha: Hadley D. Johnson, 1856), 62.

4. Flores, *Natural West*, 167; Frederick Jackson Turner, "The Significance of the Frontier on American History," in *Annual Report, American Historical Association 1893* (Washington DC: GPO, 1894), 39, 60.

5. Walter Prescott Webb, *The Great Plains* (Boston: Ginn, 1931), 8.

6. James C. Malin, *The Grassland of North America: Prolegomena to Its History* (Lawrence KS: privately printed, 1947), 169, 314.

7. James R. Shortridge, *Cities on the Plains: The Evolution of Urban Kansas* (Lawrence: University of Kansas Press, 2004), 6.

8. Cronon, *Nature's Metropolis*, 307.

9. For a notable critique of Turner, see Patricia Nelson Limerick, *The Legacy of Conquest*. While not subscribing to environmental determinism, many environmental historians, Flores for one, pay homage to Webb for assigning agency to nature. Edward W. Soja, *Postmetropolis: Critical Studies of Cities and Regions* (Malden MA: Blackwell, 2000), 6.

10. Susan M. Deeds, *Defiance and Deference in Mexico's Colonial North: Indians under Spanish Rule in Nueva Vizcaya* (Austin: University of Texas Press, 2003), 6. See also Elliott West, *The Contested Plains: Indians, Goldseekers, and the Rush to Colorado* (Lawrence: University of Kansas Press, 1998).

11. The implications of Jefferson's statement are discussed in Peter Boag, "Sexuality, Gender, and Identity in Great Plains History and Myth," *Great Plains Quarterly* 18 (Fall 1998): 329; the name *Nebraska* translates from its Siouan-language roots (similar in both Otoe and Omaha) as "water that is flat" and describes the area's most notable geographic feature—the Platte River.

12. Reuben Gold Thwaites, *Early Western Travel Series, 1748–1846*, vol. 17 (Cleveland: Arthur H. Clark, 1905), quoted in Webb, *The Great Plains*, 152; and W. Eugene Hollon, *The Great American Desert: Then and Now* (New York: Oxford University Press, 1966), 11.

13. *Centennial Handbook: Nebraska Territory, 1854–1954* (Lincoln: Nebraska Territorial Centennial Commission, 1954), 57; Marti-Graham Cripps, "Indian Territory," http://www.rootsweb.com/~itsac/indian-territory/indian-territory.htm; and John R. Wunder, *"Retained by the People": A History of American Indians and the Bill of Rights* (New York: Oxford University Press, 1994), 23.

14. Addison Erwin Sheldon, *Nebraska: The Land and the People* (Chicago: Lewis Publishing, 1931), 220; and Hugh J. Dobbs, *History of Gage County Nebraska* (Lincoln: Western Publishing, 1918), 32.

15. John Brinckerhoff Jackson, *American Space: The Centennial Years, 1865–1876* (New York: W. W. Norton, 1972), 173.

16. See James C. Malin, *The Nebraska Question, 1852–54* (Lawrence: privately printed, 1953), 24; Flores, *Natural West*, 115; Joan E. Lampton, "The Kansas and Nebraska Act Reconsidered: An Analysis of Men, Methods, and Motives" (PhD diss., Illinois State University, 1979), 29, 62; *Centennial Handbook*, 57; and *History of the State of Nebraska* (Chicago: Western Historical, 1882), 56.

17. Bradley H. Baltensperger, *Nebraska Geography* (Boulder CO: Western Press, 1985), 57–58.

18. Lieutenant G. K. Warren, *Preliminary Report of Explorations in Nebraska and Dakota in the Years 1855, '56 and '57* (Washington DC: GPO, 1856), 3.

19. Samuel Black, quoted in Nebraska Territorial Legislature, *Council Journal of the Legislative Assembly of the Territory of Nebraska*, 6th sess. (Nebraska City: Thomas Morton, 1860), 20; "The Future of the West," *Nebraska City News*, January 16, 1858; Timothy J. Garvey, "Strength and Stability on the Middle Border: Lee Lawrie's Sculpture for the Nebraska State Capitol," *Nebraska History* 65 (Summer 1984): 157.

20. John R. Stilgoe, *Common Landscape of America, 1580 to 1845* (New Haven CT: Yale University Press, 1982), 205, 324; and Richard White, *Land Use, Environment,*

and Social Change: The Shaping of Island County, Washington (Seattle: University of Washington Press, 1980), 77.

21. Boag, *Environment and Experience*, 38, 80, 141. See also, Patricia Lorcin, "'Africa Made Me': Gender, Imperialism, and Nostalgia in the Genesis of Literary Personality in the Settler Colonies of Algeria and Kenya," (presentation, Caroll R. Pauley Memorial Symposium, University of Nebraska–Lincoln, September 26, 2003); Flores, *Natural West*, 98.

22. U.S. Bureau of the Census, *Nebraska Territorial Census, 1854–1856, Population Census*, vol. 1 (Washington DC: GPO, 1855), 1–42; and Sheldon, *Nebraska*, 374.

23. Territorial censuses indicated about 78 percent of territorial populations were born in the United States. Pennsylvania, Ohio, Indiana, Illinois, and Iowa were the most common terminal states of emigration. This was, however, a mobile population and place of birth and socialization may have been different. Jackson, *Sense of Place*, 102; and Boag, *Environment and Experience*, 38, 2. Malin, *Grassland*, 2, 120. Baltensperger, *Nebraska Geography*, 11–15; West, *Contested Plains*, xxiv; and University of Nebraska–Lincoln, Conservation and Survey Division, *Nebraska Official Highway Map* (Lincoln: Department of Transportation, 1993). The dominant rolling topography was formed by wind-blown silt blanketing a series of glacial tills.

24. Jackson, *American Space*, 26.

25. "An Ordinance for Ascertaining the Mode of Disposing of Lands in the Western Territory, Passed May 20, 1785," TNgen Project, http://www.tngenweb.org/tnland/seven-ranges/; "Land Survey in Nebraska, from *Nebraska and the Northwest, 1881*," http://www.rootsweb.com/~necuming/survey.html; D. J. Huebner, "The U.S. Public Land Survey System (USPLSS)," 2002, http://www.utexas.edu/depts/grg/huebner/grg312/lect23.html; and Robert Cottrell, "Surveying the Federal Lands," http://www.connerprairie.org/historyonline/survey.html. See also, James C. Olson, *History of Nebraska* (Lincoln: University of Nebraska Press, 1955), 95; Cayton and Gray, "Story of the Midwest," 10; Vernon Carstensen, ed., *The Public Lands: Studies in the History of the Public Domain* (Madison: University of Wisconsin Press, 1968), 483; Kansas Society of Land Surveyors, "Original Surveys of Kansas: The Public Land Survey System," http://www.ksls.com/about_surveys.htm; and William H. Beezly, "Homesteading in Nebraska: 1862–1872," *Nebraska History* 53 (Spring 1972): 62–63.

26. Carstensen, *Public Lands*, xv, xix. See also, Jackson, *Sense of Place*, 4; William Least Heat-Moon, *PrairyErth: (a deep map)* (Boston: Houghton Mifflin, 1991), 15; William Cronon, "A Place for Stories: Nature, History, and Narrative," *Journal of American History* 78 (March 1992): 1350; and Donald Worster, "A Tapestry of Change: Nature and Culture on the Prairie," in *The Inhabited Prairie* (Lawrence: University of Kansas Press, 1998), xiii.

27. Milton E. Holtz, "Early Settlement and Public Disposal of Land in the Elkhorn River Valley, Cuming County, Nebraska Territory," *Nebraska History* 52 (Summer 1971): 125.

28. William H. Smith, *Early Days in Seward County, Nebraska* (Seward NE: Seward Independent, 1937), 7.

29. Alvin Saunders, quoted in Nebraska Territorial Legislature, *Council Journal of the Legislative Assembly of the Territory of Nebraska*, 8th sess. (Omaha: Taylor and McClure, 1862), 21–22.

30. Malin, *Nebraska Question*, 154.

31. Nebraska Territorial Legislature, *Council Journal*, 6th sess., 9, 10, 22.

32. See *Bellevue Gazette*, November 20, 1856; January 1, 1857; January 8, 1857; February 5, 1857; February 12, 1857; February 19, 1857; February 26, 1857; and March 26, 1857.

33. "Narrative of George Cale," in Hugh J. Dobbs, *History of Gage County Nebraska* (Lincoln: Western Publishing, 1918), 170–71; Theron Nye, "Early Days in Fremont," in *Nebraska Pioneer Reminiscences*, comp. Nebraska Society of the Daughters of the American Revolution (Cedar Rapids: IA: Torch Press, 1916), 86.

34. Stilgoe, *Common Landscape of America*, 341; George Miller, quoted in W. W. Cox, *History of Seward County, Nebraska and Reminiscences of Territorial History* (University Place NE: Jason L. Claflin, 1905), 81.

35. Black, quoted in Nebraska Territorial Legislature, *Council Journal*, 6th sess., 10–11.

36. Nebraska Territorial Legislature, *Council Journal*, 7th sess., 240–44.

37. Cronon, *Nature's Metropolis*, xvi.

38. Cox, *History of Seward County*, 13. See also Baltensperger, *Nebraska Geography*, 45; and Wallace Gates, "The Role of Land Speculation in Western Development," in *The Public Lands: Studies in the History of the Public Domain*, ed. Vernon Carstensen (Madison: University of Wisconsin Press, 1968), 360.

39. Ann L. Wilhite, "Cities and Colleges in the Promised Land: Territorial Nebraska, 1854–67," *Nebraska History* 67 (Winter 1986): 357; Kenneth J. Winkle, *The Young Eagle: The Rise of Abraham Lincoln* (Dallas: Taylor Trade Publishing, 2001), 43–44; and Rita Napier, "Frontier Agricultural Settlements and Government Regulation: The Town Site Preemption Act of 1844," in *Working the Range: Essays on the History of Western Land Management and the Environment*, ed. John R. Wunder (Westport CT: Greenwood Press, 1985), 113.

40. Preemption allowed settlers and, later, town builders to stake out claims and purchase them from the federal government at $1.25 an acre. See, Napier, "Frontier Agricultural Settlements," 116; and Erastus F. Beadle, *"Ham, Eggs, and Corn Cake": A Nebraska Territory Diary* (Lincoln: University of Nebraska Press, 2001), xv.

41. Cox, *History of Seward County*, 78, 80.

42. Beadle, *"Ham, Eggs, and Corn Cake,"* 30.

43. *Florence Courier*, February 5, 1857.

44. Similarly, county expansion was premature as settlements remained well east of the original survey line throughout the territorial period. Intense activities in the far western reaches of the territory due to the discovery of gold led to the formation of Colorado Territory. Despite this area's anticipated wealth, a mere two thousand people (east of the Rocky Mountains) were counted as permanent residents in 1860. Throughout its territorial period, the majority of Nebraska's population remained confined to the very fringes of the Great Plains. Wilhite, "Cities and Colleges," 330; Malin, *Nebraska Question*, 366; W. M. Warner, *Warner's History of Dakota County, Nebraska from the Days of Pioneer Settlers to the Present Time, with Biographical Sketches, and Anecdotes of Ye Olden Times* (Dakota City NE: Lyons Mirror, 1893), 49; and Baltensperger, *Nebraska Geography*, 60. Sheldon, *Nebraska*, 397.

45. The ten banks created for the territory were the Bank of Nebraska, the Bank of

Desoto, the Bank of Tekama, the Bank of Dakota, the Platte Valley Bank, the Waubeek Bank, the Nemaha Valley Bank, the Western Exchange Bank, the Fontenelle Bank of Bellevue, and the Bank of Florence. Cox, *History of Seward County*, 64, 65, 98; and Forrest B. Schrader, *A History of Washington County, Nebraska* (Omaha: Magic City Printing, 1937), 79.

46. Black, quoted in Nebraska Territorial Legislature, *House Journal*, 7th sess., 241.

47. Thomas B. Cuming, quoted in Nebraska Territorial Legislature, *Journal of the Council of the First Regular Session of the General Assembly of the Territory of Nebraska* (Omaha: Sherman and Strickland Printers, 1855), 9, 11; and Saunders, quoted in Nebraska Territorial Legislature, *Council Journal*, 8th sess., 15.

48. Shortridge, *Cities on the Plains*, 96–97.

49. Donald F. Danker, "The Influence of Transportation upon Nebraska Territory," *Nebraska History* 47 (June 1966): 194, 205; Sheldon, *Nebraska*, 266; West, *Contested Plains*, xv, 121; Baltensperger, *Nebraska Geography*, 54; Mildred Newman Flodman, *Early Days in Polk County* (Lincoln: Union College Press, 1966), 1; and *History of the State of Nebraska*, 109.

50. Nicole Etcheson, *Bleeding Kansas: Contested Liberty in the Civil War Era* (Lawrence: University of Kansas Press, 2004), 21; and Howard R. Lamar, *The Far Southwest, 1846–1912: A Territorial History*, rev. ed. (New Haven CT: Yale University Press, 1966; Albuquerque: University of New Mexico Press, 2000), 9.

51. Lampton, "Kansas and Nebraska Act Reconsidered," 84; and Mark Izard, quoted in Nebraska Territorial Legislature, *Journal of the Council*, 2nd sess., 14.

52. Nebraska Territorial Legislature, *Council Journal*, 6th sess., 46.

53. Etcheson, *Bleeding Kansas*, 7; and James B. Potts, "Frontier Solons: Nebraska's Territorial Lawmakers, 1854–67," *Great Plains Quarterly* 12 (Fall 1992): 282.

54. Nye, *Nebraska Pioneer Reminiscences*, 87.

55. Ella Pollock Minor, "Incident at Plattsmouth," in *Nebraska Pioneer Reminiscences*, comp. Nebraska Society of the Daughters of the American Revolution (Cedar Rapids: IA: Torch Press, 1916), 42.

56. Nye, *Nebraska Pioneer Reminiscences*, 87.

57. Nebraska Territorial Legislature, *Journal of the Council of the Third Legislative Assembly of the Territory of Nebraska* (Brownsville: Robert W. Furnas, 1857), 20.

58. Alvin Saunders, in Nebraska Territorial Legislature, *Council Journal of the Legislative Assembly of the Territory of Nebraska*, 10th sess. (Omaha: Taylor and McClure, 1865), 12.

59. Schrader, *History of Washington County*, 83; David Wishart, "The Death of Edward McMurty," *Great Plains Quarterly* 19 (Winter 1994): 7; and Edith Robbins, "German Immigration to Nebraska: The Role of State Immigration Agents," *Yearbook of German American Studies* 26 (1991): 94.

60. Nebraska Territorial Legislature, *Annual Message of Acting Governor Paddock to the Legislative Assembly of the Territory of Nebraska at its Twelfth Regular Session* (Omaha: Barkalow Brothers, 1867), 5, 7, 8.

61. William G. Robbins, *Landscapes and Promise: The Oregon Story, 1800–1940* (Seattle: University of Washington Press, 1997), 75.

62. Shortridge, *Cities on the Plains*, 9.

63. Shortridge, *Cities on the Plains*, 68, 97.

64. White, *Land Use, Environment, and Social Change*, 41.

65. David Peterson del Mar, *Oregon's Promise: An Interpretive History* (Corvallis: Oregon State University Press, 2003), 72; White, *Land Use, Environment, and Social Change*, 44; and Boag, *Environment and Experience*, 143–53.

66. White, *Land Use, Environment, and Social Change*, 74.

67. Lamar, *Far Southwest*, 3.

68. John M. Nieto-Phillips, *The Language of Blood: The Making of Spanish-American Identity in New Mexico, 1880s-1930s* (Albuquerque: University of New Mexico Press, 2004), 52.

69. Lamar, *Far Southwest*, 4.

70. James J. Rawls and Walter Bean, *California: An Interpretive History*, 7th ed. (Boston: McGraw Hill, 1998), 101.

71. Russell R. Elliott, *History of Nevada*, 2nd ed. (Lincoln: University of Nebraska Press, 1987), 61, 402.

72. Matt Garcia, *A World of Its Own: Race, Labor, and Citrus in the Making of Greater Los Angeles, 1900–1970* (Chapel Hill: University of North Carolina Press, 2001), 4; See also, Susan Kollin, *Nature's State: Imagining Alaska as the Last Frontier* (Chapel Hill: University of North Carolina Press, 2001), 19.

15. Architecture Crosses Region

Building in the Grecian Style

PATRICK LEE LUCAS

Much of the work to establish a national identity for the nineteenth-century American nation was accomplished in the trans-Appalachian West, a region that incorporated present-day Kentucky and Tennessee; the Northwest Territory states of Ohio, Indiana, and Illinois, and parts of southern Michigan; as well as both Mississippi and Alabama, which were together sometimes referred to as the Frontier South. Social historians described this trans-Appalachian region as a place where diverse peoples occupied and transformed the landscape into a national model. Susan Gray examines how "Yankees" moved west and reconstructed familiar communal institutions and thus transferred ethnic identity to shape a new regional identity.[1] Nicole Etcheson, like Gray, evaluates the presence of both "Yankees" and "Southerners" who migrated to the trans-Appalachian West and whose ideas refashioned the region as something different than regions south and east. Despite their diverse geographic origins, settlers "transported a traditional social order to a new environment and . . . progressively transformed the landscape in ways compatible with their own priorities."[2] Each of these historians suggests that civic institutions, created by diverse populations through a common vision of community within the region, actually contributed to a stronger sense of nationalism. Other historians support this position that the

West was a crossing ground for streams of settlers emigrating from the Northeast and the South, and that the West emerged as a release valve for sectional differences bubbling up as early as the first decade of the nineteenth century.[3]

The cultural work performed by the settlers from other regions of the nation resulted in "new forms and new values to satisfy the deep and enduring need for community," forms and values that represented both the region of the West and the nation as a whole.[4] Despite the relative isolation and provincial nature of the trans-Appalachian West landscape and its cities, communities there organized themselves in remarkably similar fashion. People often moved in family units and established the same kinds of cultural institutions (churches, organizations, clubs, etc.) as they had in the East or in Europe, while simultaneously displacing the Native Americans who had previously occupied the landscape. Most significant for purposes of this analysis, they chose to emulate Hellenistic Athens in their architecture. Though classical building forms existed both in the East and the West, the Grecian style curried more favor in the western states as a symbol for both a return to the core of ancient civilization and as a symbol for an optimistic future for the region within the national framework. Architecture simultaneously united the West with the nation in the classical mode but divided the West as a particular subset in the Grecian idiom.

Grecian-style buildings gave a sense of unity that belies the diversity apparent in historical accounts that characterize the antebellum North and South as fundamentally different places. Architecture illustrates that the built environment and these regional landscapes were more similar than different. The architecture of the trans-Appalachian West demonstrates that the early republic might be best conceptualized as a unified West rather than the conventional North-South division adopted by historians to explain the Civil War. Furthermore, architecture helps demonstrate the importance of order to nineteenth-century Americans, especially in the trans-Appalachian West, a region in the midst of rapid transformation from Native American occupation to an American "wilderness" ripe for exploitation and settlement.

The architecture of the antebellum Frontier South and the Old

Northwest demonstrates the cultural similarity of these two areas of the nation. West of the Appalachian Mountains, as Northerners and Southerners purchased newly available public lands and created new communities, they performed remarkably similar cultural work by relying on a common architectural style. In the construction of buildings designed to look like structures of ancient Greece, nineteenth-century Americans manufactured and perpetuated connections to the past, in order to claim cultural meanings associated with the world's first democracy and the glories of Athens. The Grecian style imprinted idealized notions of order, gentility, nation, region, and democratic values on the nineteenth-century trans-Appalachian landscape. Grecian style defined the people of the trans-Appalachian West, their communities, their region, and their place within the nation; Grecian-style architecture also put into built form a model for both the western region and the nation.

The buildings provide a strategy to question the assumptions historians have made about the divided and regional nature of antebellum society. Buildings constructed in the trans-Appalachian West suggest that the cultural claims advanced by communities defined the landscape as *one* region. Because much of the cultural activity that took place in Middle America was quite similar, the reality of the antebellum trans-Appalachian West as a single region belies the differences inherent in a historical model that separates the Old Northwest from the Frontier South. In both North and South, the federal government formed territories and established rules for land division and sale and admission to the Union. People established links to the East through trade and the consumer market as well as through cultural activity that fostered a series of urban outposts in a landscape perceived as a wilderness. Moreover, Americans who emigrated from the East and new European immigrants attempted to define who they were in the creation of western communities, and disparate cultures acquired a similar cultural vocabulary in a distinctive landscape when concepts of the nation were in formation. The buildings, with their fleeting meanings and particular circumstances of construction, show a nation in transition from a republic inherited from the nation's founders to a fully realized democratic nation ruled by common men rather than an educated elite.

Nationalism, a necessary precondition for the development of a regional consciousness, took many forms in the trans-Appalachian West but is perhaps best understood in the construction of Grecian-style buildings for governmental, ecclesiastical, commercial, and residential purposes. People constructed Grecian-style buildings throughout the trans-Appalachian West to emulate the temples of ancient Greece and to deploy through those buildings social and political meanings tied to the ancient democracy. Both in the North and the South, white-columned porticos erected in front of plain, cube-like buildings made public statements about the cultural sophistication and political aspirations of building occupants. Found throughout the landscape, such buildings provided a common architectural language that was adapted freely to all types of structures. Through Grecian-style buildings, people suggested inherent external meanings of stability, rationality, and balance in a world marked by impermanence and disorder.

The Grecian style arose almost simultaneously between 1770 and 1820 in localities throughout the world from St. Petersburg, Russia, to the banks of the Danube River in central Europe as well as in Australia and the United States. By erecting structures in the same style, designers, builders, and owners in trans-Appalachian communities simultaneously brought international and national dimensions to a regional sense of place.

While some buildings of the early nineteenth century were exact copies from one or more of the architectural treatises and stylebooks available, most buildings were a combination of individual elements borrowed from these works and first-hand observation. The Grecian style, like similar classical styles before it, centered on the notion of orders with proportioned columns and prescribed elements (e.g., bases, shafts, capitals) as the articulation system for buildings. The result of the use of these consistent orders and their derivative building elements tied together the character of these structures of the trans-Appalachian West to those throughout the United States and abroad. Grecian-style architecture offered a unified set of building blocks that could be constantly manipulated to create houses, business buildings, churches, and institutional structures. With endless variations on general themes, because all parts related to a system of understanding buildings, everyone could build their own temple in their own town and generally people understood what the building meant.

The early-nineteenth-century attraction to Greek culture follows two earlier classical revivals. During the Italian Renaissance, interest in classical building and architectural orders resulted when a large number of commissions were supported by patrons in Italian cities (most notably Florence) and throughout the Italian countryside. Renaissance painters, sculptors, artists, and architects drew inspiration from ancient classical history and lore; and these works reflected the glories and the tragedies of the ancient civilizations. The collected works of architects such as Bramante, Brunelleschi, Michelangelo, and Palladio helped spread the influence of Italian Renaissance buildings to continental Europe, England, and North America as well as Russia. In 1571 Palladio published *The Four Books of Architecture* as a guide to classical buildings. This treatise was a well-used source for buildings throughout the world from the sixteenth century to present day. The buildings, paintings, and sculpture of Renaissance Italy similarly served as models for scores of visitors to the country and as inspiration for generations of artists, architects, and builders throughout the world.

The second classical revival occurred by the middle of the eighteenth century, spurred on by the interest in and the actual excavation of Herculaneum and Pompeii in the 1730s and 1740s. Archaeological investigations of these sites, supported by collectors in Europe and the United States, first focused on Rome. By the latter part of the nineteenth century, Greece was identified popularly as the "Mother of Rome," turning attention from Roman sites to Grecian digs and investigations. Architects Nicholas Biddle and Joseph Allen Smith, for example, spent much of the year 1806 measuring buildings of the Acropolis. These gentlemen joined a large number of American architects, authors, designers, and artists (and their European peers) who visited Greece and its environs, documenting their travels in journals and in artistic works.[5]

The general fascination with Hellenistic culture in the early nineteenth century was chiefly caused by the growth of historical archaeology in Greece. Greek buildings stood alongside Roman buildings as even older and purer examples of the classical idiom emulated by individuals and groups throughout the United States and the world. Moreover, Greece was thrust upon the world stage with its struggle for independence in the 1820s. Citizens of the United States were particularly interested in this struggle, given their own revolutionary activities fifty years earlier. Above all, nineteenth-century Americans used classical history to establish a context of antiquity for the young United States. Classical buildings, place names, decorative arts objects, and classical references in rhetoric helped set a stage to borrow freely from the past to create an idyllic and hopeful future.

Nineteenth-century citizens not only absorbed ideas about ancient civilization from material culture, they also learned of Greece and ancient history through classical texts and studies in schools, academies, and colleges throughout the United States. And no education was considered complete without a grand tour of Europe and the ancient civilizations of Greece and Rome. Newspapers by the 1840s suggested that "Lovers of art flock from the most distant parts of the world to the Acropolis and dwell with rapture on its unrivalled beauties and seek to inhale, amid the ruins that surround them, a portion of the spirit by which they were conceived."[6] Greece was conceived as a model civilization not only to be visited but to be emulated by republican citizens within the United States. This responsibility centered on upperclass Americans, who were able to build houses and collect goods in the Grecian style. Moreover, due to increased inexpensive fabrication of goods and the simultaneous rise of guide books and taste manuals, the middle class was also able to purchase and use Grecian-style goods and construct Grecian-style buildings. For the first time, Grecian-style culture aligned in these two classes, extending the reach of the Grecian style beyond the walls of the mansions of the rich to the broader population. Thus, the Grecian style represented a first DEMOCRATIC style to have widespread application throughout the nation.[7]

For example, Grecian style helped American men and women restyle themselves by introducing gentility into the life of the nation. Mrs. Basil Hall, an Englishwoman, visited Boston in 1827 and, in moving from a social function at Mrs. Ticknor's to a "rout," recounted that "There were refreshments of various kinds handed round, and the Ice instead of being in one great pillar was in glasses, as is in fashion in England. At Albany I was told that this is considered very ungenteel, their favorite phrase, for in America everything is genteel or ungenteel."[8] Hall's statement captures a sense of Americans' struggles with the rules and images of their new nation. Should they follow the rules of behavior established in Europe and, most especially, in England? Should Americans wear clothes, collect goods, and inhabit houses and buildings based on European fashions? Alternatively, should republican citizens dismiss European rules, modes, and fashions and establish others? Should they cast the rules aside altogether?

In the eighteenth century, people were increasingly concerned with stylishness, taste, beauty, and politeness. As the century progressed, plain and utilitarian buildings and furnishings yielded to more decorative and opulent modes as the power of the colonial gentry increased. After the American Revolution, gentility spread to a broad middle class via rules that dictated the conduct of these new democratized "aristocrats." Volumes on etiquette explained how people should hold their bodies, dress, eat, and converse in pleasing ways; and guidebooks illustrated the types of buildings appropriate to such genteel people. This democratization of gentility had an impact on nearly every form of behavior and aspect of the physical environment. People remodeled or constructed new houses and yards, public buildings, and churches with rules similarly established in architectural guidebooks. Entrepreneurs constructed factories to supply household furnishings to vast new markets whose emergence reflected the new knowledge and refined taste of American citizens. Throughout the nation, city officials landscaped parks and planted trees to demonstrate their refined nature in contrast to the rural landscapes outside of these communities. These efforts reflected the collective exertion of the American people to re-mold themselves into a new society on the world stage, with buildings and landscapes transformed by gentility and democracy.[9]

Mrs. Hall's observation, "in America everything is genteel or ungen-teel," not only demonstrated the growing concern for gentility but provides a way to conceive of different people and places in a diverse nineteenth-century nation. Her comment sheds light on the struggles of Americans to come to terms with their self-images, both the pro-jected images of the nation within an emerging world order and the domestically aimed or interregional images captured in the nation's regions. Mrs. Hall illustrates that differences could be observed be-tween places, as distinctions made them either "genteel or ungenteel." An 1822 article in the *North American Review* amplified this view through the notation of regional differences among the nation's citi-zens—a "greater variety of specific character" than ever before: "the highminded, vainglorious Virginian, living on his plantation in baro-nial state . . . the active, enterprizing money-getting merchant of the East . . . the Connecticut peddler . . . vending his 'notions' at the very ends of the earth . . . and the long shaggy boatmen 'clear from Ken-tuck.'"[10] Through the revelation of some notions of nineteenth-cen-tury regional stereotypes, this *North American Review* article demon-strates a similar sense of difference in place and in people throughout the United States. The December 1824 editorial of the *Kaskasia Re-publican* noted a growing sense of regional identity as well: "The man of the East is but an inert biped—a mere baby in comparison [with the Westerner]. Yet strange as it may seem, these beings, whose senses are as obtuse as a pumpkin, whose dialecticks are of the dandy-obscure, and who have 'no more talents than a turnip,' are self-class'd as the first order of men! Let them enjoy the illusion."[11]

Westerners held strong opinions about more established Easterners and sought to distinguish the West as a place of hard work where men could rise through their own efforts and become fully engaged citizens of the United States. In 1817, when Morris Birkbeck ventured west of the Appalachian Mountains, he was surprised by the large number of immigrants there and wrote that "Old America seems to be breaking up and moving westward."[12] From West and East and from North and South, people struggled to create themselves, and to identify one another, their communities, and the nation.

The nation's physical environment, part of the early-nineteenth-century processes of self-identification, contained fledgling communities constructed within idealized frameworks of Hellenistic culture as places of commerce and centers of government. The buildings reflected the aspirations and ideals of Americans who sought to overlay a web of gentility across an increasingly democratic landscape. The tensions encapsulated within these buildings and communities shifted as conceptions of who was included and excluded became embedded in the larger notions of American nationhood. Temple-style civic structures found throughout the nation's regions stood as oppositional contentions about "democracy" within the country.

Despite significant opportunities to change architectural styles in the reconstruction of the federal capital, Roman-style buildings dominated Washington DC and stood for the lofty republican ideals of the Revolution, in a nation ruled by an educated elite to whom the common person was expected to defer. Designed and constructed over several decades of the early nineteenth century, the U.S. Capitol features a massive dome—a decidedly Roman form—at the center of its composition: central authority represented with a central dome. By contrast, in the state capitals and in other western communities, a greater variety of motifs was used in classical structures to represent democracy, ranging from towers (Indiana and Tennessee) to small domes (Illinois, Kentucky, and Iowa). Grecian-style buildings most especially resonated with the ideas of "democratized" republican citizens who contributed to the wealth and health of the nation in its hinterlands. Greek-inspired buildings helped to define the means through which the land, the people, and the economy were democratized. As the early nineteenth-century Old Northwest and Frontier South were landscapes of intercultural interaction, with Easterners moving west, immigrants from Europe, and Native Americans, the identities of place and people were in flux. The placement of classical buildings—"temples of democracy"—in these landscapes represented significant cultural work to shape the character of both the land and the people. These buildings, based on Old World models, helped transform people into ideal republican citizens. They helped democratize communities by offering classical and ordered settings for the everyday work of a great nation. They helped construct the Old Northwest and the Frontier South as archetypal landscapes at the same time as they fashioned a consolidated national identity. Buildings east and west of the Appalachian Mountains were constructed for the same reasons—demonstrations of order on the landscape and manifestations of the democratic government in tangible form.

The architectural landscape of the new republic of the trans-Appalachian West—state capitol buildings, academic halls, churches, business buildings, and houses—revealed how the revolutionary rhetoric of eighteenth-century republican ideology evolved in both shared and competing notions of nineteenth-century democracy. The nation's founders, particularly men like Washington, Adams, and Jefferson, supported a limited democracy that demanded deference and emphasized the importance of a government led by an educated elite. West of the Appalachian Mountains the populace promoted alternative visions of an open, democratized society and the buildings that were constructed by them bore remarkable similarity.

Through architecture, people in the trans-Appalachian West democratized the region into a people's landscape. Gone were the social and political restrictions and allegiances of the East. In their place, people of the trans-Appalachian West introduced more pure and simple Grecian-style structures, made reference to temples of ancient Greece, and thus associated these buildings with an open and democratic society. Though trans-Appalachian buildings shared some of the same general classicized vocabulary as their counterparts in the East, particularly in the nation's Capitol, the buildings helped distance the people of the trans-Appalachian West from those in the East. Where both western and eastern structures displayed order, balance, and symmetry, frontier structures were built in the open style of Athenian democracy with broad, accessible staircases and sheltering porticos that provided pathways that could be ascended by all people. Grecian-style architecture configured the frontier landscape, both North and South, as remarkably similar and in direct opposition to the landscape of the East, a landscape adorned with Roman-style buildings and places. For its architecture and the ideologies these buildings stood for, the antebellum trans-Appalachian West frontier constituted a unique region and was not merely a westward expansion of the plantation South or colonial New England. The trans-Appalachian West, when viewed as a vacant wilderness, nurtured and encouraged the development of communities visually shaped by architectural styles of Athenian Greece and even nicknaming practices that literally and aurally reinforced associations with Athenian Greece.[13]

Within the geographic space of the Old Northwest and the Frontier South, Americans believed they could create a true democracy based on an idealized version of Hellenistic culture. Because the people in both the Old Northwest and the Frontier South attempted cultural work that introduced and replicated Grecian-style architecture throughout the geographic area, the notion that the North and South of the antebellum West were fundamentally different can be questioned. The material culture approach of this paper suggests that the Grecian-style buildings of the nineteenth-century trans-Appalachian West tell a different story than the historians writing about this geographic space. Whereas historians have tended to isolate differences in the North and South, the buildings show commonalities in the process of community formation.

In the nineteenth century, communities imagined themselves as places of commerce and civility in order to attract people and bring economic prosperity. These towns used classical nicknames as one way to transform communities and establish a "genius loci" for the place that could be understood by citizens in all walks of life. Cities thus invented themselves as "Athens"; and Grecian-style buildings appropriately clothed these settlements in visual rhetoric, supplying them with a democratic backdrop for their stage upon which the actions of a fully functioning ideal community were played out. Just as the Hellenistic Athens was associated with worldly, well-read appreciators of art, nineteenth-century communities sought to become "well-dressed" by association with the name.

Not only did residents of the trans-Appalachian West co-opt the Grecian style to materialize the Athens nickname, Grecian-style buildings represented efforts by individuals—designers and owners alike—to engage in the development of a *national* vocabulary for design. The Grecian style provided a common language many understood because it was so prevalent in the nation and because of nineteenth-century citizens' familiarity with the Grecian style through stylebooks, archaeological records, newspaper stories, and other sources. As abstract signs, the Grecian-style buildings encapsulated elaborate messages and the mindsets of the people who designed, built, lived, and worked within them. These buildings transformed the democratic experiment into physical form.

In the democratization of a republican state, people of the trans-Appalachian West selected the Grecian style rather than the Roman style buildings of the nation's capital. The West claimed the mantle of political authority and created an architecture that spoke in the language of democracy. As political commentary in built form, the Grecian style established an architectural order that was copied across a diverse landscape.

Public and private buildings utilized the same architectural language. Grecian-style buildings established classical rhetoric that had resonance in the worlds of politics, education, religion, and commerce. This was a language that spoke in direct competition with the East and with Europe. And yet, in shaping communities in the nineteenth century, settlers were carrying the cultural baggage of Europe along with ideas of democracy. Their sense of identity was tied into European standards and opinions.[14] People sought to validate the democratic experience of the New World by Old World measures. Rather than replicate the Old World precisely, however, American citizens transformed the classical building styles of the ancient world into something different.

The middle class adopted the style and constructed buildings with ornate columns, cornices, and porches, rivaling on a lesser scale some of the upper-class residences in the region. Even when an owner could not afford highly ornate carved columns, builders fashioned square columns with simple details to stand as public expressions of the style on more vernacular dwellings. Thus, ever more common Grecian-style cottages coexisted alongside more-traditional, high-style forms of the architectural language on public buildings and houses of the wealthy. This was true of communities nicknamed "Athens" throughout the trans-Appalachian region—towns like New Harmony, Crawfordsville, Jacksonville, Cincinnati, Lexington, Nashville, Tuscaloosa, and Holly Springs—and places in between.

People chose classical garb as much to disassociate from the surrounding wilderness as they did to ensure economic prosperity in the future. In displaying "mainstream" behavior, owners of both public and private Grecian-style buildings fit in with their neighbors and with the vision of the nation as a great democracy, something of a model for the world. In a landscape perceived as a primeval forest populated by hostile Indians, Grecian-style buildings stood as symbols of progress and power. The structures provided a means to manipulate local, regional, and national images in order to "uncivilize" the Indians and remake the Frontier South and the Old Northwest as a wilderness. Travel writers and community boosters both had a stake in representing western communities in a positive light, cultural activity often done at the expense of making the land around the communities a tangled wilderness to elevate the level of sophistication and civility of the community itself.

The trans-Appalachian West, a vast territory, represented an opportunity to construct a new nation on "unsettled" land. In a time when the nation struggled to come to terms with the democratic experiment proposed by the revolutionary generation, people looked for a national vocabulary that would define who they were as individuals and as American citizens. People were interested in creating order from disorder, classifying and compartmentalizing the landscape and reducing wilderness. People turned to the Grecian style as one means

PLACE IS POLITICAL

to stabilize the mobility and fluidity of the nation where people were cut off from the roots of family and community in their effort to settle the land. Americans established in the landscape of the trans-Appalachian West a tightly prescribed set of values that swept aside previous notions of the nation, its landscape, its regions, and its people.

Though localized realities were far more nuanced, people generally asserted that the East was a civilized place with developed communities and businesses fully integrated into market activity—a stratified and refined place with great wealth and progressive spirit. The South was a different place altogether, for it relied on a slave-based economy and, by mid-nineteenth-century standards, was backward thinking, mired in the past and doomed to failure. There were relatively few communities of substantial size in the region; much of the economic and social activity was focused on the plantation and small farm. In this way, the South shared the common characteristic of localized, somewhat-autonomous economic and social organization. But the South was different than the West because the South was divided into farms and plantations whereas the West was still perceived as a wilderness landscape. Though we know the reality and the extent of wilderness in the West was far from wild, this characteristic did distinguish the West from the South and the East in the minds of antebellum Americans.

Edward Ayers and Peter Onuf, along with Stephen Nissenbaum and Patricia Nelson Limerick, explore the evolution of ideas about region in the United States from the country's founding to present day with the goal of understanding regions and the importance of regionalism to the nation in general. These authors together address the resurgence of regionalism and regional studies in American history and suggest that the reappearance of regionalism in the last several decades is a direct result of Americans having "lost faith in national innocence and the national state" and "grown dubious of a transcendent national character and American exceptionalism." As a result, "many Americans have decided that places closer to home deserve their loyalty" and attention.[15] The authors make important assertions about regional difference in climate and land, in ethnicity and ethnic interaction, in relations to the nation and the economic system, and in cultural beliefs and expressions. They do so to lay the foundation to link regionalism with nationalism: "Consciousness of difference, the identification of economic interests or of cultural patterns that could divide Americans along regional lines, depended on a common context that had not existed before the Revolutionary conflict. Nationalism came first and was the necessary precondition for the development of a regional consciousness."[16] Taking this departure, it seems, then, that regional difference helps to define the United States as a nation. In this context, it is interesting to rethink the importance of the trans-Appalachian West as a cultural norm and as a national icon.[17]

According to Andrew Cayton, "regions are all about social identity. What matters most is who people think they are, or more specifically, who they think they are not."[18] Certainly, regional names are far more than simple place labels. They are cultural symbols that carry implications for the nation and for the regions within the United States. Community studies, particularly those of the last decade, assert that the trans-Appalachian West is a cultural meeting place, where North and South fuse to produce corn-belt culture. Because "North, South, Midwest, and West are largely nineteenth-century terms, created in response to nineteenth-century perceptions and problems, most of them revolving around questions of race and federal authority,"[19] it is now time to reconceptualize the Old Northwest and the Frontier South as a trans-Appalachian region, one where the greater Ohio Valley is unified with the Ohio River as an artery in the middle of the region. In this way, the trans-Appalachian might be conceptualized as a series of overlapping zones with different cultural work occurring in each zone—sometimes overlapping another zone, sometimes repeating the cultural work of a previous zone. This place is distinct in terms of geography and contains land use patterns, reflective of the time of European settlement. Perhaps, then, regionalism is reinforced by cultural activity, which is, in turn, reinforced by geographic difference. These differences are underscored through the formation of political and social institutions and through diverging streams of migration.

These diverse peoples brought with them to the trans-Appalachian West, and afterwards fashioned there, strong ideologies about life and business which are pervasive even today.

The regions and subregions described herein, and in historiography on regional history, shift and change through time. It is possible to support the boundaries of each region and subregion with data from innumerable sources. By the same token, each region and subregion can be disassembled and re-created in a slightly different manner by an alternative analysis of the same data. Considering these multiple views of scholarly work and its constitution, it is appropriate that narrators of history embrace the very fluidity of these boundaries. It is not so important that specific definitions of given regions stand the test of time throughout American history. Instead, what is important is that regional work and identity be considered within the national frame, as well as local work and identity within the regional frame. Historians should support the shifting borders of the locality and region to the best of their ability, recognizing that these boundaries fluctuate and that their movement is part of what makes history interesting. In this more honest way, regional and local approaches to history are both valid and appropriate in the broader field of historical inquiry. Without taking into account regional and local history, the danger exists of whitewashing an accurate story of the development of locality, region, and nation, and the agency of human beings in this shifting process. Regional architecture, a common link across the landscape of the antebellum trans-Appalachian West, thus helps uncover further linkages among localities and regions north and south, linkages that help describe the simultaneous shaping of individual, community, regional, and national identities on a world stage.

Notes

1. Gray, *Yankee West*.

2. Etcheson, *Emerging Midwest*; Faragher, *Sugar Creek*, 237.

3. Stephen Aron, *How the West Was Lost: The Transformation of Kentucky from Daniel Boone to Henry Clay* (Baltimore: Johns Hopkins University Press, 1996); Anne Norton, *Reflections on Political Identity* (Baltimore: Johns Hopkins University Press, 1988); Smith, *Virgin Land*; and David Waldstreicher, *In the Midst of Perpetual Fetes:*

The Making of American Nationalism, 1776–1820 (Chapel Hill: University of North Carolina Press, 1997).

4. Don H. Doyle, *The Social Order of a Frontier Community: Jacksonville, Illinois 1825–1870* (Chicago: University of Illinois Press, 1978), 259. For a discussion of regional and national identities existing simultaneously for the West, see Waldstreicher, *Midst of Perpetual Fetes*, who maintains that westerners "claim their difference from those at the center, complain of mistreatment, and boast of their superiority" (270).

5. The Society of Dilettanti, founded in 1733 in England, sponsored the publication of printed materials following general interest in archaeological investigations. These publications, in turn, influenced architects and builders and the erection of Grecian-style residences, business buildings, churches, and institutional structures. Perhaps the most widespread and popular book was Nicholas Revett, *Antiquities of Athens*, 4 vols. (n.p., 1762–1816). This significant body of measured drawings of ancient sculpture and buildings in turn inspired additional publications of measured drawings as well as style manuals and guidebooks for carpenters and builders. *The Antiquities of Athens* was available not only in England but was readily purchased by architects and builders in the United States. Other eighteenth-century publications available in American shops included Robert Adam's *Ruins of the Palace of the Emperor Diocletian at Salatro in Dalmatia* (1764), John Wood's *Ruins of Palmyra* (1753) and *Ruins of Balbec* (1757), and Thomas Major's *Ruins of Paestum* (1768).

6. *Nashville Daily Orthopolitan*, January 8, 1846.

7. For an elaboration of the class argument, see Richard Bushman, *The Refinement of America: Persons, Houses, Cities* (New York: Alfred A. Knopf, 1992). On democratization, see Gordon S. Wood, *The Radicalism of the American Revolution* (New York: Alfred A. Knopf, 1992); and Nathan Hatch, *The Democratization of American Christianity* (New Haven CT: Yale University Press, 1989).

8. Cited in Hermann Warner Williams, *Mirror to the American Past: A Survey of American Genre Painting, 1750–1900* (Greenwich: New York Graphic Society, 1973), 46–47.

9. Richard Bushman stresses that these visions of a more elegant life both complemented and competed with other American values associated with evangelical religion, republicanism, capitalism, and the work ethic. Bushman, *Refinement of America*.

10. "The Spy," *North American Review* 15 (July 1822): 252.

11. *Kaskasia Republican*, December 14, 1824, cited in Etcheson, *Emerging Midwest*, 10.

12. Cited in Doyle, *Social Order of a Frontier Community*, 1.

13. In the eighteenth and early nineteenth century, the western country of the North American continent was stereotypically viewed as an unrefined, backward, and underdeveloped area in comparison to a more culturally and socially advanced Northeast and Southeast. Andrew Cayton and Frederika Teute define the "backcountry," or "western country," as the land west of English settlement, literally everything to the west of the colonies. But, sometime in the late eighteenth century and the early nineteenth century, this land began to be referred to as the "frontier." By the middle of the nineteenth century, more distinct regional cultures had formed the Frontier South and the Northwest Territory, both sometimes referred to together as the "Old West," as a

replacement for earlier names for Middle America. The terms "Midwest" and "Middle West" did not come into everyday usage to describe this area until the twentieth century. The earliest use of the term is from the writings of Timothy Flint. After decades of little or no use, the term next appeared in Kansas and Nebraska newspaper editorials in the 1880s, denoting the middle of the West or the high plains then being settled. The Midwest migrated east, so that by World War I, it and the Old Northwest Territory, were indivisible. Andrew R. L. Cayton and Frederika Teute, *Contact Points: American Frontiers from the Mohawk Valley to the Mississippi, 1750–1830* (Chapel Hill: University of North Carolina Press, 1998); and Timothy Flint, "Religious Character of the Western People," *Western Monthly Review*, 1827, 207.

14. Americans looked to France rather than to England for a model and for cues. Napoleonic buildings and empire style furniture held greater resonance in the nation than their English counterparts. Wendy A. Cooper, *Classical Taste in America, 1800–1840* (New York: Abbeville Press, 1993).

15. Ayers and Onuf, introduction to *All Over the Map*, 8.

16. Ayers and Onuf, introduction to *All Over the Map*, 10.

17. This is a central theme in Shortridge, *Middle West*. Wanda Corn also takes up this theme in her essay "The Birth of a National Icon: Grant *Wood's American Gothic*," in *Reading American Art*, ed., Marianna Doezema and Elizabeth Milroy (New Haven CT: Yale University Press, 1998). See also Gray, *Yankee West*; and Etcheson, *Emerging Midwest*.

18. Andrew Cayton, "Commentary on 'The Peristence of Regional Labels in the United States: Reflections from a Midwestern Perspective'" in *The New Regionalism: Essays and Commentaries*, ed., Charles Reagan Wilson (Jackson: University of Mississippi Press, 1998), 64.

19. Cayton, "Commentary," 66.

16. Societies and Soirees

Musical Life and Regional Character in the South Atlantic

MICHAEL SAFFLE

Except for a few individuals and events—the activities of Charles Theodor Pachelbel in 1740s Charleston; the presence of the Moravians in eighteenth- and early-nineteenth-century North Carolina (as well as Pennsylvania); and the 1930s, 1940s, and 1950s pop songs of Savannah-born Johnny Mercer—historians have largely ignored musical life in what was recently proclaimed the South Atlantic Region of the United States: the Carolinas, Florida, Georgia, Puerto Rico, Virginia, and the American Virgin Islands.[1] This is especially true of the almost 150 years separating today from the end of the Civil War; there are more books in print about antebellum music in Charleston, South Carolina, than about contemporary musical life in Atlanta, Miami, and Savannah combined.[2]

Perhaps, though, this is to be expected. The South Atlantic emerged as a more or less distinct musical region prior to the Civil War—a region more accomplished in many respects than the rest of the South; more private in its practices; and more aristocratic in its bearing than many other parts of our nation. After 1865 these differences gradually disappeared, although traces of them persisted into the 1940s and may survive today. In large part, then, any history of *distinctive* South Atlantic musical life must look to the past—and not just any "past," but the antebellum eighteenth and nineteenth centuries. Fortunately, a wealth of published and unpublished information about these centuries exists; to some extent information can also be extrapolated from other parts of our nation and the world.

The thesis illustrated in the following pages is that, for several centuries, the musical South Atlantic flourished *especially* and *characteristically* in private circumstances, insofar as both "cultivated" and "vernacular" circumstances are concerned.[3] I consider examples of antebellum South Atlantic musical life largely in the following terms: the sophisticated seaboard towns such as Charleston and Savannah; the aristocratic character and geographical isolation of rural life; the importance of slavery, race prejudice, and ethnic practices and products as "privatizing" musical factors; the roles played by religious attitudes and institutions; and, to a lesser extent, the cultural isolation that long separated even the largest South Atlantic cities from musical undertakings more common in other parts of our nation and abroad. Finally, I speculate briefly upon the course of the South Atlantic's more recent and increasingly complex musical-cultural development. At no point do I intend to imply that the musical South Atlantic is or has ever been *altogether* different from *every* other part of our nation. Rather, I explore those differences that have distinguished—and, perhaps, continue to distinguish—"South Atlantic" from "southern" (as well as "American") in musical terms.

Is it possible to distinguish South Atlantic musical practices from those associated with other parts of the United States? My answer is a qualified "yes." This does not mean, however, that any one musical distinction between the South Atlantic and the rest of our nation is necessarily clear, contemporary, or always applicable. Jazz and blues, for instance, are an important part of musical life in present-day Richmond; but jazz has much more often—and with good reason—been associated with New Orleans and Chicago, just as the blues have more often been associated with the Mississippi Delta, Memphis, and Kansas City.[4] Atlanta, Georgia; Charleston, South Carolina; and Roanoke, Virginia, possess symphony orchestras today; but those of Boston, Philadelphia, and New York boast longer and more-prestigious histories.[5] Even the folk songs and bluegrass sounds of the southern

Appalachians belong as much to Kentucky and Tennessee as they do to Virginia and the Carolinas.

To attempt an outline of South Atlantic musical history as well as a definition of South Atlantic musical practices is, however, to accept the possibility of establishing meaningful *regional* definitions devolving upon culture in addition to nature. This is a problematic undertaking; but geographers, historians, linguists, and politicians have been dividing up the world into regions for millennia. For historians of every age, as Norman Davies suggests, selection has always been necessary; it has also been "always difficult, and always unsatisfactory" in one way or another.[6] Davies explains how "Europe" evolved as a concept from antiquity to the recent past, with boundaries—real or imaginary—that incorporate a multitude of perspectives. For some individuals and eras, ethnicity has been of crucial importance; for others, politics; for still others, commerce and agriculture, or religious affiliation. Thus, the Romans were concerned with viticulture—theirs was primarily the Europe in which wine grapes grew—(warm South vs. cold North); the Middle Ages, with Christianity (Catholic vs. Orthodox, followed in Western regions by Catholic vs. Protestant); the Nazis, with regions of racial "purity" and "impurity" (Germans vs. Jews and Slavs); and cold war politicians, with "imperialism" and "totalitarianism" (the North American Free Trade Agreement vs. the Warsaw Pact).[7]

Local history may provide "an interesting solution" to some of the dilemmas facing scholars attempting to deal with enormous areas and variegated groups of people.[8] As Davies points out, local history draws upon "the familiar and the down-to-earth," encourages "individual explorations and research," and "is relatively resistant" to nationalistic and ideological pressures. It is also especially well suited "to subjects such as the family," yet it can serve specialists "as the basis for far-flung international theorizing." In other words, "narrowness of one kind provides an opportunity for breadth of a different kind."[9]

Regional history, of course, is only one way of doing local history. Regions are often more like continents than families: they may not be altogether "familiar," nor can they accurately and easily be understood.

PLACE IS POLITICAL

Nor does geography, physical or political, altogether determine the lives of those who live within its distinctions. Scholars must incorporate both cultures of place and peoples, to paraphrase a cautionary observation about Appalachia by Henry Shapiro.[10] Too, the notion of region seems especially problematic where North American melting-pot attitudes are concerned.

Precedents exist, however, for defining parts or regions of the United States. For Hector St. John de Crèvecoeur, author of *Letters from an American Farmer*, the British colonies of the New World could be divided into three sections according to length of European settlement and certain geographic, economic, and political characteristics. "Those who live near the sea," Crèvecoeur wrote in 1782, "feed more on fish," which "renders them more bold and enterprising." These comparatively sophisticated town and city dwellers "see and converse with a variety of people; their intercourse with mankind becomes extensive." "Those who inhabit the middle settlements," Crèvecoeur continues (referring in this instance to regions inland of the coast of Massachusetts—and, one might add, inland Virginia and the Carolinas) "must be very different," because their rank and circumstances as "independent freeholders must inspire them with sentiments, very little known in Europe among a people of the same class." As citizens, they tend to be litigious and to demand fair treatment from their governors and preachers; as businessmen, they are "careful and anxious to get as much as they can."[11] (These "yeomen and poor whites" comprised between 80 and 90 percent of "all small farmers in the antebellum South."[12]) Finally, Crèvecoeur "arrives near the great woods, near the last inhabited districts," where men and women—pioneers all—often "appear to be no better than carnivorous animals of a superior kind," subsisting on the "flesh of wild animals" and whatever grain they can grow.[13]

Frederick Jackson Turner expanded upon these distinctions in "The Significance of the Section" and elsewhere. For Turner, "there is and always will be a sectional geography in America based fundamentally upon geographic regions"; the settlers who constructively poured "their plastic pioneer life into geographic molds" must inevitably be shaped by the physical realities confronting them.[14] Nevertheless, Turner reminds us that cultural generalizations devolving exclusively upon physical geography or economic interests are always oversimplified. By the 1920s, if not earlier, a host of other factors as well as geography and economics—"ideals and psychology," for instance, and "inherited intellectual habits" and "conceptions of right and wrong"—had made such phrases as "New England, the Middle [Atlantic] States, the South, the Middle West," and so on "as common names as Massachusetts or Wisconsin."[15]

Geographically, the South Atlantic consists of coastal plains, piedmont, and highlands as well as swamps, islands, and a few hardwood hammocks. Ethnically—this holds true especially for the decades prior to the Civil War—a great many South Atlantic European Americans were of or descended from English, Scots-Irish, Celtic, and German stock. (Today, many more are Hispanic American, African American, or Asian American.) The northern and mid-Atlantic are generally characterized by colder temperatures and rockier soil. Their populations have long been more ethnically variegated—although, with the exception of New York (at least until recently), there were fewer Hispanics than in the Caribbean and (prior to the 1920s) fewer blacks than in Georgia or the Carolinas. It may be significant that several identifiable "regional patterns of ethnicity" that have persisted throughout the twentieth century and into the twenty-first include both "old stock Americans (black and white)" throughout the South.[16] In any event, other parts of our nation are more often associated, say, with Asian Americans or, in the case of the Midwest, with Scandinavian and Polish Americans.

On the other hand, the South Atlantic cannot altogether be distinguished geographically and ethnically from other portions of the former Confederacy, which also are coastal or swampy or Appalachian. These portions, however, were mostly settled later; they were not, in one sense of the word, "colonial." Prior to the 1830s, for example, only western Georgia and North Carolina in the South Atlantic remained unsettled, whereas much of Alabama and most of Mississippi were settled only after that date.[17] Thus, as early as 1817, one

PLACE IS POLITICAL

Carolinian reported that "the *Alabama Feaver* [*sic*] rages here with great violence and has *carried off* vast numbers of our Citizens."[18] But until the 1880s Florida's peninsular regions, also in the South Atlantic, "remained the last great frontier east of the Mississippi"; and like Louisiana, a French colony, Florida, Puerto Rico, and the American Virgin Islands had distinctive economic, political, and cultural antecedents extending well beyond the British Empire.[19]

To a considerable extent, then, the South Atlantic was and still is part of the South. Prior to the Civil War all of what subsequently became the Confederacy was less thoroughly industrialized than New England, and industrial growth throughout "Dixie" was further interrupted after 1865.[20] This is scarcely surprising because, "as the eighteenth century passed into the nineteenth . . . the population [of the United States] did not move south"; for this and other reasons, the South became "increasingly isolated from the rest of the nation and from Europe."[21] Southern states and communities also established public-education programs somewhat later than their Northern contemporaries; after the Civil War, Southern schools were much more systematically segregated. In 1840 the United States Census Report confirmed that American literacy rates varied from 95 to 99 percent of the adult population of New England to only 72 percent in North Carolina (excluding slaves).[22] Later nineteenth-century schools attended by Southern blacks were more often organized through churches. Among whites, even elementary educational institutions frequently enjoyed "the support of individual benefactors"—a situation much less common in other parts of the country.[23]

Perhaps no other attitude has more thoroughly shaped America than has racial prejudice. Although all but omnipresent, racial divisiveness has been called "the central theme of *Southern* history." That "common resolve, indomitably maintained" that the South "shall be and remain a white man's country."[24] As D. R. Hundley acknowledged in 1860, the antebellum Southern "gentleman" was unmistakably "exclusive in his tastes and associations." Although such individuals "sometimes possess[ed] strong and deep-seated prejudices of caste," there were "thousands of Southern slaveholders more democratic in their instincts than these very ultra Republicans; for while the former wear homespun every day and work side by side with their slaves, the latter are the very pinks of propriety, array themselves in the most unexceptionable silks and broadcloth, and turn up their nose at the 'vulgar herd' with as much disdain as the most aristocratic Oligarch in the whole land."[25] In other words, prejudice about race and class was by no means exclusively a Southern preoccupation. Nevertheless, other regional differences existed, contributing to segregated sociability, and were acknowledged by critics like Hundley, who notes that antebellum Southerners sent their sons "to the University" but preferred to educate their daughters "at home."[26] This was increasingly less true in the North, where many of our nation's first colleges for women were established.[27]

Among the "ideals" and "inherited intellectual habits" separating one part of the United States from another are musical practices. Regional definitions have long taken these differences into account. "As early as 1889," for instance, James Mooney "called attention to the southern mountain regions of the eastern United States" as a resource for the collecting of folk songs and folklore. As an economically less-developed region, its music and stories were of interest precisely because "the processes of civilization" elsewhere had altered the "cultural patterns" typical of earlier American life.[28] Similarly, a century or so ago, the frontier increasingly came to be defined in musical circles as the archetypal location and source of cowboy songs.[29] Dixie was instead linked with musical allusions to slavery, plantation life, and "the War of Southern Independence"—even when, as in the case of Stephen Foster's *Old Folks at Home* or Patrick Gilmore's *When Johnny Comes Marching Home Again*, the tunes were actually composed by natives of Pittsburgh, Pennsylvania (Foster), and Galway, Ireland (Gilmore).[30]

Regional distinctions of these kinds are often loaded with stereotypical baggage or are of dubious geoeconomic distinctiveness. Just as the southern highlands, for instance, have long been accepted as the home of "primitive people as yet unchanged by immigration and uncontaminated by modern civilization," so the Deep South and Dixie

PLACE IS POLITICAL

have long been accepted—by northerners especially, but also in southern gothic literature (including some of William Faulkner's novels)—as defeated and morally degenerate places.[31] The meaning of terms such as *Appalachia*, the *southern highlands*, and the *rural upland South*, as well as their physical boundaries and social characteristics, have been—and continue to be—hotly debated by scholars.[32]

One political, social, and aesthetic phenomenon that does seem characteristic of the South Atlantic states and territories—especially prior to the Civil War but also (though to a declining extent) after 1865—is *private* music making. *Private* refers to music made during or intended for gatherings closed to the general public: domestic get-togethers, cotillions, and other assemblages made up exclusively of blacks or whites, rich or poor, tourists or "locals." Such gatherings are about more than merely gaining admission; often, observers are excluded from participation. Private music making is *exclusive*: prerequisites include membership in a family or clan, in a race or class, in a political, social, or spiritual organization.

For example, shortly before the outbreak of the Civil War, Marion Harland visited Richmond's First African Baptist Church. "The choir of the 'Old African' was one of the shows of the city," Harland informs us. "Visitors from Northern cities who spent the Sabbath in Richmond seldom failed to hear the famed choir. . . . George F. Root, who heard [it] more than once while he was our guest, could not say enough of the beauty of the anthem-hymn 'Jerusalem, My Happy Home' as given by the colored band. He declared that one soloist had 'the finest natural tenor he ever heard.'"[33] Yet even Root (much less Mrs. Harland) could not have *joined* the "Old African" choristers. Nineteenth-century society did not encourage white composers and tourists to model their public behavior upon those of black musicians.

The title of the present article, "Societies and Soirees," suggests two prototypical circumstances for private musical practices, especially those of the antebellum era. *Societies* are social organizations that encourage music making without making it available to everyone. *Soirees* refers to more informal, even spontaneous opportunities for intimate music making, including serenades, sing-alongs, square dances, church services, socials, and the like. *Soiree* and *soiree party* also appear in conjunction with celebrations that originated under slavery in the Virgin Islands and other parts of the South and Caribbean regions. Although originally more oratorical and religious than musical, these "riotous occasions" later incorporated elements of variety shows and featured such instruments as bum drums or bone drum (fife and drum) ensembles.[34] What all these activities had (and to some extent still have) in common was their spontaneity; they were less frequently associated with publicity of various kinds, nor were they often taken seriously (at least not in the sense that a symphony concert may be said to be "serious"). More than a few soirees, in fact, were considered less than genteel, and all of them were separated—geographically, ethnically, and so on—from society as a whole.

Antebellum music making especially among African American slaves was private in precisely these ways. Although visitors to Southern plantations "rarely" wrote about slaves "without mentioning their music, for this was [perhaps] their most splendid vehicle of self-expression," those same visitors often heard only what slaves (or their masters) wanted them to hear.[35] Spontaneous slave music making was seldom accessible to the general public.[36] No wonder scholars are unable to determine today whether the "birth of the blues" took place in a given state or decade, much less in a particular town, county, or year. More revealing are the reminiscences of former slaves—for example, Solomon Northup's account of square dancing, fiddling, and other ring-play activities.[37] Unfortunately, accounts like Northup's were long ignored by historians, even though slave "dance calls"— which "differed from their European counterparts" in that they took the shape of "rhymed 'raps'"—must have gradually influenced American square dancing overall.[38]

Of course, private music making was not the exclusive property of the antebellum South Atlantic (or even the South), nor was it limited to slaves. America's early musical life generally was rural and domestic, because America herself began as a nation of farmers. Nineteenth-century Americans attended square dances in Maine and Minnesota as well as the Carolinas; fiddles were played in the parlors of California and Texas as well as Florida and Georgia. But in New England, attitudes that gave rise to common plots of ground and town meetings also encouraged the establishment of public concerts. In the South, aristocratic landowners as well as African Americans were more likely to join forces privately in order to entertain themselves and their families. Distances and technological developments also played an important role in determining the regional character of antebellum American musical life. Frederick Law Olmstead, who visited the "seaboard slave states" during the 1850s, had real trouble getting from one place to another south of Richmond, Virginia—and this at a time when he was able to travel in some comfort by train between Boston, New York, and Philadelphia.[39] Race played its part too: encountering a "negro funeral procession" one Sunday afternoon, Olmstead listened to "a wild kind of chant" sung by the mourners but also paid close attention to another "white man," an "apparently indifferent spectator." "I judged he was a police officer," Olmstead concludes, "or some one procured to witness the funeral" in order to "destroy" any "opportunity" of slaves "conspiring to gain their freedom."[40] Spectators such as Olmstead were rare, however; and while racial lines regarding social events of all kinds were firmly drawn—in the North, too—they were even more firmly placed in the South.

This tendency was reinforced by the fact that, at least until after World War II, the South in general "retained too many rural traits to allow sufficient development of those features of urban culture required for an artistic flowering above the level of folk expression." The pace of development devolving upon urbanization, immigration, and comparatively greater economic prosperity seems to have brought more kinds of music at earlier dates to more people outside the South. Instead, many urban Southerners especially contented themselves "with adopting Northern ideas, in the realms of the beautiful and the decorative"; as a consequence, or so historian Francis Simkins has dismissively maintained, the region "between the [Potomac River and the Rio Grande] represented one of the barren territories of twentieth century civilization."[41] Simkins is correct, though, in maintaining that the South's rural character meant that its "most original contribution to music [overall] was its Negro folk songs."[42] No music is more private than folk music; it has always been made largely in homes, farms, taverns, and other domestic and amateur venues.

Even today, songs of home remain more common throughout Appalachia (much of which belongs to the South Atlantic) than elsewhere—suggesting, as Bill Malone has pointed out, that "the system of moral values" associated with rural isolation and the nuclear family "still has relevance" to regional as well as national value systems.[43] Several of the United States' most celebrated singing families came from South Atlantic states, the well-known Carter Family among them.[44] Appropriately enough, "country music"—personified initially by the Carters and Jimmy Rodgers—is still epitomized by many as having begun and been discovered in the South Atlantic (actually, on its edge, in Bristol, Virginia and Tennessee) before being commercialized in Nashville, New York, and other urban centers.[45] All this began in 1927, by which time Atlanta had established a decade-old reputation as a center of "old-timey" music.[46] Atlanta's fiddle contests—themselves celebrations of values "squarely at odds" with those Atlantans had come to prize "in their New South"—were later taken up by radio and to some extent contributed, albeit indirectly, to such subsequent musical-commercial phenomena as the Grand Ole Opry.[47]

South Atlantic musical life, however, has long possessed cultivated as well as vernacular character. Simkins exaggerates even when he describes late-nineteenth- and early-twentieth-century southern choirs and orchestras as "almost always mediocre and amateur."[48] Eighteenth-century Charleston, Richmond, and Savannah, along with such nearby cities as Annapolis, Maryland, boasted performers and ensembles every bit as good as those of contemporary Philadelphia and Boston.[49] Yet it's true that fewer cultural capitals grew up during the nineteenth century in the tidewater and piedmont than in places like the Midwest. Even Charleston, "one of the major cities in the colonial era, lost ground to newer northern cities after the Revolution."[50] Still, throughout the nineteenth and early twentieth centuries, there were always a few well-publicized paid events in Charleston and other South Atlantic cities, though a great many of them had to be imported.[51]

PLACE IS POLITICAL

But in the nineteenth-century South and especially the South Atlantic coast, it was not so much new imports or attitudes toward music that determined regional developments as much as comparatively rural conditions—smaller and fewer cities and towns—and racial distinctions. As colonial cities developed, certain musical activities first became possible, then grew more sophisticated, then—sometimes—more secular. Boston's cultivated musical history between the 1720s and the 1840s, for example, has been epitomized as "symphony overtak[ing] psalmody."[52] To some extent this transformation was politically motivated; as Michael Broyles explains, members of New England's "older gentry in particular sought to use music to create a republican vision of American society." In Boston and elsewhere, especially after 1840, musical activities "such as concert attendance, membership in musical organizations, and patronage itself, closely followed class lines"; at the same time, "radically new attitudes about music [and musical taste] became the norm."[53]

Now consider the musical evolution of Alexandria, Virginia. Concert life in that city can be documented as far back as the mid-eighteenth century, a period when virtually all of the British colonies boasted their own accomplished ensembles, most of them involved with public performances. By 1799 the "Gentlemen of Alexandria and its vicinity" had met to organize a regular season of dances on behalf of the region's wealthier white residents.[54] Similar organizations also grew up in eighteenth-century Philadelphia, Boston, and Baltimore. The short-lived Tuesday Club of Annapolis, Maryland, for example, boasted in Thomas Bacon one of the colonies' first cultivated composers; among its other members were composers Alexander Malcolm and William Thornton and author Alexander Hamilton.[55] Yet cultivated music seems mostly to have withered away in Annapolis and Alexandria well before 1861; in Boston and elsewhere—including Charleston, South Carolina—it flourished.

Without the Handel and Haydn Society of Boston, for instance, a great many important European choral works never would have been heard in nineteenth- and twentieth-century America. Almost from its inception in 1815, the Handel and Haydn was devoted to *public* audiences and *paid* public performances. Charleston's St. Cecilia Society was a rather different organization. Founded in 1762, Charleston's club was originally limited to 120 wealthy, white, male members. Election to the St. Cecilia Society required the support of two-thirds of the existing membership. After 1763 it also required the payment of £35 (an enormous sum!) as an initiation fee; in addition, all members paid annual dues. The Society's bylaws specified that, except in the case of "as many ladies as [each member] considers proper" (and for each lady a ticket had to be issued), "no other person is to be admitted [to concerts, dinners, and other activities] except strangers [to Charleston], and they only by tickets from a manager, signed and directed as before specified."[56]

In terms of some of the St. Cecilia Society's activities, Charleston's eighteenth-century musical life was more advanced than Boston's, as were the musical lives of Annapolis, Alexandria, and a few other South Atlantic urban centers. From the outset, though, clubs like the St. Cecilia Society were fundamentally more aristocratic and more exclusionary in terms of income and race, and they tended to remain that way. A few antebellum singing societies even eventually challenged law and order—which is to say they acted on behalf of themselves instead of the "public good." In 1850s Richmond, Virginia, the "large and talented German glee club" was only one of several similar organizations. Occasionally, competition grew up among such clubs. On one occasion, for instance, members of the German glee club "made complaint to [the mayor] . . . that about midnight on Wednesday evening, while engaged in serenading a friend . . . the night watch had interfered with and put a stop to their musical performances, stating that they must cease their singing in the *public* streets." The Germans alleged that "the Armory and other bands were allowed to serenade in different parts of the city, and were not interfered with—and desired to know whether they were to be made the exception, and debarred a privilege granted to other musical organizations."[57]

On the other hand, nineteenth-century Boston's socioeconomic elite—which, like its South Atlantic counterparts, "had few reservations" about maintaining its position and created institutions in which "membership and privileges were tightly controlled—did little initially to foster musical activity.[58] Yet public activities especially after 1840 not only made Boston the hub of nineteenth-century American cultivated culture, but they also transformed American attitudes toward what later came to be known as "good" music especially among the middle classes. When the Handel and Haydn's chorus gave its first recorded concert on Christmas night in 1815, "an estimated one thousand *customers*" were "electrified" by the music they heard.[59] Note the word "customers": admission to the concert in question was available to anyone who could pay the price. Note, too, the publicity accorded the same concert in the local press. Antebellum Southern newspapers also published announcements and reviews even of certain private musical events, but their readerships and geographical distribution were much more limited, their cultural *reportage* more circumstanced. Neither before nor after the Civil War, for instance, did Charleston produce a newspaper as prestigious as Boston's *Evening Post* or (later) *Globe*. Nor were published announcements of private musical events equated with invitations to admission. Instead, they informed the hoi polloi of what their "betters" were up to.

Antebellum music in the South Atlantic was instead much more widely disseminated through churches and church-related institutions than through concerts and social events. Richmond's "Old African" choir was set apart from the community surrounding it; and in other instances too, Southern religious music was created and performed only by members of its own community. At Bethesda, an orphanage built during the early 1740s in Georgia, for example, the daily routine for inmates included psalm singing at 6:00 a.m., hymns before or after many meals (including breakfast), and evening suppers at which "the Masters and the Misstress [sic] attend" to the children "and sing with them."[60] It goes without saying that different denominations created their own hymnals and hymns—in the North, too, but especially in the South. The various schools of shape note singing were largely Southern, and several South Atlantic cities boasted music publishing houses that survived into and even through the Civil War years.[61]

As in Boston, different classes were involved with Southern music in one way or another. A great many plantation owners and other ante-bellum South Atlantic "aristocrats" were active musically—but again mostly at home. The estate of John Carlyle, who died in 1780 Alex-andria, included "2 Old Trumpets & 1 French horn" and "1 fife."[62] Carlyle's children were set to studying music; Sally Carlyle, evidently an industrious student, nevertheless complained that she found "Thro Bass . . . very deficult [*sic*]" and confessed she was "in want of some agreeable tunes that I can Learn myself."[63] In a later letter addressed by Maria Bryan Harford to Julia Ann Bryan Cumming of Mt. Zion, Georgia, on Christmas Eve 1840, the private acquisition of music skills continues: Ms. Harford's nephew Julien "has been a charming little boy during the visit. . . . I am honouring your request that he should attend to his music, so far as to be teaching him the rules which can never be too thoroughly learned, and I have moved the piano in this room, that I may hear him practice."[64] Julia Ann herself took music lessons in 1827, Maria the following year.[65] The diaries of Keziah Bre-vard, the owner of a substantial plantation east of Columbia, South Carolina, mention little about music outside of references to church services; yet her estate boasted "One (1) new Piano" and "One (1) old Piano"—the former valued at $150, the latter at $10.[66] Although Brevard's diary covers only the years 1860–1861, it seems plausible that the old piano had been purchased, and almost certainly used, for decades prior to her death in 1885 and possibly well before the Civil War began. Behind other apparently less-privileged doors lay further material evidence of antebellum South Atlantic music making and its role in sustaining class position. O. J. Hammong, a visitor to Tal-lahassee during the 1840s, expected to find "splendid houses in the city" but was instead "astonished by . . . the incongruity of ill-con-structed log cabins that were furnished with pianos, sofas, tables, rich sideboards, Turkish rugs, and cut glass."[67] Similar stories might be told of finding instruments and music lessons in the antebellum New England and the Middle West, of course; but those of the South (and South Atlantic) have perhaps been less widely disseminated. In con-tradistinction to cultivated Boston, stories of "uncouth" and "illiter-ate" Southerners linger in the American imagination.

Prior to emancipation, African American slaves also entertained themselves—often, as already noted, out of sight of their European American masters and guests. Frequently forbidden in many circumstances to play or sing, lest they manage to communicate secretly with one another, slaves nevertheless sometimes entertained the men and women who owned them, which contributed to the birth of minstrelsy. Blacks and whites rarely performed together anywhere. Antebellum Caribbean and Southern fife and drum groups, for instance, were always African American ensembles (although they entertained blacks as well as whites); their music was a pastiche of military marches and "European dance form[s] like the quadrille or reel."[68] Before the end of the 1860s few blacks were educated anywhere in the United States; in fact, it was a crime in many parts of antebellum America to teach slaves reading and writing. Nor, again, did more than a handful of blacks learn to make cultivated music until after the Civil War. These factors also contributed to certain kinds of musical isolation.

With slaves, however, came unique melodies and methods of singing, along with new and hitherto unknown instruments. Thomas Jefferson noted that the "instrument proper to [slaves] is the Banjar," which had been "brought hither from Africa, and which is the original of the guitar, its chords [i.e., strings]" being tuned to the same intervals as the four lower strings of that more "refined" instrument.[69] By the middle of the eighteenth century, banjos had spread through the Carolinas to Georgia and probably to Florida. Therefore, the South Atlantic region, by way of western Africa, may well have given the world one of its more popular musical instruments. Yet for decades, banjos were seldom heard except on plantations. And not until the 1870s did spirituals, performed in public and for profit by the Fisk Jubilee Singers and a few other "authentic" ensembles, leave the homesteads and fields of what formerly had been the Confederacy.[70]

Other folk traditions—which is to say other private forms of musical performance and enjoyment (including versions of the Scots-Irish ballads more often associated with the southern highlands)—spread during the eighteenth and nineteenth centuries from Virginia to Georgia. Ballads became associated with Appalachia, especially the region's

South Atlantic eastern edge; they also spread throughout several regions of the United States. British ballads, as "sung by both black and white residents," were found by Elsie Clews Parsons on several South Atlantic coastal islands as late as the 1930s. These melodies included "The Cruel Brother," "Young Beichan," and "The Maid Freed from the Gallows."[71] Researchers in Florida and the Bahamas have also found that, although "story lines were kept for a few ballads . . . more often, local characters or imaginary incidents rounded out the tale" with "devils, witches, or [talking] animals" appearing in many lyrics.[72] Examples such as these illustrate how local concerns and customs help define private musical practices within those regions, including the South Atlantic, that initiate or accept them.

Serenades, today all but extinct, also provided residents of the South Atlantic (as well as other parts of the United States and much of Europe) with music in a host of intimate circumstances. The diary of Emma Holmes is full of musical chitchat concerning domestic musical delights in and around Charleston. On September 18, 1861, for example, she notes that "[l]ast night Isaac gave us the long promised serenade. The moonlight was brilliant, and just at twelve we were woke by the arrival of a Jersey waggon [sic], carrying a piano & the performers." Willie Walker played the piano, she notes; "Edwin [White] the 'fairy-flute' & Messrs. George & John Read on the violin [sic]."

> The two first pieces were delicious waltzes, to which I have often danced, & one particularly has been haunting me ever since. . . . Soon [too] we were rewarded by a most exquisite gem from Travatore [sic], a duet, in which the violins and flute strove to see which could *talk* the sweetest. I never heard any music but theirs which made you feel as if you heard the different speakers. . . . It is really an exquisite pleasure to hear such music, and it is heightened by the scene & the time, all blending into a perfect whole. They gave sixteen serenades, beginning at Hattie's at half past ten & not getting home till five o'clock.[73]

Olmstead, who chanced one evening in a small town upon an impromptu "negro" serenade, observed that the young men in question sang "with great skill and taste—better than I ever heard a group of young men in a Northern village, without previous arrangement." After two of the men had "danced the 'juba,'" while the rest whistled and applauded," one said to the rest, "Come, gentlemen, let's go in and see the ladies."[74] Serenaders and other amateur Southern musicians were often more skillful and even cultivated than one might expect. In a brief essay on "The Musical Talent of Negroes," Olmstead observes that a "gentleman in Savannah . . . had heard more than one negro . . . whistling the most difficult [opera] arias, with perfect accuracy."[75] As these accounts and others demonstrate, rural music making in the antebellum South Atlantic was at least sometimes a cultivated activity, complete with exquisite performances and excerpts from Verdi operas.

Finally, music has always coexisted with dancing, and dancing has often been private—not merely in the interpersonal sense of that word (one thinks of courtships and other sentimental situations), but in terms of geographic isolation in schooling and setting. Quadrilles, contradanses, square dances, and similar forms of homemade entertainment were widespread throughout the antebellum South Atlantic as well as other regions. Lizzie Brown, daughter of the Thomas Brown who served as governor of Florida from 1849 to 1853, describes how she and her sister "danced the Spanish dance and waltz [in Tallahassee] long before it was allowed in America [sic]," thanks in part to the academy "for instruction in the elegant art of dancing" that taught quadrilles, caledonias, mazurkas, polkas, and waltzes.[76] Slaves, too, danced in isolated circumstances. All racial segregation is a form of privacy, whether imposed from within or without.

What of today—or, at least, of late-nineteenth- and twentieth-century musical practices in the South Atlantic? Societies and social clubs persisted in parts of the region well into the twentieth century, although their exclusivity seems gradually to have lessened as portions—especially of Virginia, the Carolinas, and Georgia—became more urban and modern. In 1906, for instance, the Musical Arts Club was established in Charleston. This organization gave public concerts and sponsored fund-raising events, including a performance of Gilbert and

Sullivan's *Trial by Jury* in 1911 that earned enough money to rent a hall on King Street; in 1920 the club moved to a hall at the rear of the Circular Church on Meeting Street. Among its activities, the Musical Arts boasted "an associate department . . . whereby non-active members might enjoy the musicale, and other benefits." The club also organized a chorus, which presented such works as Mendelssohn's psalm settings, Rossini's *Stabat mater*, and Samuel Coleridge-Taylor's *Hiawatha's Wedding-Feast* at public concerts.[77] The existence of this last work on a Southern program exemplifies a certain lessening of racial tensions following the Civil War; Coleridge-Taylor was perhaps the most successful of early twentieth-century African American art composers.

Increasingly, black residents of the South Atlantic region took up European music making after 1865. Consider the home of the Reverend L. R. Nochols, in which a newspaper reporter was entertained during the 1880s in "a well-furnished and cozy parlor, containing a large new piano and half a dozen oil paintings."[78] In a contemporaneous black Charleston household, two sisters "not only played the piano competently but also," according to a visitor, "had admirably solved the sweet mysteries of Shubert's [*sic*] and Bach's most difficult music."[79] For fifty years and more after World War II, well-to-do African American women in such places as Orangeburg, South Carolina, have enjoyed "the leisure time to do volunteer social work through various clubs," while even poor women, as well as men, continue to take part in church-related activities.[80] Such activities, which often include music, continue today—not only in the South Atlantic, of course, but there too.

In 1974 the American Music Conference survey identified 34 million musical amateurs in all parts of our nation, 3 million more than in 1970. According to their researches, 42 percent of all U.S. households then boasted "at least one musical amateur," and observed that one 1970s amateur in five could play an instrument.[81] Statistics such as these suggest that homemade music continues to be popular everywhere, but in the South Atlantic it may still retain a folk character. In 1947 Earl Leaf reported that some of Puerto Rico's early musical traditions—and, it seems likely, those of other South Atlantic areas—survived especially in vernacular circumstances. "Superior and exciting dancing," for example, could still "be seen at such [Puerto Rico] hot spots as Jack's, New Carioca, Copacabana and the Savoy Club" after World War II, although it was no longer "native in origin." On the other hand, the *seis chorreo*, which was based on old Andalusian dances, was "still danced by the simple folk of the mountains during the Christmas holidays"; so was the *marianda*.[82]

Leaf also reported that "the old folk" still met "in the hills and valleys of the three U.S. Virgins [the Virgin Islands], on holidays and Saturday nights, to get giddy and frivolous on rum and let themselves go as far as they dare" in dancing twentieth-century versions of the *bamboula*. Leaf himself witnessed a "score of grannies and grandpaps . . . kicking up the dust while an ancient drum, played by two beaters simultaneously, was giving the rhythm. Two or three couples were dancing in the middle of a circle of others who were chanting, clapping their hands, drinking rum and eating hot-dogs all at once." Leaf was surprised to learn that the *ka* drum, which many scholars had believed extinct throughout the West Indies, remained in use but was never displayed "in public." Fortunately for him, local people granted him permission to photograph the drum and themselves. "Self-conscious at first," Leaf reports that "they soon forgot me and danced for sheer joy. . . . One could well visualize the *bamboula* dances of yesteryear as one watched these island elders perform. Singing, chanting, dancing, drinking, they were all a little crazy—and very happy."[83]

In spite of such facts, we cannot overlook the many and diverse musical changes that have taken place throughout the United States as a whole since 1865. In the case of Puerto Rico, "migration to and from Venezuela, Mexico, and Cuba" influenced several of that island's musical practices; so did the importation by United States Army soldiers of dance-band and big-band music during World War II.[84] Even more recently, "a modern receptivity to English-language popular culture," including various forms of popular music, has come to "underlie a clear degree of cultural unity" throughout the American Virgin Islands.[85]

Furthermore, parts of the South Atlantic and contiguous areas have recently assumed leadership roles in public music making. The Country Music Association, for instance, was founded in Nashville, Tennessee, in 1958, in order "to protect and regain old markets and to penetrate mainstream urban popular markets." Its success in marketing country music in the 1960s and 1970s, together with the first public bluegrass festivals, resulted in the spread of this formerly regional form to much of the United States as well as Canada, Japan, and Europe.[86] For more than seventy years, and with considerable success, Moose Lodge No. 773 of Galax, Virginia, has sponsored a "Fiddler's Convention" that continues to introduce "old-time" and contemporary artists to a broader, fee-paying public. This regional growth in public music making, albeit music that had developed in what had been formerly largely private forums, demonstrates how standardization and globalization continue to encroach upon regional distinctions, just as they did in the orchestras and choirs of the eighteenth and nineteenth centuries. At the same time, it demonstrates how regional musical practices persist and adapt themselves to changing national and world circumstances.

Today, global technology is transforming or obliterating many local practices. At the same time, increased contact with and knowledge of nonwestern music—combined with the development of sequencing software for personal computers; the proliferation of iPods; the growth of portable digitalized music libraries; and, perhaps most significantly, "a drastic splintering of audiences"—have fueled the development of so many musical subcultures.[87] This has helped spawn so much cultural fragmentation that "the center seems to be fading and the margins acquiring new vitality and worth" throughout the United States as a twenty-first-century nation.[88] Although the bamboula probably disappeared during the nineteenth century and certainly was a memory in Puerto Rico when Leaf visited the Caribbean half a century ago, the South Atlantic has held on to some of its traditional musical attitudes, even as it has developed new and distinctive musical practices both public and private.

Notes

I would like to thank both the South Atlantic Humanities Center and Virginia Polytechnic Institute and State University for funding that enabled me to attend "Regionalism and the Humanities" in Lincoln, Nebraska, in November 2003, at which conference a preliminary version of the present article was presented as a paper.

1. For information about this geopolitical region, as defined by the National Endowment for the Humanities for research and funding purposes—and on behalf of the South Atlantic Humanities Center as one example of such purposes in action—see South Atlantic Center, www.southatlanticcenter.org. The author is a South Atlantic Humanities Center Fellow.

2. See John Joseph Hindman, "Concert Life in Ante Bellum Charleston," 2 vols. (PhD diss., University of North Carolina at Chapel Hill, 1971); and Nicholas Michael Butler, "Votaries of Apollo: The St. Cecilia Society and the Patronage of Concert Music in Charleston, South Carolina, 1766–1820" (PhD diss., Indiana University, 2004).

3. *Cultivated* and *vernacular* are employed by musicologists such as H. Wiley Hitchcock to distinguish between European and local traditions, attitudes, and practices. The New York Philharmonic, for example, would be considered "cultivated," whereas square-dancing and the songs of Johnny Mercer would be "vernacular." I have employed these terms similarly throughout this work. See Hugh Wiley Hitchcock, *Music in the United States: An Introduction*, 3rd ed. (Englewood Cliffs NJ: Prentice-Hall, 1988).

4. For many experts, blues and jazz began in the Deep South before spreading to such northern or central cities as Chicago, Detroit, Kansas City, New York, and Philadelphia. See, for example, Charles Joyner, *Shared Traditions: Southern History and Folk Culture* (Urbana: University of Illinois Press, 1999), esp. 193–207, "The Sounds of Southern Culture: Blues, Country, Jazz, and Rock."

5. As late as 1930, for instance, only eight out of sixty-two symphonic ensembles "classified as of second rank [much less first] were located in the South," and of these Dallas's orchestra—southern but not South Atlantic—was perhaps the best-known. Francis Butler Simkins, *The South, Old and New: A History, 1820–1947* (New York: Alfred A. Knopf, 1947), 362. Regarding today's first-rank American orchestras, consider that the New York Philharmonic was established in 1842 and the Atlanta Symphony, only in 1945.

6. Norman Davies, *Europe: A History* (Oxford: Oxford University Press, 1996), 30. Like mine, Davies's discussion deals with regional distinctions and divisions proposed and widely accepted some time ago, long before transnational corporations began to exert global sway and "the domination of territory" stood central to what Barbara Ellen Smith calls "the hegemony of capital. Because of this [new] structural reality," she continues, "global capitalism in the present era [has recently become] highly destructive of place." Barbara Ellen Smith, "The Place of Appalachia," *Journal of Appalachian Studies* 8, no. 1 (2002): 43.

7. Davies, *Europe*, 7–46.

8. Davies, *Europe*, 34.

9. Davies, *Europe*, 34–35.

10. Henry D. Shapiro, "Appalachian Culture," in *The Encyclopedia of Southern*

Culture (Chapel Hill: University of North Carolina Press, 1989), 1100, quoted and briefly discussed in Helen Hollingsworth, "The Land of Appalachia: From Encounter to Perception," in *Appalachia Inside Out*, vol. 1, *Conflict and Change*, ed. Robert J. Higgs and others (Knoxville: University of Tennessee Press, 2002), 32.

11. Hector St. John de Crèvecoeur, *Letters from an American Farmer and Sketches of Eighteenth-Century America* (New York: New American Library, 1963), 65.

12. William J. Cooper Jr. and Thomas E. Terrill, *The American South: A History*, 2nd ed. (New York: McGraw-Hill, 1996), 258–59.

13. Crèvecoeur, *Letters from an American Farmer*, 66. Some of Crèvecoeur's distinctions were based on historical facts; the 1760s Regulator Riots in the Carolinas, for example, testify to demands mostly by farmers for more efficient government and protection from Indians.

14. Frederick Jackson Turner, "The Significance of the Section in American History," in *Frontier and Section: Selected Essays of Frederick Jackson Turner*, ed. Ray Allen Billington (Englewood Cliffs NJ: Prentice-Hall, 1961), 126, 131. Turner's essay "The Significance of the Section in American History" was originally published in March 1925.

15. Turner, "Significance of the Section," 133–35.

16. Richard Crawford, *A History of America's Musical Life* (New York: W. W. Norton, 2001), 784.

17. See Cooper and Terrill, *American South*, 259.

18. Quoted in Malcolm J. Rohrbough, *The Trans-Appalachian Frontier: People, Societies, and Institutions, 1775–1850* (New York: Oxford University Press, 1978), 156 (italics in the original).

19. Gary R. Mormino, "Peninsular Florida," in *Encyclopedia of American Social History*, ed. Mary Kupiec Cayton, Elliott J. Gorn, and Peter W. Williams, 3 vols. (New York: Charles Scribner's Sons, 1993), 2:1062.

20. The region did not altogether lack industry and modern transportation, however; railroads linked many Southern cities prior to 1861, and "prominent southern industries included ironworks, tobacco processing, and textiles." Cooper and Terrill, *American South*, 307.

21. Orville Vernon Burton, "Sectional Conflict, Civil War, and Reconstruction," in *Encyclopedia of American Social History*, ed. Mary Kupiec Cayton, Elliott J. Gorn, and Peter W. Williams, 3 vols. (New York: Charles Scribner's Sons, 1993), 1:131.

22. Quoted in William J. Gilmore-Lehne, "Literacy," in *Encyclopedia of American Social History*, ed. Mary Kupiec Cayton, Elliott J. Gorn, and Peter W. Williams, 3 vols. (New York: Charles Scribner's Sons, 1993), 3:2419.

23. Burton, "Sectional Conflict," in *Encyclopedia of American Social History*, ed. Mary Kupiec Cayton, Elliott J. Gorn, and Peter W. Williams, 3 vols. (New York: Charles Scribner's Sons, 1993), 1:146.

24. Ulrich B. Phillips, "The Central Theme of Southern History," *American Historical Review* 34 (October 1928): 31 (italics added).

25. D. R. Hundley, *Social Relations in Our Southern States* (New York: Henry B. Price, 1860), 69, 71.

26. Hundley, *Social Relations*, 72. Residents of the antebellum South Atlantic were

proud of their distinctive differences from other parts of the United States. And—sad but true—they were proud of slavery, which many of them believed (and with some reason) exempted "so large a portion of our citizens from the necessity of bodily labor, that we have a greater proportion than any other people, who have leisure for intellectual pursuits, and the means of attaining a liberal education." William Harper, *Memoir on Slavery, Read Before the Society for the Advancement of Learning of South Carolina* (Charleston: James S. Burges, 1838), 101, 126. For observations on musical practices among Charleston's antebellum "aristocrats," including Harper, see Maurie D. McInnis, *The Politics of Taste in Antebellum Charleston* (Chapel Hill: University of North Carolina Press, 2005), esp. 277–79.

27. This was not true, however, for the very first college: that institution, the Georgia Female College, opened on December 23, 1836. Vassar opened only in 1861; Smith, in 1889.

Again, slavery played its part in South Atlantic notions of education. "Authorities" such as J. S. Buckingham inveighed throughout the 1830s and 1840s against Northern schoolbooks, "books, whose very tone & spirit are hostile to [Southern] institutions." J. S. Buckingham, *The Slave States of America* (London: Fisher, Son, 1842), quoted in McInnis, *The Politics of Taste*, 92. No wonder many South Atlantic parents, even those who lived in urban areas, strove to keep their children close to home.

28. See James Mooney, "Folk-Lore of the Carolina Mountains," *Journal of American Folk Lore*, 1889, 95, quoted in Henry D. Shapiro, *Appalachia on Our Mind: The Southern Mountains and Mountaineers in the American Consciousness, 1870–1920* (Chapel Hill: University of North Carolina Press, 1978), 244.

29. See John Avery Lomax, *Cowboy Songs and Other Frontier Ballads* (New York: Sturgis and Walton, 1910). For Turner, too, the story of the American frontier was "the history of the colonization of the Great West." Turner, "Significance of the Section," 37.

30. For a discussion of Foster's and Gilmore's careers, as well as of Irish American music in general (and, to a limited extent, of its similarities with certain aspects of African American music), see Michael Saffle, "Across a Great Divide: Irish American Music and Musicians of the Civil War Era," in *Bugle Resounding: Music and Musicians of the Civil War Era*, ed. Bruce C. Kelley and Mark A. Snell (Columbia: University of Missouri Press, 2004), 169–201 passim. NB: whether Gilmore composed "When Johnny Comes Marching Home Again" is open to doubt; even its tipping (a rhythmic-melodic figure) and modal inflections are by no means exclusively Irish. Saffle, "Across a Great Divide," 186. It is in cases like this one that regional distinctions often break down or need to be reconsidered.

31. Shapiro, *Appalachia on Our Mind*, 245.

32. Among musicological studies that employ the second term is Mellinger Edward Henry, ed., *Folk-songs from the Southern Highlands* (New York: J. J. Augustin, 1938). Among those that employ the third is Neil V. Rosenberg, "Bluegrass," in *The Garland Encyclopedia of World Music*, vol. 3, *The United States and Canada*, ed. Ellen Koskoff (New York: Garland, 2001), 168. For three definitions of *Appalachia* as a region bounded by political, social, and cultural factors—those of John C. Campbell (1910), the Ford Foundation (1950), and the Appalachian Regional Commission

(1965)—see Bruce Ergood, "Toward a Definition of Appalachia" in *Appalachia: Social Context, Past and Present*, ed. Bruce Ergood and Bruce E. Kuhre, 3rd ed. (Dubuque IA: Kendall/Hunt, 1991), 39–49.

33. Marion Harland, *Autobiography* (New York: Harper and Bros., 1910), 234, quoted in Albert Stoutamire, *Music of the Old South: Colony to Confederacy* (Rutherford NJ: Fairleigh Dickinson University Press, 1972), 169.

34. Roger D. Abrahams, "Afro-Caribbean Culture and the South: Music with Movement," in *The South and the Caribbean*, ed. Douglass Sullivan-González and Charles Reagan Wilson (Jackson: University Press of Mississippi, 2001), 105–6.

35. Kenneth M. Stampp, *The Peculiar Institution: Slavery in the Ante-Bellum South* (New York: Alfred A. Knopf, 1978), 368.

36. Exceptions, largely limited to urban observations, include accounts of voodoo dances and dancing the bamboula "in Place Congo." See Eileen Southern, *The Music of Black Americans: A History*, 3rd ed. (New York: W. W. Norton, 1997), 135–40.

37. See Solomon Northup, *Twelve Years a Slave* (Auburn NY: Derby and Miller, 1853), 216–17.

38. John F. Szwed and Morton Marks, "The Afro-American Transformation of European Set Dances and Dance Suites," *Dance Research* 20, no. 1 (Summer 1988): 33. For a detailed discussion of this and other slave musical practices, see Roger D. Abrahams, *Singing the Master: The Emergence of African American Culture in the Plantation South* (New York: Pantheon, 1992).

39. Frederick Law Olmstead, *A Journey in the Seaboard Slave States, with Remarks on their Economy* (New York: Dix and Edwards, 1856), 24.

40. Olmstead, *Journey in the Seaboard Slave States*, 24, 27.

41. Simkins, *South, Old and New*, 365.

42. Even the most "celebrated" Negro spirituals "were not adequately recorded or appreciated until Northerners William Francis Allen, Charles Prichard Ware, and Lucy McKim Garrison published in 1867 *Slave Songs of the United States*." Simkins, *South, Old and New*, 363.

43. Bill C. Malone, *Don't Get Above Your Raisin': Country Music and the Southern Working Class* (Urbana: University of Illinois Press, 2002), 54. For a lengthy and interesting discussion of home and "mountain music," see Malone, *Don't Get Above Your Raisin'*, 53–88 passim.

44. Among several excellent accounts of the Carters and their several careers, see Mark Zwonitzer and Charles Hirshberg, *Will You Miss Me When I'm Gone? The Carter Family and Their Legacy in American Music* (New York: Simon and Schuster, 2002).

45. "Whereas Rodgers can now be seen to be the Father of Modern Country Music, in that he pioneered the Nashville crooner tradition, then the Carter Family must be the Patron Saints of Traditional Country Music, as their style and repertoire provide much of the nucleus of that branch of country music which has always remained apart from the well-defined patterns of commercial success determined by Nashville, Tennessee." John Atkins, "The Carter Family," in *Stars of Country Music: Uncle Dave Macon to Johnny Rodriguez*, ed. Malone and Judith McCulloh (Urbana: University of Illinois Press, 1975), 95. The event that brought the Carters and Rodgers together,

PLACE IS POLITICAL

of course, was the August 1, 1927, recording session in Bristol, organized by Ralph Peer, a talent scout for the Victor Talking Machine Company.

46. See Gavin James Campbell, "The Georgia Old Time Fiddling Contest," in *Music and the Making of a New South* (Chapel Hill: University of North Carolina Press, 2004), chap. 3, 100–142 passim.

47. Campbell, "Georgia Old Time Fiddling Contest," 140.

48. Simkins, *South, Old and New*, 367.

49. Annapolis and nearby Baltimore are almost "South Atlantic." They are geographically close to Virginia; they are tidewater towns; like Richmond and Charleston, they declined as cultural centers during the first half of the nineteenth century. Both Baltimore and Annapolis were also musically important throughout the colonial era. See Lubov Keefer, *Baltimore's Music: The Haven of the American Composer* (Baltimore: J. H. Furst, 1962), esp. 1–20; and John Barry Talley, *Secular Music in Colonial Annapolis: The Tuesday Club, 1745–56* (Urbana: University of Illinois Press, 1988).

50. Allan Kulikoff, "The Southern Tidewater and Piedmont," in *Encyclopedia of American Social History*, ed. Mary Kupiec Cayton, Elliott J. Gorn, and Peter W. Williams, 3 vols. (New York: Charles Scribner's Sons, 1993), 2:1024.

51. See Simkins, *South, Old and New*, 362.

52. Michael Broyles, *"Music of the Highest Class": Elitism and Populism in Antebellum Boston* (New Haven CT: Yale University Press, 1992), 313. Broyles situates his observations within the early nineteenth century; I extend that span backward to the early eighteenth, when the first singing schools opened in New England.

53. Broyles, *"Music of the Highest Class,"* 93.

54. *Alexandria Gazette*, May 11, 1799, quoted in Larry Steven Allen, "Musical Life in Old Town Alexandria, Virginia, 1749–1814" (master's thesis, American University, 1979), 81.

55. Not to be confused with the Alexander Hamilton who co-wrote the Federalist Papers and served as the secretary of the treasury.

56. Quoted in Elizabeth P. Simons, *Music in Charleston from 1732 to 1919* (Charleston SC: John J. Furlong and Son, 1927), 13–14.

57. *Richmond Dispatch*, August 6, 1852 (italics added), quoted in Stoutamire, *Music of the Old South*, 181.

58. Broyles, *"Music of the Highest Class,"* 97–98.

59. Crawford, *America's Musical Life*, 293 (italics added), quoted in Charles Callahan Perkins and John Sullivan Dwight, eds., *History of the Handel and Haydn Society of Boston, Massachusetts* (Boston: A. Mudge and Son, 1883), 1:39.

60. Ron Byrnside, *Music in Eighteenth-Century Georgia* (Athens: University of Georgia Press, 1997), 84–85.

61. See, for example, Kirsten M. Schultz, "The Production and Consumption of Confederate Songsters," in *Bugle Resounding: Music and Musicians of the Civil War Era*, ed. Bruce C. Kelley and Mark A. Snell (Columbia: University of Missouri Press, 2004), 133–68. Most of the songbooks Schultz identifies were published in Atlanta, Richmond, and other South Atlantic cities; a few were published in Mobile, Alabama; New Orleans, Louisiana; and other places in the Confederacy.

62. Allen, "Old Town Alexandria," 13.

63. Allen, "Old Town Alexandria," 13–14.

64. Maria Bryan Harford to Julia Ann Bryan Cumming, Mt. Zion, Georgia, December 24, 1840, in *Tokens of Affection: The Letters of a Planter's Daughter in the Old South*, ed. Carol Blesner (Athens: University of Georgia Press, 1996), 320.

65. In good Southern—which, at least in this case, is to say South Atlantic—fashion, both women stayed at home throughout the Civil War. Whether Julien attended college, I do not know; but we do know he served as a Confederate soldier, was captured at the Battle of Gettysburg, and died in prison at Johnson's Island, Ohio, in March 1864. See Blesner, *Tokens of Affection*, 40, 77, and 376.

66. John Hammond Moore, ed., *A Plantation Mistress on the Eve of the Civil War: The Diary of Keziah Goodwyn Hopkins Brevard, 1860–1861* (Columbia: University of South Carolina Press, 1993), 128.

67. Quoted in Wiley L. Housewright, *A History of Music and Dance in Florida, 1565–1865* (Tuscaloosa: University of Alabama Press, 1991), 189.

68. Abrahams, "Afro-Caribbean Culture," 106.

69. Quoted in Byrnside, *Music in Eighteenth-Century Georgia*, 11.

70. Information about African American spirituals and their early dissemination outside the South (and South Atlantic) may be found in William Francis Allen, Charles Pickard Ware, and Lucy McKim Garrison, *Slave Songs of the United States* (New York: A. Simpson, 1867; repr. 1995); and T. F. Seward, *Jubilee Songs as Sung by the Jubilee Singers of Fisk University* (New York: Biglow and Main, 1872). From these years on, the musical world much more frequently and thoroughly interpenetrated the South Atlantic, just as the musical South Atlantic reached out to the world.

71. These songs were also known respectively as Child ballads 11, 53, and 95. For additional information about these traditional, well-researched folksongs and tales, see Francis James Child, *English and Scottish Popular Ballads*, ed. George Lyman Kittredge, 5 vols. (Boston: Houghton Mifflin, 1883–1898).

72. Housewright, *Music and Dance in Florida*, 251.

73. John F. Marszalek, ed., *The Diary of Miss Emma Holmes, 1861–1866* (Baton Rouge: Louisiana State University Press, 1979), 91, entry for September 18, 1861.

74. Olmstead, *Journey in the Seaboard Slave States*, 551.

75. Olmstead, *Journey in the Seaboard Slave States*, 552–53. Although Olmstead included his observations about slaves and music making in the Alabama chapters of his *Journey*, he incorporated information from his South Atlantic travels too.

76. See Bertram H. Groene, "Lizzie Brown's Tallahassee," *Florida Historical Quarterly* 23, no. 2 (October 1969): 167, quoted in Housewright, *Music and Dance in Florida*, 185.

77. Simons, *Music in Charleston*, 69–71.

78. Bernard E. Powers Jr., *Black Charlestonians: A Social History, 1822–1885* (Fayetteville: University of Arkansas Press, 1994), 178.

79. Powers, *Black Charlestonians*, 178.

80. Kibibi Voloria C. Mack, *Parlor Ladies and Ebony Drudges: African American Women, Class, and Work in a South Carolina Community* (Knoxville: University of Tennessee Press, 1999), 171.

81. Christopher Pavlakis, *The American Music Handbook* (New York: Free Press, 1974), 587.

82. Earl Leaf, *Isles of Rhythm* (New York: A. S. Barnes, 1948), 202.

83. Leaf, *Isles of Rhythm*, 136, 140–41.

84. Hector Vega Drouet, "Puerto Rico," in *The Garland Encyclopedia of World Music*, vol.2, *South America, Mexico, Central America, and the Caribbean*, ed. Dale A. Olsen and Daniel E. Sheehy (New York: Garland, 1998), 940.

85. Sheehy, "The Virgin Islands," in *The Garland Encyclopedia of World Music*, vol.2, *South America, Mexico, Central America, and the Caribbean*, ed. Dale A. Olsen and Daniel E. Sheehy (New York: Garland, 1998), 968–69.

86. Rosenberg, "Bluegrass," 163.

87. See Crawford, *America's Musical Life*, 823–24. Terryl L. Givens, *The Viper on the Hearth: Mormons, Myths, and the Construction of Heresy* (New York: Oxford University Press), 164.

88. Terryl L. Givens's observations are moral and ethical rather than musical, but his discussion holds good for a variety of contemporary situations.

Contributors

Ginette Aley is assistant professor of early American history at the University of Southern Indiana. Her most recent publication is in *Ohio History* entitled "A Republic of Farm People: Women, Families, and Market-Minded Agrarianism in Ohio, 1820s–1830s." She is currently revising her dissertation into a book manuscript under contract with Kent State University Press entitled "Narrating an Early American Borderland: John Tipton and the West of the Early Republic."

Stephen C. Behrendt is George Holmes Distinguished Professor of English at the University of Nebraska–Lincoln. He has published widely on British Romantic literature, art, and culture, with a special emphasis in recent years on the recovery and reassessment of women writers. He is also the author of several volumes of original poetry, including his most recent volume *History*.

Mark Busby is director of the Center for the Study of the Southwest and the Southwest Regional Humanities Center. He is the Jerome H. And Catherine E. Supple Professor of Southwestern Studies and professor of English at Texas State University–San Marcos. He has authored and edited numerous books on southwestern literature and culture and has written one novel, *Fort Benning Blues*. His latest book, edited with Terrell Dixon, is *John Graves, Writer*.

Cheryll Glotfelty is associate professor in the Literature and Environment Program of the English Department at the University of Nevada, Reno. She coedited with Harold Fromm *The Ecocriticism Reader: Landmarks in Literary Ecology* and has published widely on western American literature.

Barbara Handy-Marchello is associate professor emerita of the History Department at the University of North Dakota. She is author of *Women of the Northern Plains: Gender and Settlement on the Homestead Frontier, 1870–1930*, which won the Caroline Bancroft History Prize for 2006. She continues her current research on Linda Warfel Slaughter.

Wendy J. Katz is associate professor of art history at the University of Nebraska–Lincoln and a Fellow of the Center for Great Plains Studies. Her publications include *Regionalism and Reform: Art and Class Formation in Antebellum Cincinnati* and articles in *Winterthur Portfolio*, *Prospects*, *American Studies*, and *Nineteenth-Century Studies*.

Kurt E. Kinbacher completed his PhD in May 2006 and is a lecturer and postdoctoral researcher in the History Department at the University of Nebraska–Lincoln. He recently published "Life in the Russian Bottoms: Community Building and Identity Transformation among Germans from Russia in Lincoln, Nebraska, 1876 to 1926" in the *Journal of American Ethnic History*.

Patrick Lee Lucas is assistant professor of interior architecture at the University of North Carolina Greensboro. He holds a PhD in American studies from Michigan State University. He has received numerous grants relating to dissertation work and to the preparation of a manuscript entitled "Athens on the Frontier: Grecian-Style Architecture in the Valley of the West, 1820–1860." Active in history, American studies, and design organizations, Patrick Lucas has given numerous papers at conferences throughout the United States and abroad. He is the author of "Lexington's Wolf Wile Department Store: A Mid-Century Achievement in Urban Architecture," which appeared in the *Kentucky Review*.

Timothy R. Mahoney is professor of history at the University of Nebraska–Lincoln. He is the author of *Provincial Lives: Middle Class Experience in the Antebellum Middle West*. He is project administrator of the Plains Humanities Alliance of the Center for Great Plains Studies.

Larry W. Moore is an independent writer in Frankfort, Kentucky (which is also home to several Vachel Lindsay cousins). He did graduate study in the history of science and medicine at the University of Kentucky and spent a year abroad studying the life and work of Hermann Hesse, supported by a grant from the German government. He presented a paper on Vachel Lindsay at the 2005 Illinois History Conference. A digital artist as well as published poet, photographer, and translator, he is cofounder of Broadstone Media--a cultural promotion company, publishing books under the Broadstone Books imprint and managing an art gallery among other ventures.

Annie Proulx is the author of four novels: *Postcards*, *The Shipping News*, *Accordion Crimes*, and *That Old Ace in the Hole*. She has won the Pulitzer Prize, National Book Award, and a PEN/Faulkner award. She lives in Wyoming.

Guy Reynolds is professor of English at the University of Nebraska–Lincoln, where he also directs the university's Cather Project. He is the author, most recently, of *Apostles of Modernity: American Writers in the Age of Development*.

Mark A. Robison is associate professor of English at Union College in Lincoln, Nebraska. His essay "Recreation in World War I and the Practice of Play in One of Ours" appears in *History, Memory, and War*, volume six of *Cather Studies*.

Michael Saffle received a PhD in music and humanities from Stanford University in 1977 and joined the faculty of Virginia Tech a year later; today he teaches arts and humanities courses as well as colloquia on behalf of Tech's University Honors Program. In addition to publishing books and articles on a variety of subjects, Professor Saffle has served as editor for American biographical entries for "Die Musik in Geschichte und Gegenwart." In April 2007 he won the William E. Wine Award, Tech's top "career" teaching prize.

William Slaymaker teaches philosophy and literature at Wayne State College, Nebraska and specializes in environmental ethics and ecocriticism.

Maggie Valentine, professor of architecture and interior design at the University of Texas at San Antonio, holds a PhD in architecture and urban planning from the University of California at Los Angeles. She is the author of *The Show Starts on the Sidewalk: An Architectural History of the Movie Theatre, Starring S. Charles Lee*, several essays on architecture in popular culture, and a series of oral histories exploring the design process with architects and members of the Taliesin Fellowship.

Edward Watts teaches English and American studies at Michigan State University. His most recent books are *An American Colony: Regionalism and the Roots of Midwestern Culture* and *In This Remote Country: Colonial French Culture in the Anglo-American Imagination, 1780–1860.*

Nicolas S. Witschi is associate professor of English at Western Michigan University, where he teaches American realism and modernism, the American West, culture studies, and film. He is the author of *Traces of Gold: California's Natural Resources and the Claim to Realism in Western American Literature* and of essays on Henry James and Mary Austin, and he is presently writing a book about the autobiographical writings of famous gunfighters and the development of the western as a literary genre.

Index

Gray, Susan: on regional histories, xvi, xxiv, 95, 169, 178, 180; on shaping regionality, 101, 274
"Great American Desert," 254, 258
Great Basin Desert, 239, 242–43
Great Plains: alternating imaginings of, 235; boosterism writing about, 111–23; dependence on eastern markets, xv, 97–98, 235; as Great American Desert, 111, 115, 254, 258; impact of extractive industries, 38–39; Indian territories in, 110; influences on American traits, 252; native grasses of, 37, 38, 39, 40; naturalist writings on, 3; nature writings on landscapes and life, 28–41; regional identity of, xvi–xvii, xxii; revising agricultural practices, 38, 39, 40; settlement of, 252, 254; soils of, 39; states associated with, 153
Greene, Graham, 9
Greenspun, Hank, 245
Greenwood, Grace, 115
Grove, Frederick Phillip, 8
gunfights, staged, 127–41

Hagerman, A. R., 258
Hall, James, 183
Hall, Mrs. Basil, 280, 281
Hall, Roger A., 135
Halttunen, Karen, xxi, xxviin27
Hamilton, Alexander, 303, 317n55
Hammong, O. J., 306
Handel and Haydn Society of Boston, 303–4, 305
Handy Guide for Beggars, A (Lindsay), 219
Handy-Marchello, Barbara, xiv, xxiii, 76–77, 110–23, 146
Hanover NE, 197–98, 199, 201
Hard Rock Cafe, 238
Hardy, Thomas, 8
Harford, Maria Bryan, 306
Harland, Marion, 299
Harney, Corbin, 241
Harper's, 84, 244
Hart, Fred, 244
Harte, Bret, 132

Harvey House, 70–71
Hazard, Lucy Lockwood, 87
Hazen, W. B., 120, 122, 126n22
"Heart of Texas," 48
Hegeman, Susan, 80
Hellenistic culture, architectural influences of, 274–89
Hemingway, Ernest, 10
Henri, Robert, 217
Henry, Bentley's servant, 101
herons, 31
Hidatsa Indians, 110
Higgs, Gerald B., 131, 135
High Country News, 245
"Hill Country," 46, 48
Hillerman, Tony, 10
Hindraker, Eric, 169
Hispanic populations, 239
History of the American Frontier, 1763–1893 (Paxson), 86
History of the English Speaking Peoples (Churchill), 172
Hoagland, Edward, 12
hoaxing, journalistic, 132–33
Hofstra, Warren, xvi, xxviin16
hogan, 63, 64
Hogan, Paul, 184
Hollon, Eugene, 48
Holmes, Emma, 308
homogenization, xxiii, xxiv
Hoosier Chronicle, A (Nicholson), 81
Hoover, Dwight W., 194
Hopkins, Sarah Winnemucca, 241
Howells, William Dean, 175, 176
Hudson Valley Regional Review, The, 158
humanist environmentalism, xxiii
humanist geography, xvi
humanities: defining, 164; geographic determinism, xii, xiii, xiv; study of regions, xii
Humphrey, William, 49
Hundley, D. R., 297, 298
Hurt, James, 170
hybrid space, 9
hypercolonies, 168–69, 174, 177

Ida Stockdale, 116